THE HANDBOOK OF
FINANCIAL
MODELING

THE HANDBOOK OF
FINANCIAL MODELING

The Financial Executive's Reference Guide to Accounting, Finance and Investment Models

John Guerard/H. T. Vaught

Probus Publishing Company
Chicago, Illinois

Library of Congress Cataloging-in-Publication Data

Guerard, John.
   The handbook of financial modeling.

   Includes index.
   1. Corporations—Finance—Mathematical models.
2. Accounting—Mathematical models. 3. Investments—
Mathematical models. I. Vaught, H.T. II. Title.
HG4012.G84 1988 658.1'5'0724 87-32868

ISBN 0-917253-45-0

Printed in the United States of America

1 2 3 4 5 6 7 8 9 0

Contents

v

Acknowledgments

The authors are grateful for the support of many family and friends during the development of this handbook. We would like to acknowledge the support of Julie, Richard, and Katherine Guerard. Professor David Leahigh of Lehigh University, a long-time office-mate of one of the authors, wrote the appendix to chapter ten. We gratefully acknowledge Glen Hansen's assistance in running the Stone and Miller cash forecasting. Although the handbook was written on our own time, our directors at Drexel Burnham Lambert, Inc. and Peat, Marwick, Mitchell & Co., George Douglas, Hugh Feehan, and Thomas Richards have been extremely supportive. William Alpert of the Donner Foundation, Bernard Morin and William Kehoe of the University of Virginia, Al Bean, David Sanchez, and Eli Schwartz of Lehigh University, Lewis Spellman of the University of Texas, George McCabe of the University of Nebraska, and Mustafa Gultekin of the University of North Carolina are thanked for their support of our project. Additional helpful research suggestions on several chapters came from our friends in industry: Ken and Sheila Lawrence of AT & T., Ross Tartell at CIBA—GEIGY; James Sykes at Air Products and Chemicals, Inc.; David Baker; and Carl Ratner at Standard & Poor's Corporation.

The authors are especially grateful to Professor William Damon, at Vanderbilt University, and Professor Bernell Stone, at Brigham Young University, who read drafts of many of the chapters in the handbook. The book is much better as a result of their assistance. Any errors remaining are the sole responsibility of the authors. James Sykes, of Air Products and Chemicals, Inc., allowed the authors access to the SAS system with which most of our statistical analysis was performed. Jim's support was instrumental in developing the research papers on which chapters seven, twelve, and seventeen are based.

The authors are grateful to the people at Probus who guided us throughout the development of this handbook, constantly reminding us of our audience. They were very helpful and extremely patient.

We hope that the readers enjoy this handbook as well as finding it very useful. Many an hour in the evening went into writing the book. We often worked with a cold Molson in hand, watching the Yankees (and Cubs) on the television, after the family had gone to bed. We hope that our readers enjoy and learn from the handbook; after all, is there anything better than a good beer while analyzing Box-Jenkins, simultaneous equation systems, latent root regressions, and goal programing models?

Introduction

The purpose of this book is to familiarize the financial manager, treasurer, or comptroller with many recently developed tools of financial decision making. The field of financial management is changing rapidly, and it is often necessary for a manager to reach for a reference book to become reacquainted with models used in financial analysis. Our hope is that this book will become a useful reference for the financial executive.

Assuming that the reader is familiar with the basic theory of corporate finance and control, we proceed to the model-building process after only a brief review of the basic points. Each chapter (1) introduces the theory to be analyzed in a selected model, (2) discusses the assumptions on which that model is based, and (3) develops and estimates the model. We believe that numerical examples will be useful to financial managers; we include examples of computer output as well as references to software packages that are available to aid managers in the decision-making process.

We begin Part I, on assessing the present and future health of a firm, with a chapter on the analysis of financial statements. Chapter 1 examines the income statement and the balance sheet and presents many ratios useful for probing the condition of a firm. We examine the firm's sources and uses of funds by analyzing its statement of changes in financial position. By examining the actual financial statements of well-known corporations, Chrysler and Chevron, we hope to emphasize the significance of ratio analysis in the real world.

Traditional financial analysis relies heavily upon the projection of income statements and balance sheets into the future to gain insights into the management of current assets and liabilities and to predict a firm's needs to enter the capital market. In Chapter 2 we apply regression analysis to forecast sales and the percentage-of-sales approach to develop financial statements. We introduce the time series (ARIMA) analysis of Professors Box and Jenkins and use time series modeling to forecast daily cash collections. In Chapters 2 and 3 we employ SAS®, a user-friendly (IBM) mainframe software system for statistical analysis. In Chapter 4 we

1

present the Altman Z bankruptcy model, which invokes discriminant analysis and financial ratios to assess a firm's financial condition.

Part II deals with the cost of capital and with capital budgeting. Chapter 5 covers the calculation of the cost of capital on the basis of the Gordon-Shapiro framework and the Capital Asset Pricing Model (CAPM); it also examines the problem of project selection. Chapter 6 discusses the effect of leverage on the cost of capital and the optimal use of debt. Recent studies have shown that firms make decisions on dividends, investments, and the funding of research and development projects all at the same time. Equation modeling and estimation are introduced in Chapter 7 to show how the interactions of financial decisions can be included in the development of a strategic planning model of the firm. The SAS system is used to evaluate the simultaneous equation model of the firm, and SAS/OR, an algorithm for solving linear programming models, is applied in developing a reasonable allocation of corporate resources.

Part III is concerned with portfolio theory. In Chapter 8 we introduce Markowitz mean-variance analysis, analyze the basic theory of risk and return, and develop the idea of the efficient frontier. Systematic risk, measured by a firm's beta, is presented in Chapter 9, and examples involving Air Products, Exxon, and IBM illustrate the statistical basis of the CAPM. The portfolio theory of bonds is discussed in Chapter 10, emphasizing Malkiel's bond theorems, elasticity, and duration. We include an appendix on duration and yield curve analysis to aid the reader. The Black and Scholes Option Pricing Model (OPM), widely used on Wall Street, is introduced in Chapter 11. Portfolio return distribution models, including covered call writing with protective paths, advanced by Merton, Scholes and Gladstein, and Bookstaber and Clarke are discussed in Chapter 11.

Recent evidence suggests that analyst forecasts may be improved by combining them with time series forecasts to produce composite models. Since the weighting scheme of analyst forecasts highly correlated with time series (Box-Jenkins) forecasts may be very unstable, an equal weighting scheme for building composite earnings models is advocated in Chapter 12. Chapter 13 briefly summarizes the literature on the efficient markets hypothesis and discusses the implications for stocks, bonds, options, and analysts in an efficient market.

Part IV deals with long-term financial decisions. Chapter 14 introduces and develops the theory of conglomerate mergers. The cash flow approach to mergers is the focus of Chapter 15, in which the use of forecasts of sales, income, and discounted cash flow are applied to the problem of ascertaining a reasonable value for a merger candidate. Chapter 15 allows the reader to review the forecasting and pro forma analysis presented in Chapter 2, the cost of capital and capital budgeting of Chapter 6, and the equity valuation theories implicit in Chapters 5, 10, and 14. A further topic treated in Chapter 15 is Mobil Corporation's acquisition of Superior Oil Company in 1984. A brief introduction to leasing is presented in Chapter 16.

For firms that grow with the economy, a dependable GNP forecast may be advantageously combined with sales forecasts and pro forma statement analyses. Chapter 17 illustrates the combination of composite modeling with regression analysis to develop the 'best' possible statistical model for forecasting GNP.

Chapter 1

Financial Statement Analysis

In this chapter, we discuss how ratio analysis may be used to identify possible problems for the firm's management with respect to liquidity, profitability, leverage, and efficiency measures. A corporate financial officer would use this information to determine whether the firm's financial statements and ratios are significantly different from an industry average or average of all industrial firms. A rational corporate plan must be developed from knowledge of the firm's future financing opportunities, including the issuance of debt and equity. The firm's sources and uses of funds show how the firm generates its cash flow and how corporate resources are allocated.

Ratio analysis is used by commercial institutions from whom the firm may wish to borrow and investors who are possible purchasers of the firm's debt and equity. Management may desire to re-allocate corporate resources if it lags the industry or manufacturing firms' average. Relative performance measures such as those shown in the respective (liquidity, profitability, leverage, and efficiency) classes are widely used in the financial community.

Chrysler and Chevron are used as example firms.

Information Needs of Users of Financial Statements

The primary users of financial statements include the following:

- Credit grantors (trade creditors, banks, savings and loan associations, insurance companies, etc.);
- Equity investors (individual investors, pension funds, mutual funds, etc.);
- Managers (or others concerned with the effects of management decisions on financial performance); and

5

- Acquisition and merger analysts (or others interested in how a combination of two or more businesses will result in increased value).

Each of these users has different needs, purposes, and objectives when evaluating financial statements. For example, the equity investor looks primarily to prospects of future earnings and changes in those earnings. The credit grantor, on the other hand, is concerned primarily with specific security provisions of the loan, the fair market value of assets pledged, and repayment of principal and interest.

Source and Limitations of the Data Used for Most Analysis

The primary sources of data for most financial analysis are accounting statements. There are certain characteristics of accounting data that analysts should understand.

First, most accountants conform to a basic convention that accounting determinations are subject to objective verification. Since the cost of an asset arrived at by arm's length bargining may generally be objectively determined by inspection, it is claimed that the cost figure enjoys an objectivity surpassing any subsequent unrealized appraisal of value. Primarily for this reason, accounting adheres, with few exceptions, to the cost concept. Use of the cost concept is an important limitation of the usefulness of accounting statements. Cost balances do not, in most cases, represent current market values. Yet the users of financial statements usually look for an assessment of value, and for this purpose, historical cost balances are of very limited usefulness. The analyst must also be aware of valuation bases other than cost that are used in financial statements.

Second, because of the provisional nature of financial reports there is reliance on estimates for a large part of the data. To be useful, accounting information must be timely, therefore, determinations of financial condition and results of operations must be made frequently. But this frequency of report, particularly on the results of operations, requires a great deal of estimation; and the greater the potential errors of estimation, the greater the amount of uncertainty that is introduced into the statements. Examples of estimates include the following:

- Amount and timing of collections of receivables;
- Warranty claims expense;
- Percentage completion of various contracts;
- Future sales prices and volume of inventory;
- Estimated life and the salvage value of fixed assets.

These are limitations of accounting data. Although there are many others that are not discussed here, the point of this section, is to make the analyst aware of the limitations of the data that are being used to draw conclusions on financial performance.

Major Types of Financial Statements

The major types of financial statements are:

- Balance sheet (statement of financial condition);
- Income statement (results of operations); and
- Statement of changes in financial position.

These are discussed in the paragraphs that follow.

Balance Sheet

The balance sheet shows all assets, liabilities, and capital accounts in a convenient format. This format is:

Assets			*Liabilities and Equity*		
Cash		1,000	Accounts Payable		750
Accounts Receivable					
Gross Accounts					
Receivable	1,000				
Less: Uncollectible					
Accounts	100				
Net Accounts Receivable		900			
Inventory					
Raw Materials	100				
Work in process	200				
Finished Goods	300				
Total Inventory		600			
Total Current Assets		2,500	Total Current Liabilities		750
Property, Plant, Equipment			Long Term Debt		750
Gross Property, Plant and					
Equipment	1,200				
Less Depreciation:	800				
Net Property, Plant, Equipment		400	Stockholders Equity		
			Common Stock	1,000	
Intangible Assets		50	Retained	500	
			Earnings		
					1,500
Deferred Charges		50			
Total Assets		3,000	Total Liabilities and Stockholders Equity		3,000

On the left side of the balance sheet are the assets and unexpired costs in which the resources of the enterprise are invested at a point in time. On the right side are the sources from which these invested funds were financed, that is, the liabilities and the equity.

Generally, the assets that are categorized as current (cash, accounts receivable, inventory, securities not held as investment) are summarized on the balance sheet. Similarly, the liabilities that are categorized as current (accounts payable, other trade accounts payable, wages payable, payments on long-term debt occurring during the current operating cycle) are summarized as well. Since the current liabilities represent a short-term claim against the enterprise, the balance sheet shows the current assets generally available to meet these claims.

Income Statement

The income statement does not show the account balances as of a certain date, but rather shows the cumulative activity in the revenue, cost, and expense accounts for the period reported upon. It is a report on the dynamic aspects of the enterprise—the results of operations. The final net income (or loss) is added to or deducted from capital through the Retained Earnings account. Thus, the net results of operations are incorporated in the balance sheet through their inclusion in the capital accounts. One of the best measures of performance during the year is net income. But there are many limitations in relying on this measure alone in evaluating performance. Specifically, the net income realized one year does not necessarily reflect a long-term trend. In fact, in some cases income in a single period can be boosted by selling assets at a profit. This type of profit is misleading in that it is not produced from ongoing operations; it is not likely to be repeated in following years. Thus, conclusions about performance that are based solely on net income may be misleading.

Statement of Changes in Financial Position

This statement, which is of major importance and interest to the financial analyst, is designed to explain the changes in financial position that occur from one balance sheet date to another.

Types of Conclusions and Analysis

Most of the measures identified in this chapter provide some insight into the overall evaluation of a company. However, like most statistically oriented evaluations, they must be examined as a whole and not in isolation. While one ratio may be excellent, others may be poor. The overall analysis may be simply good. It is important to point out that even after all the ratios for a single company are calculated and reviewed they measure only past performance. The analyst must look deeper into the expected future performance. Is the past performance expected to continue? Or has management identified certain changes that will occur? If changes are to occur, what specifically are they? How will they affect financial performance? The evaluation of performance is difficult and, as mentioned earlier, cannot be drawn from a single number but rather must be based on a variety of sources about the economy, the industry, and of course, the financial statements of the specific enterprise being examined.

Often, when ratios are used as a measure of performance it is necessary to establish benchmarks for comparison. If the ratios for two companies in completely different industries are the same, this condition could be favorable for one company and unfavorable for the other. Thus, when evaluating ratios it is necessary to place them in the context of the previous history of the firm being evaluated, to compare them with those of the industry the firm is in, and finally to consider the overall economy in the periods being evaluated. A little thought and common sense go a long way in helping evaluate financial ratios. Often, ratios will not provide an answer to all that is being undertaken by the firm but they are excellent indicators and provide considerable insight into the overall operations of the firm.

Common Techniques for Analysis for Income Statement and Balance Sheet

One way in which income can be measured is by comparing the capital balances at the beginning and end of a period. Since capital is the excess of assets over liabilities, the problem of income determination is inseparable from the problem of asset and liability measurement. The process of measuring income involves two basic steps: 1) identification of the revenues that may be correctly attributable to the period reported and 2) relating the corresponding costs with the revenues of the period either through direct association with the cost of the products sold or by assignment as expenses properly applicable as period costs.

Common Size Statements

In the analysis of financial statements, it is often helpful to find out the proportion of a total that a single item or subgroup represents. On the balance sheet, the assets as well as the liabilities and capital are each expressed as 100 percent, and each item in these categories is expressed as a percentage of the respective totals. Similarly, in the income statement net sales are set at 100 percent and every item in the statement is expressed as a percentage of net sales. The analytical technique that relies upon expressing the individual components as part of the total (100 percent) is called common size statement analysis.

Common Ratios Used

There are a number of ratios that may be used in income statement analysis. We divide our analysis into the following categories of ratios:

- Profitability;
- Efficiency;
- Leverage; and
- Liquidation.

Each of the ratios are numbered sequentially. In the following sections we discuss each of the ratios.

A. Profitability ratios help the analyst evaluate the profitability of a firm.

   1. Net Profit Margin or Net Income/Revenues. This ratio identifies the percentage of profit earned relative to revenues (or sales). This is one of the most common measures of profitability and is very commonly employed. This ratio is calculated as follows:

$$\frac{\text{Net Income}}{\text{Revenues}}$$

A Net Profit Margin on Revenues of 10 percent means that $10 of after tax profit is generated for every $100 of sales. The percentage of net profit margin that is obtained will often vary significantly by industry. For example, the grocery stores in the food industry typically have low profit margins (for example three percent) and high turnover whereas jewelry stores often have high profit margins (for example greater than 50 percent) and low turnover. There is often a close relationship between the profit and the profit margin and inventory turnover (see the ratio under 10 below for a description of the inventory turnover ratio). In fact, firms can vary the net income and turnover factors to achieve the volume of profits desired. For example, a jewelry store could cut the profit margin (for each item of jewelry sold) and increase the volume of items sold hoping to make up the lost profit due to the reduced margin by increased volume.

2. Return on Equity. This ratio identifies the level of profits relative to total equity. This ratio is a measure of the effectiveness or productivity of invested capital in terms of earning profits. This ratio is calculated as follows:

$$\frac{\text{Net Income}}{\text{Book Value of Equity}}$$

The return on equity is a good measure of how effectively the firm's managers have employed invested capital. Stockholders often base share purchase (or sell) decisions on the return on equity.

3. Return on Assets. This ratio identifies the level of profits relative to assets. It identifies the productivity of assets in terms of the asset's earning power. This ratio is calculated as follows:

$$\frac{\text{Net Income}}{\text{Total Assets}}$$

This ratio is similar to the return on equity calculation but does not show the impact of leverage.

4. Taxes Paid/Net Income Before Taxes. This ratio identifies the tax paid by the firm relative to its pretax income.

$$\frac{\text{Taxes}}{\text{Net Income Before Taxes}}$$

This measure could be used to measure how effectively a firm manages its income tax expense.

B. Efficiency ratios help the analyst evaluate how efficiently companies are using their assets.

5. Sales to Assets. This ratio shows the extent to which assets are put to use in generating sales:

$$\frac{\text{Sales}}{\text{Average Total Assets}}$$

This ratio identifies how many times total assets must change in order to support the sales volume for the firm.

6. Sales to Net Working Capital. Since working capital can be adjusted more rapidly and more easily than total assets, given fluctuations in sales it may be a better measure of how well assets are employed. This ratio is calculated as follows:

$$\frac{\text{Sales}}{\text{Average Net Working Capital}}$$

This ratio measures the extent of working capital required for a given sales volume.

7. Inventory Turnover. This ratio identifies the number of times in a year that the inventory must be replaced in order to sustain a given sales volume. It measures the efficiency with which inventory is used. Obviously, whether the resulting ratio is favorable or unfavorable or bad depends upon the products in the inventory. For perishable items like milk or produce the turnover will be higher than for nonperishable higher priced items, such as heavy farm equipment. The inventory turnover is calculated as follows:

$$\frac{\text{Cost of Goods Sold}}{\text{Average Inventory}}$$

8. Days of Cash on Hand. It is often useful to know how large a cash reserve a firm has. For example, a firm having $10 million cash on hand may appear to be in a good position, but, if the firm has $20 million of cash expenditures each day the picture does not look so good. A measure of the cash reserve factor is:

$$\frac{\text{Cash}}{\text{Average Daily Expenditures from Operations}}$$

Most financial statements do not identify 'Average Daily Expenditures from Operations,' therefore in most cases it must be derived. A rough measure of average daily expenditures from operations is Cost of Goods Sold (per year)/360 days per year.

9. Average Collection Period. The average amount of time required to collect receivables is a good measure of the degree to which receivables can be readily converted into cash. The average collection period is calculated as follows:

$$\frac{\text{Average Accounts Receivable}}{\text{Average Sales per Day}}$$

Average accounts receivable may be approximated by adding the beginning and ending balances and dividing the sum by two.

Average Sales per Day is calculated as Annual Sales/360. An average collection period of say, 10 days means that on average its takes 10 days between the time a sale is earned and the time the cash is actually collected for the sale.

10. Average Payment Period. The amount of time required for the firm to pay trade receivables is a good measure of the extent to which other firms provide financing for the firm under analysis. The prompter the payment the fewer days the credit is providing for financing. A rough measure of the average payment period is the ratio:

$$\frac{\text{Average Accounts Payable}}{\text{Cost of Goods Sold per Day}}$$

The denominator in this equation may require some further analysis for each company. For example, depending upon the information available, the denominator may more appropriately be labeled Expenditures on Trade Credit. If it is possible to more appropriately define the denominator based on information available then of course, the resulting ratio has a greater value.[1]

C. Leverage ratios summarize the firm's position relative to borrowed capital. There are several ratios that provide insight into the degree of leverage and its effect on financial health. These include the following:

11. Debt Ratio. The debt ratio measures the ratio of long-term debt to total long-term capital. Since long-term lease payments or agreements also represent a commitment of the firm's resources, they are included in the numerator of this ratio.

$$\frac{\text{Long-Term Debt} + \text{Value of Leases}}{\text{Long-Term Debt} + \text{Value of Leases} + \text{Equity}}$$

12. Debt-Equity Ratio. The ratio of debt to equity is another measure of the amount of debt in the firm's capital structure but relative to equity rather than to total capital. It is calculated as follows:

$$\frac{\text{Long-Term Debt} + \text{Value of Leases}}{\text{Equity}}$$

---

[1]One could additionally calculate the average total asset life ratio and other measures of asset efficiency. It is often difficult to develop a reasonable comparison (outside of an industry average) for performance evaluation.

The last two ratios rely upon book value, not market value. Quite a different picture may result by using market values rather than book values. The financial analyst may want to look at these two ratios, using book value in one series of calculations and market value in another series.

13. Times Interest Earned. The times interest earned ratio measures the extent to which interest payments are covered by Earnings Before Interest and Taxes (EBIT) plus depreciation. It is calculated as follows:

$$\frac{\text{EBIT} + \text{Depreciation}}{\text{Interest}}$$

The point of this ratio is to measure the risk that the firm won't have money to pay interest. If EBIT falls below interest obligations, the firm won't have to worry about taxes, since interest is paid before the firm pays income taxes. The firm's regular interest payments must be made in order to avoid default. Thus, this ratio measures how safe the firm is in terms of making these payments.

D. Liquidity Ratios. These ratios summarize the firm's ability to pay current debt. There are two ratios that provide insight into the extent to which a firm could liquidate its current debt. These ratios include the following:

14. Current Ratio. The current ratio measures the extent to which current assets could liquidate current liabilities. There is a certain degree of simplicity involved in the use of this ratio. Basically, the ratio assumes that all current assets (cash, accounts receivable, inventory, and investments) are liquid. To some extent, this is true. While all these categories of assets may not be liquidated on a days notice most categories could be liquidated over a relatively brief period of time. The exception, of course, is inventory. If a firm has a large investment in obsolete inventory then the firm would not likely be capable of liquidating the inventory at book value to pay current liabilities. The ratio is calculated as follows:

$$\frac{\text{Current Assets}}{\text{Current Liabilities}}$$

15. Quick Ratio. The quick ratio measures the extent to which liquid current assets (all current assets less inventory) could liquidate current liabilities. The ratio is calculated as follows:

$$\frac{\text{Current Assets-Inventory}}{\text{Current Liabilities}}$$

E. Common Stock Valuation. The basis of modern stock valuation techniques and models is present value theory. This approach maintains that the present value of a share of stock is equal to the sum of all dividends expected to be received from it, discounted to the present at an appropriate rate of interest. The normal procedure in dynamic models is to state the price of a stock as the present value of a stream of dividends, with each component of this stream discounted at the rate k. One of the best known dynamic stock valuation models is that developed by Gordon and Shapiro. In their model, $E(t)$ denotes the earnings per share of an enterprise at time t, b is the dividend payout ratio, k is the market discount rate (the cost of capital), and g is the projected annual growth rate of earnings. The formula for the justified market price (P_{cs_e}) of the company's stock is

$$P_{cs_e} = \frac{bE(t)}{k - g}$$

$$P_{cs_e} = \frac{\text{Current Dividend}}{\text{Discount Rate} - \text{Growth Rate}}$$

There are many ratios used for evaluating the market value of a company and the related value of equities. Some of these are discussed below.

16. Payout Ratio. The payout ratio represents the proportion of earnings that is paid as dividends.

$$\frac{\text{Dividends per Share}}{\text{Earnings per Share}}$$

Thus, 1 minus the payout ratio equals the proportion of earnings plowed back into the ongoing operation of the business.

17. Price Earnings (P/E) Ratio. The P/E ratio, a common measure of the premium placed on a company by investors, is calculated as follows:

$$\frac{\text{Stock Price}}{\text{Earnings per Share}}$$

18. Market to Book Ratio is the ratio of the market value per share to the book value per share:

$$\frac{\text{Market Value per Share}}{\text{Book Value per Share}}$$

The book value equals proceeds from the sale of common stock plus retained earnings. For example, a ratio of 1:10 means that the firm's market value is 10 percent more than investments made by past and present stockholders.

Ratio Usage—Benefits and Pitfalls

There are many uses of ratios, however, the financial analyst must know and understand the power of ratios as well as their limitations. In general ratios provide a good indication of the financial health of a firm. However, it is important to realize that ratios are static—they only represent the situation at a point in time. In particular, to compute one ratio, for example, net income for one year, and draw any conclusions about the long-term health of a firm would be fallacious. It is more important to examine trends (for example, analyze net income over the last five years and the forecast for net income over the next three-five). Using ratios to help analyze and pinpoint trends is helpful. Even though this will provide insight there is usually the need to temper the numerical analysis with some qualitative judgment about the trend. For example, while the published forecast for net income over the next five years may point out a significant growth rate, the forecast may be soft and subject to a number of political and economic factors that may radically alter the estimate. These factors should be recognized by the analyst.

Chrysler Corporation Example

This is a sample case involving Chrysler Corporation, the third largest U.S. motor vehicle producer engaged primarily in the manufacturing, assembly, and sale of passenger cars, trucks, and parts in North America. In this case, we illustrate the calculation of the ratios we previously explained. We introduce several basis observations concerning changes in Chrysler revenues, profits, and leverage. The 18 ratios are then calculated during the 1976–1985 period.

In 1985 Chrysler acquired Gulfstream Aerospace Corporation for $642 million. This added a major producer of jet aircraft to the corporation.

Relevant income data is shown below:

Chrysler Income Data (Millions $)

Year Ended 12/31 Yr	REV	OI	CE	DEP	I	EBT	NI
1976	$15,538	$1,055	$424	$402	$181	$544	$328
1977	$16,708	$710	$723	$388	$202	$218	$125
1978	$13,618	$144	$671	$352	$166	($286)	($205)
1979	$12,002	($489)	$749	$401	$275	($1,102)	($1,097)
1980	$9,225	($771)	$835	$567	$405	($1,670)	($1,710)
1981	$10,882	$250	$456	$451	$406	($460)	($476)
1982	$10,045	$518	$374	$433	$339	($68)	($69)
1983	$13,240	$1,358	$1,057	$457	$267	$704	$302
1984	$19,573	$2,790	$1,247	$564	$184	$2,430	$1,496
1985	$21,256	$2,424	$1,663	$476	$268	$2,370	$1,635
10 Yr Totals	$142,087	$7,989	$8,199	$4,491	$2,693	$2,680	$329

REV = Revenue
OI = Operating income
CE = Capital expenditures
DEP = Depreciation
I = Interest expense
EBT = Earnings before taxes
NM = Not meaningful
NI = Net income

CHRYSLER ANALYSIS:
1. Let us begin our Chrysler analysis by examining revenue growth and net income during the 1976-1985 period. We will then calculate the previously discussed ratios for Chrysler.
   a. Calculated on a percentage basis, year-to-year growth in revenue is as follows:

1976-1977	7.5%
1977-1978	-18.5%
1978-1979	-11.9%
1979-1980	-23.1%
1980-1981	18.0%
1981-1982	-7.7%
1982-1983	31.8%
1983-1984	47.8%
1984-1985	8.6%

Year-to-year revenue changes are significant. Significant swings in revenue have occurred. Given that the auto industry has a high degree of fixed costs, there is a great deal of operating leverage. The compound revenue growth during these years is as follows:

$$\frac{\$21,256}{\$15,538} = 1.368 = \text{Compound Value interest factor of a lump sum for 8 years.}$$

During this nine-year period the annualized growth per year was 3.5 percent.

Year-to-year changes in net income are even more significant than the revenue savings.

Year-to-Year		% CHANGES NI	% CHANGES REV	% CHG (NI) / % CHG (REV)
1976	1977	-61.9%	7.5%	-8.2%
1977	1978	-264.0%	-18.5%	14.3
1978	1979	435.1%	-11.9%	-36.7
1979	1980	55.9%	-23.1%	-2.4
1980	1981	-72.2%	18.0%	-4.0
1981	1982	-85.5%	-7.7%	11.1
1982	1983	-537.7%	31.8%	-16.9
1983	1984	395.4%	47.8%	8.3
1984	1985	9.3%	8.6%	1.1

The swings in net income are larger than the changes in revenue because of high operating costs and a high amount of debt in Chrysler's capital structure. Weston and Copeland (1986) refer to this relationship as the degree of combined leverage. In fact, the change in net income ranges from little more than 1 to nearly 37 times the percentage change in revenue. The auto industry has a high degree of fixed costs and although the amount of leverage is high, Chrysler was able to cut its break-even point from 2.4 million cars in 1979 to 1.2 million cars in 1985.

During this period Chrysler was spending quite a bit on capital expenditures. Almost every year capital expenditures exceeded depreciation by an average factor of more than 1.8 to 1. The excess of capital expenditures relative to depreciation tends to reduce Chrysler's cash flow from operations. This could mean that new equipment and other capital is much more expensive than the old equipment being replaced or more likely it means that Chrysler is embarking on capital expansion (enhancing its equipment facilities). In fact, Chrysler embarked on a five-year $12.5 billion capital expansion program for new products and plant modernization beginning in 1980.

One should analyze the patterns exhibited by earnings per share and the stock price to notice the effects of leverage and high fixed costs of profitability and the stock price.

		Stock Price		
Yr	EPS	High	Low	Arithmetic Average
1976	$3.63	$14.875	$6.875	$10.875
1977	$1.38	$14.750	$8.250	$11.500
1978	($2.36)	$9.125	$5.500	$7.313
1979	($11.45)	$7.750	$3.750	$5.750
1980	($17.33)	$7.750	$2.750	$5.250
1981	($4.79)	$5.125	$2.000	$3.563
1982	($0.85)	$12.500	$2.375	$7.438
1983	$1.57	$22.750	$9.375	$16.063
1984	$7.83	$22.500	$13.875	$18.188
1985	$9.38	$31.375	$19.875	$25.625

The patterns in earnings per share are so erratic it is very difficult to draw conclusions other than one obvious one about the degree of risk involved in Chrysler's stock because of such erratic earnings patterns. The great variability in the earnings of Chrysler tend to produce a higher cost of equity and capital than would be the case for a firm with stable earnings (Malkiel and Cragg (1970)). The stock price changes are also quite erratic as evidenced by the swings in the price per share.

The percentage change in earnings and share price from year to year are calculated and shown below.

From	To	EPS Percentage Changes	Share Price Percentage Changes
1976	1977	−62.0%	5.7%
1977	1978	−271.0%	−36.4%
1978	1979	385.2%	−21.4%
1979	1980	51.4%	−8.7%
1980	1981	−72.4%	−32.1%
1981	1982	−82.3%	108.8%
1982	1983	−284.7%	116.0%
1983	1984	398.7%	13.2%
1984	1985	19.8%	40.9%

Using percentage changes probably does not produce as good a measure as the standard deviation. The standard deviation of the series is enormous (823.7) relative to the mean EPS value of −$1.30.

Let us calculate the degree of financial leverage based on the information available which shows the relationship between the firm's operating income, its EBIT, and its net income. The larger the degree of financial leverage, the greater will be return on equity of the firm, ceterus paribus (for firms with positive earnings)

$EBIT/(EBIT − I)$ = Degree of financial leverage

	EBIT − I	I	EBIT	EBIT/(EBIT − I)
1976	$544	$181	$725	1.33272
1977	$218	$202	$420	1.92660
1978	($286)	$166	($120)	0.41958
1979	($1,102)	$275	($827)	0.75045
1980	($1,670)	$405	($1,265)	0.75748
1981	($460)	$406	($54)	0.11739
1982	($68)	$339	$271	−3.9852
1983	$704	$267	$971	1.37926
1984	$2,430	$184	$2,614	1.07572
1985	$2,370	$268	$2,638	1.11308

The resulting number, the degree of financial leverage illustrates the percentage change in earnings given a change in operating income.

Relevant balance sheet data is shown below:

Chrysler Balance Sheet Data (Millions $)							
Year Ended 12/31 Yr	Cash	CA	CL	TA	LTD	CE	TC
1976	$572	$3,878	$2,826	$7,074	$1,048	$2,815	$4,014
1977	$409	$4,153	$3,090	$7,668	$1,253	$2,925	$4,319
1978	$523	$3,562	$2,486	$6,981	$1,204	$2,710	$4,242
1979	$474	$3,121	$3,232	$6,653	$992	$1,599	$2,938
1980	$297	$2,861	$3,029	$6,618	$2,483	($138)	$3,014
1981	$404	$2,601	$2,419	$6,270	$2,059	($601)	$2,907
1982	$897	$2,369	$2,113	$6,264	$2,189	($419)	$3,205
1983	$1,069	$2,754	$3,454	$6,772	$1,104	$1,143	$2,469
1984	$1,700	$3,980	$4,116	$9,063	$760	$3,306	$4,088
1985	$2,798	$5,313	$4,729	$12,605	$2,366	$4,215	$6,973

In this section we will illustrate the calculation of a number of ratios using Chrysler Corporation. In some cases, the ratios are not meaningful. In those conditions we have indicated this in the narrative explanation that accompanies each ratio. In addition, we have identified the automobile industry and S&P 400 ratios as a basis for comparison and evaluation of Chrysler during the 1982–1985 period.[2]

The order of presentation of the ratios follows the order previously presented in this chapter.

CA = Current Assets
CL = Current Liabilities
TA = Total Assets
LTD = Long Term Debt
CE = Common Equity
TC = Total Capitalization
NM = Not Meaningful
REV = Revenues

Let us calculate Chrysler's net profit margin:

---

[2]Averages for the S&P 400 and automobile industry can easily be calculated for the entire 1976–1985 period. We compare the Chrysler ratios to the industry and industrial benchmarks only to illustrate the Chrysler recovery. Chrysler ratios for the 1976–1985 period are used in Chapter 4 in the Altman Z bankruptcy analysis to assess the financial health of Chrysler.

Year	REV	NI	Chrysler Net Profit Margin	Automobile Industry	S&P 400
1976	$15,538	$328	2.1%		
1977	16,708	125	.7%		
1978	13,618	(205)	−1.5%		
1979	12,002	(1097)	−9.1%		
1980	9,225	(1710)	−18.5%		
1981	10,882	(476)	−4.4%		
1982	10,045	(69)	−.7%	−22.4%	4.0%
1983	13,240	302	2.3%	−6.7%	4.2%
1984	19,573	1496	7.6%	2.8%	4.9%
1985	21,256	1635	7.7%	−3.2%	4.0%

Comparison to Automobile Industry Average: Chrysler has out performed the automobile industry during the 1982–1985 period by earning a larger profit margin on its sales.[2]

Comparison to S&P 400: Chrysler's profits margin on sales lagged the average of the 400 largest industrial firms in 1982 and 1983. However, Chrysler's profit margin greatly exceeded the industrial averages in 1984 and 1985. One can again see the effects of high fixed costs on profitability.

1. Let us calculate the return on equity (net income/common equity)

Yr	EBT	NI	CE	NBT/CE	Chrysler NI/EQ	Automobile Industry	S&P 400
1976	$544	$328	$2,815	19.3%	11.7%		
1977	$218	$125	$2,925	7.5%	4.3%		
1978	($286)	($205)	$2,710	NM	NM		
1979	($1,102)	($1,097)	$1,599	NM	NM		
1980	($1,670)	($1,710)	($138)	NM	NM		
1981	($460)	($476)	($601)	NM	NM		
1982	($68)	($69)	($419)	NM	NM	1.8%	10.7%
1983	$704	$302	$1,143	61.6%	26.4%	21.5%	10.9%
1984	$2,430	$1,496	$3,306	73.5%	45.3%	26.3%	14.1%
1985	$2,370	$1,635	$4,215	56.2%	38.8%	17.8%	11.2%

Return on equity (either calculated on a pretax or after-tax basis) yields results that are consistent with the profit swings incurred by Chrysler. The high of 45 percent return on equity was offset by the less than positive results in the years 1978–1982.

Comparison to Automobile Industry Average: In the years for which comparison data are used Chrysler outperforms the industry.

Comparison to S&P 400: In the years for which comparison data are used Chrysler outperforms the industrial average.

3. Let us calculate the return on assets (net income/total assets)

Yr	EBT	NI	TA	EBT/TA	NI/TA	Automobile Industry	S&P 400
1976	$544	$328	$7,074	7.7%	4.6%		
1977	$218	$125	$7,668	2.8%	1.6%		
1978	($286)	($205)	$6,981	−4.1%	−2.9%		
1979	($1,102)	($1,097)	$6,653	−16.6%	−16.5%		
1980	($1,670)	($1,710)	$6,618	−25.2%	−25.8%		
1981	($460)	($476)	$6,270	−7.3%	−7.6%		
1982	($68)	($69)	$6,264	−1.1%	−1.1%	7.5%	4.7%
1983	$704	$302	$6,772	10.4%	4.5%	11.1%	4.9%
1984	$2,430	$1,496	$9,063	26.8%	16.5%	8.3%	6.0%
1985	$2,370	$1,635	$12,605	18.8%	13.0%	0.7%	4.5%

Return on assets (either calculated on a pretax or after-tax basis) yields results that are consistent with the profit swings incurred by Chrysler. The return on assets is substantially less than the return on equity for Chrysler during the 1983–1985 period because of Chrysler's use of debt. The high of 25.8% return on assets was offset by the less than positive results in the years 1978–82.

This ratio measures the profitability of assets in generating returns. The return on assets is not always high, this can be expected in a highly capital intensive industry like the auto industry.

Comparison to Automobile Industry Average. In the years for which comparison data are available Chrysler outperforms the industry.

Comparison to S&P 400. In the years of comparison data, Chrysler outperforms the S&P 400.

4. Let us calculate the percentage of taxes paid relative to net income before taxes.

Yr	EBT	NI	Taxes (EBT-NI)	Taxes/EBT
1976	$544	$328	$216	39.7%
1977	$218	$125	$93	42.7%
1978	($286)	($205)	($81)	28.3%
1979	($1,102)	($1,097)	($5)	0.5%
1980	($1,670)	($1,710)	$40	−2.4%
1981	($460)	($476)	$16	−3.5%
1982	($68)	($69)	$1	−1.5%
1983	$704	$302	$402	57.1%
1984	$2,430	$1,496	$934	38.4%
1985	$2,370	$1,635	$735	31.0%

5. Let us calculate the sales-to-assets ratio.

Yr	REV	TA	Chrysler REV/ TA	Automobile Industry	S&P 400
1976	$15,538	$7,074	2.2		
1977	$16,708	$7,668	2.2		
1978	$13,618	$6,981	2.0		
1979	$12,002	$6,653	1.8		
1980	$9,225	$6,618	1.4		
1981	$10,882	$6,270	1.7		
1982	$10,045	$6,264	1.6	1.5	1.18
1983	$13,240	$6,772	2.0	1.7	1.16
1984	$19,573	$9,063	2.2	1.8	1.23
1985	$21,256	$12,605	1.7	1.6	1.14

Comparison to Automobile Industry Average. In the years of comparison data, Chrysler outperforms the industry, showing efficient usage of assets.

Comparison to S&P 400. In the years for which comparison data are available Chrysler generally outperforms the S&P 400.

6.   Let us calculate the sales to net working capital ratio. First, we will illustrate the calculation of net working capital.

Yr	CA	CL	Net Working Capital
1976	$3,878	$2,826	$1,052
1977	$4,153	$3,090	$1,063
1978	$3,562	$2,486	$1,076
1979	$3,121	$3,232	($111)
1980	$2,861	$3,029	($168)
1981	$2,601	$2,419	$182
1982	$2,369	$2,113	$256
1983	$2,754	$3,454	($700)
1984	$3,980	$4,116	($136)
1985	$5,313	$4,729	$584

The net working capital position provides a measure of the amount by which current assets exceed current liabilities.

Second, we will illustrate calculation of the sales to net working capital (NWC) ratio.

Yr	Revenue	NWC	Chrysler	Automobile Industry	S&P 400
1976	$15,538	1052	14.8		
1977	$16,708	1063	15.7		
1978	$13,618	1076	12.7		
1979	$12,002	−111	−108.1		
1980	$9,225	−168	−54.9		

Yr	Revenue	NWC	Chrysler	Automobile Industry	S&P 400
1981	$10,882	182	59.8		
1982	$10,045	256	39.2	370	9.66
1983	$13,240	−700	−18.9	23.23	9.07
1984	$19,573	−136	−143.9	20.7	9.73
1985	$21,256	584	36.4	45.1	9.94

Comparison to Automobile Industry Average. In the years for which comparison data are used Chrysler does not perform as well as the industry. The lack of liquidity supports the relative riskiness of Chrysler.

Comparison to S&P 400. In the years for which comparison data are used Chrysler is not as liquid as the average firm in the S&P 400.

7. Let us calculate the inventory turnover.

   In this example, not enough data is available to calculate this ratio for all years. In order to illustrate this calculation we have obtained the inventory balance for two years: 1985 and 1986. We will illustrate calculation of this ratio for only these two years.

	INVENTORY (Millions)	Sales (Millions)	Days per Yr	Sales per Day (Millions)
1986	1699.6	$22,586	360	62.73888
1985	348.9	$21,256	360	59.04444

	INVENTORY TURNOVER	S&P 400	AUTO INDUSTRY
1986	27	4.89	10.85
1985	6	4.9	9.8

In 1986 Chrysler's inventory turnover was far better than either the auto industry or the S&P 400. However, in 1985 the ratio was not as good. Clearly, in 1986 Chrysler did a good job managing its inventory.

8. Days of Cash on Hand. This ratio could be approximated in this example by computing average daily expenditures as simply computed 'cash expenditures'/360.

1 CE	2 IE	3 REV	4 OI	5 Expenditures From Operations	6 Total Expenditures (COL 1+2+5)
$424	$181	$15,538	$1,055	$14,483	$15,088
$723	$202	$16,708	$710	$15,998	$16,923

1 CE	2 IE	3 REV	4 OI	5 Expenditures From Operations	6 Total Expenditures (COL 1+2+5)
$671	$166	$13,618	$144	$13,474	$14,311
$749	$275	$12,002	($489)	$12,491	$13,515
$835	$405	$9,225	($771)	$9,996	$11,236
$456	$406	$10,882	$250	$10,632	$11,494
$374	$339	$10,045	$518	$9,527	$10,240
$1,057	$267	$13,240	$1,358	$11,882	$13,206
$1,247	$184	$19,573	$2,790	$16,783	$18,214
$1,663	$268	$21,256	$2,424	$18,832	$20,763

Average Daily Expenditures = Expenditures/360

Annual Expenditures (Millions)	Days Per Year	Expenditures Per Day (Thousands)	Cash Balance (Millions)	Days of Cash on Hand
$15,088	360	$42	$572	13.6
$16,923	360	$47	$409	8.7
$14,311	360	$40	$523	13.2
$13,515	360	$38	$474	12.6
$11,236	360	$31	$297	9.5
$11,494	360	$32	$404	12.7
$10,240	360	$28	$897	31.5
$13,206	360	$37	$1,069	29.1
$18,214	360	$51	$1,700	33.6
$20,763	360	$58	$2,798	48.5

The number of days of cash on hand has increased significantly having improved to the point of having over 48 days of cash on hand. This indicates the cash management process at the firm has significantly improved over this period of time.

9. Let us calculate the average collection period. In this example, not enough data is available to calculate this ratio for all years. In order to illustrate this calculation we have obtained the accounts receivable balance for three years: 1984, 1985, and 1986. We will illustrate calculation of this ratio for only these three years.

	A/R ($ Millions)	REV ($ Millions)	Days per Yr	Sales per Day ($ Millions)
1985	207.5	$21,256	360	59.04444
1986	372.5	$22,586	360	62.73888

Average Collection Period = AR/Sales per day

1985	4
1986	6

Comparable industry or S&P 400 comparison data are not available.

10. Average Payment Period. This ratio could be approximated in this example by computing average cost of goods sold per day.
     Average cost of goods sold per day

REV	OI	Cost of Goods Sold ($ Millions)		Cost of Goods Sold Per Day ($ Millions)
$15,538	$1,055	$14,483	360	40.2
$16,708	$710	$15,998	360	44.4
$13,618	$144	$13,474	360	37.4
$12,002	($489)	$12,491	360	34.7
$9,225	($771)	$9,996	360	27.8
$10,882	$250	$10,632	360	29.5
$10,045	$518	$9,527	360	26.5
$13,240	$1,358	$11,882	360	33.0
$19,573	$2,790	$16,783	360	46.6
$21,256	$2,424	$18,832	360	52.3

Avg A/P	Avg COGS per Day	Avg Payment Period
$2,826	40.2	70.2
$3,090	44.4	69.5
$2,486	37.4	66.4
$3,232	34.7	93.1
$3,029	27.8	109.1
$2,419	29.5	81.9
$2,113	26.5	79.8
$3,454	33.0	104.6
$4,116	46.6	88.3
$4,729	52.3	90.4

11. Let us calculate the debt ratio.

Year	LTD	CE	Debt Equity +	Percentage	Auto Industry	S&P 400
1976	$1,048	$2,815	$3,863	27.1%		
1977	$1,253	$2,925	$4,178	30.0%		
1978	$1,204	$2,710	$3,914	30.8%		
1979	$992	$1,599	$2,591	38.3%		
1980	$2,483	($138)	$2,345	105.9%		
1981	$2,059	($601)	$1,458	141.2%		
1982	$2,189	($419)	$1,770	123.7%	39.0%	42.0%
1983	$1,104	$1,143	$2,247	49.1%	25.0%	39.0%
1984	$760	$3,306	$4,066	18.7%	15.0%	40.0%
1985	$2,366	$4,215	$6,581	36.0%	16.0%	43.0%

12.   Let us calculate the debt-equity ratio.

Year	LTD	Equity	Percentage	Automobile Industry	S&P 400
1976	$1,048	$2,815	37.2%		
1977	$1,253	$2,925	42.8%		
1978	$1,204	$2,710	44.4%		
1979	$992	$1,599	62.0%		
1980	$2,483	($138)	−1799.3%		
1981	$2,059	($601)	−342.6%		
1982	$2,189	($419)	−522.4%	39.0%	42.0%
1983	$1,104	$1,143	96.6%	25.0%	39.0%
1984	$760	$3,306	23.0%	15.0%	40.0%
1985	$2,366	$4,215	56.1%	16.0%	43.0%

Comparison to Automobile Industry Average. In the years for which comparison data are available Chrysler generally has a much higher debt level than the industry. Serving to increase its return on equity.

Comparison to S&P 400. In the years for which comparison data are available Chrysler has a much higher debt ratio than the S&P 400.

13.   Let us calculate the times fixed charged coverage ratio (sometimes called times interest earned—if the only fixed charge being analyzed is interest).

Year	EBIT	I	Chrysler Ratio	Automobile Industry	S&P 400
1976	$725	$181	1.9		
1977	$420	$202	1.4		
1978	($120)	$166	0.4		
1979	($827)	$275	−0.6		
1980	($1,265)	$405	−0.7		
1981	($54)	$406	0.5		
1982	$271	$339	0.9	1.09	3.05
1983	$971	$267	2.0	4.8	3.4
1984	$2,614	$184	4.2	7.58	3.58
1985	$2,638	$268	4.2	5.75	3.16

Comparison to Automobile Industry Average. In the years for which comparison data are used Chrysler has a much lower fixed charge coverage ratio than the industry reflecting the relative degree of risk associated with Chrysler.

Comparison to S&P 400. In the years for which comparison data are available Chrylser has differing results compared to the S&P 400. In some years the ratio is higher (for example in 1985 and 1984) whereas in other years the ratio is lower.

14. Let us examine the liquidity of Chrysler. Calculate the current ratio (current assets/current liabilities).

YR	CA	CL	Chrysler Current Ratio	Automobile Industry Current Ratio	S&P 400 Current Ratio
1976	$3,878	$2,826	1.4		
1977	$4,153	$3,090	1.3		
1978	$3,562	$2,486	1.4		
1979	$3,121	$3,232	1.0		
1980	$2,861	$3,029	0.9		
1981	$2,601	$2,419	1.1		
1982	$2,369	$2,113	1.1	1.01	1.49
1983	$2,754	$3,454	0.8	1.2	1.51
1984	$3,980	$4,116	1.0	1.22	1.46
1985	$5,313	$4,729	1.1	1.09	1.47

Comparison to Automobile Industry Average. In the years for which comparison data are used Chrysler is often fairly close to the industry averages. This means their ability to liquidate debt is about equivalent to the industry average.

Comparison to S&P 400. In the years for which comparison data are available Chrysler generally does not show as strong a current ratio as the S&P 400.

15. Let us calculate the modified quick ratio (cash/current liabilities):

YR	Cash	CL	Quick Ratio	Automobile Industry Quick Ratio	S&P 400 Quick Ratio
1976	$572	$2,826	0.2		
1977	$409	$3,090	0.1		
1978	$523	$2,486	0.2		
1979	$474	$3,232	0.1		
1980	$297	$3,029	0.1		
1981	$404	$2,419	0.2		
1982	$897	$2,113	0.4	0.55	0.85
1983	$1,069	$3,454	0.3	0.78	0.93
1984	$1,700	$4,116	0.4	0.83	0.85
1985	$2,798	$4,729	0.6	0.72	0.79

The quick ratio or acid test measures the degree to which cash could be used (say in the event of an emergency) to pay off current liabilities. The quick ratios is found by subtracting the inventory from total current assets and dividing the result by total current liabilities. The quick ratio should exceed one. We will use a similar measure: Cash/Current Liabilities. Obviously, Chrysler's modified quick ratio does not look good. In the years 1976–81 Chrysler did not have enough cash to pay off more than 10-20% of its current liabilities.

Comparison to Automobile Industry Average. In the years for which comparison data are used Chrysler is less than the industry averages. This means their ability to liquidate debt quickly does not appear to be as good as the industry average.

Comparison to S&P 400. In the years for which comparison data are available Chrysler generally does not show as strong a current ratio as the S&P 400.

16.   Calculate the payout ratio.

YR	EPS	Dividends	Payout Percentage
1976	$3.63	N/A	0.0%
1977	$1.38	$0.40	29.0%
1978	($2.36)	$0.38	−16.1%
1979	($11.45)	$0.09	−0.8%
1980	($17.33)	$0.00	0.0%
1981	($4.79)	$0.00	0.0%
1982	($0.85)	$0.00	0.0%
1983	$1.57	$0.00	0.0%
1984	$7.83	$0.38	4.9%
1985	$9.38	$0.44	4.7%

Most mature manufacturing firms have a payout ratio of 40 percent.

17.   Calculate the price/earnings ratio.

	Arithmetic Avg Price	EPS	Chrysler P/E Ratio	S&P 400		Auto	
				High	Low	High	Low
1976	$10.875	$3.63	3.0				
1977	$11.500	$1.38	8.3				
1978	$7.313	($2.36)	−3.1				
1979	$5.750	($11.45)	−0.5				
1980	$5.250	($17.33)	−0.3				
1981	$3.563	($4.79)	−0.7				
1982	$7.438	($0.85)	−8.8	13.92	8.05	135.4	65.58
1983	$16.063	$1.57	10.2	14.7	9.84	6.44	3.99
1984	$18.188	$7.83	2.3	12	8.39	4.4	3.15
1985	$25.625	$9.38	2.7	16.37	11.04	5.32	3.83

Generally, Chrysler's P/E is lower than the auto industry and the S&P 400.

Calculate the dividend yield.
18.   Let us calculate the market-to-book ratio.

	Market Value	Book Value Common Equity ($ Millions)	No. Shares Thousands	Book Value Share	Mkt/ Book Value	Auto Industry
1976	$10.875	$424	NA	NA	NA	
1977	$11.500	$723	136	$5.32	2.2	
1978	$7.313	$671	139	$4.83	1.5	
1979	$5.750	$749	147	$5.10	1.1	
1980	$5.250	$835	150	$5.57	0.9	
1981	$3.563	$456	158	$2.89	1.2	
1982	$7.438	$374	172	$2.17	3.4	1.06
1983	$16.063	$1,057	261	$4.05	4.0	1.17
1984	$18.188	$1,247	278	$4.49	4.1	1
1985	$25.625	$1,663	261	$7.49	3.4	0.84

NA = Not Available

Chrysler generally appeared better than the industry and the S&P 400. This seems to indicate the high degree of trust the American public placed in Chrysler's ability to get back on its feet after experiencing financial difficulties.

In the following sections we illustrate the calculation of some other financial ratios that may be of interest in this example.

Let us calculate net interest expense relative to total debt. In the ratios below we have calculated both the proportions of interest expense relative to long-term debt and interest expense relative to current debt to try and arrive at an average interest rate paid on borrowed money. Obviously, neither figure is exactly correct. The first ratio may overstate the interest rate since some short-term debt may have required interest payments that are due. The second ratio may understate the amount of interest relative to debt since not all short-term borrowings (trade credit) require the payment of interest.

YR	I	LTD	CL	I/LTD	I/LTD+CL
1976	$181	$1,048	$2,826	17.3%	4.7%
1977	$202	$1,253	$3,090	16.1%	4.7%
1978	$166	$1,204	$2,486	13.8%	4.5%
1979	$275	$992	$3,232	27.7%	6.5%
1980	$405	$2,483	$3,029	16.3%	7.3%
1981	$406	$2,059	$2,419	19.7%	9.1%
1982	$339	$2,189	$2,113	15.5%	7.9%
1983	$267	$1,104	$3,454	24.2%	5.9%
1984	$184	$760	$4,116	24.2%	3.8%
1985	$268	$2,366	$4,729	11.3%	3.8%

Calculation of this ratio leads to some interesting results. In 1985, year interest expense as a percentage of long-term debt expense comes to 11.3 percent. This appears to be reasonable. However, the 1979 calculation doesn't look as reasonable. In that year the long-term debt dropped to $992 million (a significant decrease and unlike the size of debt in other years). It is reasonable to assume in that year a larger proportion of financing was handled through short-term borrowing. That short-term borrowing probably was subject to interest payments.

In the following steps we illustrate calculation of other ratios that were not previously explained in the text. These are for additional information.

One could calculate the percentage of fixed assets relative to total assets and current assets to total assets. Current Assets are identified and therefore fixed assets could be easily calculated as total assets minus current assets. The ratios are shown below.

YR	CA	TA	CA/TA	FA/TA
1976	$3,878	$7,074	54.8%	45.2%
1977	$4,153	$7,668	54.2%	45.8%
1978	$3,562	$6,981	51.0%	49.0%
1979	$3,121	$6,653	46.9%	53.1%
1980	$2,861	$6,618	43.2%	56.8%
1981	$2,601	$6,270	41.5%	58.5%
1982	$2,369	$6,264	37.8%	62.2%
1983	$2,754	$6,772	40.7%	59.3%
1984	$3,980	$9,063	43.9%	56.1%
1985	$5,313	$12,605	42.1%	57.9%

One could calculate the percentage of long-term debt relative to the total capital structure.

YR	LTD	TC	Percentage
1976	$1,048	$4,014	26.1%
1977	$1,253	$4,319	29.0%
1978	$1,204	$4,242	28.4%
1979	$992	$2,938	33.8%
1980	$2,483	$3,014	82.4%
1981	$2,059	$2,907	70.8%
1982	$2,189	$3,205	68.3%
1983	$1,104	$2,469	44.7%
1984	$760	$4,088	18.6%
1985	$2,366	$6,973	33.9%
		Average	43.6%

In 1980 debt constituted a very high percentage of total capital (over 80 percent). In other years the percentage is more reasonable, given the industry and economy. The average over the period of time examined is 43.6 percent.

Analysis of the Statement of Changes in Financial Position

The purpose of this section is to continue the introduction of some common concepts and techniques for evaluating the financial performance of a business organization. The previous section concentrated on the income statement and balance sheet whereas this section discusses the Statement of Changes in Financial Position.

As indicated in the previous section there are several measures of financial health. We concentrated on some measures that identified the ability of an enterprise to meet its obligations and its ability to expand and grow; both of these depend upon adequate levels of liquid funds. The Statement of Changes in Financial Position (SCFP) provides information on funds flow in a business enterprise. Specifically, it identifies the sources and uses of working capital over a period of time. The statement also provides information about major financing and investment activities that do not involve sources and uses of working capital.

This section of the appendix is organized into the following topics:

- Liquidity Concepts and Reporting Requirements
- Construction of the Statement of Changes in Financial Position— Working Capital Focus
- Explanation of the Statement of Changes in Financial Position—Cash Focus
- Example: Analysis of Chevron Corporation's SCFP.

Liquidity Concepts and Reporting Requirements

Liquidity is the key to the financial survival of any firm. If the firm cannot pay bills as they come due, the very existence of the financial enterprise is in question. Even beyond simple survival, the firm must have cash to sustain operations and to expand. The two best-recognized measures of liquidity are working capital and cash. In this discussion the term "funds" is equivalent to working capital. The Statement of Sources and Uses of Working Capital (funds) explains the change in the level of working capital between two dates.

Years ago, the Statement of Sources and Uses of Working Capital was sufficient for financial reporting purposes. Over time, however, investors, creditors, and other users of financial statements found flaws in the construction of the statement. It was inadequate. The inadequacy centered on the fact that important financing and investing transactions do not involve either working capital or cash. For example, acquisition of a plant financed through long-term debt does not affect working capital. The end result is that the accounting community, through APB Opinion 19, broadened the financial reporting requirements by requiring the Statement of Changes in Financial Position as one of the three basic financial statements (the income statement and balance sheet are the other two major statements).[3]

Explanation of the Statement of Changes in Financial Position—Working Capital Focus

The statement focuses on changes in working capital or on changes in cash and cash equivalents. The FASB has recommended that the cash focus be used in practice, and the trend is to emphasize the cash focus statement rather than the working capital statement. We will describe these two forms. First, we will describe the SCFP-Working Capital Focus. Because this approach corresponds to the traditional concept of the SCFP, we will devote more space to discussing it. Either statement, regardless of focus, includes major financing and investing transactions that do not involve funds or cash such as the following:

- Issuance of securities to acquire property or other long-term assets
- Conversion of long-term debt or preferred stock into common stock
- Other nonmonetary exchanges

Because an understanding of this statement requires a grasp of the principles and methods that underlie its preparation, we describe these in this section.

For purposes of illustration the balance sheet may be summarized as follows:

Current Section

Current Assets   Current Liabilities

Noncurrent Section

Fixed Assets   Long Term Liabilities
Other Assets   Deferred Credits
Equity Accounts

Given this division, the following guidelines apply in the preparation of the SCFP:

---

[3]APB opinion 19, *Reporting Changes in Financial Position*. APB No. 19 was superseded by Statement of Financial Accounting Standards (FASB) No. 95, *Statement of Cash Flows*, 1987.

1. A *net change* in the current section can be explained **only** by changes in the accounts of the noncurrent section. These are the only changes with which the SCFP is concerned. For example, a net increase in working capital must be explained by a change in the noncurrent portion of the balance sheet; there is no other source from which this change could be derived.
2. Internal changes *within* the current section are not relevant because the statement indicates the *net* change in working capital. For example, the purchase of short-term securities or inventory for cash merely involves a change in the composition of working capital but not a net change in the amount of working capital. Similarly, the retirement of short-term debt through the payment of cash has no effect on the noncurrent section of the balance sheet—the working capital is unchanged. APB Opinion 19 does, however, require a separate statement explaining the net changes in the working capital composition.
3. Similarly, internal changes *within* the noncurrent section have no effect on working capital. However, some changes within the noncurrent section are significant financial transactions, and consequently, the SCFP includes these.

The statement format is, simply expressed, as follows:

> *Sources of funds:*
>   Funds provided by operations:
>   Net Income
>   Changes not requiring funds in the current period:
>   Depreciation
>   Amortization
>   Sale of fixed assets
>   Issue of capital stock in conversion of debt
>   Sale of capital stock
>   Total sources of funds
> *Uses of funds:*
>   Purchases of fixed assets
>   Payment of dividends
>   Repayment of long term debt
>   Conversion of debt into capital stock
>   Total uses of funds
>   Decrease in working capital
>   (working capital will have decreased if total
>   sources are less than total uses)
>   Increase in working capital
>   (working capital will have increased if total
>   sources exceed total uses)

While the statement format is helpful to know, it does not specifically explain the position of each component. In the following pages we will explain each individual account in the statement.

Sources of Funds:

Funds provided by operations represent the summary of all funds provided by operations. The components of funds provided by operations are identified below.

a. Net income is obviously the major source of funds provided by operations. The ongoing operation of the business is expected to generate funds. Thus, this is typically the major component of funds provided by operations.

b. Even though net income is the major source of funds provided by operations the number represented by net income needs to be adjusted for items that provide funds but are subtracted from net income. Examples include the following:

- **Depreciation** is an expense that is an accrued expense subtracted from income in arriving at net income. Depreciation is not a **cash** expense. Rather, it is an even allocation of the cost of an asset over time with no cash consequences in any one year. Thus, when net income is identified as a component of funds provided by operations it should be adjusted for depreciation since depreciation is not a cash expense. The amount of depreciation normally deducted from gross income should be added back to net income to identify the total funds provided from operations.

- **Amortization** is also an expense that is subtracted from income in arriving at net income. Thus, the figure for funds provided from operations needs to be adjusted for this noncash expense. There are many different categories of intangibles whose costs are evenly allocated over time.

Examples of other amortized items include:

- **amortization of bond premiums**—the amount of bond premium is subtracted from net income;

- **amortization of bond discount**—the amount of bond discount is added back to net income;

- **warranty expenses**—the amount of warranty expense needs to be added back to net income;

- **deferred income tax expense**—the amount of the expense is added back to net income;

- **amortization of leasehold improvements**—the amount of expense is added back to net income;

- **subscription income**—the amount of subscription income is subtracted from net income.

c. **Sale of fixed assets**—This is a transaction that provides funds. Regardless of whether the transaction is a gain or loss for financial accounting purposes the transaction, nevertheless, provides funds. Thus, any sale of fixed assets should be included in total funds provided.

d. **Capital stock issued in conversion of debt**—This is a transaction that affects total funds flow in the broader concept required by APB Opinion 19.

e. **Sale of capital stock**—This is also a transaction that affects total funds flow in the broader concept required by APB Opinion 19.

f. **Total Sources of Funds**—This is merely a total of all sources of funds.

Uses of Funds:

a. **Purchase of a fixed asset** for cash or a liability or otherwise financed is reported as a use of funds.

b. **Payment of dividends** represents a use of funds. Note that the entire amount of net income is included as a source and the amount actually paid in dividends is reported as a use. There is no netting of these two amounts since reporting both amounts provides additional information as to the actual amounts of the source and use of funds, respectively.

c. **The repayment of long-term debt** is considered a use of funds.

d. **Debt converted into capital stock**—If convertible debt is outstanding and is converted into capital stock, this transaction should be reported as a use of funds.

e. **Total uses of funds**—This is merely the total uses of funds.

Increase in Working Capital or Decrease in Working Capital

Working capital will have increased if total sources exceed total uses (not including working capital changes). Working capital will have decreased if total sources are less than total uses (not including working capital changes).

Now that we have explained the components of this statement, let's review an example.

Sources of funds:			
Funds provided by operations			
Net income		$280,000	
Charges not requiring funds in the current period			
Depreciation	$24,000		
Amortization of	16,000	40,000	$320,000
Sale of fixed assets			$180,000

Issue of capital stock in conversion of debt	$ 5,000
Sale of capital stock	$ 25,000
Total sources of funds	$430,000
Uses of funds	
Purchases of fixed assets	$214,000
Payment of dividends	$150,000
Repayment of long-term debt	$ 5,000
Conversion of debt into capital stock	$ 5,000
Total uses of funds	$374,000
Increase in working capital	$ 56,000

Having read the statement we can answer several questions:

1. What was the primary use of funds during the period?

   The purchase of fixed assets accounted for 57 percent ($214,000/$374,000) of funds used.

2. What was the dividend payout ratio?

   The dividend payout was 54 percent ($150,000/$280,000)

3. What was the primary source of funds? Secondary source?

   The primary source was net income from operations. This provided 65 percent of the total sources ($280,000/$430,000)

   The secondary source was the sale of fixed assets, which provided 42 percent ($180,000/$430,000) of total funds. This is particularly important, since the sale of fixed assets is usually not a recurring transaction from year to year. Without these funds the total sources would have been $250,000 ($430,000 − $180,000) and there would have been a net decrease in working capital for the period.

4. What was the total change in the capital accounts of the firm?

   Debt decreased by $5,000 because of repayment.

   Debt decreased by $5,000 because the debt was converted into capital stock.

   Capital stock increased by $5,000 and debt decreased by $10,000. Thus, there was a net decrease of $5,000 in the total.

By now, you can probably think of other questions you might also ask. The usefulness of this statement is that it identifies what happens to the funds that go in and out of a business during the year. This statement is helpful to the financial analyst because it provides considerable insight into the investing and financing activities of a business.

Explanation of the Statement of Changes in Financial Position—Cash Focus

The cash focus statement is an extension of the working capital focus. In the case of the working capital focus the changes in current assets and liabilities were explained by changes in the noncurrent accounts. Since in the cash focus statement we identify only the changes in cash, it follows that the preparation of the cash focus statement involves, in addition to the procedures followed in the preparation of the working capital statement, an explanation of changes in all current assets and liabilities with the exception of cash and cash equivalents.

Example Analysis—Chrysler and Chevron

In the following pages we will present two different firms' financial statements. Both Chevron's and Chrysler's Statement of Changes in Financial Position will be reviewed. The statement is followed by some sample analysis that is performed on the statement.

References

Malkiel, B.G., and Cragg, J. 1970. "Expectations and the Structure of Share Prices," *American Economic Review*, 6: 601–617.

Weston, J.F., and Copeland, T.E. 1986. *Managerial Finance*, Eighth Edition. Chicago: CBS Publishing Co.

Chrysler—Consolidated Statement of Changes in Financial Position

	1984	1985	1986
Funds Provided by Operations			
Earnings before extraordinary items	$1,496	$1,635	$1,403
Depreciation and amortization	$554	$476	$544
Equity in Earnings of unconsolidated subsidiaries	($126)	($256)	($299)
Deferred taxes on income	$22	$546	$699
Other	$5	$119	$171
Changes in working capital affecting operations	$1,951	$2,520	$2,518
(Increase) decrease in inventories and other current assets	($596)	$102	($149)
Increase in accounts payable and accrued expenses	$1,029	$310	$487
Net Change	$433	$412	$338
Extraordinary item-utilization of tax loss carryforwards	$884		
Net Change in noncurrent assets and liabilities	$3	$39	($365)
Funds Provided by Operations	$2,387	$2,971	$2,491
Funds Provided by (Used in) Investment Activities			
Purchase of Gulfstream		($672)	
Increase in investments and advances	($253)	($548)	($15)
Sale of property, plant, and equipment	$40	$29	$22
Expenditures for property, plant, and equipment	($800)	($1,043)	($1,312)
Expenditures for special tools	($447)	($492)	($749)
Other		$13	($1)
Funds Used in Investment Activities	($1,460)	($2,713)	($2,055)
Financing Activities			
(Decrease) increase in short term debt (includes current maturities of long term debt and capital lease obligations)	$411	($151)	($1,164)
New long term debt and capital lease borrowings	$10,100	$1,148	$896
Reductions and reclassifications in long term debt and capital lease obligations	($489)	($6,416)	($708)
Other			
(Decrease) increase in certain accounts, primarily non-current liabilities	($57)	$6	($540)

Chrysler (*Continued*)

	1984	1985	1986
Miscellaneous	($48)	($270)	$15
Net (Decrease) Increase in Cash, Marketable Securities and Cash Investments	$10,271	($8,099)	($3,485)

1. The major task in this analysis will be to analyze funds from operations. Earnings before extraordinary items provided a relatively large percentage of the total funds from operations (greater than 50 percent). Other sources included depreciation and deferred taxes on income.

Cash from Operations			
Earnings before extraordinary items	62.7%	55.0%	56.3%
Depreciation and amortization	23.2%	16.0%	21.8%
Equity in Earnings of unconsolidated subsidiaries	NA	NA	NA
Deferred taxes on income	0.9%	18.4%	28.1%
Other	0.2%	4.0%	6.9%

Chevron—Consolidated Statement of Changes in Financial Position

	1984	1985	1986
Cash from Operations			
Net Income	$1,534	$1,547	$715
Depreciation, depletion, and amortization	$2,453	$2,915	$2,787
Exploration expense, dry hole costs and the expense portion of capital projects	$1,138	$1,126	$965
Deferred income taxes	$407	$470	$76
Distributions greater than (less than) equity in affiliates' earnings	$67	$239	($33)
Gains on sales of selected operations, net of current taxes		($388)	($38)
Asset write-offs, net of current taxes	$80	$202	$102
Other charges to net income that did not use cash	$170	$251	$75
Cash from Operations Before Working Capital Changes	$5,849	$6,362	$4,649

Chevron—Consolidated Statement (*Continued*)

	1984	1985	1986
Decrease (increase) in operating working capital:			
Accounts and notes receivable	$18	$791	$1,505
Inventories	$250	$401	$229
Prepaid expenses and other current assets	($48)	($258)	$348
Accounts Payable	($470)	($491)	($1,476)
Income and other taxes payable	$328	($114)	($1,335)
Cash from Operations- Working Capital Changes	$78	$329	($729)
Total Cash from Operations	$5,927	$6,691	$3,920
Cash Dividends	($818)	($818)	($818)
Investment Activities			
Acquisition of Gulf Corporation in 1984	($10,326)		
Capital and exploratory expenditures	($4,572)	($3,810)	($2,689)
Proceeds from sale of selected operations	$451	$3,233	$829
Other properties plant and equipment sold or retired	$268	$45	$175
Net decrease (increase) in long term receivables and deferred charges	($35)	$151	$47
Financing Activities			
(Decrease) increase in short term debt (includes current maturities of long term debt and capital lease obligations)	$411	($151)	($1,164)
New long term debt and capital lease borrowings	$10,100	$1,148	$896
Reductions and reclassifications in long term debt and capital lease obligations	($489)	($6,416)	($708)
Other			
(Decrease) increase in certain accounts, primarily non-current liabilities	($57)	$6	($540)
Miscellaneous	($48)	($270)	$15
Net (Decrease) Increase in Cash, Marketable Securities and Cash Investments	$812	($191)	($37)

Chevron—Analysis of Statement of Changes in Financial Position

1. As a first step we will analyze cash from operations. Net income provided a relatively small percentage of total cash from operations. The major source was depreciation, depletion, and amortization as illustrated in the computations below.

Cash from Operations			
Net Income	26.2%	24.3%	15.4%
Depreciation, depletion, and amortization	41.9%	45.8%	59.9%
Exploration expense, dry hole costs and the expense portion of capital projects	19.5%	17.7%	20.8%
Deferred income taxes	7.0%	7.4%	1.6%
Distributions greater than (less than) equity in affiliates' earnings	1.1%	3.8%	−0.7%
Gains on sales of selected operations, net of current taxes		−6.1%	−0.8%
Asset write-offs, net of current taxes	1.4%	3.2%	2.2%
Other charges to net income that did not use cash	2.9%	3.9%	1.6%
Cash from Operations Before Working Capital Changes	100.0%	100.0%	100.0%

2. As a second step we examine the changes in operating working capital. In this section we recast the changes in working capital into the components causing increases and the components causing decreases. Finally, we produce a common size statement of this portion of the statement.

From the SCFP: Decrease (increase) in operating working capital:			
Accounts and notes receivable	$18	$791	$1,505
Inventories	$250	$401	$229
Prepaid expenses and other current assets	($48)	($258)	$348
Accounts Payable	($470)	($491)	($1,476)
Income and other taxes payable	$328	($114)	($1,335)
Cash from Operations Arising from Working Capital	$78	$329	($729)

Information Recast from the SCFP: Increases in Working Capital + A Common Size Statement

Increase in Working Capital

Chevron—Analysis of Statement (*Continued*)

Accounts and notes receivable	$18	$791	$1,505
Inventories	$250	$401	$229
Prepaid expenses and other current assets			$348
Income and other taxes payable	$328		
Total Increases	$596	$1,192	$2,082
Increase in Working Capital (Expressed as percentages)			
Accounts and notes receivable	3.0%	66.4%	72.3%
Inventories	41.9%	33.6%	11.0%
Prepaid expenses and other current assets			16.7%
Income and other taxes payable	55.0%		
Total Increases	100.0%	100.0%	100.0%

Information Recast from the SCFP: Decreases in Working Capital + A Common Size Statement

Decrease in Working Capital			
Prepaid expenses and other current assets	($48)	($258)	
Accounts Payable	($470)	($491)	($1,476)
Income and other taxes payable		($114)	($1,335)
Total Decreases	($518)	($863)	($2,811)
Net Change in Working Capital	$78	$329	($729)
Decrease in Working Capital (Expressed as percentages)			
Prepaid expenses and other current assets	9.3%	29.9%	
Accounts Payable	90.7%	56.9%	52.5%
Income and other taxes payable		13.2%	47.5%
Total Decreases	100.0%	100.0%	100.0%

3. As a third step we examine the components of total cash from operations.

Cash from Operations Before Working Capital Changes	98.7%	95.1%	118.6%
Cash from Operations Arising from Working Capital	1.3%	4.9%	−18.6%
Total Cash from Operations	100.0%	100.0%	100.0%

4. As a fourth step we examine the relative percentage of dividends to total cash from operations. The resulting percentage will be compared to the payout ratio (calculated using net income).

Cash Payout Percentage			
Cash Dividends	($818)	($818)	($818)
Cash from Operations	$5,927	$6,691	$3,920
Percentage	13.8%	12.2%	20.9%
Net Income Payout Percentage			
Cash Dividends	($818)	($818)	($818)
Net Income	$1,534	$1,547	$715
Percentage	53.3%	52.9%	114.4%

Chevron—Analysis of Statement (*Continued*)

5. As a fifth step we will examine the status of the investment activities of the firm. For each of these years, the firm's major investments were Gulf Oil and Capital and exploratory expenditures. For the oil industry a portion of the exploratory expenditures are capitalizable and hence are classified as investment activity. In fact, of the three-year total investment of $16,233, over 63 percent was the investment in Gulf Corporation.

Investment Activities

Acquisition of Gulf Corporation in 1984	($10,326)		
Capital and exploratory expenditures	($4,572)	($3,810)	($2,689)
Proceeds from sale of selected operations	$451	$3,233	$829
Other properties plant and equipment sold or retired	$268	$45	$175
Net decrease (increase) in long term receivables and deferred charges	($35)	$151	$47
Total	($14,214)	($381)	($1,638)
3 yr total			($16,233)
Gulf investment			63.6%

6. As a sixth step we analyze the net (decrease) increase in cash marketable securities and cash investments. We will see that the change computed in the Statement of Changes in Financial Position exactly matches the change if we had computed this change from the balance sheet as illustrated below.

Net (Decrease) Increase in Cash, Marketable Securities and Cash Investments (as reported on the SCFP)	($37)

as reported on the Consolidated Balance Sheet

	for the year ending	
	1985	1986
Current Assets		
Cash	$502	$145
Marketable Securities and Cash investments	$2,666	$2,986
Total Cash, Marketable securities & investments	$3,168	$3,131
Change in accounts from 1985 to 1986		($37)
(this matches the amounts reported in the SCFP)		

Summary of Common Ratios

A. Profitability ratios help the analyst evaluate the profitability of a firm.
   1. Net Profit Margin or Net Income/Revenues:

$$\frac{\text{Net Income}}{\text{Revenues}}$$

   2. Return on Equity

$$\frac{\text{Net Income}}{\text{Book Value of Equity}}$$

   3. Return on Assets

$$\frac{\text{Net Income}}{\text{Total Assets}}$$

   4. Taxes Paid/Net Income Before Taxes:

$$\frac{\text{Taxes}}{\text{Net Income Before Taxes}}$$

B. Efficiency ratios help the analyst evaluate how efficiently companies are using their assets.
   5. Sales to Assets:

$$\frac{\text{Sales}}{\text{Average Total Assets}}$$

   6. Sales to Net Working Capital:

47

$$\frac{\text{Sales}}{\text{Average Net Working Capital}}$$

7. Inventory Turnover:

$$\frac{\text{Cost of Goods Sold}}{\text{Average Inventory}}$$

8. Days of Cash on hand:

$$\frac{\text{Cash}}{\text{Average Daily Expenditures from Operations}}$$

9. Average Collection Period:

$$\frac{\text{Average Accounts Receivable}}{\text{Average Sales per Day}}$$

Average Sales per Day is calculated as Annual Sales/360.

10. Average Payment Period:

$$\frac{\text{Average Accounts Payable}}{\text{Cost of Goods Sold per Day}}$$

C. Leverage ratios help the analyst summarize the firm's position relative to borrowed capital.

11. Debt Ratio:

$$\frac{\text{Long-Term Debt + Value of Leases}}{\text{Long-Term Debt + Value of Leases + Equity}}$$

12. Debt-Equity Ratio:

$$\frac{\text{Long-Term Debt + Value of Leases}}{\text{Equity}}$$

13. Times Interest Earned:

$$\frac{\text{EBIT + Depreciation}}{\text{Interest}}$$

14. Earnings Variability Measure:

$$\frac{\text{Standard deviation (EBIT } t + 1 - \text{EBIT } t)}{\text{Average EBIT}}$$

D. Liquidity Ratios help the analyst asset the degree of liquidity of a firm.

    15. Current Ratio:

$$\frac{\text{Current Assets}}{\text{Current Liabilities}}$$

    16. Quick Ratio:

$$\frac{\text{Current Assets} - \text{Inventory}}{\text{Current Liabilities}}$$

E. Common Stock Valuation ratios help the analysts evaluate a firm's stock valuation.

$$V = \frac{bE(t)}{k - g}$$

$$V = \frac{\text{Current Dividend Rate}}{\text{Discount Rate} - \text{Growth Rate}}$$

    17. Payout Ratio:

$$\frac{\text{Dividends per Share}}{\text{Earnings per Share}}$$

1 minus the payout ratio equals the proportion of earnings plowed back into the ongoing operation of the business.

    18. Price Earnings (P/E) Ratio:

$$\frac{\text{Stock Price}}{\text{Earnings per Share}}$$

    19. Market to Book Ratio:

$$\frac{\text{Market Value per Sahre}}{\text{Book Value per Share}}$$

Chapter 2

Regression Analysis and Forecasting Models

In this chapter, we discuss the use of regression analysis to make forecasts. A *forecast* is merely a prediction about the future (such as a weather forecast). Financial forecasts span a broad range of areas, and each of the forecasts is of interest to a number of people and departments in a firm. A sales manager may wish to forecast sales (either in units sold or revenues generated). This prediction is of interest to the operations (manufacturing) department in order to predict the materials and time needed to create the product. A corporate financial officer would be interested in the amount of cash required to support the projected level of sales. Securities analysts try to predict future earnings. An investment advisor might want to predict the future variability of the stock and bond markets. The government is often interested in projections of the trade or budget deficits. In short, forecasts are used on a daily basis to make a wide variety of financial decisions.

There are a variety of ways to make forecasts. One could consult tarot cards or be guided solely by one's intuition. Recent years have seen the explicit search for "megatrends" which, presumably, might continue into the future. Yet another alternative, *regression analysis*, is discussed in this chapter. Regression analysis is one technique with which to analyze quantitative (as opposed to qualitative) data to make forecasts. As a brief introduction to regression analysis, consider the graph on page 52.

The horizontal line is called the X axis and the vertical line the Y axis. Regression analysis looks for a relationship between the X variable (sometimes called the "independent" or "explanatory" variable) and the Y variable (the "dependent" variable). For example, X might be the aggregate level of personal disposable income in the United States and Y

51

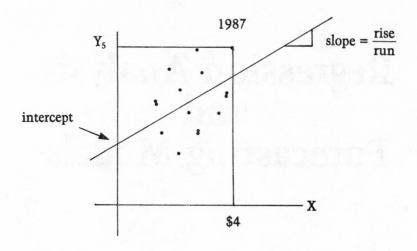

would represent the number of cars sold in the United States. By looking up these numbers for a number of years in the past, we can plot points on the graph. Each point represents one year. In 1987, personal disposal income was $4 and the number of cars sold was 5.

More specifically, regression analysis seeks to find the "line of best fit" through the points. The term "best" has a very specific meaning in this context, which is discussed in the appendix to this chapter. Basically, the regression line is drawn to best approximate what relationship there may be between the two variables. Techniques for estimating the regression line (i.e., its intercept on the Y axis and its slope) are the subject of this chapter.

Forecasting using the regression line assumes that the relationship which existed in the past between the two variables will continue to exist in the future. There may be times when this assumption is inappropriate; the forecaster must be aware of this potential pitfall.

Once the regression line has been estimated, the forecaster must provide an estimate of the level of the independent variable in the future. For example, if we were going to use the regression line in the graph above to forecast the number of cars sold in 1988, we must first estimate what the level of personal disposable income will be in 1988. We then plug this estimate into the regression equation. The output is our forecast of the number of cars sold.

Regression analysis can be expanded to include more than one independent variable; this is called *multiple regression*. For example, the forecaster might believe that the number of cars sold depends not only on personal disposable income but on the level of interest rates as well.

Historical data on these three variables must be obtained, then a *plane* of best fit estimated. With estimates of the future level of personal disposable income and interest rates, a forecast of number of cars sold can be made.

Regression capabilities are found in a wide variety of software packages and hence are available to anyone with a microcomputer. Lotus 1-2-3, a popular spreadsheet package, can do simple or multiple regressions. Many statistics packages can do not only regressions, but other quantitative techniques such as those discussed in Chapter 3 (Time Series Analysis and Forecasting).

The management of a firm must be able to develop an accurate forecast of its operations for the future. The future may involve the next quarter, year, or five years. Sales is one of the most important variables to be forecast because the balance sheet and income statements may be generated from a percentage-of-sales method. When the firm has made a reasonable sales forecast it will be able to prepare an income statement and balance sheet for the future. The determination of sales and cash flow will aid the firm in its economic decision to issue corporate liabilities. In this chapter we will employ least squares regression to forecast the firm's sales and derive its financial statements.

In simple regression analysis, one seeks to measure the statistical association between two variables, X and Y. Regression analysis is generally used to measure how changes in the independent variable, X, influence changes in the dependent variable, Y. Regression analysis shows a statistical association or correlation among variables, rather than a causal relationship among variables.

Simple linear least squares regression is a reasonable tool to use in the forecasting of sales. Least squares regression assumes the past is the proxy for the future. The sales of the firm in the future will be determined by the same variables and magnitudes of the variables' influence as those that have determined the sales of the past. When one uses regression analysis, one seeks to examine the statistical association between two variables, so one may forecast using the regression analysis only if the association remains reasonably stable. This is an assumption which, if violated, can make a forecast of sales look absurd. The failure to foresee an oil embargo or a change in Federal Reserve policy is a weakness of many economic models. Least squares regression on a firm's sales is powerless against major economic catastrophes, but it can point a reasonable direction for the firm to pursue.

Once a sales forecast has been calculated, the manager must determine if any external funds need to be acquired from the capital market. An income statement and balance sheet can be derived from the sales figure using a percentage-of-sales method. The financial statements will indicate the firm's external funds needed. The rational manager will borrow funds from the capital market only if these funds cannot be generated internally.

The regression line represents the hypothesized relationship between sales, the dependent variable, and time, the

$$Y_t = \alpha + \beta X_t + \varepsilon_t \qquad (1)$$

The regression line assumes that the error term, ε_t, has an expected value of zero (the property of being unbiased) and is uncorrelated with the dependent variable (time, in this example). Formally,

$$E(\varepsilon_t) = 0, \qquad (2)$$

$$COV(\varepsilon_t, X_t) = 0 \qquad (3)$$

where E = expected value, and COV = covariance of two variables. Moreover, the error term has to be normally distributed and a constant variance (no outliers or fat tails).

Let us analyze the past ten years of data of the Chrysler Corporation using ordinary least squares (OLS) regression. Ordinary least squares analysis can be used to obtain regression estimates of α and β in the equation $Y = a + bX$ where Y is sales and X is time, in this example, and forecast sales in future periods.

One can forecast sales for Chrysler by using ten years of sales data to estimate the relationship between sales and time and project that relationship into future periods.

Historic Data

Year	Chrysler Sales ($billions)
1985	21.256
1984	19.573
1983	13.240
1982	10.045
1981	10.822
1980	9.225
1979	12.002
1978	13.618
1977	16.708
1976	15.538

One can model the relationship between Chrysler sales and time by transforming the year variable into a time variable with 1976 being the year 1, 1977 being year 2, . . . , and 1985 being year 10. The ordinary least sales equation for Chrysler sales is:

$$\text{Chrysler Sales} = a + b \text{ Time}$$

In the OLS methodology developed in appendix 3,

$$b = \frac{N\left(\sum XY\right) - \sum X\left(\sum Y\right)}{N\left(\sum X^2\right) - \left(\sum X\right)^2} \text{ and } a = \bar{Y} - b\bar{X}. \tag{4}$$

If one applies the OLS methodology to the Chrysler data using a standard microcomputer program such as ESP or SCA-PC, one obtains the following model:

Method		(t)	(4.31)	(.88)
OLS	Chrysler Sales =	12,024 +	.396 Time,	$R^2 = .089$,

$$D - W = 0.78, \text{ s.e.} = 4.082.$$

Ordinary Least Squares Regression Analysis of Chrysler Sales

Chrylser Sales	Time	Regression Output:		
21.256	10.000	Constant		12.024
19.573	9.000	Std Err of Y Est		4.082
13.240	8.000	R Squared		0.088
10.045	7.000	No. of Observations		10.000
10.822	6.000	Degrees of Freedom		8.000
9.225	5.000			
12.002	4.000	X Coefficient(s)	0.396	
13.618	3.000	Std Err of Coef.	0.449	
16.708	2.000			
15.538	1.000			

Source: Lotus Spreadsheet Regression

There is no statistically significant relationship between Chrysler sales and time; the absolute value of the t-statistic of the time variable (.88) is less than the critical value of the t-statistic, 1.86, at the 10 percent level. However, the Durbin-Watson (D-W) statistic indicates that the regressive model errors are not normally distributed and are positively first-order correlated. The Durbin-Watson statistic should be approximately two since the statistic is $2(1 - r)$ where r is the correlation coefficient between the current and one period lagged error terms. The very low Durbin-Watson statistic is below the approximate critical value of 1.08 and thus the Cochrane-Orcutt (CORC) iterative procedure should be employed to correct the serial correlation. The application of the CORC procedure produces normally distributed error terms and a statistically significant relationship between Chrysler sales and time. The t-statistic of 2.11 indicates that the sales and time series are statistically correlated at the 10 percent level. The Durbin-Watson statistic of 1.77 is such that one cannot reject the null hypothesis of normally distributed error terms. The CORC-estimated rho of .795 indicates an almost first-difference of the data.

Method	(t)	(−.99)	(2.11)
CORC	Chrysler Sales =	−15.673 +	3.289 Time,

$$\hat{\rho} = .795, R^2 = .688, D - W = 1.77, \text{s.e.} = 2.535.$$

In 1986, the time variable will be at year 11 and the sales forecast is:

$$\text{Chrysler Sales, 1986} = \hat{Y} = -15.673 + 3.289\ (11)$$

$$\hat{Y} = 20.506 \text{ billion.}[1]$$

The 95 percent confidence interval for Chrysler's sales in 1986 are thus: management has a 95 percent probability that sales will fall within the $14.193–$26.819 billion interval.

One might question the appropriateness of an ordinary least squares regression analysis with a glance at Chrysler's data. One possible alterna-

---

[1]The 1986 sales forecast for Chrysler may look a bit absurd given its growth during the 1980–1985 period; however, one must be aware that the regression line estimation may be changed by the selection of the years in the estimation.

tive is the use of nonlinear least squares (NLLS) analysis which also is developed in the regression appendix.

$$\log \text{Chrysler Sales} = \log a + \log bX \qquad (5)$$

The normal equations for NLLS can be solved to yield the following estimates for $\log a$ and $\log b$.

$$\log a = \frac{\sum (\log Y)}{N} \qquad (6)$$

$$\log b = \frac{\sum (X \log Y)}{\sum X^2}$$

The application of the NLLS analysis to the Chrysler data produces a statistically insignificant relationship between the log of Chrysler sales and time:

Method		
	(12.69)	(.65)
NLLS	$\log$ Chrysler Sales = 2.504	+ .002 Time

$$R^2 = .050, \; D - W = 0.58, \; \text{s.e.} = .289.$$

NLLS seeks to estimate sales growth as a function of time. The NLLS analysis is plagued by serial correlation. The CORC-estimated NLLS regression line is:

Method		
	(.82)	(1.86)
CORC, NLLS	$\log$ Chrysler Sales = .858	+ .198 Time,

$$\hat{\rho} = .777, \; R^2 = .639, \; D - W = 1.90, \; \text{s.e.} = .188.$$

The 1986 (CORC-estimated) NLLS-forecasted Chrysler Sales is $20.822 billion and the 95 percent confidence intervals are $13.040–$28.60 billion. If one examines the relative R^2's between CORC-adjusted OLS and NLLS analyses, one notices that the methods are essentially equal;

however, the NLLS analysis standard error is 1.568 which is considerably less than the OLS standard error.

This may seem confusing to the reader because the standard error of the NLLS regression is reported as .188. The regression model errors from NLLS must be transformed to the same unit (taking the anti-log of the errors) and the standard error of the transformed NLLS errors is 1.568.

Pro Forma Statement Analysis

One can forecast Chrysler Sales according to the CORC-estimated nonlinear least squares regression line and use a percent-of-sales method to develop *pro forma* income statement and balance sheets. Let us assume that Chrysler will maintain its 1985 current assets- and current lia-bilities-to-sales ratios for 1986. Furthermore, let us assume that the 1985 net income-to-sales ratio will be maintained in 1986. An abbreviated 1985 balance sheet for Chrysler was:

Chrysler Balance Sheet, December 31, 1985

Cash	147.6	Accounts Payable	2504.5
Marketable Securities	2649.9	Short-term Debt	195.3
Accounts Receivable	207.5	Other	2029.4
Inventories	1862.7	Current Liabilities	4729.2
Other	445.8	Notes Payable	2337.9
Current Assets	5313.5	Other Long-term	
Net Property, Plant	4639.6	Liabilities	1322.9
Investments	2652.2	Common Stock	153.2
Total Assets	12,605.3	Additional Paid	
		in Capital	1943.2
		Retained Earnings	2153.3
		Treasury Stock	(34.4)
		Total Liabilities	
		and Equity	12,605.3

If net property and plant, investments, and long-term liabilities and equity do not increase proportionally with sales, the balance sheet may be expressed as a percentage of sales as follows:

Chrysler Percentage of Sales

Cash	0.69	Accounts Payable	11.78
Marketable Securities	12.47	Short-term Debt	0.92
Accounts Receivable	0.98	Other	9.55
Inventories	8.76	Current Liabilities	22.49
Other	2.10	Notes Payable	00.00
Current Assets	25.00	Common Equity	00.00
Net Property, Plant	00.00	Total Liabilities	
Investments	00.00	and Equity	22.49
Total Assets	25.00		

In 1985, Chrysler earned a $1.635 billion (7.6 percent of sales) net income and paid a dividend of $.66625 per share. If one expects Chrysler's sales to be $20.822 in 1986, net income should be $1.602 billion if net income continues to be 7.69 percent of sales. Furthermore, a 1985 dividend payout ratio of 7.1 percent in 1985 would produce total dividends of $.1137 billion of 1986, leaving $1.4883 billion in 1986 retained earnings for possible reinvestment, mergers, or additional capital investment. If current assets and liabilities remain 25.00 and 22.25 percent of sales, respectively, the 1986 *pro forma* balance sheet for Chrysler is:

Cash	143.7	Accounts Payable	245.3
Marketable Securities	2596.5	Short-term Debt	19.2
Accounts Receivable	204.1	Other	1988.5
Inventories	182.4	Current Liabilities	4362.9
Other	437.3	Other Liabilities	1295
Current Assets	5206	Long-term Debt	2366
Fixed Assets	7292	Common Equity	5703.3
Total Assets	12,498	Total Liabilities	
		and Equity	13,997.2

The imbalance in the *pro forma* statements is created because Chrysler generated more funds than it needed on current assets and fixed assets.

Let us further examine the imbalance in the *pro forma* balance sheet. Chrysler generated more funds through the production of retained earnings and current liabilities financing than it spent on the expansion of current assets. If the current assets-to-sales ratio, *CA/S*, is less than the current liabilities-to-sales ratio, *CL/S*, plus the retained earnings increase-to-sales, *dRE/S*, then the firm will not need to issue additional equity or long-term debt.[2] Weston and Copeland (1986) refer to this imbalance as the external funds needed (*EFN*) of the firm.

---

[2]The initial financing needs are increased dollar-for-dollar as capital expenditures (an increase in fixed assets) occur.

$$EFN = \frac{CA}{S}(dS) - \frac{CL}{S}(dS) - P(1 - d)S$$

where dS = change in sales,

                   P = profit margin, net income/sales,

and $1 - d$ = retained earnings/net income.

For Chrysler in 1986, unless Chrysler expanded its fixed assets or retooled, its *EFN* is ($1.4992 billion).

EFN = .25 ($20,822 − $21.256) − .2225 (−434) − (0.076) (.929) 20,822

     = −11.935 − 1470.12 = (1482.1)

The negative *EFN* for Chrysler represents "excess" funds that may be used for additional dividends or repurchasing long-term debt or equity.[3]

Multiple Regression

Several economic variables may influence the variable that one is interested in forecasting. For example, the levels of the Gross National Product, personal disposable income, or price indices can assert influences on the firm. Multiple regression is an extremely easy statistical tool for researchers and management to employ due to the great proliferation of computer software—many applicable for the microcomputer. The general form of the two-independent-variable multiple regression is:

$$Y_t = \beta_1 + \beta_2 X_{t2} + \beta_2 X_{t3} + \varepsilon_t, t = 1, \ldots, N \qquad (7)$$

In matrix notation multiple regression can be written:

$$\hat{Y} = X\beta + \varepsilon \qquad (8)$$

Multiple regression requires unbiasedness, that the expected value of the error term is zero, and that the X's are fixed and independent of the error term. The error term is an identically and independently distributed normal variable. Least squares estimation of the β coefficients yields:

---

[3]Chrysler used its excess funds in 1986 to increase its plant and equipment by $1.3121 billion and incur retooling expenditures of $749 million (as we discussed in Chapter 1).

$$\hat{\beta} = \{\hat{\beta}_1, \hat{\beta}_2, \hat{\beta}_3\} \tag{9}$$

$$Y = X\hat{\beta} + e$$

Multiple regression, using the least squared principle, minimizes the sum of the squared error terms:

$$\sum_{i=1}^{N} e_i^2 = e'e \tag{10}$$

$$(Y - X\hat{\beta})'(Y - X\hat{\beta})$$

To minimize the sum of the squared error terms, the squared error term function must be differentiated with respect to $\hat{\beta}$ and the partial derivative set equal to zero.[4]

$$\frac{\partial(e'e)}{\partial\hat{\beta}} = -2X'Y + 2X'X\hat{\beta}$$

$$-2X'Y + 2X'X\hat{\beta} = 0$$

$$2X'X\hat{\beta} = 2X'Y$$

$$\hat{\beta} = \frac{X'Y}{X'X} = (X'X)^{-1}X'Y$$

The normal equations for the two-variable case can be written:

$$\sum Y = n\hat{\beta}_1 + \hat{\beta}_2\sum X_2 + \hat{\beta}_3\sum X_3$$

$$\sum X_2 Y = \hat{\beta}_1\sum X_2 + \hat{\beta}_2\sum X_2^2 + \hat{\beta}_3\sum X_2\sum X_3$$

$$\sum X_3 Y = \hat{\beta}_1\sum X_3 + \hat{\beta}_2\sum X_2 X_3 + \hat{\beta}_3\sum X_3^2$$

The sample moments will aid the solution of the multiple regression equation system.

---

[4]The reader is referred to J.L. Murphy, *Introductory Econometric* (Homewood, Ill: R.D. Irwin, 1973) for an excellent treatment of matrix algebra and multiple regression.

$$\begin{pmatrix} Y'Y & Y'X \\ X'Y & X'X \end{pmatrix} = \begin{pmatrix} M_{YY} & M_{YX_2} & M_{YX_3} \\ M_{X_2Y} & M_{X_2X_2} & M_{X_2X_3} \\ M_{X_3Y} & M_{X_3X_2} & M_{X_3X_3} \end{pmatrix}$$

The Texas-Typical-Oil firm has the following sales and industry price index history.

Year	Sales	Price Index
1977	$ 200,000,000	90
1978	400,000,000	93
1979	750,000,000	95
1980	1,000,000,000	100
1981	1,200,000,000	102
1982	1,500,000,000	106
1983	1,800,000,000	110
1984	2,500,000,000	112
1985	3,300,000,000	114
1986	4,500,000,000	118

To make calculations easier, sales will be denoted in millions of dollars. (See Table 2-1.)

$$M_{YY} = 10(46,082,500) - (17,150)^2 = 166,702,500$$

$$M_{X_2X_2} = 10(385) - (55)^2 = 825$$

$$M_{X_3X_3} = 10(108,978) - (1,040)^2 = 8180$$

$$M_{YX_2} = 10(129,550) - (17,150)(55) = 352,250$$

$$M_{YX_3} = 10(1,893,050) - (17,150)(1,040) = 1,094,500$$

$$M_{X_2X_3} = 10(5,979) - (55)(1,040) = 2,590$$

$$X'X = \begin{bmatrix} 825 & 2,590 \\ 2,590 & 8,180 \end{bmatrix} = \begin{bmatrix} M_{X_2X_2} & M_{X_2X_3} \\ M_{X_3X_2} & M_{X_3X_3} \end{bmatrix}$$

$$X'Y = \begin{bmatrix} 352,250 \\ 1,094,500 \end{bmatrix} = \begin{bmatrix} M_{YX_2} \\ M_{YX_3} \end{bmatrix}$$

To find the inverse of $X'X$, the determinate of $X'X$ must be found.

$$|X'X| = (825)(8,180) - (2,590)^2 = 40,400$$

The adjoint of $X'X$ is:

Table 2-1

Sales, Y	Year, X_2	X_2	Price Index, X_3	Y^2	$X_2 X_3$	X_2^2	X_3^2	YX_2	YX_3
200	1977	1	90	40,000	90	1	8,100	200	18,000
400	1978	2	93	160,000	186	4	8,649	800	37,200
750	1979	3	95	562,500	285	9	9,025	2,250	71,250
1,000	1980	4	100	1,000,000	400	16	10,000	4,000	100,000
1,200	1981	5	102	1,440,000	510	25	10,404	6,000	122,400
1,500	1982	6	106	2,250,000	636	36	11,236	9,000	159,000
1,800	1983	7	110	3,240,000	770	49	12,100	12,600	198,000
2,500	1984	8	112	6,250,000	896	64	12,544	20,000	280,000
3,300	1985	9	114	10,890,000	1,026	81	12,996	29,700	376,200
4,500	1986	10	118	20,250,000	1,180	100	13,924	45,000	531,000
17,150 $\sum_{i=1}^{N}$		55	1,040	46,082,500	5,979	385	108,978	129,550	1,893,050
1,715.0 Means		5.5	104.0						

$$\begin{bmatrix} 8,180 & -2,590 \\ -2,590 & 825 \end{bmatrix}$$

The inverse of $X'X$ is found by dividing the adjoint of $X'X$ by the determinant of $X'X$.

$$(X'X)^{-1} = \frac{1}{40,400}\begin{bmatrix} 8,180 & -2,590 \\ -2,590 & 825 \end{bmatrix} = \begin{bmatrix} .2025 & -.0641 \\ -.0641 & .0204 \end{bmatrix}$$

$$\hat{\beta} = \begin{bmatrix} \hat{\beta}_2 \\ \hat{\beta}_3 \end{bmatrix} = (X'X)^{-1}X'Y$$

$$= \begin{bmatrix} .2025 & -.0641 \\ -.0641 & .0204 \end{bmatrix}\begin{bmatrix} 352,250 \\ 1,094,500 \end{bmatrix}$$

$$\hat{\beta}_2 = 71,330,625 - 70,157.45 = 1,173.175$$

$$\hat{\beta}_3 = -22,579.225 + 22,327.80 = -251.425$$

$$\hat{\beta}_1 = \bar{Y} - \hat{\beta}_2\bar{X}_2 - \hat{\beta}_3\bar{X}_3$$

$$= 1,715 - (1,173,175)5.5 - (-251,425)104$$

$$= 1,715 - 6,452,46 + 26,148.20$$

$$= 21,410.74$$

The multiple regression estimating equation is:

$$\hat{Y}_t = 21,410.74 + 1,173.175(X_{2t}) - 251.425(X_{3t})$$

In terms of the original data, the Texas-Typical-Oil Company's sales estimation equation can be written:

$$\hat{Y}_t = 21,410,740,000 + 1,173,175,000X_{2t} - 251,425,000X_{3t}$$

To forecast the company's sales for 1987, the industry's price index for output must be known.[5]

---

[5]The application of the SAS regression package (proc reg) produces the following (approximately equal) estimate:

$$\hat{Y}_t = 19,472,055 + 1,154,703X_{2t} - 231,806,930X_{3t}$$
$$(t) \qquad\qquad (1.84) \qquad\qquad (-1.16)$$
$$F = 39.18, R^2 = .918$$

The significance of the individual variables can be tested by performing t-tests on the X_2 and X_3 coefficients. In multiple regression, the t-values are calculated:

$$t = \frac{\hat{\beta}_i - \beta_i}{\sqrt{\sum_{i=1}^{N} e_i^2/(N-k)}\sqrt{a_{ii}}}$$

where $\sqrt{\sum_{i=1}^{N} e_i^2/(N-k)}$ = square root of the mean square of the residual

$\sqrt{a_{ii}}$ = the variable's diagonal element of $(X'X)^{-1}$

The t-values for the coefficients of X_2 and X_3 are:

$$t_2 = 1.84$$

$$t_3 = 1.16$$

The calculated t-values are less than the critical t-value for $(N-k)$ degrees of freedom of 2.365. Thus neither variable in the multiple regression equation is statistically significant at the 10 percent level.

It might seem strange that the F-value for the firm's multiple regression model rejects the null hypothesis of no association while the individual t-tests reject the statistical significance of both variables. The unusual result is probably due to the existence of multicollinearity, where the independent variables are not independent. The existence of multicollinearity means that the least squares regression results are still unbiased but are inefficient as they do not have the minimum variance among the linear, unbiased estimators. The higher variances from multicollinearity increase the standard errors of the coefficients, reducing the t-values. The multicollinearity can be shown by the correlation coefficient between time and the industry's price level of output.

$$r_{23} = \frac{M_{X_2X_3}}{\sqrt{M_{X_2X_2}}\sqrt{M_{X_3X_3}}} = \frac{2590}{\sqrt{825}\sqrt{8,180}} = .997$$

The extreme correlation between the independent variables makes the variables linear functions of the other independent variables.[6] The least

---

[6] Severe multicollinearity is present because the condition number exceeds 30 and the variance-decomposition proportions of the third eigenvalue exceed .50 (among X_2, X_3, and the intercept). D. Belsley, "Collinearity and Forecasting," *Journal of Forecasting* 3 (1984), 183–196.

DEP VARIABLE: SALES

ANALYSIS OF VARIANCE

SOURCE	DF	SUM OF SQUARES	MEAN SQUARE	F VALUE	PROB>F
MODEL	2	15303143.56	7651571.78	39.178	0.0002
ERROR	7	1367106.44	195300.92		
C TOTAL	9	16670250.00			

ROOT MSE	441.9286	R-SQUARE	0.9180
DEP MEAN	1715	ADJ R-SQ	0.8946
C.V.	25.76843		

PARAMETER ESTIMATES

VARIABLE	DF	PARAMETER ESTIMATE	STANDARD ERROR	T FOR HO: PARAMETER=0	PROB > |T|	TOLERANCE	VARIANCE INFLATION
INTERCEP	1	19472.05446	17323.69099	1.124	0.2981	.	0
TIME	1	1154.70297	628.83704	1.836	0.1089	0.00598516	167.04208
PRICE	1	-231.80693	199.70477	-1.161	0.2838	0.00598516	167.04208

COLLINEARITY DIAGNOSTICS

NUMBER	EIGENVALUE	CONDITION NUMBER	VAR PROP INTERCEP	VAR PROP TIME	VAR PROP PRICE
1	2.871221	1.000000	0.0000	0.0001	0.0000
2	0.128753	4.722310	0.0001	0.0066	0.0000
3	0.0000260	332.013	0.9999	0.9933	1.0000

Source: SAS Output

squares line cannot isolate separate explanatory roles between the independent variables.

The firm's multiple regression estimation line does explain 83 percent of the firm's variation in sales and should be of use to the firm. Our model is of use as the F-value for the model rejected the null hypothesis of no correlation existing statistically among the variables.

References

Belsley, D. 1984. Collinearity and Forecasting. *Journal of Forecasting* 3: 183–196.

Johnston, J. 1972. *Econometric Methods*, 2nd ed. New York: McGraw-Hill Co.

Mansfield, E. 1987. *Statistics for Business and Economics.* 3rd ed. New York: W.W. Norton & Company.

Miller, Irwin and John E. Freund. 1965. *Probability and Statistics for Engineers.* Englewood Cliffs, N.J.: Prentice-Hall.

Murphy, James L. 1973. *Introductory Econometrics.* Homewood, Ill: Richard D. Irwin, Inc.

Weston, J.F. and T.E. Copeland. 1986. *Managerial Finance.* Chicago: CBS Publishing Co.

Appendix to Chapter 2

An Introduction to Linear Regression Models

This appendix introduces the reader to a more formal construction of simple linear regression and multiple regression. Simple linear regression and multiple regression analysis is used to forecast corporate sales.

The case of simple, linear, least squares regression may be written in the form:

$$Y = \alpha + \beta X + \varepsilon \tag{1}$$

where Y, the dependent variable, is a linear function of X, the independent variable. The parameters α and β characterize the population regression line and ε is the randomly distributed error term. The regression estimates of α and β will be derived from the principal of least squares. In applying least squares, the sum of the squared regression errors will be minimized; our regression errors equal the actual dependent variable minus the estimated value from the regression line. If Y represents the actual value and Y the estimated value, their difference is the error term, e. Least squares regression minimized the sum of the squared error terms. The simple regression line will yield an estimated value of Y, $\hat{Y}$ by the use of the sample regression:

$$\hat{Y} = a + bX \tag{2}$$

In the estimation equation a is the least squares estimate of α and b is the estimate of β. Thus, a and b are the regression constants that must be estimated. The least squares regression constants (or statistics) a and b are unbiased and efficient (smallest variance) estimators of α and β. The

69

error term, e_i, is the difference between the actual and estimated dependent variable value for any given independent variable values, X_i.

$$e_i = \hat{Y}_i - Y_i \tag{3}$$

The regression error term, e_i, is the least squares estimate of ε_i, the actual error term.[1]

To minimize the error terms, the least squares technique minimizes the sum of the squares error terms of the N observations,

$$\sum_{i=1}^{N} e_i^2 \tag{4}$$

The error terms from the N observations will be minimized. Thus, least squares regression minimizes:

$$\sum_{i=1}^{N} e_i^2 = \sum_{i=1}^{N} [Y_i - \hat{Y}_i]^2 = \sum_{i=1}^{N} [Y_i - (a + bX_i)]^2 \tag{5}$$

To assure that a minimum is reached, the partial derivatives of the squared error terms function

$$\sum_{i=1}^{N} [Y_i - (a + bX_i)]^2$$

will be taken with respect to a and b.

$$\frac{\partial \sum_{i=1}^{N} e_i^2}{\partial a} = 2 \sum_{i=1}^{N} (Y_i - a - bX_i)(-1)$$

$$= -2 \left(\sum_{i=1}^{N} Y_i - \sum_{i=1}^{N} a - b \sum_{i=1}^{N} X_i \right)$$

---

[1]The reader is referred to an excellent statistical reference, such as Irwin Miller and J.E. Freund, *Probability and Statistics for Engineers*, (Englewood Cliffs, NJ: Prentice-Hall, 1965).

$$\frac{\partial \sum_{i=1}^{N} e_i^2}{\partial b} = 2 \sum_{i=1}^{N} (Y_i - a - bX_i)(-X_i)$$

$$= -2\left(\sum_{i=1}^{N} Y_i X_i - \sum_{i=1}^{N} X_i - b \sum_{i=1}^{N} X_i^2\right)$$

The partial derivatives will then be set equal to zero.

$$\frac{\partial \sum_{i=1}^{N} e_i^2}{\partial a} = -2\left(\sum_{i=1}^{N} Y_i - \sum_{i=1}^{N} a - b \sum_{i=1}^{N} X_i\right) = 0 \qquad (6)$$

$$\frac{\partial \sum_{i=1}^{N} e_i^2}{\partial b} = -2\left(\sum_{i=1}^{N} YX_i - \sum_{i=1}^{N} X_1 - b \sum_{i=1}^{N} X_i^2\right) = 0$$

Rewriting these equations, one obtains the normal equations:

$$\sum_{i=1}^{N} Y_i = \sum_{i=1}^{N} a + b \sum_{i=1}^{N} X_i \qquad (7)$$

$$\sum_{i=1}^{N} Y_i X_i = a \sum_{i=1}^{N} X_1 + b \sum_{i=1}^{N} X_1^2$$

Solving the normal equations simultaneously for a and b yields the least squares regression estimates;

$$\hat{a} = \frac{\left(\sum_{i=1}^{N} X_i^2\right)\left(\sum_{i=1}^{N} Y_i\right) - \left(\sum_{i=1}^{N} X_i \sum_{i=1}^{N} X_i Y_i\right)}{N\left(\sum_{i=1}^{N} X_i^2\right) - \left(\sum_{i=1}^{N} X_i\right)^2},$$

$$\hat{b} = \frac{N\left(\sum_{i=1}^{N} X_i Y_i\right) - \left(\sum_{i=1}^{N} X_i\right)\left(\sum_{i=1}^{N} Y_i\right)}{N\left(\sum_{i=1}^{N} X_i^2\right) - \left(\sum_{i=1}^{N} X_i\right)^2}. \qquad (8)$$

An estimation of the regression line's coefficients and goodness of fit also can be found in terms of expressing the dependent and independent variables in terms of deviations from their means, their sample moments. The sample moments will be denoted by M.

$$M_{XX} = \sum_{i=1}^{N} x_i^2 = \sum_{i=1}^{N} (X_i - \bar{X})^2$$

$$= N \sum_{i=1}^{N} X_i - \left(\sum_{i=1}^{N} X_i \right)^2$$

$$M_{XY} = \sum_{i=1}^{N} x_i y_i = \sum_{i=1}^{N} (X_i - \bar{X})(Y_i - \bar{Y})$$

$$= N \sum_{i=1}^{N} X_i Y_i - \left(\sum_{i=1}^{N} X_i \right)\left(\sum_{i=1}^{N} Y_i \right)$$

$$M_{YY} = \sum_{i=1}^{N} y_i^2 = \sum_{i=1}^{N} (Y - \bar{Y})^2$$

$$= N \left(\sum_{i=1}^{N} Y_i^2 \right) - \sum_{i=1}^{N} (Y_i)^2$$

The slope of the regression line, b, can be found by:

$$b = \frac{M_{XY}}{M_{XX}} \tag{9}$$

$$a = \frac{\sum_{i=1}^{N} Y_i}{N} - b \frac{\sum_{i=1}^{N} X_i}{N} = \bar{y} - b\bar{X} \tag{10}$$

The standard error of the regression line can be found in terms of the sample moments.

$$S_e^2 = \frac{M_{XX}(M_{YY}) - (M_{XY})^2}{N(N-2)M_{XX}}$$

$$S_e = \sqrt{S_e^2} \tag{11}$$

The major benefits in calculating the sample moments is that the correlation coefficient, r, and the coefficient of determination, r^2, can easily be found.

$$r = \frac{M_{XY}}{(M_{XX})(M_{YY})}$$

$$R^2 = (r) \tag{12}$$

The coefficient of determination, R^2, is the percentage of the variance of the dependent variable explained by the independent variable. The coefficient of determination cannot exceed 1 nor be less than zero. In the case of $R^2 = 0$, the regression line's $Y = Y$ and no variation in the dependent variable is explained. If the dependent variable pattern continues as in the past, the model with time as the independent variable should be of good use in forecasting.

The firm can test whether the a and b coefficients are statistically different from zero, the generally accepted null hypothesis. A t-test is used to test the two null hypotheses:

$$H_{0_1} = \alpha = 0$$

$$H_{A_1} = \alpha/0$$

$$H_{0_2} = \beta = 0$$

$$H_{A_2} = \beta/0$$

The *HO* represents the null hypothesis while *HA* represents the alternative hypothesis. To reject the null hypothesis, the calculated t-value must exceed the critical t-value given in the t-tables in the appendix. The calculated t-values for a and b are found by:

$$t_a = \frac{a - \alpha}{S_e} \sqrt{\frac{N(M_{XX})}{M_{XX} + (N\bar{X})^2}}$$

$$t_b = \frac{b - \beta}{S_e} \sqrt{\frac{(M_{XX})}{N}} \tag{13}$$

The critical t-value, t_c, for the .05 level of significance with $N - 2$ degrees of freedom, can be found in a t-table in any statistical econometric text.

if $t_a > t_c$, then reject H_{0_1},

if $t_b > t_c$, then reject H_{0_2},

The null hypothesis that =0 can be rejected and therefore is statistically different from zero. The t-value of b leads to the rejection of =0, and is statistically different from zero. One has a statistically significant regression model if one can reject H_{O_2}.

We can create 95 percent confidence intervals for a and b, where the limits of a and b are:

$$a + t\alpha/_2 S_e \sqrt{\frac{(N\bar{X})^2 + M_{XX}}{N(M_{XX})}}$$

$$b + t\alpha/_2 S_e \sqrt{\frac{N}{M_{XX}}} \tag{14}$$

To test whether the model is a useful model, an F-test is performed where:

$$H_0 = \alpha = \beta = 0$$

$$H_A = \alpha/\beta = 0$$

$$F = \frac{\sum_{i=1}^{N} Y^2 \div 1 - \beta^2 \sum_{i=1}^{N} X_i^2}{\sum_{i=1}^{N} e^2 \div N - 2} \tag{15}$$

As the calculated F-value exceeds the critical F-value with $(1, N - 2)$ degrees of freedom of 5.99 at the .05 level of significance, the null hypothesis must be rejected. The 95 percent confidence level limit of prediction can be found in terms of the dependent variable value:

$$(a + bX_0) + t\alpha/_2 S_e \sqrt{\frac{N(X_0 - \bar{X})^2}{1 + N + M_{XX}}} \tag{16}$$

Autocorrelation

An estimated regression equation is plagued by the first-order correlation of residuals. That is, the regression error terms are not white noise (random) as is assumed in the general linear model, but are serially correlated where

$$\varepsilon_t = \rho\varepsilon_{t-1} + U_t \qquad t = 1, 2, \ldots N \qquad (17)$$

ε_t = regression error term at time t,

ρ = first-order correlation coefficient and

U_t = normally and independently distributed random variable.

The serial correlation of error terms, known as autocorrelation, is a violation of a regression assumption and may be corrected by the application of the Cochrane-Orcutt procedure.[2] Autocorrelation produces unbiased, the expected value of parameter is the population parameter, but inefficient parameters. The variance of the parameters are biased (too low) among the set of linear unbiased estimators and the sample t and F-statistics are too large. The Cochrane-Orcutt (CORC) procedure was developed to produce the best linear unbiased estimators (BLUE) given the autocorrelation of regression residuals. The CORC procedure uses the information implicit in the first-order correlative of residuals to produce unbiased and efficient estimators

$$Y_t = \alpha + \beta X_t + \varepsilon_t$$

$$\hat{\rho} = \frac{\sum e_{t,} e_t - 1}{\sum e_t^2 - 1}. \qquad (18)$$

The dependent and independent variables are transformed by the estimated rho, $\hat{\rho}$, to obtain more efficient ordinary least squares estimates:

$$Y_t - \rho Y_{t-1} = \alpha(1 - \rho) + \beta(X_t - \rho X_{t-1}) + u_t \qquad (19)$$

The Cochrane-Orcutt procedure is an iterative procedure that can be repeated until the coefficients converge. One immediately recognizes that as ρ approaches unity the regression model approaches a first-difference model.

The Durbin-Watson, D-W, statistic was developed to test for the absence of autocorrelation:

$$H_0: \rho = 0$$

---

[2]Cochrane, D. and G.H. Orcutt. 1949. "Application of Least Squares Regression to Relationships Containing Autocorrelated Error Terms," *Journal of the American Statistical Association* 44:32-61.

One generally tests for the presence of autocorrelation ($\rho = 0$) using the Durbin-Watson statistic:

$$\text{D-W} = d = \frac{\sum_{t=2}^{N} (e_t - e_{t-1})^2}{\sum_{t=2}^{N} e_t^2} \tag{20}$$

The e's represent the ordinary least squares regression residuals and a two-tailed tail is employed to examine the randomness of residuals. One rejects the null hypothesis of no statistically significant autocorrelation if:

$$d < d_L \text{ or } d > 4 - d_u$$

where

d_L is the "lower" Durbin-Watson level

and

d_u is the "upper" Durbin-Watson level.

The upper and lower level Durbin-Watson statistic levels are given in Johnston (1972). The Durbin-Watson statistic is used to test only for first-order correlation among residuals.

$$d = 2(1 - \rho). \tag{21}$$

If the first-order correlation of model residuals is zero, the Durbin-Watson statistic is 2. A very low value of the Durbin-Watson statistic, $d < d_L$, indicates positive autocorrelation between residuals and produces a regression model that is not statistically plagued by autocorrelation.

The inconclusive range for the estimated Durbin-Watson statistic is

$$d_L < d < d_u \text{ or } 4 - d_u < 4 - d_u.$$

One does not reject the null hypothesis of no autocorrelation of residuals if $d_u < d < 4 - d_u$.

One of the weaknesses of the Durbin-Watson test for serial correlation is that only first-order autocorrelation of residuals is examined, one should plot the correlation of residual with various time lags

$$\text{corr } (e_t, e_{t-k})$$

to find higher-order correlations among residuals.

In a nonlinear least squares (NLLS) model, one seeks to estimate an equation in which the dependent variable increases by a constant growth rate rather than a constant amount.[3] The nonlinear regression equation is:

$$Y = ab^X \qquad (22)$$

$$\text{or } \log Y = \log a + \log BX$$

The normal equations are derived from minimizing the sum of the squared error terms (as in ordinary least squares) and may be written as:

$$\sum(\log Y) = N(\log a) + (\log b)\sum X \qquad (23)$$

$$\sum(X \log Y) = (\log a)\sum X + (\log b)\sum X^2$$

If $\sum X = 0$, as we may do when we are forecasting sales, the normal equations simplify to:

$$\sum(\log Y) = N(\log a)$$

$$\sum(X \log Y) = (\log b)\sum X_2 \qquad (24)$$

The solutions to the simplified NLLS estimation equation are:

$$\log a = \frac{\sum(\log Y)}{N}$$

and $\qquad (25)$

$$\log b = \frac{\sum(X \log Y)}{\sum X^2}$$

---

[3]The reader is referred to C.T. Clark and L.L. Schkade, *Statistical Analysis for Administrative Decisions* (Cincinnati: South-Western Publishing Company, 1979) for an excellent treatment of this topic.

Multiple Regression

It may well be that several economic variables influence the variable that one is interested in forecasting. For example, the levels of the Gross National Product (GNP), personal disposable income, or price indices can assert influences on the firm. Multiple regression is an extremely easy statistical tool for researchers and management to employ due to the great proliferation of computer software. The general form of the two-independent variable multiple regression is:

$$Y_t = \beta_1 + \beta_2 X_{2t} + \beta_3 X_{3t} + \varepsilon_t, \ t = 1, \ldots, N \tag{26}$$

In matrix notation multiple regression can be written:

$$Y = X\beta + \varepsilon \tag{27}$$

Multiple regression requires unbiasedness, the expected value of the error term is zero, and the X's are fixed and independent of the error term. The error term is an identically and independently distributed normal variable. Least squares estimation of the coefficients yields:

$$\hat{\beta} = (\hat{\beta}_1, \hat{\beta}_2, \hat{\beta}_3)$$
$$Y = X\hat{\beta} + e \tag{28}$$

Multiple regression, using the least squared principle, minimizes the sum of the squared error terms:

$$\sum_{i=1}^{N} e_i^2 = e'e \tag{29}$$

$$(Y - X\hat{\beta})'(Y - X\hat{\beta})$$

To minimize the sum of the squared error terms, one takes the partial derivative of the squared errors with respect to $\hat{\beta}$ and the partial derivative set equal to zero.

$$\partial \frac{(e'e)}{\partial \beta} = -2X'Y + 2X'X\hat{\beta} = 0$$

$$\hat{\beta} = (X'X)^{-1}X'Y \tag{30}$$

Alternatively, one could solve the normal equations for the two-variable to determine the regression coefficients.

$$\sum Y = \hat{\beta}_1 N + \hat{\beta}_2 \sum X_2 + \hat{\beta}_3 \sum X_3$$

$$\sum X_2 Y = \hat{\beta}_1 \sum X_2 + \hat{\beta}_2 X_2^2 + \hat{\beta}_3 \sum X_2 \sum X_3 \qquad (31)$$

$$\sum X_3 Y = \hat{\beta}_1 \sum X_3 + \hat{\beta}_2 \sum X_2 X_3 + \hat{\beta}_3 \sum X_3^2$$

References

Cochrane, D. and G.H. Orcutt. 1949. Application of Least Squares Regression to Relationships Containing Autocorrelated Error Terms. *Journal of the American Statistical Association.* 44:32-61.

Johnston, J. 1972. *Econometric Methods.* 2nd ed. New York: McGraw-Hill.

Mansfield, E. 1987. *Statistics for Business and Economics.* 3rd ed. New York: W.W. Norton & Company.

Miller, Irwin, and John E. Freund. 1965. *Probability and Statistics for Engineers.* Englewood Cliffs, N.J.: Prentice-Hall.

Murphy, James L. 1973. *Introductory Econometrics.* Homewood, Ill.: Richard D. Irwin, Inc.

Chapter 3

Time Series Analysis
and
Forecasting Models

The last chapter outlined a variety of regression techniques and showed how to apply them to forecasting. In this chapter, we expand the discussion to include models which are more sophisticated than conventional regression techniques. The underlying concept is much the same, however: the use of historical data to make forecasts about the future.

In time series analysis one searches for systematic changes over time (hence the name) in the variable to be forecast. Unlike regression analysis, there is no reference to any relationship with another variable in (univariate) time series analysis. (Alternatively, one could think of the independent variable as being lagged (past) values of the variable.) As a very simple example, an analysis of historical data on cash collections by a firm might reveal that the amount of cash collected has risen by about 2 percent each year. A reasonable forecast of next year's cash collections would thus be 102 percent of this year's collections. Of course, as always, the accuracy of this forecast will depend on the extent to which the trends of the past are continued in the future.

This chapter discusses three types of time series models. It should be noted that more sophisticated forecasting techniques do not always result in more accurate forecasts. Simulations of past forecasting accuracy and hands-on experience with a variety of forecasting models are important in helping the forecaster identify the model(s) to be used.

In the past fifteen years computer software has been developed to allow managers easy access to relatively sophisticated forecasting methods. Managers can forecast financial variables using regression analysis, as we discussed in the previous chapter, or use a more statistically sophisticated set of time series models popularized by Professors Box and Jenkins (1970). The moving average-autoregressive (ARMA)

81

models of Box and Jenkins have become known as "time series" models and can be estimated by many statistical packages discussed and examined in this chapter. Managers can use time series models to develop *pro forma* statements as we did using regression in the previous chapter. Accountants and accounting researchers have developed a very large literature on the subject of forecasting corporate earnings per share, summarized in Hopwood and McKeown (1986). The comptroller and vice-president of finance of an industrial company should be very interested in forecasting earnings because earnings are a major determinant of stock prices and the cost of capital [Lewellen (1969), Malkiel (1981), and Weston and Copeland (1986)].

In this chapter we will illustrate the time series modeling process by analyzing the cash collections series of a *Fortune 100* firm and the Chrysler Corporation earnings per share (eps) series. We want to stress the importance of being able to develop effective time series models at very low costs and modeling efforts. Many economic series, such as Gross National Product (GNP), and corporate earnings per share (eps), follow near-random-walk with drift series [Granger and Newbold (1986)]. The random-walk with drift framework is similar to a very simple first-order exponential smoothing model [Montgomery and Johnson (1976)].

We can use the random-walk with drift framework as a benchmark for measuring forecasting efficiency.

The basic framework for the ARMA model is:

$$\phi(B)Z_t = C + \theta(B)a_t \qquad (1)$$

where $\phi(B)$ represents how the current value of the series is expressed as a function of previous values of series Z; $\theta(B)$ represents how the current value of the series is expressed as a function of previous values of the error terms; B represents the backshift operator, i.e., $BZ = Z$; and C is the constant. In a more formal notation:

$$\phi(B)Z_t = C + \theta(B)a_t$$

$$\phi(B) = 1 - \phi_1 B^1 - \phi_2 B^2 \ldots -\phi_p B_p \qquad (2)$$

$$\theta(B) = 1 - \theta_1 B^1 - \theta_2 B^2 - \ldots - \theta_q B^q.$$

In a random walk model, such as one adequate to describe GNP or corporate earnings series, the current value of the series, Z_t, is equal to the previous value of the series plus a random change (shock) in the current period, a_t. In the Box-Jenkins ARMA notation, the random walk model is a first-order autoregressive process, an $AR(1)$ process (with an assumed $\phi_1 = 1$).

$$Z_t = Z_{t-1} + a_1$$

or $$Z_t - Z_{t-1} = a_t \tag{3}$$

or $$(1 - B)Z_t = a_t$$

If the series follows a random-walk with drift process, the change in the series is written as a function of the current shock term and the previous shock term, a_{t-1}.

$$(1 - B)Z_t = a_t - \theta_1 a_{t-1}$$

or $$(1 - B)Z_t = (1 - \theta_1 B)a_t \tag{4}$$

The reader will note that the series analyzed to stationarity first-differenced (to produce a constant variance model). Most economic series are transformed to a constant variance model by differencing the series [Granger and Newbold (1986)]. Instead of differencing the series, one could have estimated the autoregressive term. A first-difference model assumes that the first-order autoregressive parameter is unity. In an $AR(1)$ model, the correlation coefficients between the current and previous values of the series is very high (in many cases the correlation coefficient is near one) and the correlation coefficients between the current value of the series and successive series lags tend to decay slowly. The correlation coefficients between the current value of the series and successive time lags is known as the autocorrelation function. The partial autocorrelation function examines the relationship between the current value of the series and the time lags in the series holding constant the previous relationships. That is, the partial autocorrelation for time $t - 2$ holds constant the correlation coefficient between the series at time t and $t - 1$. In an $AR(1)$ process, if the series follows a random-walk, the partial autocorrelation between the series at time t and $t - 2$ should be approximately zero because the second time period lag adds no additional statistically significant information to the correlation coefficient between time t and $t - 1$. In an $AR(p)$ process, the autocorrelation function estimates decay slowly while the partial autocorrelation function estimates "cut off" after lag p. In an $MA(q)$ process, the autocorrelation function cuts off after lag q while the partial autocorrelation function decays slowly. In a mixed order autoregressive-moving average

(ARMA) process, both the autocorrelation and partial autocorrelation function estimates decay slowly.

The Box-Jenkins methodology is set forth in their seminal treatment of time series analysis, entitled *Time Series Analysis: Forecasting and Control*. Their methodology is well-used in accounting and finance. An appendix is included to reacquaint the reader to the theory and practical modeling practices of time series analysis.

The Forecasting of Cash Collections

The purpose of this example is to employ automatic forecasting systems to forecast daily cash collections for a *Fortune 100* manufacturing firm. The firm's forecasting of cash collections is an integral element in efficiently managing the firm's cash position because knowledge of the net cash inflow can be incorporated into the Miller-Orr (1966) control limit model [Stone (1972)]. Furthermore, Miller and Stone (1985) and Kallberg and Parkinson (1984) have recently applied sophisticated time series modeling to cash management problems.

Many statistical methods can be employed in analyzing the cash collections series; in this example, moving average (MA) and simple exponential smoothing (E1) and univariate time series (BJ) models are estimated and forecast. Initially models are estimated over the first three quarters of 1982 and the fourth quarter of 1982 is reserved as the post-sample forecasted period. The time series and exponential smoothing models are forecasted over three-week forecast horizons during the fourth quarter. The models are reestimated and reforecast over four three-week horizons (the fourth post-sample period contains the final four weeks of 1982).

When one attempts to identify and estimate univariate time series models such as in this example, one assumes that only the previous values of the series and/or its error terms (the random shocks discussed in the appendix to this chapter) are useful in the model building process. In regression analysis, one attempts to find statistically significant associations among variables; in univariate time series modeling, one models and forecasts a series using only the series history. Time series analysis is extremely easy to use given the excellent software now available for performing the analysis. We use the Autobox system, marketed by Automatic Forecasting Systems, Inc. (AFS), and SCA-PC system marketed by Scientific Computing Associates (SCA) in this chapter. It is now very easy to forecast variables such as Gross National Product (GNP) or the money supply simply by obtaining data from the *Federal Reserve Bulletin* or the *Economic Report of the President*, inputing the data on a personal computer (using the DOS system to create an ASCII file), and identify and estimate models. One can easily enter the data, develop a model, and forecast the series in 30 minutes. One only needs to change one or two lines of programming language to estimate time series models, moving averages, or exponential smoothing models.

The modeling and forecasting of a cash collections series should illustrate the importance of reserving a post-sample period to test one's modeling efforts. Carbone and Makridakis (1986) have noted that many sophisticated models fail to outperform very simple models in post-sample forecasting.

The Models

The models used in this example are (1) the time univariate series model put forth by Box and Jenkins (1970); (2) a twenty-day equally-weighted moving average; and (3) a simple first-order exponential smoothing model. We also briefly examine an outlier-augmented time series model to model outliers into a traditional time series model. A twenty day moving average method is employed to provide a very simplistic forecast. The twenty-day equally-weighted moving average procedure is selected because the firm is principally concerned with analyzing the previous month's cash collections. The twenty-day moving average forecast, $M(20)$, may be written as:

$$\sum_{j=t-s+1}^{t} x_j \qquad (5)$$

A second model, a simple first-order exponential smoothing model is used in the general form:

$$S_{t+1} = S_t + \alpha(X_t - S_t) \qquad (6)$$

where S = (old) forecast made for time t,

X = actual series value at time t,

S = (new) forecast made for time $t + 1$,

and α = smoothing parameter.

The reader is referred to Kallberg and Parkinson (1984) for a complete discussion of alternative cash forecasting models.

The modeler of a univariate time series model seeks to identify and estimate models using autocorrelation and partial autocorrelation function estimations that are statistically different from zero (see the appendix for a review of time series modeling). The estimated autocorrelation and partial autocorrelation function are shown in Table 3-1. Because

Table 3-1 Autocorrelation Function Estimates

Series						*lags*						
	1	2	3	4	5	6	7	8	9	10	11	12
∇ Collections	.163	−.119	−.139	−.075	.094	.110	−.097	−.091	−.099	.045	.141	−.029
∇̄ Collections	−.316	−.176	−.051	−.054	.093	.132	−.119	−.001	−.091	.031	.165	−.031
∇² Collections	.143	−.511	−.262	−.065	.199	.167	−.080	−.143	−.120	.090	.235	−.025
∇ Collections**.5	.163	−.119	−.139	−.075	.094	.110	−.097	.080	−.099	.045	.121	.076
∇ Bills	−.147	−.016	.038	.045	.141	.010	.057	.069	.040	.090	.032	−.027
∇̄ Bills	−.549	.034	.021	−.061	.115	−.081	.016	.020	−.036	.008	.052	.017
∇² Bills	−.104	−.527	.076	.032	.067	−.028	−.040	.020	−.045	.018		

Series	13	14	15	16	17	18	19	20	21	22	23	24
∇ Collections	−.143	−.029	.034	.050	.100	−.036	−.125	−.112	.179	.168	.090	−.107
∇̄ Collections	−.143	.027	.032	−.026	.115	−.027	−.193	.101	.041	.032	.015	−.030
∇² Collections	−.201	−.043	.052	.075	.128	−.106	−.239	.049	.182	.105	.013	−.097
∇ Collections**.5												
∇ Bills	.095	.024	.001	.085	.067	.122	−.073	.098	.115	.035	.126	.023
∇̄ Bills	.041	−.021	−.046	.042	−.033	.113	−.163	.071	.038	−.069	.088	−.057
∇² Bills	.034	−.056	−.078	.017	.095	.029	−.164	.024	.086	−.038	.090	−.037

		lags											
	1	2	3	4	5	6	7	8	9	10	11	12
∇ Collections	.163	-.149	-.097	-.053	.091	.054	-.126	-.022	-.082	.049	.074	-.077
$\bar{\nabla}$ Collections	-.316	-.306	-.269	-.314	-.205	-.017	-.106	-.040	-.158	-.145	.023	.026
∇^2 Collections	.143	-.542	-.103	-.399	.096	-.225	.009	-.220	-.144	-.065	.026	-.148
∇ Collections **.5												
∇ Bills	.163	-.149	-.097	-.053	.091	.054	-.126	.080	-.082	.049	.142	.111
$\bar{\nabla}$ Bills	-.148	-.039	.030	.057	.162	.062	.076	.082	.052	.085	-.098	-.098
∇^2 Bills	-.549	-.382	-.273	-.312	-.158	-.154	-.142	-.096	-.110	-.148	-.071	-.112
$\bar{\nabla}$ Bills	-.104	-.543	-.092	-.369	.008	-.280	.002	-.225	-.090	-.207		

	13	14	15	16	17	18	19	20	21	22	23	24
∇ Collections	-.090	.035	.017	-.029	.084	-.021	-.083	.165	.112	.104	.113	.095
$\bar{\nabla}$ Collections	-.094	-.054	-.006	-.114	.010	.053	-.169	-.070	-.055	-.056	-.030	.084
∇^2 Collections	-.095	-.056	-.123	-.077	.060	-.228	-.157	-.102	-.130	-.100	-.005	.003
∇ Collections **.5												

there are 195 observations in the estimation period, the standard error of the autocorrelation and partial autocorrelation estimates is .071($1/\sqrt{195}$) and the estimated function coefficients must exceed .143 to be statistically significant at the 5 percent level (2 × .071). One would expect to find moving average operators at lags 1, 2, and 20 to be statistically significant. The completely estimated [Guerard and Lawrence (1985)] model for the cash collections series, BJU, is:

$$CC = 19.389 + (1 + .126B - .149B^2 + .176B^{20} + .243B^{21})a_t$$
[s.e.]   [.073]   [.073]   [.075]   [.074]

The estimated mean square error of the model is 118.5.

The univariate cash collections time series model may be estimated in the tradition of Box and Jenkins involving an automatic forecasting system, the Autobox system, described in Reilly (1980) and shown in Table 3–2. The initial univariate cash collections time series model, estimated using 195 daily observations during the first three quarters of 1982, is an AR(2) time series model.[1] The mean square error of the automatically estimated univariate time series model for cash collections is 119.9. Thus, one must take a close look at the relative cost of developing a model versus the ease of using an automatic procedure. The AR(2) process estimation is substantiated in estimation periods 1-226 and 1-241. The automatic univariate Box and Jenkins model has significantly lower sample mean square error rather than first-order exponential smoothing process and the twenty-day moving average models estimated with the Autobox system. The simple exponential smoothing model constant is approximately equal to .10.[2] Although the Box-Jenkins and exponential smoothing models are initially estimated and reestimated three times, the univariate model produces the lowest sample variance of the exponential smoothing and moving average models but

---

[1]In an AR(2) time series model in which the current value of the series, X_t, is expressed as a linear combination of the two previous values of the series X_{t-1} and X_{t-2} plus a randomly distributed error term:

$$X_t = \phi_1 X_{t-1} + \phi_2 X_{t-2} + U_t$$

For the AR(2) process, it is well known [Box and Jenkins (1970)] that:

$$\phi_2 = \frac{\rho - \rho_1^2}{1 - \rho_1^2} \text{ and } \phi_1 = \frac{\rho_1(1 - \rho_2)}{1 - \rho_1^2}$$

[2]An ARMA-estimated first-order exponential smoothing model, ARMA(0,1,1) model, produced a slightly higher sample mean square error than did the simple smoothing constant model presented in the analysis.

Table 3-2 Model Estimations Summary and Post-Sample Forecasting Error

Observations	Models	R^2	Mean Square Errors	Degrees of Freedom
1-195	MA: M(20)	.000	145.9	154
El: $S_{t+1} = S_t + .11(X_t - S_t)$		.000	139.8	193
BJ: $X_t = 1.941 + .208X_{t-1} - .153X_{t-2}$		.058	119.9	190
(S.e) $\quad$ [.071] $\quad$ [.070]				

Post-Sample Period	Models	Absolute Values of Forecasting Errors	
		$\bar{X}$	$\bar{\sigma}$
196-211	MA	8.204	4.122
	El	8.038	4.382
	BJ	8.281	5.031

			Mean Square Errors	Degrees of Freedom
1-211	M(20)	.000	146.9	170
$S_{t+1} = S_t + .10(X_t - S_t)$		.000	140.8	209
$X_t = 1.914 + .221X_{t-1} - .149X_{t-2}$		.061	117.0	206
[.070] $\quad$ [.069]				

Post-Sample Period	Models	Absolute Values of Forecasting Errors	
		$\bar{X}$	$\bar{\sigma}$
212-226	MA	7.690	4.952
	El	7.633	4.993
	BJ	8.474	5.420

			Mean Square Errors	Degrees of Freedom
1-226	M(20)	.000	141.4	185
$S_{t+1} = S_t - .11(X_t - S_t)$		.000	136.3	224
$X_t = 1.874 + (1 + .225B)a_t$		.043	116.3	216
[.067]				

Post-Sample Period	Models	Absolute Values of Forecasting Errors	
		$\bar{X}$	$\bar{\sigma}$
227-241	MA	8.953	7.681
	El	9.360	7.902
	BJ	10.415	7.583

			Mean Square Errors	Degrees of Freedom
1-241	M(20)	.000	141.8	200
$S_{t+1} = S_t + .10(X_t - S_t)$		.000	137.5	239
$X_t - 1.852 + .250X_{t-1} - .163X_{t-2}$		.073	115.6	236
$\cdot$ [.064] $\quad$ [.063]				

(continued)

Table 3-2 (*Continued*)

Post-Sample Period	Models	Absolute Values of Forecasting Errors	
		$\bar{X}$	$\bar{\sigma}$
242–261	MA	6.946	5.050
	E1	7.189	5.156
	BJ	7.232	5.180

relatively higher post-sample forecasting errors (although forecasting errors are not statistically different as measured by the *t*-test) in each of the post-sample periods. One must be aware of the differences between modeling efficiency and forecasting efficiency.[3] Carbone and Makridakis (1986) have examined the changing nature of data and argued that simple exponential smoothing models may be reasonable long-run post-sample forecasting models because they track the changing mean of the process.

An Outlier Series Model Analysis of Cash Collections

The univariate time series model was deemed adequately fitted on the basis of residual plots and the Ljung-Box statistic. There were only 11 observations that lie outside the 95 percent upper and lower confidence intervals. The number of outliers is not unexpected given the 195 observations used in the initial model estimation. However, the presence of outliers conveys information that the modeler may use to forecast daily collections.

The application of outlier analysis techniques, using the Autobox system to the cash collections forecasting problems produces five inter-

---

[3]The post-sample forecasting efficiency analysis may be further developed. A transfer function model of cash collections may be constructed by using the billings series of the *Fortune 100* firm as the input to the collections model. The cross-correlation coefficient between cash collections and billings is 0.243 at lag one (highly significant). The estimated transfer function model is:

$$V_{cc} = 19.773 + (1 + .110B - .020B^2 + .189B^{20} + .243B^{21})a_t$$
[s.e.] [1.123]   [.074]   [.075]   [.076]   [.074]

$$+ .529 \text{ billings}_t + .312 \text{ billings}_{t-1}$$
[.071]   [.070]

The estimated mean square error is 86.7, representing a very large reduction in the estimated model variance during the sample modeling period. However, no statistically significant forecasting improvement is found during the post-sample periods.

ventions. The model identified pulse intervention variables at observations 32 (President's Day) and 133 (July 6th); step intervention variable are identified at observations 5 and 153. The identification of pulse intervention variable for holidays is well documented in the time series literature [Box and Tiao (1975), Liu (1980, 1983), Bell and Hillmer (1983), and Cleveland and Devlin (1982)] and is an alternative to the mixed-effect model of Miller and Stone (1985). The most important outlier variable is a seasonal pulse observation identified to occur every five observations, beginning at observation eight. The weekly seasonal pulse is in relative accord with the firm's policy of billing on the second Monday of the month and receiving the cash, on average, on the following day.

$$V_{cc} \cdot \cdot .5 = 15.343 + (1 - .180B^{10})a_t + .823X_1$$
$$[\text{s.e.}] \qquad\qquad\qquad [.071] \qquad [.241]$$

$$-4.094X_2 + 1.611X_3 - 3.329X_4 - .665X_5$$
$$[1.378] \qquad [.686] \qquad [1.359] \qquad [0.229]$$

where

$$X_1 = \begin{cases} 0, & T \neq 8, 13, 18, \ldots \\ 1, & T = 8, 13, 18, \ldots \end{cases}$$

$$X_2 = \begin{cases} 0, & T \neq 133 \\ 1, & T = 133 \end{cases}$$

$$X_3 = \begin{cases} 0, & T < 5 \\ 1, & T > 5 \end{cases}$$

$$X_4 = \begin{cases} 0, & T \neq 32 \\ 1, & T = 32 \end{cases}$$

$$X_5 = \begin{cases} 0, & T > 153 \\ 1, & T < 153 \end{cases}$$

The mean square error variance is 115.8, representing a slight reduction in the variance produced by the traditionally estimated univariate time series model. However, the outlier model does not significantly outperform the traditional time series model in forecasting collections in the first post-sample period.[4] Second, preliminary evidence suggests that the

---

[4]The intervention analysis model produces an average mean square forecasting error of 8.513 during the first post-sample forecasting period (observations 196–211) whereas the automatic time series model without outliers produces an average mean square forecasting error of 8.281.

seasonal pulse intervention variable may not be found in the reestimation of the model during the post-sample periods.

There are no statistically significant differences in the time series models' forecasting errors.

Practical Benefits of an Automatic Forecasting System

The use of an automatic forecasting system in forecasting cash collections, such as Autobox, is an excellent tool with which management can easily (and with little expense) develop relatively sophisticated time series models. Data entry can be accomplished at the keyboard or from ASCII files and is easily done. The automatically estimated time series models with and without intervention analysis did not outperform simple exponential smoothing models in the post-sample forecasting of cash collections; however, given the results of Carbone and Makridakis (1986), this is not surprising. The primary benefits (to this author) of the automatically estimated time series models are the calculations of the optimal Box-Cox (1964) transformation and outlier detection routines. The automatic estimation of the Box-Cox lambda is very helpful in lieu of the mean-range plots advocated in Jenkins (1979). The outlier detection algorithm produces models that may not be evident from examining plotted data. The data transformation and outlier routines are well worth the cost of the package.

An alternative approach to the use of outlier time series modeling techniques is to use the Stone and Wood (1977) and Stone and Miller (1987) frameworks for daily cash forecasting. The Stone and Wood standard month daily cash forecasting model used an additive model to characterize the daily cash flow pattern, CF_{tw}.

$$CF_{tw} = a_t + b_w$$

where a_t = proportion of monthly cash flow occurring on workday t in the absence of any day of the week effect,

and b_w = proportion of monthly cash flow occurring on day of the week effect (w = 1 for Monday, 5 for Friday).

The (OLS) estimation of the additive cash forecasting model for the first three quarters of the 1982 cash collections series produces the regression coefficients shown on the following page.

The Stone and Wood additive model set the Friday day of the week variable equal to zero to prevent perfect collinearity [Stone and Miller (1987)]. One notes that the additive model correctly identifies the second Tuesday of the month (the t-statistical on the Tuesday variable is 3.57

Table 3-3 Estimated Additive Model

Variable	Regression coefficient	(t)
Intercept	15.592	(2.67)
Monday	.311	(0.14)
Tuesday	7.861	(3.57)
Wednesday	2.651	(1.19)
Thursday	.019	(.01)
Day of the Month		
1	.069	(.01)
2	−10.650	(−1.60)
3	−12.874	(−1.89)
4	1.448	(0.21)
5	−7.614	(−1.14)
6	−10.159	(−1.49)
7	14.909	(2.19)
8	.712	(0.11)
9	−1.450	(−.22)
10	−2.875	(−.42)
11	−1.252	(−.18)
12	5.486	(.82)
13	5.141	(.75)
14	9.825	(1.44)
15	4.712	(0.71)
16	6.222	(0.93)
17	5.559	(0.81)
18	4.198	(0.61)
19	5.557	(0.83)
20	3.724	(0.55)
21	8.525	(1.25)
22	6.583	(0.99)
23	−3.021	(−.45)
24	−3.991	(−.59)
25	−1.202	(−.18)
26	−3.771	(−.57)
27	−.709	(−.10)
28	7.975	(1.17)
29	10.964	(1.60)
30	12.401	(1.81)

and day seven is statistically significant, $t = 2.19$). The additive model produces an R^2 of 0.408 and a mean square error of 92.5, slightly larger than the transfer function cash collections model but less than the outlier cash collections model. If one uses the mean absolute percentage errors (MAPE) for the fourth quarter of 1982 to measure post-sample forecasting efficiency, the additive model is (significantly) superior to the univariate, transfer function, and outlier time series models.

The Stone and Wood additive model produces the lowest MAPE of the models developed in this chapter. A multiplicative model has been put forth by Stone and Miller (1987) to reflect cash discounts, but that analysis is not examined in this chapter.

Table 3-4 Mean Absolute Percentage Errors

Model	MAPE
BJU	3.406
Eq 1	3.336
Transfer Function	3.436
Outlier	3.504
Additive Model	1.416

An Introduction to the Time Series Modeling of Earnings: The Case of Chrysler

Let us continue building time series models by examining the corporate earnings models developed in the accounting literature. We will estimate quarterly eps models for the Chrysler Corporation during the 1979.1 to 1986.4 period. Although time series specialists advocate the use of 40–50 observations for estimating models, it has been shown that only using 24 observations is adequate in modeling corporate earnings [Lorek and McKeown (1978)]. Corporate earnings per share (eps) tend to follow a random-walk with drift process, and ARIMA (0,1,1) process [Albrecht, Lookabill, and McKeown (1977) and Watts and Leftwich (1977)]. The annual random (or random-walk with drift) earnings series may be written as:

$$(1 - B)X_t = (1 - \theta_1 B)a_t \tag{7}$$

where:

the backshift operator: $BX_t = X_{t-1}$.
θ_1 is the first order moving average parameter.

A random walk with drift quarterly series may be written as:

$$(1 - \phi_1 B)(1 - B^4)X_t = (1 - \theta_1 B)(1 - \theta_4 B^4)a_t \tag{8}$$

where:

ϕ_1 = the first-order autoregressive parameter,
θ_1 is the first-order moving average parameter,
θ_4 is the quarterly moving average operator, and $(1 - B^4)$ is the 4th seasonal difference.

Equation (8) can become a pure random walk series if ϕ_1 is unity and the constant is zero [Granger and Newbold (1986)]. Little (1962) put forth the hypothesis that earnings changes are random and the bulk of the empirical evidence supports the random nature of earnings [Ball and Watts (1979)]. Brown and Rozeff (1979) held that an AR(1) parameter and a MA (4) parameter should be estimated; the Brown and Rozeff lacks only the MA (1) parameter from the traditional random-walk with drift formulation. Griffin (1977) advocated first-differencing quarterly series data in equation (8) rather than estimating ϕ_1. Foster (1977) argued that only a constant and AR(1) parameter should be estimated. The empirical evidence does not support the superiority of either the Foster, Griffin or Brown and Rozeff modifications of the near-random-walk nature of equation (8) [Lorek (1979) and Hopwood and McKeown (1986)]. We will estimate the full form of equation (8) in this study, referring to equation (8) as the (near) random walk with drift, RWD, process of quarterly earnings per share.

If one estimates the autocorrelation and partial autocorrelation functions for Chrysler eps during the 1979.1 to 1986.4 characterized by decaying autocorrelation function, suggesting a first-order autoregressive scheme, an AR(1) or a first-difference model (see Table 3–5 for function estimates). Furthermore, the autocorrelation and partial autocorrelation function estimates of the first-difference Chrysler eps series have large autocorrelations at lags 1 and 4, suggesting that a seasonal (quarterly) difference also is appropriate. Therefore, because a quarterly seasonal difference should be estimated with a first-difference model, one should expect the random-walk with drift model to be appropriate for the Chrysler eps series [Granger and Newbold (1986)].

If one estimates the various time series models using the Chrysler Corporation data during the 1979.1 to 1986.4 period, one finds that Chrysler's earnings per share follow a near-random-walk process (complete time series models are shown in Table 3–6). This is particularly interesting given Chrysler's near-bankruptcy condition of 1980. The Foster model estimation shows a moderately large (.547) and statistically significant AR(1) parameter. The R^2 of .657 indicates that the model is a reasonably "good" fit and a residual plot does not indicate but two observations (the residuals from observations 10 and 28) outside of the 95 percent confidence interval. See Table 3–6 for complete time series model estimations. The Brown and Rozeff model representation is not that terribly different from the Foster formulation; the AR(1) parameter is statistically significant and larger than the Foster model estimate but the MA(4) term is not statistically significant. A constant is not estimated in the Brown and Rozeff formulation which produces an R^2 of .642. The Griffin model estimation produces a slightly lower R^2 (.585) than the Brown and Rozeff and Foster representations; one might have expected

Table 3–5 Autocorrelation and Partial Autocorrelation Function Estimates Chrysler eps

Function	Series	lags							
		1	2	3	4	5	6	7	8
ACF	X_t	.85	.77	.67	.59	.42	.31	.22	.15
PACF	X_t	.85	.18	−.06	−.03	−.35	−.01	.05	.09
ACF $(1-B)$	X_t	−.26	.01	−.02	.29	−.26	−.10	−.09	.05
PACF $(1-B)$	X_t	−.26	−.07	−.04	.30	−.12	−.21	−.22	−.11
ACF $(1-B^4)$	X_t	.55	.26	.05	−.25	−.35	−.25	−.12	−.17
PACF $(1-B^4)$	X_t	.55	−.05	−.11	−.32	−.11	.09	.07	−.29

Table 3–6 Complete Univariate Time Series Models for Chrysler eps

Model	series	constant	(t) AR(p)	(t) MA(q)	R^2	Forecasts	outliers, type(period)	(t) estimate
Brown and Rozeff	$(1 - B^4)X_t$		(4.59) .702(1)	(1.27) .302(4)	.642	1987.1 $2.73 1987.2 3.62 1987.3 1.76 1987.4 2.21	IO (1981.2) AO (1984.4)	(4.40) 6.29 (3.00) 2.53
Griffin	$(1 - B)(1 - B^4)X_t$		(.30) .066(1) (2.92) .529(4)		.586	1987.1 2.91 1987.2 3.80 1987.3 1.89 1987.4 2.40	IO (1981.2)	(3.73) 5.93
Foster	$(1 - B^4)X_t$	(1.66) .670	(3.99) .547(1)		.657	1987.1 3.16 1987.2 4.40 1987.3 2.88 1987.4 3.58	IO (1981.2) AO	(4.16) 6.21 (3.39) 2.79
RWD	$(1 - B^4)X_t$		(3.76) .713(1)	(.10) .027(1) (1.25) .304(4)	.642	1987.1 2.73 1987.2 3.61 1987.3 1.75 1987.4 2.21	IO (1981.2)	(4.40) 6.30

this given the AR(1) parameter estimates of approximately 0.70 in the Brown and Rozeff and Foster models whereas the Griffin first-difference imposes a first-order autoregressive parameter of 1.00. If one estimates the near-random-walk form found in equation (9), one finds that the MA(1) and MA(4) parameters are not statistically significant. The AR(1) parameter is .713, the R^2 is .641, and the ARMA model residuals are normally distributed.

The Brown and Rozeff, Griffin, Foster and random-walk drift models contain several (one or two) outliers that slightly improve upon traditional time series models. The SCA-PC program is used to identify and estimate additional outliers, AO (those that affect only one observation) and innovational outliers, IO (those that affect the memory of the system). The traditional time series models have an innovational outlier in 1981.2 (as Chrysler recovered from near-bankruptcy) and some have an additive outlier in 1984.4 (a very good quarter for Chrysler). The reader is referred to Hillmer, Bell and Tiao (1983) for a complete description of outlier analysis.

Summary and Conclusions

An automatic time series modeling system is used to forecast daily cash collections. The traditional univariate time series model produces lower sample variances than the simple moving average and first-order exponential smoothing in the sample periods variances; however, the post-sample error variances are not statistically different. Furthermore, an outlier model is identified involving holiday effects and offers managers an alternative to Miller and Stone's standard month formulation. The Chrysler eps series is modeled and follows a random-walk with drift process during the 1979.1 to 1986.4 period. This is quite surprising when one considers the unusual history of Chrysler in the late 1970s and early 1980's.

References

Albrecht, W.S., L.L. Lookabill and J.C. McKeown. 1977. The Time Series Properties of Annual Earnings. *Journal of Accounting Research* 15: 226–244.

Ball, R., and R. L. Watts. 1979. Some Additional Evidence on Survival Biases. *Journal of Finance* 34: 197–206.

Ball, R., and R.L. Watts. 1972. Some Time Series Properties of Accounting Income Numbers. *Journal of Finance* 27: 663–681.

Beaumont, C., E. Mahmoud, and V.E. McGee. 1985. Microcomputer

Forecasting Software: A Survey. *Journal of Forecasting* 4: 305–311.

Bell, W. 1983. A Computer Program (TEST) for Detecting Outliers in Time Series. 1983. American Statistical Association meeting, Business & Economic Statistics Proceedings, 624–639.

Bell, W.R. and S.C. Hillmer. 1983. Modeling Time Series with Calendar Variation. *Journal of the American Statistical Association* 78: 526–534.

Box, G.E.P. and G.M. Jenkins. 1970. *Forecasting and Control Time Series Analysis*. San Francisco: Holden-Day.

Box, G.E.P. and G.C. Tiao. 1975. Intervention Analysis with Applications to Economic and Environmental Problems. *Journal of the American Statistical Association* 70: 70–79.

Box, G.E.P. and D.R. Cox. 1964. An Analysis of Transformations. *Journal of the Royal Statistical Society* B 26: 211–243.

Brown, L.D. and M.S. Rozeff. 1978. The Superiority of Analyst Forecasts as Measures of Expectations: Evidence from Earnings. *Journal of Finance* 33: 1–16.

Brown, L.D. and M.S. Rozeff. 1979. Univariate Time Series Models of Quarterly Earnings Per Share Behavior. *Journal of Finance* 34: 13–21.

Carbone, R. and S. Makridakis. 1986. Forecasting When Pattern Changes Occur Beyond the Historical Data. *Management Science* 32: 257–271.

Cleveland, W.S. and S.J. Devlin. 1980. Calendar Effects in Monthly Time Series: Detection by Spectrum Analysis and Graphic Methods. *Journal of the American Statistical Association* 75: 487–496.

Collins, W.A. and W.S. Hopwood. 1980. A Multivariate Analysis of Annual Earnings Forecasts Generated from Quarterly Forecasts of Financial Analysts and Univariate Time Series Models. *Journal of Accounting Research* 18: 390–406.

Foster, G. 1977. Quarterly Accounting Data: Time Series Properties and Predictive Ability Results. *The Accounting Review* 52: 1–21.

Fox, A.J. 1972. Outliers in Time Series. *Journal of the Royal Statistical Society* B, 34: 350–363.

Griffin, P.A. 1977. The Time Series Behavior of Quarterly Earnings: Preliminary Evidence. *Journal of Accounting Research* 15: 71–83.

Guerard, J.B., D.P. Reilly, and K.D. Lawrence. 1985. Forecasting Daily Cash Collections. Presented at the Symposium on Cash, Treasury, and Working Capital Management, Montreal, Canada, July 29, 1985.

Hillmer, S.C. and G.C. Tiao. 1982. An ARIMA-Model-Based Approach to Seasonal Adjustment. *Journal of the American Statistical Association* 77: 63–70.

Hopwood, W.S., and J.C. McKeown, and P. Newbold. 1984. Time Series Forecasting Models Involving Power Transformations. *Journal of Forecasting* 3: 57–61.

Hopwood, W.S. and J.C. McKeown. 1986. *Univariate Time-Series Analysis of Quarterly Earnings: Some Unresolved Issues.* American Accounting Association.

Hopwood, W.S. and P. Newbold. 1981. Power Transformations in Time Series Models of Quarterly Earnings per Share. *The Accounting Review* 56: 927–933.

Hopwood, W.S. 1980. On the Automation of the Box-Jenkins Modeling Procedures: An Algorithm with an Empirical Test. *Journal of Accounting Research* 18: 289–296.

Hillmer, S.C., W.R. Bell, and G.C. Tiao. 1983. Modeling Considerations in Seasonal Adjustment of Economic Time Series. *Applied Time Series Analysis of Economic Data.* Ed., A. Zellner. Washington, D.C.: U.S. Department of the Commerce, Bureau of the Census.

Jenkins, G.M. 1979. Practical Experiences with Modeling and Forecasting Time Series. *Forecasting.* Ed., O.D. Anderson. Amsterdam: North-Holland.

Kallberg, J.G. and K.L. Parkinson. 1984. *Current Asset Management: Cash, Credit and Inventory.* New York: John Wiley & Sons, Inc.

Lewellen, W.G. 1969. *The Cost of Capital.* Belmont, CA: Wadsworth.

Liu, Lon-Mu. 1980. Analysis of Time Series and Calendar Effects. *Management Science* 26: 106–112.

Liu, Lon-Mu. 1986. Identification of Time Series Models in the Presence of Calendar Variation. *International Journal of Forecasting* 2: 357–372.

Lorek, L.S. 1979. Predicting Annual Net Earnings with Quarterly Earnings Time-Series Models. *Journal of Accounting Research* 19: 190–204.

Malkiel, B. 1981. *A Random Walk Down Wall Street*. New York: W.W. Norton.

Miller, M.H. and D. Orr. 1966. A Model of the Demand for Money by Firms. *Quarterly Journal of Economics* 79: 413-435.

Miller, T.W. and B.K. Stone. 1985. Daily Cash Forecasting and Seasonal Resolution: Alternative Models and Techniques for Using the Distribution Approach. *Journal of Financial and Quantitative Analysis* 20: 335-351.

Montgomery, D.C. and L.A. Johnson. 1976. *Forecasting and Time Series Analysis*. New York: McGraw-Hill.

Reilly, D.P. 1980. Experiences with an Automatic Box Jenkins Modelling Algorithm. *Time Series Analysis*. Ed., O. D. Anderson. Amsterdam: North-Holland.

Stone, B.K. 1972. The Use of Forecasts and Smoothing in Control Limit Models for Cash Management. *Financial Management* 1: 72-84.

Stone, B. K. and T. W. Miller. 1987. Daily Cash Forecasting with Multiplicative Models of Cash Flow Patterns. *Financial Management* 16: 45-54.

Watts, R.L. and R.L. Leftwich. 1977. The Time Series of Annual Accounting Earnings. *Journal of Accounting Research* 15: 254-271.

Weston, J.F. and T.E. Copeland. 1986. *Managerial Finance*. Chicago: The Dryden Press.

ARMA Modeling: An Introduction

One of the most widely used techniques for short-term forecasting is the autoregressive integrated moving average, ARMA, model put forth by Professors G.E. Box and G.M. Jenkins.[1] The ARMA, or univariate time series, model was developed to forecast discrete time series. That is, the set of observations are generated sequentially in time and the observations are taken at a fixed time interval. The time series model is used to forecast future series values that are not deterministic and can be described only in terms of a probability distribution. A statistical time series that is described in terms of probability distributions is referred to as a stochastic process. In analyzing a statistical time series, one must be concerned with the question of stationarity, in which the process generating the time series has a constant mean, μ, and variance, σ^2. Stationarity implies that the n observations of a time series, Z, Z_1, Z_2, $Z_3, \ldots, Z_n$ have statistical properties unaffected by changing time. That is, the series fluctuates randomly about a fixed or constant mean

$$\mu = E[Z_t].$$

The mean of the process can be found by estimating the mean of the time series

$$\bar{Z} = \frac{1}{N} \sum_{t-1}^{N} Z_t.$$

The variance of a stationary stochastic process measures the variability of the series about its constant mean

---

[1]The reader is referred to G.E. Box and G.M. Jenkins, *Time Series Analysis: Forecasting and Control*, Revised Edition (Oakland: Holden-Day, 1976) for a complete treatment of time series analysis.

$$\sigma_Z^2 = E[(Z_t - \mu)^2]$$

and is estimated by

$$\hat{\sigma}_Z^2 = \frac{1}{N} \sum_{t=1}^{N} (Z_t - \bar{Z})^2.$$

Basic Statistical Properties

The time series modeling approach of Box and Jenkins involves the identification, estimation, and forecasting of stationary (or series transformed to stationarity) series through the analysis of the series autocorrelation and partial autocorrelation functions.[2] Stationarity implies that the joint probability $[p(Z)]$ distribution $P(Z_{t_1}, Z_{t_2})$ is the same for all times t, t_1, and t_2 where the observations are separated by a constant time interval. The autocovariance of a time series at some lag or interval, k, is defined to be the covariance between Z_t and Z_{t+k}

$$\gamma_k = \text{cov}[Z_t, Z_{t+k}] = E[(Z_t - \mu)(Z_{t+k} - \mu)].$$

One must standardize the autocovariance, as one standardizes the covariance in traditional regression analysis, before one can quantify the statistically significant association between Z_t and Z_{t+k}. The autocorrelation of a time series is the standardization of the autocovariance of a time series relative to the variance of the time series, and the autocorrelation at lag k, ρ_k, is bounded between $+1$ and -1.

$$\rho_k = \frac{E[(Z_t - \mu)(Z_{t+k} - \mu)]}{\sqrt{E[(Z_t - \mu)^2]E[(Z_{t+k} - \mu)^2]}}$$

$$= \frac{E[(Z_t - \mu)(Z_{t+k} - \mu)]}{\sigma_Z^2} = \frac{r_k}{r_0}.$$

The autocorrelation function of the process, $\{\rho_k\}$, represents the plotting of r_k versus time, the lag of k. The autocorrelation function is symmetric about series and thus $\rho_k = \rho_{-k}$; thus, time series analysis normally examines only the positive segment of the autocorrelation function. One may also refer to the autocorrelation function as the correlogram. The statistical estimates of the autocorrelation function are

---

[2]This section draws heavily from Box and Jenkins, *Time Series Analysis*, Chapters 2 and 3.

calculated from a finite series of N observations, $Z_1, Z_2, Z_3, \ldots, Z_n$. The statistical estimate of the autocorrelation function at lag k, r_k, is found by

$$r_k = \frac{C_k}{C_0}$$

where

$$C_k = \frac{1}{N} \sum_{t=1}^{N-k} (Z_t - \bar{Z})(Z_{t+k} - \bar{Z}), \ k = 0, 1, 2, \ldots, K.$$

C_k is, of course, the statistical estimate of the autocovariance function at lag k. In identifying and estimating parameters in a time series model, one seeks to identify orders (lags) of the time series that are statistically different from zero. The implication of testing whether an autocorrelation estimate is statistically different from zero leads one back to the t-tests used in regression analysis to examine the statistically significant association between variables. One must develop a standard error of the autocorrelation estimate such that a formal t-test can be performed to measure the statistical significance of the autocorrelation estimate. Such a standard error, S_e, estimate was found by Bartlett and, in large samples, is approximated by

$$\text{Var}\,[r_k] \cong \frac{1}{N}, \text{ and}$$

$$S_e[r_k] \cong \frac{1}{\sqrt{N}}.$$

An autocorrelation estimate is considered statistically different from zero if it exceeds approximately twice its standard error.

A second statistical estimate useful in time series analysis is the partial autocorrelation estimate of coefficient j at lag k, ϕ_{kj}. The partial autocorrelations are found in the following manner:

$$\rho_j = \phi_{k1}\rho_{j-1} + \phi_{k2}\rho_{j-2} + \ldots + \phi_{k(k-1)}\rho_{jk-1} + \phi_{kk}\rho_{j-k} \quad j = 1, 2, \ldots, k$$

or

$$\begin{bmatrix} 1 & \rho_1 & \rho_2 & \cdots & \rho_{k-1} \\ \rho_1 & 1 & \rho_1 & \cdots & \rho_{k-2} \\ \vdots & \vdots & \vdots & \cdots & \vdots \\ \rho_{k-1} & \rho_{k-2} & \rho_{k-3} & \cdots & 1 \end{bmatrix} \begin{bmatrix} \phi_{k1} \\ \phi_{k2} \\ \vdots \\ \phi_{kk} \end{bmatrix} \begin{bmatrix} \rho_1 \\ \rho_2 \\ \vdots \\ \rho_k \end{bmatrix}$$

The partial autocorrelation estimates may be found by solving the above equation systems for $k = 1, 2, 3, \ldots k$.

$$\phi_{11} = \rho_1$$

$$\phi_{22} = \frac{\rho_2 - \rho_1^2}{1 - \rho_1^2} = \frac{\begin{vmatrix} 1 & \rho_1 \\ \rho_1 & \rho_2 \end{vmatrix}}{\begin{vmatrix} 1 & \rho_1 \\ \rho_1 & 1 \end{vmatrix}}$$

$$\phi_{33} = \frac{\begin{vmatrix} 1 & \rho_1 & \rho_1 \\ \rho_1 & 1 & \rho_2 \\ \rho_2 & \rho_1 & \rho_3 \end{vmatrix}}{\begin{vmatrix} 1 & \rho_1 & \rho_2 \\ \rho_1 & 1 & \rho_1 \\ \rho_2 & \rho_1 & 1 \end{vmatrix}}$$

The partial autocorrelation function is estimated by expressing the current autocorrelation function estimate as a linear combination of previous orders of autocorrelation estimates

$$\hat{r}_j = \hat{\phi}_{k1} r_{j-1} + \hat{\phi}_{k2} r_{j-2} + \ldots + \hat{\phi}_{k(k-1)} r_{j+k-1} + \hat{\phi}_{kk} r_{j-k} \quad j = 1, 2, \ldots, k.$$

The standard error of the partial autocorrelation function is approximately

$$\mathrm{Var}\,[\hat{\phi}_{kk}] \cong \frac{1}{N}, \text{ and}$$

$$S_e[\phi_{kk}] \cong \frac{1}{\sqrt{N}}.$$

The Autoregressive and Moving Average Processes

A stochastic process, or time series, can be repeated as the output resulting from a white noise input, a_t.[3]

$$\tilde{Z}_t = a_t + \psi_1 a_{t-1} + \psi_2 a_{t-2} + \ldots$$

$$= a_t + \sum_{j=1}^{\infty} \psi_j a_{t-j}.$$

The filter weight, ψ_j, transforms input into the output series. One normally expresses the output, $\tilde{Z}_t$, as a deviation of the time series from its mean, μ, or origin

$$\tilde{Z}_t = Z_t - \mu.$$

The general linear process leads one to represent the output of a time series, $\tilde{Z}_t$, as a function of the current and previous value of the white noise process, a_t which may be represented as a series of shocks. The white noise process, a_t, is a series of random variables characterized by

$$E[a_t] \cong 0$$

$$\text{Var}\,[a_t] = \sigma_a^2$$

$$\gamma_k = E[a_t a_{t+k}] = \sigma_a^2 \quad k \neq 0$$
$$0 \quad k = 0.$$

The autocorrelation function of a linear process may be given by

$$\gamma_k = \sigma_a^2 \sum_{j=0}^{\infty} \psi_j \psi_{j+k}.$$

The backward shift operator, B, is defined as $BZ_t = Z_{t-1}$ and $B^j Z_t = Z_{t-j}$. The autocorrelation generating function may be written as:

$$\gamma(B) = \sum_{k=-\infty}^{\infty} \gamma_k B^k$$

---

[3]Please see Box and Jenkins, *Time Series Analysis*, Chapter 3, for the most complete discussion of the ARMA(p,q) models.

For stationarity, the ψ weights of a linear process must satisfy that $\psi(B)$ converges on or lies within the unit circle.

In an autoregressive, AR, model, the current value of the time series may be expressed as a linear combination of the previous values of the series and a random shock, a_t.

$$\tilde{Z}_t = \phi_1 \tilde{Z}_{t-1} + \phi_2 \tilde{Z}_{t-2} + \ldots + \phi_p \tilde{Z}_{t-p} + a_t$$

The autoregressive operator of order P is given by

$$\phi(B) = 1 - \phi_1 B^1 - \phi_2 B^2 - \ldots - \phi_p B^p$$

or

$$\phi(B)\tilde{Z}_t = a_t$$

In an autoregressive model, the current value of the time series, $\tilde{Z}_t$, is a function of previous values of the time series, $\tilde{Z}_{t-1}, \tilde{Z}_{t-2}, \ldots$ and is similar to a multiple regression model. An autoregressive model of order p implies that only the first p order weights are non-zero. In many economic time series, the relevant autoregressive order is one and the autoregressive process of order p, $AR(p)$ is written as

$$\tilde{Z}_t = \phi_1 \tilde{Z}_{t-1} + a_t$$

or

$$(1 - \phi_1 B)\tilde{Z}_t = a_t, \text{ implying}$$

$$\tilde{Z}_t = \phi^{-1}(B)a_t.$$

The relevant stationarity condition is $|B| \leqslant 1$ implying that $|\phi_1| < 1$. The autocorrelation function of a stationary autoregressive process,

$$\tilde{Z}_t = \phi_1 \tilde{Z}_{t-1} + \phi_2 \tilde{Z}_{t-2} + \ldots + \phi_p \tilde{Z}_{t-p} + a_t,$$

may be expressed by the difference equation

$$P_k = \phi_1 \rho_{k-1} + \phi_2 \rho_{k-2} + \ldots + \phi_k \rho_{k-p} k > 0$$

or expressed in terms of the Yule-Walker equations as

$$\rho_1 = \phi_1 + \phi_2 \rho_1 + \ldots + \phi_p \rho_{p-1}$$

$$\rho_2 = \phi_1\rho_1 + \phi_2 + \ldots + \phi_p\rho_{p-2}$$

$$\rho_p^= = \phi_1\rho_{p-1} + \phi_2\rho_{p-2} + \ldots + \bar{\phi}_p$$

For the first-order *AR* process, *AR*(1)

$$\rho_k = \phi_1\rho_{k-1} = \phi_1^k.$$

The autocorrelation function decays exponentially to zero when ϕ_1 is positive and oscillates in sign and decays exponentially to zero when ϕ_1 is negative.

$$\rho_1 = \phi_1$$

and

$$\sigma_2 = \frac{\sigma_a^2}{1 - \phi_1^2}.$$

The partial autocorrelation function cuts off after lag one in an *AR*(1) process. For a second order *AR* process, *AR*(2)

$$\tilde{Z}_t = \phi_1\tilde{Z}_{t-1} + \phi_2\tilde{Z}_{t-k} + a_t$$

with roots

$$\phi(B) = 1 - \phi_1 B - \phi_2 B^2 = 0$$

and, for stationarity, roots lying outside the unit circle, ϕ_1 and ϕ_2 must obey the following conditions

$$\phi_2 + \phi_1 < 1$$

$$\phi_2 - \phi_1 < 1$$

$$-1 < \phi_2 < 1.$$

The autocorrelation function of an *AR*(2) model is

$$\rho_k = \phi_1\rho_{k-1} + \phi_2\rho_{k-2}$$

The autocorrelation coefficients may be expressed in terms of the Yule-Walker equations as

$$\rho_1 = \phi_1 + \phi_2\rho_1$$

$$\rho_2 = \phi_1\rho_1 + \phi_2$$

which implies

$$\phi_1 = \frac{\rho_1(1 - \rho_2)}{1 - \rho_1^2}$$

$$\phi_2 = \frac{\rho_2 - \rho_1^2}{1 - \rho_1^2}$$

and

$$\rho_1 = \frac{\phi_1}{1 - \phi_2} \text{ and } \rho_2 = \phi_2 + \frac{\phi_1^2}{1 - \phi_2}.$$

For a Stationary $AR(2)$ process,

$$-1 < \rho_1 < 1$$

$$-1 < \rho_2 < 1$$

$$\rho_1^2 < \tfrac{1}{2}(\rho_2 + 1).$$

In an $AR(2)$ process, the autocorrelation coefficients tail off after order two and the partial autocorrelation function cuts off after the second order (lag).[4]

In a q-order moving average (MA) model, the current value of the series can be expressed as a linear combination of the current and previous shock variables

$$\tilde{Z}_t = a_t - \theta_1 a_{t-1} - \ldots - \theta_q a_{t-q}$$

---

[4]A stationary $AR(p)$ process can be expressed as an infinite weighted sum of the previous shock variables

$$\tilde{Z}_t = \phi^{-1}(B)a_t.$$

In an invertible time series, the current shock variable may be expressed as an infinite weighted sum of the previous values of the series

$$\theta^{-1}(B)\tilde{Z}_t = a_t.$$

$$= (1 - \theta_1 B_1 - \ldots - \theta_q B_q)a_t$$

$$= \theta(B)a_t$$

The autocovariance function of a q-order moving average model is

$$\gamma_k = E[(a_t - \theta_1 a_{t-1} - \ldots - \theta_q a_{t-q})(a_{t-k} - \theta_1 a_{t-k-1} - \ldots - \theta_q a_{t-k-q})]$$

The autocorrelation function, ρ_k, is

$$\rho_k = \begin{cases} \dfrac{-\theta_k + \theta_1 \theta_{k+1} + \ldots + \theta_{q-k}\theta_q}{1 + \theta_1^2 + \ldots + \theta_q^2} & k = 1, 2, \ldots, q \\ \\ 0 & k > q \end{cases}$$

The autocorrelation function of a $MA(q)$ model cuts off, to zero, after lag q and its partial autocorrelation function tails off to zero after lag q. There are no restrictions on the moving average model parameters for stationarity; however, moving average parameters must be invertible. Invertibility implies that the π weights of the linear filter transforming the input into the output series, the π weights lie outside the unit circle.

$$\pi(B) = \psi^{-1}(B)$$

$$= \sum_{j=0}^{a} \phi^j B^j$$

In a first-order moving average model, $MA(1)$

$$\tilde{Z}_t = (1 - \theta_1 B)a_t$$

and the invertibility condition is $|\theta_1| < 1$. The autocorrelation function of the $MA(1)$ model is

$$\rho_k = \dfrac{-\theta_1}{1 + \theta_1^2} \quad \begin{array}{l} k = 1 \\ k \geqslant 2. \end{array}$$

The partial autocorrelation function of an $MA(1)$ process tails off after lag one and its autocorrelation function cuts off after lag one.

In a second-order moving average model, $MA(2)$

$$\tilde{Z}_t = a_t - \theta_1 a_{t-1} - \theta_2 a_{t-2}$$

the invertibility conditions require

$$\theta_2 + \theta_1 < 1$$

$$\theta_2 - \theta_1 < 1$$

$$-1 < \theta_2 < 1$$

The autocorrelation function of the $MA(2)$ is

$$\rho_1 = \frac{-\theta_1(1 - \theta_2)}{1 + \theta_1^2 + \theta_1^2}$$

$$\rho_2 = \frac{-\theta_2}{1 + \theta_1^2 + \theta_1^2}$$

and

$$\rho_k = 0 \text{ for } k \geqslant 3.$$

The partial autocorrelation function of an $MA(2)$ tails off after lag two.

Mixed Autoregressive-Moving Average Processes

In many economic time series, it is necessary to employ a mixed autoregressive-moving average (ARMA) model of the form

$$\tilde{Z}_t = \phi_1 \tilde{Z}_{t-1} + \ldots + \phi_p \tilde{Z}_{t-p} + a_t - \theta_1 a_{t-1} - \ldots - \theta_q a_{t-q}$$

or

$$(1 - \phi_1 B - \phi_2 B^2 - \ldots \theta_p B^p)\tilde{Z}_t = (1 - \theta_1 B - \theta_2 B^2 - \ldots - \theta_q B^q)a_t$$

that may be more simply expressed as

$$\phi(B)\tilde{Z}_t = \theta(B)a_t$$

The autocorrelation function of the ARMA model is

$$\rho_k = \phi_1 \rho_{k-1} + \phi_2 \rho_{k-2} + \ldots + \phi_p \rho_{k-p}$$

or

$$\phi(B)\rho_k = 0.$$

The first-order autoregressive-first order moving average operator ARMA(1,1) process is written

$$\tilde{Z}_t - \phi_1 \tilde{Z}_{t-1} = a_t - \theta_1 a_{t-1}$$

or

$$(1 - \phi_1)\tilde{Z}_t = (1 - \theta_1 B)a_t.$$

The stationary condition is $-1 < \phi_1 < 1$ and the invertibility condition is $-1 < \theta_1 < 1$. The first two autocorrelations of the ARMA (1,1) model is

$$\rho_1 = \frac{(1 - \phi_1\theta_1)(\phi_1 - \theta_1)}{1 + \theta_1^2 - 2\phi_1\theta_1}$$

and

$$\rho_2 = \phi_1\rho_1$$

The partial autocorrelation function consists only of $\phi_{11} = \rho_1$ and has a damped exponential.

Non-Stationary (Integrated) ARMA Models

An integrated stochastic progress generates a time series if the series is made stationary by differencing (applying a time-invariant filter) the data. In an integrated process, the general form of the time series model is

$$\phi(B)(1 - B)^d X_t = \theta(B)\varepsilon_t$$

where $\phi(B)$ and $\theta(B)$ are the autoregressive and moving average polynominals in B of orders p and q, ε_t is a white noise error term, and d is an integer representing the order of the data differencing. In economic time series, a first-difference of the data is normally performed.[5] The application of the differencing operator, d, produces a stationary ARMA(p,q)

---

[5]Box and Jenkins, *Time Series Analysis*, Chapter 6; C.W.J. Granger and Paul Newbold, *Forecasting Economic Time Series*, Second Edition (New York: Academic Press, 1986), pp. 109–110, 115–117, 206.

process. The autoregressive integrated moving average ARMA, model is characterized by orders p,d and q [ARMA(p,d,q)]. Many economics series follow a random walk with drift, an ARMA $(0,1,1)$ may be written as:

$$\bar{V}^d X_t = X_t - X_{t-1} = \varepsilon_t + b\varepsilon_{t-1}.$$

An examination of the autocorrelation function estimates may lead one to investigate using a first-difference model when the autocorrelation function estimates decay slowly. In an integrated process, the corr $(X_t, X_{t-\tau})$ is approximately unity for small values of time, τ.

ARMA Model Identification in Practice

Time series specialists use many statistical tools to identify models; however, the sample autocorrelation and partial autocorrelation function estimates are particularly useful in modeling. Univariate time series modeling normally requires larger data sets than regression and exponential smoothing models. It has been suggested that at least 40–50 observations be used to obtain reliable estimates.[6] One normally calculates the sample autocorrelation and partial autocorrelation estimates for the raw time series and its first (and possibly second) differences. The failure of the autocorrelation function estimates of the raw data series to die out as large lags implies that a first difference is necessary. The autocorrelation function estimates of a $MA(q)$ process should cut off after q. To test whether the autocorrelation estimates are statistically different from zero, one uses a t-test where the standard error of $v\tau$ is

$$n^{-1/2}[1 + 2(\rho_1^2 + \rho_2^2 + \ldots + \rho_q^2)]^{1/2} \text{ for } \tau > q.[7]$$

The partial autocorrelation function estimates of an $AR(p)$ process cut off after lag p. A t-test is used to statistically examine whether the partial autocorrelations are statistically different from zero. The standard error of the partial autocorrelation estimates is approximately

$$\frac{1}{\sqrt{N}} \text{ for } K > p.$$

One can use the normality assumption of large samples in the t-tests of

---

[6]Granger and Newbold, *Forecasting Economic Time Series*, pp. 185–186.
[7]Box and Jenkins, *Time Series Analysis*, pp. 173–179.

the autocorrelation and partial autocorrelation estimates. The identified parameters are generally considered statistically significant if the parameters exceed twice the standard errors.

Estimation of ARMA Model Parameters

The ARMA model parameters may be estimated using nonlinear least squares. Given the following ARMA framework generally pack-forecasts the initial parameter estimates and assumes that the shock terms are to be normally distributed.

$$a_t = \tilde{W}_t - \phi_1 \tilde{W}_{t-1} - \phi_2 \tilde{W}_{t-2} - \ldots - \phi_p \tilde{W}_{t-p} + \theta_1 a_{t-1} + \ldots + \theta_q a_{t-q}$$

where

$$W_t = \bar{V}^d Z_t \text{ and } \tilde{W}_t = W_t - \mu.$$

The minimization of the sum of squared errors with respect to the autoregressive and moving average parameter estimates produces starting values for the p order AR estimates and q order MA estimates.

$$\frac{\partial e_t}{-\partial \phi_i}\bigg|_{\beta_0} = u_{i,t} \text{ and } \frac{\partial e_t}{-\partial \theta_i}\bigg|_{\beta_0} = X_{i,t}$$

Variable Transformation

It may be appropriate to transform a series of data such that the residuals of a fitted model have a constant variance, or are normally distributed. The log transformation is such a data transformation that is often used in modeling economic time series. Box and Cox (1964) put forth a series of power transformations useful in modeling time series.[8] The data is transformed by choosing a value of λ that is suggested by the relationship between the series amplitude (which may be approximated by the range of sub-sets) and mean.[9]

$$X_t^\lambda = \frac{X_t^\lambda - 1}{\bar{X}^{\lambda-1}}$$

[8]G.E. Box and D.R. Cox, "An Analysis of Transformations," *Journal of the Royal Statistical Society*, B 26 (1964), 211–243.
[9]G.M. Jenkins, "Practical Experience with Modelling and Forecasting Time Series," *Forecasting* (Amsterdam: North-Holland Publishing Company, 1979).

where $\dot{X}$ is the geometric mean of the series. One immediately recognizes that if $\lambda = 0$, the series is a logarithmic transformation. The log transformation is appropriate when there is a positive relationship between the amplitude and mean of the series. A $\lambda = 1$ implies that the raw data should be analyzed and there is no relationship between the series range and mean sub-sets. One generally selects the λ that minimizes the smallest residual sum of squares, although an unusual value of λ may make the model difficult to interpret. Some authors may suggest that only values of λ of $-.5, 0, .5,$ and 1.0 be considered to ease in the model building process.[10]

Seasonality

Many time series, involving quarterly or monthly data, may be characterized by rather large seasonal components. The ARIMA model may be supplemented with seasonal autoregressive and moving average terms

$$(1 - \phi_1 B - \phi_2 B^2 - \ldots - \phi_p B^p)(1 - \phi_{1,s} B^s - \ldots - \phi_{p,s} B^p S^s)(1 - B)^d$$

$$(1 - B^s)^{ds} X_t = (1 - \theta_1 B - \ldots - \theta_q B^q)(1 - \theta_{1,s} B^s - \ldots$$

$$-\theta_{q,s} B^{q,s}) a_t \text{ or } \theta_p(B) \Phi_p(B^s) \bar{V}^d \bar{V}^D_s Z_t = \theta_q(B) \theta_Q(B^s) a_t$$

One recognizes seasonal components by an examination of the autocorrelation and partial autocorrelation function estimates. That is, the autocorrelation and partial autocorrelation function estimates should have significantly large values at lags one and twelve as well as smaller (but statistically significant) values at lag 13 for monthly data.[11] One seasonally differences the data (a twelfth order seasonal difference for monthly data and estimates the seasonal AR or MA parameters.) A random walk with drift model with a monthly component may be written as

$$\bar{V}\bar{V}_{12} Z_t = (1 - B)(1 - \theta B^{12}) a_t$$

The multiplicative form of the $(0,1,1) \times (0,1,1)_{12}$ model has a moving average operator that may be written as

$$(1 - \theta B)(1 - \theta B^{12}) = 1 - \theta B - \theta B^{12} + \theta B^{13}$$

[10]Jenkins, op. cit., pp. 135–138.
[11]Box and Jenkins, Time Series Analysis, pp. 305–308.

The random walk with drift with the monthly seasonal adjustments is the basis of the "airline model" in honor of the analysis by Professors Box and Jenkins of total airline passengers during the 1949–1960 period.[12] The airline passenger data analysis employed the natural logarithmic transformation.

Model Adequacy and Diagnostic Checking

There are several tests and procedures that are available for checking the adequacy of fitted time series models. The most widely used test is the Box-Pierce test, where one examines the autocorrelation among residuals, a_t:

$$\hat{v}_k = \frac{t = \sum_{k+1}^{n} a_t a_{t-k}}{\sum_{t=1}^{n} \hat{a}_t^2}, \, k = 1, 2, \ldots$$

The test statistic, Q, should be X^2 distributed with $(m\text{-}p\text{-}q)$ degrees of freedom

$$Q = n \sum_{k=1}^{m} \hat{v}_k^2.$$

The Ljung-Box statistic is a variation on the Box-Pierce statistic and the Ljung-Box Q statistic tends to produce significance levels closer to the asymptotic levels than the Box-Pierce statistic for first-order moving average processes. The Ljung-Box statistic, the model adequacy check reported in the SAS system, can be written as

$$Q = n(n + 2) \sum_{k=1}^{m} (n - k)^{-1} \hat{v}_k^2.$$

Residual plots are generally useful in examining model adequacy; such plots may identify outliers as we noted in the chapter. The normalized cumulative periodogram of residuals should be examined.

---

[12]Box and Jenkins, op. cit.

Chapter 4

The Financial Health
of Firms:
Altman Z Model

In Chapter 1, we introduced various ways to measure financial performance. In this chapter, we trace the development of the Altman bankruptcy model which allows corporate financial officers, investors, and commercial loan officers a framework for the quantification of relative performance measures. The Altman Z model allows the calculation of a single number to assess the firm's financial health. The bankruptcy model was estimated from financial characteristics that were statistically significantly differentiated bankrupt and non-bankrupt firms. The bankruptcy model is easily calculated and uses the traditionally accepted ratios of finance that were discussed in Chapter 1.

Chrysler serves as an excellent example of the Altman Z bankruptcy model. The model identifies Chrysler as a "problem firm" as late as 1983, the year in which it repaid many loans. Bethlehem Steel also is analyzed; the bankruptcy model does not identify the severe problems of the firm in 1982–1983.

One of the major issues in corporate finance is the need to develop a systematic method with which one can assess the financial health of a firm. Management could issue debt or equity or procure a bank loan to provide the necessary funds. Management must be aware of the firm's financial health to secure a loan. Moreover, a commercial loan officer needs to try to develop a quantitative approach for granting loans. The purpose of this chapter is to review one of the premiere models for systematically analyzing a firm's financial condition: the Altman Z bankruptcy model.

Financial Ratios

Every student in a basic finance class becomes acquainted with many (approximately 15–20) ratios by which one attempts to judge the efficiency of a firm's operations. The reader is referred to Weston and Copeland (1986) for an excellent introduction to financial ratios. Let us briefly review several of the more widely used ratios. The ratios may be classified into liquidity, profitability, efficiency, and leverage. The current ratio measures the firm's relative investment in net working capital, current assets, cash, accounts receivable, marketable securities, and inventory, less its current liabilities, accounts payable, and short-term (less than 360 days) notes payable. The term *relative* was used in the previous sentence because one ordinarily compares a firm's position with that of its competitors or, preferably, with an industry average. Chrysler, for example, tended to be below industry standards for liquidity for the 1982–1986 period. The two basic liquidity measures are the current ratio and the quick ratio:

$$\text{Current ratio} = \frac{\text{Current assets}}{\text{Current liabilities}}$$

$$\text{Quick ratio} = \frac{\text{Current assets} - \text{Inventory}}{\text{Current liabilities}}.$$

Both management and corporate loan officers would prefer to see the current and quick ratios as large as possible and in excess of the industry average. There is a limitation to maximizing liquidity: many firms with large liquidity become attractive takeover targets (Harris, Stewart, and Carleton 1982).

Measures of the firm's profitability generally compare a firm's net income to its assets, net worth, or sales. One prefers to see the return on assets, equity (or net worth), or sales as large as possible.

$$\text{Return on assets} = \text{ROA} = \frac{\text{Net income}}{\text{Total assets}};$$

$$\text{Return on equity} = \text{ROE} = \frac{\text{Net income}}{\text{Stockholder equity}};$$

$$\text{Return on sales} = \text{ROS} = \frac{\text{Net income}}{\text{Net sales}}.$$

Chrysler's return on equity (ROE) substantially exceeded the industry average and average of the S&P 400 during the 1983–1986 period and was far below the respective averages during the 1977–1982 period. The net income figure reflects the financial leverage decision of the firm, as we will see in Chapter 5; that is, the net income figure is derived after subtracting taxes and interest from the firm's operating income, its EBIT. The Altman Z statistic is based on an operating income measure.

The firm's efficiency ratios measure the effectiveness of the firm's management in allocating its assets in generating sales (and profits). One of the most important efficiency ratios is the asset turnover ratio:

$$\text{Asset turnover ratio} = \frac{\text{Net sales}}{\text{Total assets}}.$$

A large asset turnover ratio implies that a firm's management is able to use a fixed amount of assets to produce more sales than the average firm in the industry. Chrysler traditionally achieved (1976–1985) a much greater asset turnover ratio than the automobile industry and S&P 400 as we saw in Chapter 1. A large asset turnover ratio greatly affects the Altman Z measure of the firm's financial health as we will shortly discuss.

The firm's debt policies are measured by various leverage ratios. Several debt measures may be useful. Most econometric analyses of the firm's financial decisions, as we will see in Chapter 6, are based on the debt-to-equity ratio, the ratio of the firm's long-term debt to the total of its stockholder equity, common stock, retained earnings, and capital paid-in-excess of par, (when the issuance price of stock exceeds its par value). Many financial economists argue that, from the lender's point of view, the relevant debt-to-equity ratio should include current liabilities in the debt figure. Altman used total debt as a criterion for describing the firm's financial health. Chrysler has used greater proportions of debt in its capital structure than the average automobile manufacturer or the typical S&P 400 firm.

The Altman Z Bankruptcy Model

To develop a model useful in assessing a firm's financial health, Altman (1968) analyzed 33 bankrupt and 33 nonbankrupt firms during the period 1946–1966. Balance sheet and income statement data provided the majority of the information to calculate 22 financial ratios that were input to a computer program that calculated a linear model to distinguish between the bankrupt and nonbankrupt firms. Altman used annual data and found that the best model for predicting corporate bankruptcy incorporates five financial ratios. The Altman bankruptcy model standardizes net working capital, EBIT, and sales by total assets to eliminate association between model error terms and firm size, known as heteroscedasticity in econometric analysis. The bankruptcy prediction model uses a debt-to-equity measure, where the market value of equity (the number of shares outstanding multiplied by the share price) is divided by total book value of debt (current liabilities plus all bonds.) Firms may suffer enormous losses for several years before their financial health is seriously threatened because of a large reserve of retained earnings. The Altman Z model uses retained earnings to take the reverse effect into account, and the term is standardized by total assets.

One would expect bankrupt firms to be significantly less liquid, have lower retained earnings, be less profitable, use more debt, and be less efficient in asset management than nonbankrupt firms. These are exactly what Altman found, using data from five years prior to bankruptcy to only one year prior to bankruptcy.[1] In the bankrupt, relative to the nonbankrupt, firms the respective variable means generally fell during the two to three years before bankruptcy. The Altman discriminant Z, which separates bankrupt and nonbankrupt firms, is

$$Z = 0.012X_1 + 0.014X_2 + 0.033X_3 + 0.006X_4 + 0.999X_5;$$

where

$$X_1 = \frac{(\text{Current assets} - \text{Current liabilities})}{\text{Total assets}} \times 100;$$

$$X_2 = \frac{\text{Retained earnings}}{\text{Total assets}} \times 100;$$

$$X_3 = \frac{\text{EBIT}}{\text{Total assets}} \times 100;$$

$$X_4 = \frac{\text{Market value of equity}}{\text{Book value of debt}} \times 100;$$

$$X_5 = \frac{\text{Sales}}{\text{Total assets}}.$$

An Altman Z value of less than 2.675 implies that the firm is in the "zone of ignorance" or is a marginal firm. An Altman Z of less than 1.7 leads

[1]Altman's *Corporate Bankruptcy in America* is a delightful monograph for profitable bedtime reading.

one to believe that the firm probably will declare bankruptcy in the next year. An Altman Z in excess of 2.70 implies that the firm is in good financial health. The Altman Z model is effective at the 95 percent level in classifying firms as bankrupt or nonbankrupt in the year prior to bankruptcy.

An Application of the Altman Z Bankruptcy Model: The Case of Bethlehem Steel

One of the largest corporate losses and closest approaches to bankruptcy in recent times was the $1.493 billion loss suffered by Bethlehem Steel in 1982. One might be curious as to how well the Altman Z bankruptcy model would have performed in predicting the near-collapse of Bethle-Steel. The data for the Altman Z calculations can be found in many sources; 10-K Reports, the Compustat tapes, Moody's *Industrial Manual,* and Standard & Poor's *The Stock Market Encyclopedia* are some of the best sources of financial data. In 1981, Bethlehem Steel enjoyed a current ratio of 1.8 and an asset turnover ratio of 1.38, which led to an Altman Z of 2.87. The calculations of the Altman Z for Bethlehem Steel were as follows:

$$X_1 = \frac{(\$1,880 - \$1,023)}{\$5,282}(100) = 16.22\%;$$

$$X_2 = \frac{\$2,256}{\$5,282}(100) = 42.71\%;$$

$$X_3 = \frac{\$609}{\$5,282}(100) = 11.53\%;$$

$$X_4 = \frac{(43.70)\$24}{(\$1,023 + \$972)}(100) = 52.6\%;$$

$$X_5 = \frac{\$7,298}{\$5,282} = 1.38;$$

$$Z = 0.012(16.22) + 0.014(42.71) + 0.033(11.53) + 0.006(52.6)$$
$$+ 0.999(1.38) = 2.87.$$

The Altman Z of 2.87 showed little indication of the enormous loss that the firm would suffer in the coming 12 months. Bethlehem Steel did not go bankrupt in 1982, but, certainly users of Altman Z would like it to show the severe distress suffered by the firm's management and its shareholders. The Altman Z of 2.87 suggests that the firm is healthy, according to the original Altman (1968) cutoff of 2.675. Altman and LaFleur (1983) later advocated a value of 3.00 as being more reliable for showing a healthy firm. In any event the Altman Z score of Bethlehem Steel in December 1981 would not lead one to assume a short position (or to buy a put) on the firm's stock. In fairness to Altman's model, although Bethlehem Steel suffered a loss of well over $1 billion, its stock price fell only from about $24 in December 1981 to $18 in December 1982.

The fall of Bethlehem Steel's current ratio to 1.40 and its negative operating earnings led to an Altman Z of 1.59 in December 1982. The calculations were

$$X_1 = 8.9\%;$$

$$X_2 = 15.8\%;$$

$$X_3 = 2.4\%;$$

$$X_4 = 34.4\%;$$

$$X_5 = 1.14.$$

An investor would not have shorted Bethlehem Steel until the final quarter of 1982, when the Altman Z fell below 1.7; the stock price did not fall below the $14 level, however, until mid-1986, when it dropped to $4. One can easily see the advantages and disadvantages of applying the Altman Z analysis to assessing the financial health of firms. The Altman Z (1) utilizes primarily income statement and balance sheet data; (2) is primarily useful in predicting bankruptcy one to three years prior to financial insolvency; (3) is relatively robust, in the sense that it works well despite limitations to be discussed in the theoretical section (i.e., non-normal data and unequal covariance matrices); and (4) may be susceptible to manipulation by management. Let us elaborate on the final point, the principal disadvantage of the model. Assume that you are seated on the board of directors of a firm suffering through a terrible year and having an Altman Z of 1.50. Many bankers, well aware of the Altman Z analysis Altman (1970) and Altman et al., 1981 are not likely to provide a loan to your firm. Moreover, it is unlikely that the firm's debt or equity issues would be well received in the marketplace. You might suggest that your firm divest itself of several divisions, thereby reducing its total assets and immediately increasing X_1, X_2, X_3, and X_5. In addition, if divisions showing losses are sold, there may be additional stimulus to X_3

(Altman and Lafleur 1983). By divestiture of enough of the firm's assets, the Altman Z could be raised to the point where it would be sufficient to obtain funding from financial institutions.

Chrysler and Near-Bankruptcy

The recent history of the Chrysler Corporation is well known. Chrysler was in a condition of near-bankruptcy when Mr. Iacocca became chairman of the corporation. The United States Congress passed the Loan Guarantee Act in December 1979 which provided for $1.5 billion of federal loan guarantees. The Altman Z-values for Chrysler, shown in Table 4-1, indicate that the Chrysler Corporation's Altman Z was relatively sound (2.62) as late as 1978. The Altman Z calculation for Chrysler is very interesting because the company performed relatively poorly on debt, liquidity, and retained earnings measures while doing relatively well on asset turnover and having a mixed record on profitability. The Altman Z measure allows the quantification of a firm's health with a "mixed" performance measure. The 1978 Altman Z value for Chrysler was slightly below the original (2.675) Altman (1968) cutoff value for nonbankrupt firms. In 1979, the Altman Z for Chrysler fell to 1.70, as noted by Weston and Copeland (1986), and indicated severe financial distress[2]. The Altman Z value for Chrysler fell substantially in 1980, reaching a level of only 0.75. The 1980 collapse in Chrysler's Z value was created by a large reduction in asset turnover, a large deficit in retained earnings, and the very poor operating performance (operating income) of the corporation. Chrysler's Z value did not indicate nonbankruptcy until 1982 when the Z-value reached 1.78 [slightly above the Altman and LaFleur (1983) cutoff value of 1.70 for bankrupt firms]. Thus, in lieu of the Altman Z-value of 1982, it is very interesting that Chrysler repaid its loan obligations of the Loan Guarantee Act in 1983. The Altman-Z value exceeded 3.00 (actually 3.12) in 1983 and climbed to almost 4.00 in 1984.

An Introduction to the Theory of Discriminant Analysis

Discriminant analysis is a statistical tool that is concerned with identifying variables that significantly separate distinct observations into discrete groups or samples (Johnson and Wichern 1982). The reader is referred to Johnson and Wichern (1982) and Morrison (1976) for ex-

---

[2]The Weston and Copeland calculation of the Altman Z produced a value of 1.51, owing to slightly different calculations of operating income. Our value was taken from *The Stock Market Encyclopedia*, published by Standard and Poor's.

Table 4-1 Altman-Z Values for Chrysler

	76	77	78	79	80	81	82	83	84	85
X_1	.149	.139	.154	-.017	-.025	.029	.041	-.103	-.015	.046
X_2	.253	.248	.233	.075	-.184	-.270	-.243	.136	.238	.238
X_3	.149	.093	.021	-.074	-.117	.040	.083	.200	.308	.192
X_4	.317	.1753	.149	.1006	.0593	.0552	.3279	.7384	.7972	.6654
X_5	2.20	2.18	1.95	1.80	1.39	1.73	1.60	1.96	2.16	1.69
Altman Z	3.41	3.10	2.62	1.70	0.75	1.55	1.78	3.13	3.97	3.17

cellent treatments of discriminant analysis. Altman wished to identify the financial characteristics distinguishing bankrupt from nonbankrupt firms. Accordingly, a firm is either bankrupt or nonbankrupt (note our discussion of Bethlehem Steel earlier in the chapter). It is assumed that the p-variables of samples 1 and 2 are randomly selected with mean vectors μ_1 and μ_2 and equal covariance matrices Σ. The covariance matrix is

$$\sum = E(X - \mu_i)(X - \mu_i)', \quad i = 1, 2. \tag{1}$$

One seeks to find a linear combination of variables, l, such that the absolute deviation between the sample means (relative to the variance of Y, the dependent variable) is maximized.

$$\frac{l'(\mu_1 - \mu_2)(\mu_1 - \mu_2)'l}{l'\sum l} = \frac{(l'\sigma)^2}{l'\sum l} \tag{2}$$

where $\sigma = \mu_1 - \mu_2$

The linear discriminant function, developed by R.A. Fisher (1936), produces the following linear combination of variables:

$$Y = l'X = (\mu_1 - \mu_2)'\sum^{-1}X \tag{3}$$

The Fisher discriminant model is useful in classifying observations within samples. An observation would be assigned to sample 1 if its X values exceed the midpoint of the two population means:

$$(\mu_1 - \mu_2)'\sum^{-1}X_0 > \tfrac{1}{2}(\bar{X}_1 - \bar{X}_2)'S^{-1}(\bar{X}_1 + \bar{X}_2) \tag{4}$$

where

$$\bar{X}_1 = E(\mu_1), \bar{X}_2 = E(\mu_2), \text{ and}$$

$$S = E\left(\sum\right).$$

The variable otherwise would be assigned to sample 2.

The linear discriminant function is defined so that the data are normally distributed and that the covariance matrices are equal. Economic data may not be normally distributed; if one uses large samples, however, then the violations of normality tend to be reduced (Altman et al. 1981). Furthermore, the common convariance assumption is developed from the following:

$$\bar{X}_1 = \left(\frac{1}{n_1}\right) \sum_{j=1}^{n_1} X_{1j}$$

$$S_1 = \left(\frac{1}{n_1 - 1}\right) \sum_{j=1}^{n_1} (X_{1j} - X_1)(X_{1j} - X_1)$$

$$\bar{X}_2 = \left(\frac{1}{n_2}\right) \sum_{j=1}^{n_2} X_{2j}$$

$$S_2 = \left(\frac{1}{n_2 - 1}\right) \sum_{j=1}^{n_2} (X_{2j} - \bar{X}_2)(X_{2j} - \bar{X}_2)$$

$$S_{\text{pooled}} = \frac{(n_1 - 1)}{(n_1 - 1) + (n_2 - 1)} S_1 + \frac{(n_2 - 1)}{(n_1 - 1) + (n_2 - 1)} S_2$$

$$= \frac{(n_1 - 1)S_1 + (n_2 - 1)S_2}{(n_1 + n_2 - 2)}$$

The linear model is:

$$Y = l'X = (\bar{X}_1 - \bar{X}_2)' S_{\text{pooled}}^{-1} X \tag{5}$$

The existence of unequal covariance matrices leads one to use a quadratic discriminant function, where the classification region, k (assign the observation to sample 1 if $k > 0$), is

$$k = \frac{1}{2} \ln \left| \frac{\sum^1}{\sum^2} \right| + \frac{1}{2} (\mu_1 \sum_1^{-1} \mu_1 - \mu_2 \sum^{-1} \mu_2) \tag{6}$$

The Altman bankruptcy model performed very well, and little improvement was obtained by the application of the quadratic discriminant model (Altman et al. 1981).

Summary and Conclusions

The Altman Z bankruptcy model represents an excellent application of a quantitative tool in financial analysis. The Altman Z is calculated using traditional income statement and balance sheet data and may be useful to management, lenders, and portfolio managers. Easily calculated, the Z value offers a quick and quantifiable assessment of a firm's financial health.

References

Altman, E.I. 1968. Financial Ratios, Discriminant Analysis, and the Prediction of Corporate Bankruptcy. *Journal of Finance* 23: 589–609.

_____. 1970. Corporate Bankruptcy Prediction and Its Implications for Commercial Loan Evaluation. *Journal of Commercial Bank Lending.*

_____. *Corporate Bankruptcy in America.* 1971. Lexington, Mass.: Lexington Books.

Altman, E.I., and R.A. Eisenbeis. 1978. Financial Applications of Discriminant Analysis: A Clarification. *Journal of Financial and Quantitative Analysis* 9: 185–95.

Altman, E.I., and J. LaFleur. 1983. Managing a Firm's Return to Financial Health. *Journal of Business Strategy*

Altman, E.I., et al. 1981. *Application of Classification Techniques in Business, Banking, and Finance.* Greenwich, Conn.: JAI Press.

Eisenbeis, R.A. 1977. Pitfalls in the Application of Discriminant Analysis in Business, Finance, and Economics. *Journal of Finance* 32: 875–900.

Fisher, R.A. 1936. The Use of Multiple Measurements in Taxonomic Problems. *Annals of Eugenics* 7: 179–188.

Harris, R.S., J.F. Stewart, and W.T. Carleton. 1982. Financial Characteristics of Acquired Firms. In *Mergers and Acquisitions: Current Problems in Perspective,* ed. M. Keenan and L. White. Lexington, Mass.: Lexington Books.

Johnson, R.A., and D.W. Wichern. 1982. *Applied Multivariate Statistical Analysis.* Englewood Cliffs, N.J.: Prentice-Hall.

Morrison, D.F. 1976. *Multivariate Statistical Analysis.* New York: McGraw-Hill.

Tollefson, J.O., and O.M. Joy. 1978. Some Clarifying Comments on Discriminant Analysis. *Journal of Financial and Quantitative Analysis* 9: 197–200.

Weston, J.F., and T.E. Copeland. 1986. *Managerial Finance.* Chicago: CBS Publishing.

Chapter 5

The Capital Asset Pricing Model (CAPM) and the Cost of Capital

The purpose of this chapter is to examine the association between the perceived risk of the firm and its borrowing costs. The firm's cost of capital is very important to the firm's management because it measures the marginal borrowing cost of the firm and the cutoff rate for project selection. A project must earn a return at least as large as the firm's cost of capital which is used as its "hurdle rate" for project acceptability. The borrowing costs of the firm may be estimated in several methods if the firm's stock price is fairly valued. In the Capital Asset Pricing Model (CAPM), the beta is the sole parameter to quantify risk in modern financial theory. The beta can be used to determine the fair market value of equity and the required rate of return on equity. The firm's return on equity represents the opportunity cost of investors who own the firm's stock (or may purchase existing or future shares). It is essential that the firm invest in projects with yields in excess of the firm's cost of capital if the wealth of stockholders is to be enhanced.

The firm's borrowing costs change as the firm alters its capital structure. The CAPM is very useful in allowing corporate financial officers and investors the ability to determine the effects of changing capital structure on equity returns and yields. The example of CAPM uses Chrysler and its possible beta change as a result of a capital structure change.

Cost of Capital: Definitions

For financial managers the relevant cost of capital is the marginal cost of capital, that is, the cost to the firm of obtaining an additional dollar of financing. The firm will take advantage of an investment opportunity only if the internal rate of return of a project exceeds the additional financing costs of the project. A project is acceptable only if the marginal benefits exceed the marginal costs. The cost of capital, then, is a hurdle rate, or a cutoff rate of return, which investment opportunities benefits must exceed in order to increase the firm's market value.

Cost of Capital: Traditional Calculations

To illustrate the traditional approach to calculating the cost of capital, we will use as an example an industrial *Fortune 500* company located in the eastern United States. The firm is in the chemical industry and uses debt liberally, having a large quantity of debt relative to its equity. Because of the increased risk associated with the use of debt, the large amount of debt serves to drive up the firm's cost of debt. Debtholders and stockholders must be compensated for bearing the increased risk created by additional debt issues, and thus the yield to debtholders and return to stockholders rises with debt financing. An increased quantity of outstanding debt increases the potential that the firm may not be able to cover the fixed cost of debt. For example, given a variation in the earnings level, say a 20 percent decline, the firm's interest coverage is decreased, potentially reducing the earnings available to stockholders, increasing the risk to the stockholders, and bidding up the return to the stockholders. In this analysis we maintain the traditional assumption that current liabilities are not costly to the firm; therefore our firm has four primary alternative sources of capital available:

* Long-term debt;
* Preferred stock;
* Common stock; and
* Retained earnings.

The firm does not intend to issue preferred stock; therefore we are reduced to the choices of long-term debt, common stock, or retained earnings to finance new investments.

The firm's new investment projects are financed by the firm's capital structure. It is generally assumed that the capital structure (that is, the relative percentage of each source of financing) remains constant. This relative percentage is presumed to be optimal for capital budgeting. This is the mix of financing alternatives that results in the least cost to the firm. Specifically, this means the financial risk of the firm is unaffected by its selection of investment opportunities. This is an important assumption of our calculations: if the firm's capital structure is not optimal, it will move toward that optimal position in an equilibrium situation.

The firm has the following capital structure:

Long-term debt	$416,100,000	(38.5%)
Common stock	$443,200,000 ⎱	(61.5%)
Retained earnings	$221,600,000 ⎰	

If we assume this firm maintains its existing mix of liabilities, then the firm will operate with debt as 38.5% of its total structure and equity financing as the remaining 61.5% of total capital. Since we assume this is the optimal capital structure, any new capital investment projects will be financed with this same mix of financial resources.

The debtholders of the chemical firm receive only a fixed dollar return in the form of semiannual interest payments. The shareholders of the firm receive a quarterly dividend payment and share directly in the firm's growth as the residual owners; the operating earnings of the firm less the interest payments to debtholders are the earnings available to the stockholders. Both the bondholders and stockholders may receive an additional return in the form of the price appreciation of their bonds and stock. The cost to the firm of obtaining the financial sources necessary for growth is the yield of those securities in the marketplace adjusted for taxes and flotation costs.

An after-tax cost of debt for the firm must be used because interest expense associated with operating income reduces the earnings subject to taxation. Thus, the government indirectly subsidizes the issuance of debt in the economy. It is necessary to adjust the costs of debt and equity to reflect flotation costs because the investment bankers charge the firm a per-share or per-bond fee for marketing securities to the public. The flotation costs represent the cost of marketing the security, and these costs are also a function of risk. The flotation costs on debt are generally less than the flotation costs on equity issues.

In the following paragraphs we describe the following components of the cost of capital:

- Cost of debt; and
- Cost of equity (including cost of retained earnings and cost of newly issued equity).

Then, we conclude with a description of the calculation of the average cost of capital.

Cost of Debt

The return on a bond to its holders is primarily determined by its coupon rate, the rate at which the firm promises to pay interest to its creditors. Generally, the interest is paid twice a year. The bondholders would ideally purchase a bond at a discount, buying when interest rates have risen above the original rate of the bond, forcing down the market price of the bond, and selling when interest rates fall and the market price of the bond has risen. The yield to maturity to the bondholders, Yd, percent must include both the interest receipts and the amortization of the bond appreciation (or depreciation).

The following formula approximates this return:

$$Yd = \frac{I + \left(\dfrac{F - Bp}{n}\right)}{\left(\dfrac{Bp + F}{2}\right)}, \tag{1}$$

where

I = Annual total of interest payments;
F = Face value of the bond (generally $1,000);
Bp = Market value of the bond;
n = Time (number of years) to maturity of the bond.

From this equation it is possible to see that when the investor purchases the bond at a discount, $Bp - F < 0$ (the purchase price is less than face value), the yield to maturity is greater than the coupon rate of the bond (the coupon rate is equal to the annual interest payment divided by the face value of the bond). If an investor purchased the bond at a premium, $Bp - F > 0$ (the purchase price exceeds the face value), then the yield to maturity is less than the coupon rate.

Another measure of the return of a bond is the current yield, which is equal to the annual total interest payment divided by the market value of the bond. The current yield does not take into account the amortization of the bond discount or premium. The yield to maturity is often used as the relevant return for the cost of debt because it does account for the amortization of the bond discount or premium.

The return or yield on a debt instrument differs from the cost to the firm of obtaining the necessary financing from that instrument in two aspects:

- The interest a firm pays on debt is deductible for tax purposes; thus, the relevant cost to the firm is the after-tax yield to maturity; and
- The firm must pay investment bankers a per-bond flotation charge for marketing its debt.

The inclusion of interest deductibility and flotation costs yields the following as the cost of debt, Kd, to the firm:

$$Kd = \frac{\dfrac{I + \left(\dfrac{F - Bp}{n}\right)}{\left(\dfrac{Bp + F}{2}\right)}}{1 - f} (1 - t) \tag{2}$$

where

f = flotation cost per bond divided by market value of the bond;

t = firm's tax rate.

Cost of Stockholders Equity

One of the components of new financing (assuming the firm maintains an optimal capital structure) is equity. The firm has two sources of equity financing:

- Retained earnings and
- New equity.

Retained Earnings

If the firm has a positive net income for the current year, then the firm must either pay dividends or reinvest the net income in the firm. The remainder of income not paid to shareholders as dividends is called retained earnings. At first glance it may seem that retained earnings do not have a cost to the firm for reinvestment; the income and associated cash flows are at hand from the fiscal year's operations. However, there is an opportunity cost to retained earnings: the firm should earn for the stockholders a return equal to that on a similar investment (that is, one of equal risk) in another firm.

There are two methods that may be used to determine the firm's cost of retained earnings. These two methods are:

- Examination of the retained earnings from the stockholder's viewpoint of internal operations; or
- Examination of the retained earnings in terms of their potential for investment in a similar firm.

Retained Earnings from the Stockholders Viewpoint of Internal Operations

The first method used to determine the cost of retained earnings entails examination of the return available from the stock itself. The firm's stockholders realize a dividend yield and stock price appreciation from the firm's operations. The stockholder receives a return from a stock investment by receiving a quarterly dividend check and/or by selling the stock for a greater amount than that paid for it. The firm's dividend yield is the annual stock dividend divided by the market value of the common stock. The stock price appreciation is approximated by the growth rate of the firm; generally, the growth in earnings per share is considered to be an approximate measure. The stockholders' expected return, ER, is represented by:

$$ER = \left(\frac{D}{P_{cs}}\right) + g \tag{3}$$

where

D = Current annual dividend;
P_{cs} = Market value of the common stock (per share);
g = Compound growth rate in earnings per share (EPS).

Retained Earnings in Terms of the Potential for Investment in a Similar Firm

The second method of determining the cost of retained earnings examines the notion of investment in stock of another similar firm. The price of the firm's common stock changes in a manner related to the price movements of other common stocks. It would indeed be tedious to examine the movement of our firm's stock relative to that of all the stocks we might believe are of similar risk. We have not defined similar risk, for that matter. Risk may be defined in terms of a stock's volatility or systematic risk. The more volatile our stock price, the greater is the risk. The risk inherent in the stock price movements is known as systematic risk, or the risk of the market, because the volatility of individual stock price movements and all stocks price movements are measured as a function of the movements of some market index. Thus, firms of similar risk are those with similar volatilities. The functional relationship between the price volatility of our stock and the market index is a regression line of the form

$$Y = a + bX, \tag{4}$$

where

Y = price movements of a particular stock;
X = movements of the market index.

The higher the slope coefficient, b, the "beta" value, the greater the risk and the higher the return on retained earnings to compensate the investors for bearing the risk. The beta coefficient used for measuring risk is a variation of the regression equation shown above. The beta coefficient is the slope of the regression line in which the holding period returns of the stock are regressed as a function of the holding period returns of the market index. The holding period returns differ from the stock price movements in that the dividend yield is included in the holding period return.

The regression on the holding period returns generates a beta coefficient identical to the beta coefficient in the Capital Asset Pricing Model (CAPM). The CAPM, yielding a required rate of return, K_{re}, is based on the trade-off between systematic risk and the return of our stock:

$$K_{re} = R_f + [E(R_m) - R_f]B_i \, ^1 \tag{5}$$

where

R_f = risk-free rate or 90-day Treasury Bill rate;

$E(R_m)$ = expected holding period return of the market;

B_i = stock beta coefficient.

The cost of retained earnings from the CAPM is equal to the cost of retained earnings from Equation (3) if the stock price is at equilibrium. That is, if the expected rate of return on the stock is equal to its required rate of return, then the stock has its equilibrium price.

New Equity

The cost of new equity financing differs from the cost of retained earnings only in that equity flotation costs must be included when new stock is issued. Flotation costs reduce the net amount received for issuing new stock; the net yield to the firm is the market value of the stock issue less the flotation costs. The cost of new equity, K_{cs}, is represented by

$$K_{cs} = \left(\frac{D}{\text{Net } P}\right) + g, \tag{6}$$

where

---

[1]The CAPM is the basis of modern capital market theory.

Net P = Market value per share of common stock less the equity flotation costs per share.

In terms of the CAPM and the cost of newly issued equity, the cost of equity may be expressed as

$$K_{cs} = \frac{R_f + [E(R_m) - R]B_f}{1 - f},$$ (7)

where

f = Flotation costs per share divided by the market value per share of common stock.

Calculation of the Average Cost of Capital

For the chemical firm previously introduced, we will illustrate the calculation of the component costs of capital. Assume the chemical firm can issue all the debt it needs at 12 percent with the $1,000 bonds sell for 97 ($970). The investment bankers require a $30 flotation cost per bond to market the issue. Thus, the firm will net a price of 94 ($940) per bond. The bonds will mature in 30 years. The firm's tax rate is 46 percent. We calculate the firm's cost of debt as (Equation 2)

$$K_d = \frac{120 + \left(\dfrac{1000 - 970}{30}\right)}{\dfrac{\left(\dfrac{1000 + 970}{2}\right)}{(1 - 30/970)}} (1 - 0.46)$$

$$= 0.068.$$

Thus, the after-tax cost of debt is 6.8 percent. Note the before-tax yield to maturity of the bond is 12.28 percent and its before-tax current yield is 12.37 percent ($120/$970). In this case the question of employing the yield to maturity or the current yield is practically moot. If the bond were selling at a substantial premium or discount and had only a few years to maturity, the difference between the two yields would not be so subtle.

The cost of retained earnings for our chemical firm can be calculated from the CAPM. First, we must calculate the firm's beta coefficient in terms of holding period returns of our firm and the returns to the market index. We will use the Standard & Poor's 500 as our market

Table 5-1 Chemical Firm and Market: Financial History

Year	Chemical Firm			Market (S&P 500)	
	Price	Dividend	EPS	Price	Dividend
1976	$ 8.83	$0.04	$0.57	$ 83.22	$2.50
1977	11.40	0.04	0.60	111.00	3.05
1978	14.06	0.05	0.66	142.00	3.06
1979	17.46	0.07	0.86	169.00	3.33
1980	22.58	0.09	1.42	210.00	3.73
1981	28.37	0.10	1.93	215.00	3.70
1982	35.93	0.12	2.26	250.00	3.88
1983	27.60	0.25	2.40	260.00	4.52
1984	27.00	0.50	2.70	262.50	5.09
1985	28.29	0.65	3.45	275.00	5.67
1986	38.26	0.80	4.07	298.00	6.30

measure. The holding period return (HPR) at time t is calculated as follows:

$$HPR_t = \frac{D_t + P_t - P_{t-1}}{P_{t-1}}. \tag{8}$$

The holding period return for the stock at time t is equal to the stock price appreciation from time $t - 1$ to time t, expressed as a percentage of the investment in the stock at time $t - 1$, P_{t-1}, plus a variation of the dividend yield. The calculations for beta are shown on the following pages.

Because it is necessary to use last year's stock price to calculate the current year's holding period return, we may only calculate holding

Table 5-2 Chemical Firm and Market: Holding Period Returns

Year	Holding Period Return	
	Chemical Firm	Market (S&P 500)
1977	29.6%	37.0%
1978	23.8	30.7
1979	24.7	21.4
1980	29.8	26.5
1981	26.1	4.1
1982	27.1	18.1
1983	−22.5	5.8
1984	−0.4	2.9
1985	7.2	6.9
1986	38.1	10.7
Average	18.3%	16.4%

period returns for the years 1977–1986. Next we will calculate the holding period returns for our chemical firm and the market index.

The expected return on the chemical firm stock is the arithmetic average of its ten holding period returns, or 0.183. The expected return on the market is its arithmetic average holding period return, 0.164 or 16.4 percent. We will now calculate the firm's beta by dividing the covariance of the stock and market returns by the variance of the market. The covariance of the stock and the market returns may be calculated as follows:

covariance $(HPR_{firm}, HPR_{market})$

$$= \frac{\sum_{n=1}^{10} [HPR_{firm} - E(HPR_{firm})][HPR_{mkt} - E(R_m)]}{N - 2} \qquad (9)$$

The covariance of the returns of the chemical firm and the S&P 500 is

$$cov(HPR_{firm}, HPR_{market}) = 0.105/8 = 0.013.$$

We divided by 8, that is, $(N - 2)$, because we have lost two degrees of freedom when we calculated the expected returns for the stock and the market. The variance of the market is calculated as follows:

$$variance(HPR_{market}) = [HPR_{market} - E(HPR_{market})]^2$$

The variance of the Standard & Poor's 500 index from 1977 to 1986 is calculated from the data in Table 5–4.

Table 5–3 Chemical Firm and Market: Covariance of Returns

Year	HPR_{firm}	$E(HPR_{firm})$	HPR_{mkt}	R_m	$HPR_{firm} - E(HPR_{firm})$ $\times HPR_{mkt} - E(R_m)$
1977	0.296	0.183	0.370	0.164	0.023
1978	0.238	0.183	0.307	0.164	0.008
1979	0.247	0.183	0.214	0.164	0.003
1980	0.298	0.183	0.265	0.164	0.012
1981	0.261	0.183	0.041	0.164	−0.009
1982	0.271	0.183	0.181	0.164	0.001
1983	−0.225	0.183	0.058	0.164	0.043
1984	−0.004	0.183	0.029	0.164	0.025
1985	0.072	0.183	0.069	0.164	0.011
1986	0.381	0.183	0.107	0.164	−0.011
Total					0.105

Table 5-4 Variance of S&P 500 Index

Year	HPR_{mkt}	$E(HPR_{mkt})$	$[HPR_{mkt} - E(HPR_{mkt})]^2$
1977	0.370	0.164	0.043
1978	0.307	0.164	0.020
1979	0.214	0.164	0.002
1980	0.265	0.164	0.010
1981	0.041	0.164	0.015
1982	0.181	0.164	0.000
1983	0.058	0.164	0.011
1984	0.029	0.164	0.018
1985	0.069	0.164	0.009
1986	0.107	0.164	0.003
Total			0.133

The variance of the returns of the market index is 0.133/9, or .0147; we must divide by $N - 1$, or 9, because we have calculated the expected return of the market.

The beta is calculated as follows:

$$\beta = \frac{\text{Covariance for chemical firm}}{\text{Variance for the market}}$$

$$= \frac{0.013}{0.015} = 0.893.$$

Keep in mind that the beta calculated from the holding period returns may be quite different from one calculated from weekly price changes.[2]

The cost of retained earnings may be calculated by the CAPM equation to be 9.3 percent, based on an average 90-day Treasury Bill rate of 6.8 percent from 1971 to 1980.

$$k_{re} = 0.068 + \{0.164 - 0.068\}0.893 = 0.1537.$$

The cost of retained earnings may also calculated to be 0.270 or 27.0 percent from Equation (3); if one assumes that the stock is selling for its fair market value.

$$k_{re} = \frac{0.80\{1.244\}}{38.26} + 0.244 = 0.270,$$

---

[2]The *Value Line* beta for our sample firm was 1.25 at the time of our estimation.

where g, the growth rate, is the nine-year growth in earnings per share (geometric mean):

$$g = \sqrt[9]{\frac{\$4.07}{\$0.60}} - 1 = 0.244.$$

(There are nine years of growth because we have 10 years of data.)

We must now reconcile the vast difference between the two calculations of the costs of retained earnings for the firm. From the CAPM we know that the price of the chemical firm's stock is not at equilibrium. The firm's expected return (the arithmetic average of the last ten holding period returns, see Table 5-2) is 18.3 percent and its required rate of return is 15.37 percent. Thus, the firm's stock is undervalued and should be purchased. The stock should be bid up to an equilibrium level at which its expected return is 15.37 percent, which is the firm's relevant cost of retained earnings.

We could go further and calculate the differences between the actual market value and the expected market value with the equation

$$P_{CSe} = D/(k - g). \tag{9}$$

If the expected value exceeds the market value, then the firm may be undervalued and its stock should be purchased. If the calculated value is less than the market value, then the firm may be overvalued and its stock should be sold.

The firm's cost of equity can be calculated if we know the flotation costs per share. Let's assume that the stock, currently selling at $38.26 per share, will bring a net price of $31.68 after the investment bankers have taken out their flotation charges. The $6.58 difference between the market price per share and the net price per share represents a flotation cost of 17.23 percent on the equity. From Equation (7), the chemical firm's cost of newly issued equity is

$$k_{cs} = \frac{k_{re}}{1 - f} = \frac{0.1537}{1 - .1723} = .1857.$$

Calculation of the Weighted Average Cost of Capital

Since we have calculated the component costs of capital, we may now calculate the firm's weighted average cost of capital. Recall that the chemical firm has a 38.5 percent debt capitalization and a 61.5 percent equity capitalization. The firm's equity component may be subdivided into 41 percent common stock and 20.5 percent retained earnings. The weighted average cost of capital for the firm is calculated by multiplying the respective financing instruments' weights by their costs and summing up the costs over the number of investments. Assume that debt financing can be obtained at 25 basis points above the Treasury rate and that the tax rate is 40 percent. In this example, the weighted average cost of capital, K_a is:

Instrument	Weight	Cost	Weighted Cost
Debt	0.385	0.04095	0.0158
Common Stock	0.410	0.1857	0.0761
Retained Earnings	0.205	0.1537	0.0315
Total (weighted average cost)			0.1234

The weighted average cost of capital does not have a proper use in capital budgeting or project selection. We have calculated it solely to give the reader a ballpark figure for the marginal cost of capital. The cost merely reflects the average cost of obtaining the necessary financing for growth.

The Marginal Cost of Capital

The marginal cost of capital reflects the cost of the last dollar of the necessary financing obtained. There is one major point of discontinuity in a graph of the firm's marginal cost of capital: there is a break in the curve when the retained earnings are expended and common stock must be issued. In 1980 the chemical firm earned a net income of $115.5 million and paid dividends of $22.8 million. Thus, for 1981, $92.7 million is available for reinvestment or for dividend extras. The $92.7 million of reinvestable equity funds could support a total capital level of $150.7 million in 1981; the amount of reinvestable funds divided by the percentage of equity yields the total capital spending level that can be reached before new equity must be issued. The break point in the marginal cost of capital is calculated as

$$\frac{\$92,700,000}{0.615} = \$150,731,700.$$

Below the total capital spending level of $150.7 million in 1981, the cost of equity is represented by the cost of retained earnings. The marginal cost of capital is:

Instrument	Weight	Cost	Weighted Cost
Debt	0.385	0.04095	0.015825
Retained Earnings	0.615	0.1537	0.0945
Total (K_a)			0.1100

The marginal cost of capital above the total capital spending level of $150.7 million in 1981 depends upon the cost of newly issued equity. The marginal cost of capital in this case is:

Instrument	Weight	Cost	Weighted Cost
Debt	0.385	0.04095	0.0158
Common Stock	0.615	.1857	.1142
Total (K_a)			0.1300

The marginal cost of capital is depicted graphically as follows: .1300

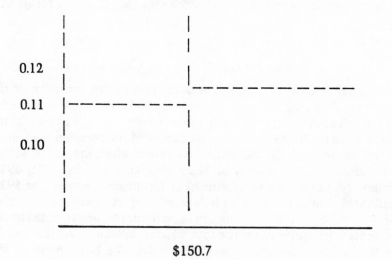

$150.7

Total Capital Spending ($ millions)

For capital budgeting purposes, as long as the chemical firm's total capital spending for 1981 is less than $150.7 million, an acceptable investment opportunity must earn at least 11 percent; once total capital spending for 1981 exceeds $150.7 million, an acceptable investment opportunity must earn 13 percent.

Capital Budgeting and the Marginal Cost of Capital

A typical problem faced by a financial manager is to select from a list of projects those that will maximize the value to the firm. Let's consider an example of how that selection process might work. Assume a financial manager is evaluating the following projects:

Project	Net Income ($millions/yr)	Depreciation ($millions/yr)	Cost ($millions)	Project Life (years)
A	$75	$10	$140	6
B	50	2.5	32	3
C	40	3	119	6
D	10	1	45	6

In order to evaluate these projects we must calculate the net present value of the cash flows associated with each and analyze their internal rates of return. Let's assume that the marginal cost of capital is 11 percent for amounts of new capital less than or equal to $151 million. For amounts above $151 million the firm will incur a cost of capital of 13 percent. At 11 percent, the net present values of these projects are as follows:

Project A: The annual cash flow (net income plus depreciation) of $85 million for six years has a net present value of $85 × 4.2305, or $359.6 million. Subtracting the cost of $140 million gives $219.6 million as the net present value of the project.

Project B: The net present value of the annual cash flow of $52.5 million for three years at 12 percent is $52.5 × 2.4437, or $128.3 million; subtraction of the cost of $32 million gives the net present value of the project as $96.3 million. To compare all the projects on a six-year time horizon, assume that Project B can be repeated after three years to yield the same net present value, but three years in the future. Discounting this sum to today at 11 percent gives $96.3 million × 0.731, or $68.8 million. Thus the total net present value of Project B is $96.3 million plus $68.8 million, or $165.1 million.

Project C: The net present value of the annual cash flow of $43 million for six years is 4.2305 × $43 million, or $181.9 million; subtracting the cost of $119 million gives the net present value of the project as $62.9 million.

Project D: Similarly, the net present value of six annual cash inflows of $11 million—that is, $46.5 million—minus the project cost of $45.0 million, gives $1.5 million as the net present value of Project D.

The results are summarized as follows:

Project	Net Present Value ($millions)
A	$219.6
B	165.1
C	62.9
D	1.5

All projects have a positive net present value. Does this mean all projects should be accepted? We will find the answer to this question is *no*. Let's examine the situation a bit more carefully. First, let's consider the firm's choice under capital rationing. Under capital rationing we assume that the firm has a maximum of only $151 million to invest. In those circumstances, the best choice is to select Projects B and C since they have the highest combined net present value. Alternatively, under capital rationing, one should select the project with the highest profitability index, P_I, where:

$$P_I = \frac{\text{Percent Value of Cash Flow}}{\text{Cost}}.$$

In terms of our four projects, one sees that Project B has the highest profitability index (at a discount rate of 11 percent). Although Project A has a higher profitability index than Project C, A's costs are prohibitive (in combination with Project B). Thus, Projects B and C should be undertaken.

Project	P_I
A	2.569
B	4.009
C	1.529
D	1.033

If the firm has unlimited access to capital, however, it experiences a cost increase after raising more than $151 million (the marginal cost of capital rises to 13 percent). Then will the choices be different? We find that the choices of investment projects will most certainly be different. Under these conditions, the first $151 million of new capital would be directed to the most profitable investments at that discount rate. This would be Projects B and C. Above $151 million the firm's choices are limited to investment in Projects A and C. At a discount of 13 percent, Project A still has a positive net present value, but Project D has a negative net present value (the internal rate of return on the project is less than the marginal cost of capital). Thus, the choices for investment projects under unlimited capital are A, B, and C. Thus, in analyzing investment projects a number of questions must be answered, including the following:

- What are the firm's marginal costs of capital?
- What is the net present value of the individual projects?
- Is the firm limited in the amount of new funds it can raise? Is equity financing limited? Is debt financing limited? If yes, what is the expected proportion of new capital?
- How are investment selections affected by the cost of capital?

Cost of Capital: Calculations Using Levered and Unlevered Betas

Beta as a measure of risk may be applied to a firm's assets, its debt, its equity, or its entire financial capital structure. Thinking of a simple balance sheet, with assets on the left and debt and equity on the right, we have the following:

Asset value	Debt value
	Equity value
Total asset value	Total firm value

The combined values of the debt and equity add to the firm's value or total asset value.

A firm may employ two types of leverage that affect the beta of the firm's stock. These two types of leverage are *operating* leverage and *financial* leverage. Operating leverage is influenced by the extent to which a firm incurs fixed charges, whereas financial leverage is influenced by the extent to which a firm incurs fixed debt charges. The concept of leverage implies that, given a percentage change in operating earnings available for fixed charges or interest only, the greater the leverage, the greater the variation in earnings available to common stockholders. When leverage increases, the beta could be expected to increase also.

Debtholders receive a portion of the cash flows generated from a firm's assets; therefore they may bear part of the asset's risk. Debtholders of the very large firms, however, bear much less risk than stockholders. Debt betas are generally assumed to be close to zero. If you owned all of the firm's securities (all of the debt and all of the stock) you would share the firm's asset value or the risk with anyone. Thus, the beta of the debt-plus-equity portfolio would equal the firm's asset beta, and the beta of a hypothetical portfolio is a weighted average of the debt and equity betas:

$$\beta_{asset} = \beta_{debt}\left(\frac{\text{Debt}}{\text{Debt} + \text{Equity}}\right) + \beta_{equity}\left(\frac{\text{Equity}}{\text{Debt} + \text{Equity}}\right).$$

In summary, a firm's asset beta reflects the business risk of the firm. Any difference between the equity and the asset betas reflects financial risk. As more debt is incurred, more risk is incurred.

A firm's decision to use more debt and less equity does not affect the firm's business risk. In this case, there would be no change in the asset beta and no change in the beta of a portfolio of all of the firm's debt and equity securities. The equity beta, however, will change. In the formula above solve for β_{equity}:

$$\beta_{equity} = \beta_{asset} + (\beta_{asset} - \beta_{debt}) \times \left(\frac{\text{Debt}}{\text{Equity}}\right).$$

If we assume the company's debt is risk-free we have

$$\beta = 0.13 + (0.13 - 0) \times \left(\frac{0.65}{0.35}\right) = 0.36.$$

If the company switched to 80% debt, the beta of the equity would also go up. On the other hand, if all of the debt were paid off, we would expect the beta to decline.

With no debt, the firm's asset and equity betas would be the same. These examples have ignored the effect of taxes, but, for now, we can conclude the following:

- Financial leverage creates financial risk; and
- Asset betas can always be calculated as a weighted average of the betas of the various debt and equity securities issued by the firm.

Example Calculation of Levered and Unlevered Beta—Chrysler Corporation

Chrysler is the smallest member of the Big Three auto manufacturers. Its earnings tend to fluctuate widely during cyclical swings of the economy. As of September 1986 its beta was estimated at 1.39 by Standard & Poor's. In this example, we will illustrate the potential effect on beta of taking on $500 million in additional debt. Thus,

$\beta_L = 1.39$ (Current beta of the leveraged firm)
$B = \$2,366$ million (Current amount of long-term debt)

S = \$4,215 million (Current amount of common equity)
t = 0.310 (Marginal tax rate)

The beta of the unleveraged firm is

$$\beta_U = \frac{\beta_L}{1 + \frac{B}{S}(1 - t)}$$

$$= \frac{1.39}{1 + \frac{2,366}{4,215}(1 - 0.310)}$$

$$= \frac{1.39}{1 + 0.5613(0.69)}$$

$$= \frac{1.39}{1.3873}$$

$$= 1.00.$$

The beta of the more fully leveraged firm (\$500 million in additional debt) is

$$\beta'_L = \beta_U\left[1 + \left(\frac{2,366 + 500}{4,215}\right)(1 - 0.310)\right]$$

$$= \beta_U[1 + 0.6799(.69)]$$

$$= 1.00(1.46851)$$

$$= 1.46$$

Thus, the beta of the leveraged firm would be projected to increase from 1.31 to 1.46 if the amount of debt were raised by \$500 million. In other words, the volatility of Chrysler's stock will increase as more debt is incurred.

Optimal Capital Structure

A firm's optimal capital structure is generally assumed to be the capital structure that currently exists, i.e., the firm is in equilibrium. If the firm does not have the optimal capital structure, it will move toward that equilibrium condition. As illustrated in the figure below, there is some mix of debt financing that will represent the least overall cost of capital. Above that percentage of debt, the overall cost of capital will rise because of the increased risk associated with the cost of debt. The other side of the optimal position represents too little use of debt, again causing the overall cost of capital to be too high because of the use of more expensive equity.

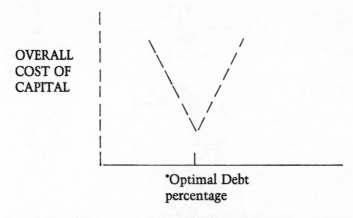

OVERALL
COST OF
CAPITAL

'Optimal Debt
percentage

DEBT PERCENTAGE AS
A PERCENT OF TOTAL
FINANCING

As an example, from the point of equilibrium—say 60 percent equity and 40 percent debt for a particular firm—increases in debt will increase the firm's overall cost of capital.

Modigliani and Miller Framework for Analyzing Cost of Capital

Some of the original work done on cost of capital was reported by Modigliani and Miller (1958). For their initial analysis a number of assumptions were made, including the absence of corporate taxes and the existence of competitive markets. They concluded the following:

- Proposition I: The market value of any firm is independent of its capital structure and is found by capitalizing its expected return at the rate appropriate to its class, and the average cost of capital to any firm is completely independent of its capital structure and is equal to the capitalization rate of a pure equity stream of its class.

- Proposition II: The expected yield of a share of stock is equal to the appropriate capitalization rate, k, for a pure equity stream in the class, plus a premium related to financial risk equal to the debt-to-equity ratio times the spread between r and k, where r is the risk-free rate.

Thus, from Proposition I we can obtain the following:

$$V = (S + D) = \bar{X}/k,$$

where

    V = market value of the firm;
    S = market value of common equity;
    D = market value of debt;
    $\bar{X}$ = expected return on assets of the company.

This equation may be restated as the average cost of capital to any firm is completely independent of its capital structure and is equal to the capitalization rate of a pure equity.

References

Arditti, F.D. 1973. The Weighted Average Cost of Capital: Some Questions on its Definition, Interpretation, and Use. *Journal of Finance* 28: 1001–1007.

Chen, A. 1978. Recent Developments in the Cost of Debt Capital. *Journal of Finance* 33: 863–883.

Fama, E.F. and M.H. Miller. 1972. *The Theory of Finance*. New York: Rinehart and Winston.

Hamada, R.S. 1969. Portfolio Analysis, Market Equilibrium, and Corporation Finance. *Journal of Finance* 24: 13–32.

Higgins, R.C. 1974. Growth, Dividend Policy and Capital Costs in the Electric Utility Industry. *Journal of Finance* 29: 1189–1201.

Jensen, M.C. and W. Meckling. 1976. Theory of the Firm: Managerial Behavior, Agency Costs and Capital Structure. *Journal of Financial Economics* 3: 11–25.

Lewellen, W.G. 1969. *The Cost of Capital*. Belmont, CA: Wadsworth.

Masulis, R.W. 1980. The Effects of Capital Structure Change of Security

Prices: A Study of Exchange Offers. *Journal of Financial Economics* 8: 139–177.

Miller, M.H. 1977. Debt and Taxes. *Journal of Finance* 32: 261–275.

Modigliani, F. and M.H. Miller. 1958. The Cost of Capital, Corporation Finance, and the Theory of Investment. *The American Economic Review* 48: 261–297.

_____. 1959. The Cost of Capital, Corporation Finance, and the Theory of Investment: Reply. *The American Economic Review* 49: 655–659.

_____. 1963. Corporate Income Taxes and the Cost of Capital: A Correction. *The American Economic Review* 53: 433–443.

Myers, S.C. 1974. Interactions of Corporate Financing and Investment Decisions—Implications for Capital Budgeting. *Journal of Finance* 29: 1–25.

Rubinstein, M.E. 1973. A Mean-Variance Synthesis of Corporate Financial Theory. *Journal of Finance* 28: 167–181.

Scott, J.H. 1976. A Theory of Optimal Capital Structure. *Bell Journal of Economics* 7: 33–54.

Werner, J. 1977. Bankruptcy Costs: Some Evidence. *Journal of Finance* 32: 337–348.

Solomon, E. 1963. *The Theory of Financial Management*. New York: Columbia University Press.

Chapter 6

The Debt/Equity Decision Model

The purpose of this chapter is to expand upon the relationship between risk and the firm's borrowing costs. Two classes of thought developed in the 1950s concerning the effect of leverage on the return on equity and value of the firm. Solomon advanced the net income approach which held that the value of the firm increased and the firm's borrowing cost decreased as debt was issued. Modigliani and Miller (M&M) held that Solomon's analysis was incomplete because the return on equity was held constant as additional debt was issued in the net income approach. M&M emphasized the operating income of the firm. The return on equity rises (linearly) as debt is issued such that the value of the firm is independent of its capital structure.

The Capital Asset Pricing Model is supportive of the M&M approach without taxes. The presence of taxes and the subsidization of interest tends to produce incentives for additional debt issuance.

The firm's choice of debt or equity issuance depends upon the level of expected sales and operating income if the earnings per share is to be maximized. Management should maximize the earnings per share of the firm if the firm's stock price is to be maximized. It is well known that management seeks to produce as high a stock price as possible.

Leverage and the Return on Equity

In the traditional determination of the cost of capital, the costs of the components of capital are assumed to be a function of the risk-free rate and a risk premium:

$$K_i = R_F + \gamma, \tag{1}$$

where

K_i = Required return on the ith component of capital;

R_F = Risk-free rate;

γ = Risk premium.

In this approach, the firm's financial risk is assumed to be constant, so that the only causes of changes in the component costs are changes in the supply and demand of each type of security or changes in the risk-free rate. γ, the risk premium, does not vary with time. Even though two firms may differ with respect to risk, firms in similar risk classes have risk premiums that are constant. The assumption of a constant risk premium, however, may not be valid, since acceptance of new projects may change the firm's financial risk and hence its risk premium.

Recall that in the traditional view, new funds always are raised in such a way as to maintain the book-value proportions in the capital structure, which is assumed to be optimal. If the firm changes its proportion of debt financing when it undertakes a new project, its risk may change, and its cost of capital also will change. Since the cost of capital is the minimum return on investments, or the discount rate applicable to cash flows generated from a project, a change in that cost may alter the value of the firm. We will consider quantitative methods that have been advanced for assessing the effect of capital-structure decisions on financial risk and corporate value.

Assumptions Made in the Analyses

In examining how the proportion of debt in the capital structure affects the value of a firm, we will assume:

1. The sale of securities incurs no transaction costs.
2. There are no income taxes.
3. Securities are traded in perfect markets.
4. The firm pays 100 percent of earnings as dividends.
5. Operating earnings remain constant.
6. The degree of leverage in a firm's capital structure is increased by issuing debt to repurchase stock.
7. There are no bankruptcy costs; that is, all assets can be sold at their economic values, which are not affected by the firm's distress.

In our analyses we employ the following notation:

EBIT = Earnings before interest and taxes, or net operating income;

I = Interest charges;

EAI = Earnings after interest;

K_d = Interest rate on debt;
K_e = Equity capitalization rate;
S = Market value of common stock;
B = Amount of debt;
V = Total value of the firm $(S + B)$;
P_{cs} = Market price of common stock, per share;
N = Number of common shares outstanding;
K_a = Weighted average cost of capital, that is, $[(B \times K_d) + (S \times K_e)]/V$.

Three Methods of Assessing How Leverage Affects Return on Equity

With the foregoing assumptions in mind, we will examine three alternative evaluations of the effect of capital structure on the value of a firm:

1. Net Income Approach;
2. Modigliani and Miller's Net Operating Income Approach; and
3. Traditional Approach.

Net Income Approach

The Net Income Approach maintains that the weighted average cost of capital declines, and the value of the firm rises, as leverage increases, because the interest rate and the cost of equity are independent of the capital structure.

Consider a firm about to change its capital structure from 100 percent equity, no debt (referred to as being unlevered, u), to 50 percent equity, 50 percent debt (becoming levered, L, or having issued long-term debt). The book value of the present equity is $40,000, represented by 1,600 shares of common stock with a par value of $25 per share. Upon incurring a debt of $20,000 (on which the interest rate will be 7 percent), the firm will use the proceeds to repurchase part of its own stock. (At the present market price of $31.25, 640 shares of stock will be acquired, so that the restructured firm will have 1,600 − 640, or 960 shares of stock outstanding. If the equity capitalization rate is 10 percent and EBIT is $5,000, the following values may be computed:

Under the NI approach, the value of the firm is determined by adding the capitalized value of earnings available to common shareholders to the market value of debt.

In the NI approach, the equity capitalization rate and the interest rate on debt are assumed to be constant for all degrees of leverage. Thus,

Table 6-1 Effects of Change in Capital Structure

	Unleveraged (without debt)	Leveraged (with debt)
Earnings before interest and taxes (EBIT)	$5,000	$5,000
Interest charges (I)	0	$1,400
Earnings after interest (EAI)	$5,000	$3,600
Equity capitalization rate (K_e)	10%	10%
Market value of common stock (EAI/K_e)	$50,000	$36,000
Amount of debt (B)	0	$20,000
Total value of firm (V)	$50,000	$56,000
Number of shares outstanding (N)	1,600	960
Market price per common share (V/N)	$31.25	$37.50
Weighted average cost of capital $(EBIT/V) = k_a$	10%	8.93%

the overall cost of capital declines as cheaper funds constitute a greater percentage of the firm's total capital. Obviously, the value is greatest and the cost of capital is least with a capital structure of 100 percent debt.

The Net Operating Income Approach of Modigliani and Miller

The Net Operating Income or Modigliani-Miller approach maintains that the overall capitalization rate of the firm is constant (the value of the firm is constant) for all degrees of leverage. Under the NOI-MM approach, the total value of the firm is determined first, and the value of equity is then derived as a residual. The NOI-MM approach maintains that the implied equity capitalization rate rises with leverage because investors penalize the firm for the greater risk associated with leverage (the PE ratio is lowered), and the cost of debt is constant. On the basis of the information in the previous example, the NOI-MM approach would value U and L as follow:

Thus, under the NOI-MM approach, capital structure decisions neither increase nor decrease the market price per share or the weighted average cost of capital.

Table 6-2

EBIT (Operating Earnings)	$5,000	$5,000
K_a	10%	10%
$V(O/K_e)$	$50,000	$50,000
B	0	$20,000
S	$50,000	$30,000
P_{cs}	$31.25	$31.25
	($50,000/1600)	($30,000/960)
k_e	10%	12%

The fundamental premise of the M&M approach is that the value of the firm remains constant, even though leverage may increase earnings per share and return on equity. As the firm uses more of cheaper debt funds, the increased risk associated with debt causes the equity capitalization rate to rise. The return on equity should be a linear function of the debt-to-equity ratio [Modigliani and Miller (1958)].

Even though the risk to equity shareholders rises as the debt ratio rises, the risk as reflected in the interest rate on debt to bondholders remains constant. This framework provides support for the conclusion that the overall capitalization rate and total value remain constant.

To provide further support for the M&M position, the NI situation cannot persist because arbitrage will drive the market price of levered and unlevered firms to the same value. According to the NI position, a firm with capital structure L will have a higher value than U. The variation of the two firms is assumed to be the following:

	U	L
EBIT	$5,000	$5,000
I	0	1,400
EAI	5,000	3,600
Ke	10%	10%
S(EBIT/Ke)	50,000	36,000
B	0	20,000
V(S + B)	50,000	56,000
B/S	0%	

M&M argue that stock in U and L are perfect substitutes and will therefore sell at the same price. If the stock of U and L have different values than arbitragers will enter the market and drive the prices together. The crucial assumption in support of the arbitrage argument is that investors are able to substitute personal leverage for corporate leverage. M&M argue that investors in L stock can obtain the same dollar return with no change in financial risk by 1) selling shares of L, 2) buying U stock, and 3) incurring personal debt. The net investment outlay for purchase of U stock is less than that required for L. Eventually, the selling of L will drive its price down; purchasers of U will drive its price up until the two values are equal. To illustrate:

If an investor owned 5 percent of L, the market value of his investment is $1,800 (36,000 × .05). The investor should sell his stock and borrow 5% of L's debt (the investor substitutes personal leverage for corporate leverage) or $1,000 (.05 × 20,000) at 7 percent interest. Then annual interest expense is $70 (1,000 × .07). The investor should buy 5 percent of U for $2,500 (50,000 × .05).

By selling L and purchasing U, the investors return on investment increases.

The dollar return earned on each stock is equal to

$$L = (\$1{,}800 \times .10) - \$180$$

$$U = (\$2{,}500 \times .10) - \$70 = \$180$$

The return on investment is equal to

$$L = \frac{\$180}{\$1{,}800} = 10\%$$

$$U = \frac{\$180}{\$2{,}500 - \$1{,}000} = 12\%$$

Obviously, by selling L and purchasing U the investor's return will increase.

The result of numerous investors taking similar actions is that the price of U is driven up, lowering its K_e; and the price of L is driven down increasing its K_e. Arbitragers continue buying and selling until there is no chance for decreasing the investment outlay and still achieving the same dollar return. The ability of investors to change their leverage position to offset the effect of corporate leverage precludes firms with differing capital structures from selling at different values.

CAPM Support for M&M. It is well known that the use of debt generally makes the ability of the firm to produce operating income in excess of its interest payments less certain. Shareholders will demand a higher return on equity as the debt issues more debt and becomes more risky. Modigliani and Miller (1958) derived a linear relationship (their proposition II) between the equity return and the debt-to-equity ratio.[1]

---

[1]The CAPM also provides support for the M&M conclusion that leverage does not affect value. The equilibrium expected return for a stock is equal to its required rate of return:

$$K_e = R_F + \frac{E(R_m) - R_F}{\sigma_m^2} [\rho_{em}\sigma_e\sigma_m]$$

and the equilibrium expected return on a debt security can be expressed as

$$K_d = R_F + \frac{E(R_m) - R_F}{\sigma_m^2} [\rho_{d,M}\sigma_d\sigma_M]$$

$$k_a = \frac{EBIT}{B + S} = \frac{EAI + I}{B + S} \tag{2}$$

$$k_a = \frac{k_e S + k_d B}{B + S}$$

$$k_e = \frac{EBIT - I}{S} = \frac{EBIT - k_d B}{S}$$

$$= \frac{k_a(B + S) - k_d B}{S}$$

$$= \frac{k_a S}{S} + \frac{(k_a - k_d)B}{S}$$

The covariance of returns between the stock of a levered firm and the market is:

$$\rho_{em}\sigma_e\sigma_m = \frac{B + S}{S}[\rho_{em}\sigma_e\sigma_m] + \left(1 - \frac{B/S}{S}\right)[\rho_{d,M}\sigma_d\sigma_M]$$

$$= \text{covariance of} \quad + \text{covariance of returns due to the}$$
$$\quad \text{returns of an} \qquad \text{use of leverage}$$
$$\quad \text{unlevered firm}$$

Substituting equation (3) into equation (1) yields the following:

$$K_e = R_F + \frac{[K_m - R_F]}{\sigma_m^2}\left[\frac{B + S}{S}(K_{em}\sigma_e\sigma_m) - \frac{B}{S}(\rho_{d,m}\sigma_d\sigma_m)\right]$$

$$K_e = R_F + \left[\frac{E(R_m) - R_F}{\sigma_m^2}\right](\sigma_{e,m}\sigma_e) + \frac{B}{S}\left[\left[\frac{E(R_m) - R_F}{\sigma_m}\right](\rho_{e,m}\sigma_e)\right.$$

$$\left. - \left[\frac{E(R_m) - R_F}{\sigma_m}\right](\rho_{d,m}\sigma_d)\right]$$

$$K_e = K_{e_u} + \frac{B}{S}(k_{e_u} - k_d)$$

where

K_{e_u} = Return on equity of the levered firm

Thus, the return on equity is a function of the degree of leverage. Therefore, the M&M consumption of homogenous risk classes is not necessary for the proof of Proposition II.

$$k_e = k_a + (k_a - k_d)\frac{B}{S} \qquad (3)$$

Relaxing the M&M Assumptions. While the M&M proof is generally regarded as theoretically sound the limited nature of the accompanying assumptions reduces its usefulness. For example, if capital markets are not perfect then market imperfections may prevent security prices from reaching the equilibrium values postulated by M&M.

Three market imperfections will be examined to determine the impact on M&M Proposition II. First consider the effect of taxes on valuation and the cost of capital. Because interest expense is a tax deductible expense the use of debt may increase total value and lower the cost of capital. The following example illustrates the effect of taxes on valuation and the cost of capital:

Net Operating Income (EBIT)	5,000	5,000
Taxes on EBIT at 46%	2,300	2,300
NOI after taxes	2,700	2,700
Ka	10%	10%
Capitalized Value of NOIAT	27,000	27,000
Interest on debt	0	1,400
After tax interest cost $(1 - t)$	0	756
Tax savings on interest	0	644
Capitalized value of tax savings	0	9,200
Total Values	27,000	36,000

M&M assert that the tax savings represent a riskless stream that is capitalized at the before tax interest rate. Thus, when taxes are considered, the total value of the firm and the market price per share rises; and the overall cost of capital declines as leverage increases. The valuations equation reformulated to include the effect of taxes on value are:

$$V_U = \frac{EBIT\,(1 - t)}{K_a} \qquad (4)$$

$$V_L = \frac{(EBIT - I)(1 - t)}{K_e} + \frac{I}{K_d} \qquad (5)$$

where

V_U = Value of unlevered firm
V_L = Value of levered firm.

Clearly the imposition of taxes on income makes increased leverage highly desirable since it will increase the firm's value.

Institutional restrictions may preclude arbitrage from working in the manner M&M hypothesize. That is, certain financial institutions are legally prohibited from incurring debt; thus homemade leverage may not be substituted for corporate leverage. If the two types of leverage are not substitutable, then arbitrage can not act to drive the prices of differently levered firms to the same value.

Furthermore, individuals may not be able to incur debt at the same interest rate as corporations. In fact, the interest rate charged to individuals is almost invariably higher than the rate charged to corporations. If the two rates of interest are not equal, arbitrage will not drive the value of two differently levered firms to the same value.

Clearly sound theoretical support exists for the NOI-M&M (Proposition II) argument as long as their assumptions are met. In reality, however, all of the assumptions are not met. For example:

1. Transaction costs do exist for trading securities.
2. Corporate income is taxable.
3. All firms do not pay 100 percent of their earnings in dividends.

Furthermore, the NOI-M&M assumption that the cost of debt is independent of leverage is not justified. One would expect the cost of debt to rise as leverage increases. Presumably, bondholders require a greater return because of an increased chance that the firm's operating earnings may not cover its interest charges. Even though the NOI-M&M argument has complete theoretical support, it bears little relationship to the real world.

Traditional Approach to the Cost of Capital

The third approach, the Traditional approach, argues that the cost of debt and the cost of equity increase as the debt ratio rises. Even though the cost of debt and the cost of equity rise as leverage increases, the increase in K_e does not always offset the benefit of using cheaper debt funds. Thus, the result of using cheaper debt funds is a decrease in the cost of capital and an increase in the market price per share. However, beyond some point the cost of capital increases and the market price per share decreases. Thus, with the traditional approach there is an optimal capital structure. Large deviations from the optimal capital structure cause the cost of capital to rise and the market price per share to decline.

To illustrate the Traditional approach assume that the equity capitalization rate for L is 11 percent. Recall that K_e was 10 percent and 12 percent under the NI and NOI approaches, respectively. Under the Traditional approach, the equity cost function increases slowly as the firm initially acquires debt, when it rises more rapidly as the debt ratio rises further. The valuation for L under the Traditional Approach is:

EBIT	$5,000
I	1,400
EBT	3,600
K_e	11%
S	32,727
B	20,000
V	57,727
K_a = EBIT/V	9.48%
P_{cs}^*	34.09

*Of course, all market price per share for L = $31.25

Thus, the firm lowered its cost of capital and increased its market price per share by increasing the degree of leverage. However, as leverage increases beyond some point, the equity capitalization rate and the cost of debt rise so that the overall cost of capital increases and the market price per share decreases.

Let us assume that the firm increases its debt by $10,000 so that the total amount of debt is $30,000. The equity capitalization rate and the cost of debt rise to 14 percent and 8 percent respectively, under the Traditional approach. The following valuations would be assigned under the three approaches:

	NI 1	TR 2		NOI-M&M 3
EBIT	5,000	5,000		5,000
I	2,100	2,400		2,100
E	2,900	2,600		2,900
K_e	10%	14%	K_a	10%
S	29,000	18,571	V	50,000
B	30,000	30,000	B	30,000
V	59,000	48,571	S	20,000
P_o	41.84	27.80		31.25

1. The firm repurchases 267 shares of stock (10,000/37.) so that the total number of shares outstanding is 960 − 267 or 693 shares.
2. The firm repurchases 293 shares of stock (10,000/34.09) so that the total number of shares outstanding is 960 − 293 or 667 shares.
3. The firm repurchases 320 shares of stock (10,000/31.25) so that the total number of shares outstanding is 960 − 320 or 640 shares.

Thus, by using excessive leverage the firm causes the market price per share to decline from $34.09 to $27.90. The problem with the Traditional approach is that while it postulates an optimum capital structure, it can not specify the exact degree of leverage at which the cost of capital is minimized and the market price per share is maximized for a specific firm.

Summary and Conclusions: Impact of Leverage on EPS and Market Price Per Share. The results of our analysis of the three approaches are summarized below:

	Net Income	Net Operating Income—M&M	Traditional
Cost of debt	Independent of Leverage	Independent of Leverage	Rises with Leverage
Cost of equity	Independent of Leverage	Rises with Leverage	Rises with Leverage
Market Price/ Share	Rises with Leverage	Constant	Rises, reaches maximum, then falls
Optimal Capital Structure	100%	No Optimal Capital Structure	A *range* exists whereby K_a is about the same value

In summary we have examined the assumption that the firm's financial risk is not affected by the acceptance of an investment project. Specifically, the effect of a firm's financing of an investment project on valuation has been examined. Three approaches were considered: the Net Income approach, the Net Operating Income—Modigliani and Miller approach, and the Traditional approach. While the NI approach bears little theoretical support, the NOI-MM approach has sound theoretical support (given its assumptions). However, when the academic assumptions of the NOI-MM approach are examined, they bear little practical significance. The Traditional approach (the most realistic of the three) argues that the cost of debt and the cost of equity rise as leverage increases, and that there is a level of debt that will maximize value and minimize the overall cost of capital.

EPS Maximization

In this section we will examine the impact of leverage on earnings per share. The NOI-MM argument that the equity capitalization rises with leverage is supported by the theory of financial leverage. The best way to analyze the effect of leverage on the cost of equity capital is to examine its impact on the level of profitability (earnings per share), the variations in profitability (earnings per share), and the rate of return on equity. In this section, we will illustrate the impact on earnings per share through several examples.

There are two alternative capital structures that will be considered: 0 percent debt and 50 percent debt. Assume that the firm has fixed costs of $500, variable costs equal 30 percent of sales, and the following probability estimates for sales:

Sales Estimate	Probability
$3,000	10%
4,000	20%
5,000	40%
6,000	20%
7,000	10%

Given that information, the level and variation in profits as well as rate of return on equity can be computed for the two alternative capital structures.

Alternative Capital Structure 1-0% Debt

Sales	3,000	4,000	5,000	6,000	7,000
Fixed Costs	500	500	500	500	500
Variable Costs	900	1,200	1,500	1,800	2,100
EBIT	1,600	2,300	3,000	3,700	4,400
Interest	0	0	0	0	0
EBT	1,600	2,300	3,000	3,700	4,400
Taxes 46%	736	1,058	1,380	1,702	2,024
Net After Tax	864	1,242	1,620	1,998	2,376
EPS	.54	.78	1.02	1.06	1.49
Return on Equity	2.76%	3.71%	4.05%	5.00%	5.94%

Alternative Capital Structure 2-50% Debt

Sales	3,000	4,000	5,000	6,000	7,000
Fixed Costs	500	500	500	500	500
Variable costs	900	1,200	1,500	1,800	2,100
EBIT	1,600	2,300	3,000	3,700	4,400
Interest	1,400	1,400	1,400	1,400	1,400
EBT	200	900	1,600	2,300	3,000
Taxes 46%	92	414	736	1,058	1,380
Net After Tax	108	486	864	1,242	1,620
EPS	.11	.51	.90	1.29	1.69
Return on Equity	.50%	2.40%	4.30%	6.20%	8.10%

This example illustrates two major points:

1. The greater the degree of leverage, the greater the variation in profit and rate of return on equity given a change in sales.
2. Given that leverage results in a greater volatility of earnings one would expect the equity capitalization to rise as investors are compensated for increased risk. Thus, the support for the M&M argument that the equity capitalization rate rises with increased leverage is given by the theory of financial leverage.

Effect of Leverage on Earnings Per Share

The results of the previous section can be generalized yet further. There will be some level of sales, beyond which debt financing will always produce a higher earnings per share and a higher return on equity than with equity financing. The break-even level of sales at which earnings per share is the same for either debt or common stock financing can be solved with the following equation:

$$EPS_{\text{bond financing}} = EPS_{\text{stock financing}}$$

$$\frac{(\text{Sales} - FC - VC - I_B)(1 - t)}{X_B} = \frac{(\text{Sales} - FC - VC - I_S)(1 - t)}{X_S} \quad (6)$$

where

> FC = Fixed costs
> VC = Variable costs
> I_B = Total interest if the asset expansion is financed with debt
> X_B = Total number of shares outstanding if the asset expansion is financed with debt
> I_S = Total interest if the asset expansion is financed with equity
> X_S = Total number of shares outstanding if the expansion is financed with equity.

Thus, the only difference between the left and right sides of the equation is interest expense and the number of shares outstanding. EBIT is the variable being factored in the equation. The solution gives the level of EBIT, beyond which debt financing will produce a higher EPS and return on equity.

Econometrics of the Debt/Equity Decision

There are no interdependencies of financial decisions from investment decisions in a perfect markets environment. However, the imperfect markets hypothesis of financial decisions holds that financial decisions are interdependent and simultaneous equations must be used to estimate the equations econometrically. The simultaneous model of the firm is necessary because the firm's financial decisions are interdependent and markets appear to be reasonably imperfect.

Dhrymes and Kurz modeled the interdependence of the dividend, investment, and new debt decisions of 181 industrial and commercial firms during the 1947–1960 period and found:

1. Strong interdependence between the investment and dividend decisions; new debt issues result from increased investments and dividends but do not directly affect them;

2. The interdependence among the two stage least squares residuals compel the use of full information (three stage least squares regression methods); and
3. The accelerator as well as profit theory is necessary to explain investment.

Even though the evidence on the perfect markets hypothesis is mixed, the majority of studies analyzing data of the 1970s and 1980s find interdependence among financial decisions. More discussion on the econometric estimation of financial decisions will be presented in the next chapter.

References

Fama, E.F. and M.H. Miller. 1972. *The Theory of Finance*. New York: Rinehart and Winston.

Hamada, R.S. 1969. Portfolio Analysis, Market Equilibrium, and Corporation Finance. *Journal of Finance* 24: 13–32.

Lewellen, W.G. 1969. *The Cost of Capital*. Belmont, CA: Wadsworth.

Modigliani, F. and M.H. Miller. 1958. The Cost of Capital, Corporation Finance, and the Theory of Investment. *The American Economic Review* 48: 261–297.

_____. 1959. The Cost of Capital, Corporation Finance, and the Theory of Investment: Reply. *The American Economic Review* 49: 655–659.

_____. 1963. Corporate Income Taxes and the Cost of Capital: A Correction. *The American Economic Review* 53: 433–443.

Rubinstein, M.E. 1973. A Mean-Variance Synthesis of Corporate Financial Theory. *Journal of Finance* 28: 167–181.

Solomon, E. 1963. *The Theory of Financial Management*. New York: Columbia University Press.

Chapter 7

Interdependencies of Financial Decisions: A Strategic Planning Model

The purpose of this chapter is to develop an econometric model of the firm's financial decisions to determine an "optimal" corporate financial plan. Evidence is presented to support the hypothesis that management simultaneously determines the dividend, capital expenditure (investment), research and development, and debt policies.

Managements often use industry averages as desired expenditure levels and produce "optimal" expenditure levels for the financial decision variables. It is not recommended that management blindly accept the expenditure levels produced by the goal programming model; however, one should be aware that corporate resource allocations affect the firm's stock price.

The chapter assumes that the reader is familiar with simultaneous equations and goal programming models. These modeling techniques are easily implemented with today's IBM mainframe computers (and personal computers in many cases). A rational strategic plan is easily developed and estimated using the interdependencies of financial decisions. A *Fortune* 200 chemical firm serves as an example of the financial interdependencies modeling approach.

Firms simultaneously determine their research and development, investment, dividend, and new debt policies. In this chapter, a strategic planning model is developed to aid in the allocation of resources. Managerial goals of paying dividends to please stockholders, pursuing capital expenditures and research and development activities to generate future profits, and minimizing the reliance upon external financing of these uses of funds are analyzed. The vice presidents of finance and research often find themselves competing for limited resources in obtaining funds for capital and R&D projects. This model seeks to allocate resources to increase the stock price. With this planning model management gains additional insights into trade-offs necessary to increase the achievement of maximizing research and development expenditures at the expense of paying dividends and undertaking investments.

The purpose of this chapter is to develop a strategic planning (a multiple criteria or linear-goal programming) model to aid management in allocating corporate resources for research and development (R&D), investment, and dividends. The firm's strategic decision makers seek to allocate resources to maximize dividends, R&D, and capital investment while minimizing the reliance upon external financing. The objective of the model is to maximize the use of funds to increase the stock price. The form of the strategic planning model is an optimization model particularly useful to the R&D manager because the manager must compete for corporate funds with the vice president of finance, who must finance capital investment projects and pay dividends. It is necessary to integrate research expenditures with corporate financial strategy.

The firm has a pool of resources, composed of net income, depreciation, and new debt issues, and this pool is reduced by dividend payments, investment in capital projects, and expenditures for research and development activities. It may be possible to pay dividends without limiting investment opportunities. Management may be able to sell as much debt (or equity) as is necessary to finance capital investment projects and not diminish funds available for dividend payments [Miller and Modigliani (1961)]. Financial decisions may be made independently of one another except that new debt is issued to finance R&D, dividends, and investment. The independence of financial decisions is known as the perfect markets hypothesis. An alternative hypothesis holds that financial decisions are interdependent. That is, the manager faces a binding budget constraint such that to increase capital investment expenditures puts pressure on the manager to reduce dividends or R&D expenditures. Simultaneous equations must be used to estimate the R&D, investment, dividend, and effective debt equations when financial decisions are not made independently. Thus, if financial decisions are made concurrently, one would expect the R&D manager to participate actively in the budgetary process. The optimization model developed in this study treats aggregate R&D expenditures as a corporate "line item" (expenditure) with corporate financial implications in the budget process. The strategic planning model of the firm is necessary because the firm's financial decisions are simultaneous and markets appear to be reasonably imperfect.

The firm's budget constraint is the basis for the development of the strategic planning model. The model is estimated with simultaneous equation system regression coefficients. The use of regression coefficients allows management to see how changes in setting one decision, such as R&D level affects other decisions and changes the optimal levels of all corporate expenditures in the model. Management seeks to minimize the underachievement of R&D, investment, and dividends and minimize the overachievement of new debt issues. Preemptive goal programming adds insight into the trade-offs inherent in analyzing various goals and priority levels. One of the principal benefits of the optimization model is to show how a crude measure of R&D activities, the industry R&D expenditures-to-assets ratio, may be further developed into a more relevant measure.

Introduction and Review of the Perfect Markets Hypothesis Literature

Miller and Modigliani (1961) formulated the perfect markets hypothesis in which the dividend decision is independent of the investment decision by deriving that the valuation process of the firm is independent of dividend policy and firm value is dependent upon investment opportunities to produce earnings, dividends, or cash flow. Additionally, the research and development and investment decisions are independent of its financing decision. The firm's dividend policy is generally maintained until a permanent change in operations (earnings) has occurred. New capital issues raise funds from which research and development, dividends, and investments are undertaken. It is assumed that dividends and investments increases lead to new capital issues. Miller and Modigliani only allow the dependence of the new debt decision upon the investment decision (or other decisions necessitating external financing).

Dhrymes and Kurz (1967) modeled the interdependence of the dividend, investment, and new debt decisions of 181 industrial and commercial firms during the 1947–1960 period and found: (1) strong interdependence between the investment and dividend decisions; (2) new debt issues result from increased investments and dividends but do not directly affect them; (3) the interdependence among the two stage least squares residuals compel the use of full information (three stage least squares regression methods); and (4) the accelerator as well as profit theory is necessary to explain investment.

The Dhrymes and Kurz study generated much interest in testing the perfect markets hypothesis. Mueller (1967) found significant interdependence among the research, advertising, dividend, and investment decisions in 67 manufacturing firms for the 1957–1960 period. Higgins

(1972) examined the Dhrymes and Kurz rejection of the perfect markets hypothesis and produced a study showing independence of the investment and dividend decisions. Fama (1974) employed time series methodology and McDonald, Jacquillat, and Nussenbaum (1975) employed a cross-sectional analysis of French firms to find little evidence of imperfect markets. McCabe (1979) criticized the Higgins and Fama studies and, using firms during the 1961–1970 period, found evidence rejecting the perfect markets hypothesis. Recent studies of large manufacturing firms by Peterson and Benesh (1983), Jalilvand and Harris (1984), and Switzer (1984) found evidence supporting the independence of the investment, dividend, and financing decisions. Guerard and McCabe (1987), Guerard, Bean, and Andrews (1987), and Guerard and Stone (1987) found interdependence between investment and new debt and between research and dividend activities. Thus, the evidence on the perfect markets hypothesis is mixed, although the majority of studies analyzing data of the 1970s find interdependence among financial decisions.

The Model

The model employs investment, dividends, and new capital financing equations to describe the budget constraint facing the manager of our manufacturing firm.[1] The manager may use his funds to undertake capitalized research and development activities dRD, new investment, NCE, pay dividends, DIV, or increase his net working capital, NWK. The firm's sources of funds are its operating cash flow, CF, composed primarily of net income, NI, plus depreciation, DEP, and the issuance of long-term debt, $dLTD$, and equity, NEQ. The firm's basic budget constraint may be written as:

$$dRD + NCE + DIV + NWK = NI + DEP + dLTD + NEQ$$

ESTIMATION EQUATION DERIVATION

DERIVATION OF AN EFFECTIVE DEBT VARIABLE

The basic one-period cash balance equation is:

$$dRD + NCE + dCA - dCL = NI + DEP + ONCE - DIV + dLTD + NEQ$$

$$(1)$$

---

[1]The model section draws heavily from Guerard and Stone (1987).

dRD = increase in capitalized R&D,

NCE = new capital investment,

dCA = increase in current assets,

dCL = increase in current liabilities,

NI = net income,

DEP = depreciation expense,

$ONCE$ = other noncash expenses and noncash adjustments,

DIV = dividend payments,

$dLTD$ = increase in long-term debt,

NEQ = net new equity issues,

CF = cash flow = $NI + ONCE$,

and NWK = increase net working capital = $dCA - dCL$,

To rewrite this equation in terms of effective debt, let:

$$dCA = dOCA + dMS + dCASH,$$
and $$dCL = dOCL + dSTD$$

where

$dOCA$ = increase in "other current assets," i.e., current assets less marketable securities and cash,

dMS = increase in marketable securities,

$dCASH$ = increase in the cash balance,

$dOCL$ = increase in "other current liabilities," i.e., increase in current liabilities other than short-term debt,

and $dSTD$ = increase in short-term debt.

Substituting these expressions into Equation (1) and rewriting gives

$$dRD + NCE + dOCA - dOCL = NI + DEP + ONCE - DIV + NEQ$$

$$+ dSTD - dMS - dCASH + dLTD$$

Rewriting this expression gives

$$dRD + NCE + dOCA - dOCL = NI + DEP + ONCE - DIV$$

$$+ NEQ + dND \qquad (2)$$

Here the variable dND is the "increase in effective debt," i.e., the increase in total debt less the increase in marketable securities and cash balance.

Let $ARE = NI - DIV$

and $dLTA = NCE - DEP$ = increase in long-term assets other than capitalized R&D

$dOWC$ = increase in "other working capital," i.e., working capital other than cash, marketable securities, and short-term debt.

Equation (2) can be rewritten as

$$dRD + dLTA + dOWC = ONCE + ARE + NEQ + dND \qquad (3)$$

Letting $dEQ = ARE + NEQ$ denote the net increase in common equity we can rewrite Equation (3) further as

$$dRD + dLTA + dOWC = ONCE + dEQ + dND \qquad (4)$$

Net Net Investment Components. Equations (3) and (4) can be viewed as basic financing-investment equations. The left-hand side is the net increase in investment organized into three categories: 1) the net increase in capitalized R&D, 2) the net increase in long-term assets other than R&D, and 3) the net increase in other working capital (inventories, and receivables less non-debt payables). This treatment of working capital has recognized that cash, marketable securities, and short-term debt are financing variables rather than operating asset-liability variables.

The equity financing has two components—retained earnings and new stock sales. An addition to retained earnings is an "equity financing decision" in the sense that the firm has decided not to pay these funds out as dividends. Thus, the addition to retained earnings adjusted by ONCE represents cash from operations that the directors decide to reinvest in the firm.

Effective debt is total debt less cash and marketable securities. It recognizes that many firms use cash and/or marketable securities as a store of financing (liquidity). For instance, they may issue long-term bonds in excess of current need, reduce short-term debt, and put any remaining surplus in cash and/or marketable securities. Thus, the "increase in effective debt" on the right-hand sides of Equations (3) and (4) represent the net investment use of debt financing in a given accounting period.

For most mature firms, ARE will be the primary source of equity financing. There will not be significant issues of new common stock. Aside from merger-acquisition uses, changes in new stock arise from executive stock options, treasury stock purchases and sales, and possibly the exercise of convertible debt options and warrants.

Equations (3) and (4) have eliminated dividends from the cash balance expression in favour of "addition to retained earnings" to focus on the financing decision. There is a one-to-one correspondence between a board of directors decision to pay dividends and a board of directors decision to retain income in the firm for reinvestment. This formulation has the merit of parallel treatment of the equity financing and net debt financing decision in that both are in the form of net increase. This form of the cash balance equations facilitates the study of cross-time variations in net equity and net debt as sources of financing, especially vis-à-vis the investment-financing interdependency issue. The development of the effective debt variable incorporates the firm's working capital decisions within a long-term optimization model. The optimization model put forth in this study is an alternative to the integrated model advanced in Burton, Damon, and Obel (1979, 1984).

Description of the Estimated Equation System

The investment equation uses the rate of profit theory in investment; Meyer and Kuh (1957) and Dhrymes and Kurz (1967) employed investment equations in net income positively affects investment. Moreover, the accelerator position on investment is estimated because of the variable's statistical significance found in Dhrymes and Kurz. The accelerator position holds that the two year growth in sales, *DSAL*, should positively affect investment. Depreciation is normally included in the investment analysis because depreciation describes the deterioration of capital in the productive process. Our chapter uses cash flows, *CF*, to incorporate both net income and depreciation effects. Investment, in an imperfect market, should increase as effective debt is issued; funds for capital expenditures increase with borrowing. Given that dividends and investment are alternative uses of funds, as dividends increase in an imperfect market one would expect investment to fall. An increase in the firm's average tax rate, *TAXR*, should reduce investment because fewer projects are profitable.

The research and development equation employed in our model reflects the work of Mansfield (1963), Mueller (1967), Grabowski (1968), Grabowski and Mueller (1972), Hambrick, MacMillan, and Barbosa (1983), Switzer (1984), and Guerard and McCabe (1987). Research and development expenditures are modeled in terms of investments, dividends, and new capital issues, to reflect the imperfect markets hypothesis. Previous one, two, and three year research and development expenditures (RD1, RD2, RD3) with previous patents, LPAT, serve as surrogates previous research and development activities. Cash flow should serve to increase research and development expenditures because the firm has the resources to pursue the activities that a smaller, less profitable firm could not afford.

Dividends should increase in an imperfect market as new debt is issued because more funds are obtained; dividends should decrease as investment increases. Dividends are a positive function of net income because income increases the firm's amount of available funds and retained earnings. An increase in net working capital should serve to decrease dividends in an imperfect market. Dividends should be a positive function of last year's dividends, LDIV, because management is reluctant to cut dividends [Fama and Babiak (1968), Lintner (1956), and Switzer (1984)]. Miller and Modigliani argue that dividends do not affect the financing of profitable investment because external funds can be raised in a perfect market. Increases in a firm's return on equity, ROE, should increase its cost of capital and serve to increase dividends because fewer investment opportunities are not profitable.

Effective debt issues were defined in the previous section; previous studies used only new debt financing because manufacturing firms traditionally finance an insignificant percent of investment with equity issues [Higgins (1972)]. New debt issues should be positively correlated with dividends and investment, as the uses of funds rise to equal the sources of funds. An increase in net income and depreciation, the firm's primary components of cash flow, should reduce the new debt issues in an imperfect market because cash flow and new debt issues are alternative sources of funds. As the one-year and average costs of debt, STKD and LTKD, and debt to equity, DE, rise, new debt financing should fall because of the additional expense.

A summary of the hypothesized equation system is:

$$NCE = F(DIV, dRD, dND, CF, TAXR) \qquad (5)$$

$$dRD = F(dRD_1, dRD_2, dRD_3, NCE, DIV, dND, NI, DEP) \qquad (6)$$

$$DIV = F(NCE, dRD, dCA - dCL, dND, LDIV, NI, ROE) \qquad (7)$$

$$dND = F(NCE, dRD, DIV, CF, STKD, LTKD, DE) \qquad (8)$$

Data and Simultaneous Equation Estimation Results

Regression analysis is used to test the independence of the financial decisions hypothesis. In an efficient or perfect market, the endogenous variables (R&D, investments, dividends, and effective debt) should not be statistically significant in the ordinary least squares equations and simultaneous equations are not necessary to estimate. A sample of 303 predominantly manufacturing firms for the 1976–1982 period is employed as the sample in the regression analysis. The firms represent a subset of the Industrial Compustat file and all financial data is drawn from the Compustat tapes. The ordinary least squares (OLS) results are not reported for the sake of brevity; the statistical significance of the endogenous variables in the OLS equations necessitates the use of two stage least squares estimation. Moreover, the residuals among the two least squares are significantly correlated (particularly between the investment and effective debt equations); thus three stage least squares regression analysis should be employed [Dhrymes (1974)]. The three-stage R&D expenditures least squares regression estimates are shown in Table 7-1. Research expenditure increases are positively associated with last year's research expenditures and net income, in accordance with the work of Switzer (1984). Dividends are an alternative use of funds in most years whereas investments are normally positively associated with increasing research activities. The negative coefficient on the effective debt variable is quite interesting; one would have expected the coefficient to have been positive. However, one finds, after examining the raw data, that the firms tend to issue debt to finance investment while holding research activities approximately constant. Switzer found no statistically significant relationship between R&D and debt financing. The dividend variable is significant in examining violations of the independence (perfect markets) hypothesis in the research activities equation. Guerard and McCabe (1987) found an inverse dividend and R&D relationship whereas Switzer found no significant relationship between the variables.

The three-stage least squares estimations of the new capital expenditures equation are shown in Table 7-2. The dividend variable is statistically insignificant in the investment equation; there is no evidence of imperfect markets with the hypothesized negative association between investments and dividends. The imperfect markets negative association between investments and dividends supported by McCabe (1979) and Peterson and Benesh (1983) is not found; moreover Switzer found no statistically significant relationship between dividends and new capital investment. The statistically significantly positive coefficient on the external funds issued variable is convincing in the investment equation and complements the work of McCabe (1979), Peterson and Benesh (1983), and Guerard and McCabe (1987); Dhrymes and Kurz (1967) and Switzer (1984) did not always find a significantly positive relationship between new debt and investments. The construction of the effective debt variable produces a lower coefficient (but still statistically significant coefficient) on the debt variable in the investment equation than

Table 7-1 Dependent Variable: R&D Three-Stage Least Square Estimates

Independent Variables	1976	1977	1978	1979	1980	1981	1982
Constant	.0000	-.0013	-.0027	.0010	-.0001	.0009	.0024
(t)	(.02)	(-1.26)	(-2.63)	(.47)	(-.03)	(.75)	(1.55)
NCE	.0613	.0249	-.0124	.0672	-.0210	.0169	.0658
	(3.73)	(2.56)	(-1.68)	(3.77)	(-1.37)	(1.89)	(5.07)
DIV	-.2172	-.0227	-.0761	-.1303	-.1156	-.0493	.0029
	(-4.08)	(-.94)	(-3.14)	(-2.47)	(-2.51)	(-1.91)	(.08)
dND	-.0100	-.0032	.0078	-.0144	.0001	-.0065	-.0209
	(-2.50)	(-1.56)	(3.59)	(-3.29)	(.02)	(-2.49)	(-6.28)
dRD_1	1.0586	1.3881	1.2797	1.3987	1.4074	1.3748	1.3987
	(9.58)	(26.03)	(17.47)	(8.96)	(18.24)	(19.89)	(14.53)
dRD_2	-.1982	-.2060	.1558	-.3359	-.2533	-.1202	-.6243
	(-1.23)	(-2.45)	(1.36)	(-1.30)	(-1.23)	(-1.06)	(-3.87)
dRD_3	.2427	-.0764	-.2595	-.0294	-.1170	-.2657	.1742
	(1.97)	(-1.21)	(-3.52)	(-.15)	(-.58)	(-3.79)	(1.60)
DEP	-.0205	.0079	.0141	-.0104	.0238	.0127	-.0162
	(-.82)	(.58)	(1.13)	(-1.51)	(1.18)	(1.60)	(-1.76)
LPAT	-.0106	.0057	.0012	-.0010	-.0098	.0258	-.0025
	(-.53)	(.68)	(.12)	(-.05)	(-.27)	(1.07)	(-.17)

Tables 7-1 thru 7-4 reproduced from Guerard and Stone with permission of *The Journal of the Operational Research Society*.

	(1)	(2)	(3)	(4)	(5)	(6)
Petroleum	-.0036 (-1.55)	-.0013 (-1.09)	.0004 (.33)	-.0035 (-1.51)	-.0014 (-.61)	-.0008 (-.56)	-.0052 (-2.77)
Construction	-.0029 (-.95)	-.0002 (-.16)	.0006 (.41)	.0000 (.01)	-.0020 (-.73)	.0003 (.19)	.0017 (.78)
Foods	-.0022 (-.40)	-.0013 (-.06)	.0007 (.35)	.0079 (.15)	-.0027 (-.70)	-.0040 (-1.62)	-.0038 (-.88)
Lumber	-.0060 (-1.62)	-.0023 (-1.24)	.0006 (.33)	-.0065 (-1.80)	.0099 (.26)	-.0017 (-.83)	-.0026 (-.88)
Rubber Products	-.0021 (-.48)	.0002 (.08)	-.0019 (-1.00)	.0006 (.15)	-.0013 (-.35)	.0005 (.22)	-.0016 (-.53)
Metals	-.0011 (-.43)	-.0013 (-.97)	-.0002 (-.13)	-.0022 (-.88)	-.0015 (-.66)	-.0010 (-.67)	-.0031 (-1.54)
Machinery	-.0047 (-1.86)	-.0012 (-.93)	.0001 (.09)	-.0018 (-.75)	-.0015 (-.67)	.0016 (1.11)	-.0034 (-1.80)
Electronics	.0062 (2.28)	.0018 (1.31)	.0033 (2.57)	.0021 (.80)	.0056 (2.35)	.0019 (1.26)	.0022 (1.12)
Instruments	-.0214 (-2.19)	.0049 (1.92)	.0061 (2.40)	-.0028 (-.57)	.0067 (1.43)	-.0114 (-3.91)	.0054 (1.21)
Chemicals	-.0032 (-1.28)	-.0022 (-1.91)	-.0019 (-1.59)	-.0019 (-.81)	-.0002 (-.09)	.0000 (.00)	.0002 (.13)
Drugs	-.0032 (-1.40)	-.0010 (-.93)	.0001 (.11)	-.0017 (.75)	-.0007 (-.34)	.0004 (.32)	-.0031 (-1.93)

Table 7-2 Dependent Variable: Capital Expenditure Three-Stage Least Squares Estimates

Independent Variables	1976	1977	1978	1979	1980	1981	1982
Constant	.0150	.0194	-.0217	-.0067	-.0312	-.0498	-.0231
(t)	(1.04)	(1.55)	(-1.22)	(-.51)	(-1.91)	(-3.23)	(-1.88)
R&D	.4037	.3216	.3527	.6775	.6158	.5122	.4867
	(2.67)	(2.48)	(2.06)	(5.01)	(4.04)	(3.58)	(3.54)
DIV	.1527	-.0524	.3221	.3908	.0613	.0413	.0389
	(.56)	(-.23)	(1.04)	(1.51)	(.21)	(.15)	(.15)
dND	.1347	.1411	.2275	.1877	.2693	.2755	.2185
	(4.56)	(6.13)	(6.74)	(7.21)	(8.39)	(9.02)	(9.11)
CF	.2929	.3076	.2906	.3150	.3205	.4367	.3197
	(4.77)	(5.62)	(4.00)	(5.73)	(5.43)	(6.53)	(6.11)
TAXR	-.0306	-.0351	.0027	-.0068	-.0014	-.0138	.0101
	(-2.39)	(-2.62)	(.13)	(-1.41)	(-.31)	(-1.31)	(2.74)
DSAL	.0102	.0066	.0071	.0101	-.0032	.0123	.0069
	(1.03)	(.73)	(.51)	(1.42)	(-.44)	(1.55)	(.79)
Petroleum	.0421	.0307	.0081	.0050	.0291	.0457	.0502
	(3.48)	(2.92)	(.58)	(.41)	(2.01)	(3.28)	(4.39)

Construction	.0189 (1.21)	.0160 (1.17)	.0416 (2.22)	-.0184 (-1.21)	-.0313 (-1.77)	.0044 (.25)	-.0411 (-2.65)
Foods	.0429 (1.51)	.0128 (.64)	.0144 (.54)	.0070 (.33)	.0160 (.63)	.0309 (1.19)	.0186 (.69)
Lumber	.0466 (2.41)	.0575 (3.38)	.0503 (2.21)	.0602 (3.29)	.0917 (4.28)	.0306 (1.40)	.0201 (1.04)
Rubber Products	.0219 (.95)	-.0100 (-.52)	.0172 (.69)	-.0007 (-.03)	.0050 (.21)	.0381 (1.58)	.0110 (.55)
Metals	.0342 (2.39)	.125 (1.03)	.0170 (1.05)	.0148 (1.13)	.0204 (1.30)	.0360 (2.30)	.0181 (1.34)
Machinery	.0347 (2.53)	.0129 (1.07)	.0226 (1.41)	.0141 (1.10)	.0246 (1.64)	.0154 (1.00)	.0188 (1.50)
Electronics	.0288 (2.22)	.0283 (2.46)	.0421 (2.72)	.0228 (1.77)	.0421 (2.77)	.0495 (3.30)	.0216 (1.62)
Instruments	.0730 (1.45)	.0353 (1.50)	.0971 (3.11)	.0216 (.87)	.0409 (1.40)	.0617 (2.08)	.0222 (.81)
Chemicals	.0443 (3.79)	.0205 (2.01)	.0203 (1.48)	.0027 (.24)	.0249 (1.89)	.0307 (2.31)	.0255 (2.29)
Drugs	.0242 (2.14)	.0194 (1.96)	.0245 (1.84)	.0132 (1.23)	.0400 (3.21)	.0293 (2.34)	.0181 (1.74)

the coefficient report in Guerard and McCabe (1987). Research expenditures are positive in the investment equation; Mueller (1967) found an inverse relationship between investments and research in his earlier piece and no relationship between the variables in his later piece with Grabowski (1972). Switzer found no significant relationship between research and investment activities. Cash flow positively affects investment while the tax rate has significantly negative coefficients in 1976 and 1977 in the investment equation. The positive coefficients on the research and dividend variables are counter to the imperfect markets hypothesis.

Dividends are positively associated with rising net income and last year's dividends, supporting the Lintner (1956) and Fama and Babiak (1968) positions. The hypothesized negative relationship between investments and dividends was realized in 1977 [as did Switzer (1984)], 1979, and 1980 in the dividend equation estimates shown in Table 7-3. Research activities are normally positively associated with rising dividends. Moreover, increasing effective debt leads to increasing dividends, a position found in McCabe (1979), Peterson and Benesh (1983), and Switzer (1984).

Effective debt issues (see Table 7-4) issued normally are in response to increasing new capital expenditures; this relationship is correct within the context of the perfect markets debate. However, we do not find complete support for a strategy in which effective debt is issued prior to capital investment (unless new effective debt is issued and drawn down in the same year). New effective debt financing is negatively associated with cash flow, dividends, and research activities. Switzer (1984) found new debt issues to be positively associated with research and negatively associated with dividend expenditures. Furthermore, debt-to-equity ratio coefficients are unexpectedly positive; Switzer's (1984) new debt issues were positively (but not significantly) associated with risk. One would expect that as the debt-to-equity ratio rises, the risk to the firm's creditors rises and normally reduces future capital issues. Moreover, interest rates do not appear to statistically influence effective debt issues, a point questioning one of the Jalilvand and Harris (1984) results of firms' timing debt issues.

Industry dummy variables are used in the financial decision regressions and are not generally statistically significant as was found in Peterson and Benesh (1983). The electronics industry tends to be significantly more aggressive than the 303-firm sample average in engaging in R&D and capital expenditures. The lumber, chemical, and drug industries also spend more than the other industries on capital expenditures. Furthermore, the electronics, lumber, chemical, and drug industries reduce effective debt relative to other industries in the sample. The regression coefficients on the statistically significant dummy variables are extremely low, partially supporting Peterson and Benesh (1983).

A Multi-Criteria Model of the Firm Decision Process

A multi-criteria model is developed from the imperfect markets hypothesis to optimally determine research, dividend, investment, and effective financing levels. The regression coefficients can serve as inputs to a multiple goal linear programming model which optimally minimizes the firm's underachievement of research and development and investment activities, dividend payments, and minimizes the over-issuance of debt. Goal programming, popularized by Lee (1972) seeks to use deviations of variables from targeted levels, attaching priority levels to the deviational variables, to extend simplistic linear programming models. Management is concerned with minimizing its underachievement of research and investment activities because future profits would be reduced; however, stockholders require certain dividend policies to maintain the stock price and relative marketability of shares. Management does not want to develop an over-dependence on the capital market to finance its growth.

Let us assume that the randomly selected chemical firm studied in Guerard and McCabe (1987) is again interested in developing a multiple goal linear programming model that minimizes the underachievement of desired research, dividends, investment, and overachievement of effective financing. Furthermore, the firm will use the 1982 two-stage least squares simultaneous equation estimates in the following model:

$$dRD - .0658NCE - .0029DIV + .0209dND - 1.3987dRD_1 + .6243dRD_2$$

$$- .1742dRD_3 + .0162DEP + d_{1j}^- - d_{1j}^+ = -.0024 + DdRD \qquad (9)$$

$$dND - 3.5694NCE - .1295DIV + 2.4169dRD + 1.3519CF - .001LTKD$$

$$- .0016STDK + d_{2j}^- - d_{2j}^+ = .1598 + DdND \qquad (10)$$

$$NCE - .0389DIV - .2185dND - .4867dRD - .3197CF - .0101TAXR$$

$$- .0069DSAL + d_{3j}^- - d_{3j}^+ = .0231 + DNCE \qquad (11)$$

$$DIV + .0083NCE - .014dND - .0515dRD - .8222LDIV$$

$$- .0394NI + d_{4j}^- - d_{4j}^+ = -.0013 + DDIV \qquad (12)$$

Table 7-3 Dependent Variable: Dividends Three-Stage Least Squares Estimates

Independent Variables	1976	1977	1978	1979	1980	1981	1982
Constant	-.0008	-.0018	-.0014	.0006	-.0030	-.0001	-.0013
(t)	(-.68)	(-1.32)	(-.79)	(.33)	(-1.92)	(-.10)	(-.68)
R&D	-.0151	.0320	-.0032	.0044	.0237	-.0123	.0515
	(-1.23)	(2.48)	(.20)	(.28)	(1.93)	(-1.41)	(2.90)
NCE	.0002	-.0182	-.0049	-.0255	-.0264	.0062	-.0083
	(.04)	(-2.25)	(-.57)	(-2.71)	(-4.00)	(1.22)	(-.81)
dND	.0041	.0041	.0046	.0099	.0125	.0015	.0140
	(1.43)	(1.48)	(1.10)	(2.46)	(3.56)	(.54)	(3.07)
LDIV	1.0053	1.1069	.9901	.8747	1.0160	1.0307	.8222
	(40.47)	(46.46)	(32.55)	(30.39)	(45.01)	(61.90)	(32.99)
NI	.0651	.0474	.0638	.1192	.0650	.0275	.0394
	(4.26)	(5.47)	(3.30)	(6.38)	(8.32)	(4.60)	(5.49)
ROE	-.0069	.0041	-.0001	-.0155	.0008	-.0010	-.0000
	(-1.04)	(2.23)	(-.01)	(-2.53)	(2.26)	(-.93)	(-.07)
Petroleum	-.0023	.0007	.0029	-.0048	.0023	.0002	.0001
	(-2.33)	(.65)	(2.22)	(-3.76)	(2.11)	(.28)	(.04)

Construction	.0022 (1.72)	.0050 (3.58)	.0005 (.28)	−.0049 (−2.92)	−.0034 (−2.50)	−.0024 (−1.20)
Foods	.0001 (.04)	.0000 (.00)	.0001 (.05)	−.0013 (−.55)	.0011 (.57)	−.0002 (−.06)
Lumber	−.0002 (−.15)	.0010 (.60)	−.0011 (−.53)	−.0015 (−.72)	.0021 (1.20)	.0013 (.54)
Rubber Products	−.0019 (−.99)	.0004 (.19)	−.0012 (−.47)	−.0012 (−.51)	.0005 (.29)	−.0025 (−1.00)
Metals	−.0021 (−1.87)	−.0009 (−.73)	−.0006 (−.41)	−.0036 (−2.42)	−.0012 (−.98)	−.0010 (−.55)
Machinery	−.0011 (−.95)	.0013 (1.11)	.0005 (.34)	−.0030 (−2.04)	.0007 (.63)	−.0007 (−.45)
Electronics	−.0021 (−1.97)	.0007 (.59)	−.0014 (−.97)	−.0048 (−3.42)	.0002 (.21)	−.0011 (−1.27)
Instruments	−.0009 (−.23)	.0027 (1.15)	−.0002 (−.06)	−.0043 (−1.54)	.0025 (1.09)	.0004 (.21)
Chemicals	−.0018 (−1.88)	−.0003 (−.27)	−.0001 (−.08)	−.0022 (−1.78)	.0013 (1.28)	−.0006 (−.70)
Drugs	−.0003 (−.35)	.0012 (1.23)	.0006 (.45)	−.0013 (−1.03)	.0009 (.94)	.0016 (2.09)

Table 7-4 Dependent Variable: Effective Debt Three-Stage Least Squares Estimates

Independent Variables	1976	1977	1978	1979	1980	1981	1982
Constant	-.3124	.0505	.1827	.1268	.1794	.2168	.1598
(t)	(-.00)	(1.34)	(5.34)	(3.64)	(5.50)	(6.67)	(4.42)
NCE	2.4368	3.1744	2.5234	3.0869	2.9955	3.1051	3.5694
	(10.69)	(12.22)	(13.08)	(14.88)	(15.82)	(16.55)	(14.07)
R&D	-1.4837	-1.5988	-1.1842	-2.4365	-2.2005	-1.8886	-2.4169
	(-3.02)	(-3.16)	(-2.31)	(-5.09)	(-4.42)	(-4.01)	(-4.21)
DIV	-.5567	-.5061	-1.2437	-1.6078	-.6889	-.1433	.1295
	(-.64)	(-.58)	(-1.41)	(-1.82)	(-.75)	(-.15)	(.12)
DE	.1646	.1127	.0475	.0621	.0005	.0006	-.0000
	(7.88)	(6.33)	(3.45)	(3.88)	(.10)	(.14)	(-.19)
CF	-.6493	-.8579	-.8679	-1.0157	-1.0127	-1.4415	-1.3519
	(-3.57)	(-4.26)	(-4.39)	(5.35)	(-5.40)	(-6.54)	(-6.42)
LTKD	.3575	.0006	-.0010	.0004	.0004	.0003	.0010
	(.00)	(.43)	(-.65)	(.36)	(.10)	(.34)	(.81)
STKD	.0000	.0001	-.0000	.0016	.0014	-.0004	.0016
	(1.21)	(.04)	(-2.22)	(1.51)	(1.14)	(1.01)	(.66)

Petroleum	−.0418 (−1.02)	.0023 (.06)	.0229 (.52)	−.0789 (−1.63)	−.1396 (−2.93)	−.1914 (−3.78)
Construction	.0873 (1.62)	−.0607 (−1.12)	.1167 (2.26)	.0966 (1.73)	−.0166 (−.29)	.1262 (1.98)
Foods	−.0813 (−.87)	−.0710 (−.90)	−.0290 (−.38)	.0838 (1.02)	−.975 (−1.15)	−.1199 (−1.05)
Lumber	−.1051 (−1.63)	−.1379 (−2.02)	−.1851 (−2.82)	−.2943 (−4.12)	−.1100 (−1.52)	−.1210 (−1.48)
Rubber Products	−.0678 (−.93)	−.0205 (−.27)	.0335 (.46)	−.0497 (−.64)	−.1162 (−1.43)	−.0715 (.87)
Metals	−.0954 (−2.17)	−.0823 (−1.75)	−.0540 (−1.18)	−.0982 (−1.99)	−.1315 (−2.61)	−.1022 (−1.82)
Machinery	−.0731 (−1.70)	−.0841 (−1.84)	−.0426 (−.97)	−.1078 (−2.26)	−.0624 (−1.26)	−.1079 (−2.10)
Electronics	−.0546 (−1.29)	−.1374 (−3.04)	−.0614 (−1.35)	−.1530 (−3.14)	−.1741 (−3.58)	−.0967 (−1.73)
Instruments	−.2978 (−1.86)	−.3389 (−3.72)	−.1086 (−1.24)	−.1738 (−1.84)	−.2097 (−2.16)	−.1373 (−1.18)
Chemicals	−.0988 (−2.57)	−.0682 (−1.68)	−.0224 (−.57)	−.1079 (−2.53)	−.1126 (−2.58)	−.1166 (−2.48)
Drugs	−.0826 (−2.32)	−.1188 (−3.20)	−.0524 (−1.44)	−.1621 (−4.18)	−.1173 (−2.94)	−.1134 (−2.63)

where

$DdRD$ = desired research and development expenditures,
$DdND$ = desired external funds issued,
$DNCE$ = desired investment,
$DDIV$ = desired dividend payments,
d_{1j}^-, d_{1j}^+ = under the overachievement of desired research expenditures,
d_{2j}^-, d_{2j}^+ = under and overachievement of desired external financing,
d_{3j}^-, d_{3j}^+ = under and overachievement of desired investment and
d_{4j}^-, d_{4j}^+ = under and overachievement of desired dividend payments.

The firm expects sales and asset achievements of $1.735 billion and $1.985 billion, respectively, in the coming year. Management calculates its desired research, external funds, investment, and dividend activities based on its 1982 industry relationships among the financial decision variables and assets. The objective function of the linear programming model may be written as:

$$\text{Min } Z = p_1 d_{1j}^- + p_2 d_{2j}^+ + p_3 d_{3j}^- + p_4 d_{4j}^-$$

The representative balance sheet and income statement on which the linear programming model is based is:

1982 Balance Sheet ($millions)

Current Assets	541.5	Current Liabilities	454.3
Fixed Assets	1253.5	Long-Term Debt	422.4
Total Assets	1795.0	Equity	918.3
		Total Liabilities and Equity	1795.0

1982 Income Statement ($millions)

Sales	1568.9
Earnings before Interest and Taxes	180.4
Interest Expense	40.0
Taxes	34.7
Net Income	105.7
Dividends	23.7

The firm incurred depreciation charges of $153.2 million, spent $302.8 million on capital expenditures, $9.4 million on research and development activities, and issued $14.12 million of long-term debt and common stock in a representative year.

The solution of the linear programming problem, assuming equal goal weights, produces underachievements in research and development, investment, and dividend activities, and no overachievement of debt financing. Guerard and McCabe (1987) relax the equal goal weighting assumption with very modest model result differences. The underachievement of external financing and research, and dividend expenditures is created because research expenditures (based on the chemical industry relationship) should normally be $74.3 million to support assets of $1985.3 million; however, optimal research expenditures should be $125.5 million. The historic firm research and development expenditures (based on the firm research-to-assets ratio) would only have been $10.40 million. Optimal external financing should equal $977.6 million whereas the average firm (in the industry) would normally have issued $116.4 million. The firm traditionally issues less than $30 million of debt; the firm would face a substantial capital shortage in the coming year. Optimal dividends should be $77.2 million whereas industry dividends would have been $58.6 million; the normal firm dividend payment of $25.80 million by the firm would probably have been far too low to maintain the stock price. Optimal capital investment should equal $328.4 million; the average firm's management traditionally would have spent $335.5 million. The overachievement of capital investment in 1982 was not found in Guerard and McCabe (1987). The multi-criteria model allows the firm to increase dividends, research, and external funding to optimal levels that avoid the management problems inherent in issuing too little new capital issues, paying too few dividends, pursuing too little investment, and engaging in too little research and development activities. The development and estimation of effective debt financing more clearly addresses the problems caused by management's reluctance to issue debt, that is, the current study finds a much larger underachievement of effective debt financing than found in Guerard and McCabe (1987). The development of the effective debt variable is primarily responsible for this improvement.

Conclusions and Summary

The rejection for the perfect markets hypothesis is found in the interdependencies among: (1) the research and development and dividend variables, and (2) the investment and effective debt variables. The empirical evidence confirms the necessity of using simultaneous equations to econometrically model the interdependencies of financial decisions. The evidence is supportive of the existence of imperfect (interdependent) markets; however, we believe that the construction of a new effective debt variable more clearly develops the basic hypothesis of financial interdependence. This study develops and estimates an optimization model to allow management insights into the trade-offs inherent in implementing an effective strategic plan.

References

Ben-Zion, U. 1984. The R&D and Investment Decision and its Relationship to the Firm's Market Value: Some Preliminary Results. In R&D, Patents, and Productivity. Ed. Z. Griliches. Chicago: University of Chicago Press.

Burton, R.M., W.W. Damon, and B. Obel. 1979. An Organizational Model of Integrated Budgeting for Short-Run Operations and Long-Run Investment. Journal of the Operational Research Society 30: 575–585.

Burton, R.M., W.W. Damon, and B. Obel. 1984. Operations Planning and Investment Strategy in the Owner Financed Firm. Optimization Models for Strategic Planning, Ed. T.H. Naylor and C. Thomas. Amsterdam: North-Holland, 1984.

Damon, W.W., and R. Schramm. 1972. A Simultaneous Decision Model for Production, Marketing and Finance. Management Science 18: 161–172.

Dhrymes, P.J. 1974. Econometrics: Statistical Foundations and Applications. New York: Springer-Verlag.

_____. 1967. Investment, Dividends, and External Finance Behavior of Firms. In Determinants of Investment Behavior. Ed. Robert Ferber. New York: Columbia University Press.

Dhrymes, P.J., and M. Kurz. 1964. On the Dividend Policy of Electric Utilities. Review of Economics and Statistics 46: 76–81.

Fama, E.F. 1974. The Empirical Relationship Between the Dividend and Investment Decisions of Firms. American Economic Review 63: 304–318.

Fama, E.F., and H. Babiak. 1968. Dividend Policy: An Empricial Analysis. Journal of the American Statistical Association 63: 1132–1161.

Grabowski, H.G. 1968. The Determinants of Industrial Research and Development: A Study of the Chemical, Drug, and Petroleum Industries. Journal of Political Economy 76: 292–306.

Grabowski, H.G., and D.C. Mueller. 1972. Managerial and Stockholder Welfare Models of Firm Expenditures. Review of Economics and Statistics 54: 9–24.

Guerard, J.B., A.S. Bean, and S. Andrews. 1987. R&D Management and Corporate Financial Policy. *Management Science* 33: 1419-1427.

Guerard, J.B., and G.M. McCabe. The Integration of Research and Development Management into the Firm Decision Process. In *Management of R&D and Engineering*. Ed. D.F. Kocaoglu. Amsterdam: North-Holland, forthcoming.

Guerard, J.B., and B.K. Stone. 1987. Strategic Planning and the Investment-Financing Behaviour of Major Industrial Companies. *Journal of the Operational Research Society*, 38: 1039-1050.

Hambrick, D.C., I.C. MacMillan, and R.R. Barbosa. 1983. Changes in Product R&D Budgets. *Management Science* 29: 757-769.

Hamilton, W.F. and M.A. Moses. 1973. An Optimization Model for Corporate Financial Planning. *Operations Research* 21: 677-692.

Higgins, R.C. 1972. The Corporate Dividend-Saving Decision. *Journal of Financial and Quantitative Analysis* 7: 1527-1541.

Jalilvand, A., and R.S. Harris. 1984. Corporate Behavior in Adjusting to Capital Structure and Dividend Targets: An Econometric Study. *Journal of Finance* 39: 127-145.

Lawrence, K.D., and J.B. Guerard. 1984. Strategic Planning and the Problem of Capital Budgeting in a Steel Firm: A Multi-Criteria Approach. In *Optimization Models for Strategic Planning*. Eds., Thomas Naylor and Celia Thomas. Amsterdam: North-Holland, 1984.

Lee, S.M. 1972. *Goal Programming for Decision Analysis*. Philadelphia: Auerbach Publishers.

Lintner, J. 1956. Distributions of Incomes of Corporations Among Dividends, Retained Earnings and Taxes. *American Economic Review* 46: 97-118.

Mansfield, E. 1963. Size of Firm, Market Structure and Innovation. *Journal of Political Economy* 71: 556-576.

Mansfield, E. 1984. R&D and Innovation. *R&D, Patents and Productivity*. Ed. Z. Griliches. Chicago: University of Chicago Press.

McCabe, G.M. 1979. The Empirical Relationship Between Investment and Financing: A New Look. *Journal of Financial and Quantitative Analysis* 14: 119-135.

McDonald, J.G., B. Jacquillat, and M. Nussenbaum. 1975. Dividend, Investment, and Financial Decisions: Empirical Evidence on French Firms. *Journal of Financial and Quantitative Analysis* 10: 741-755.

Meyer, J.R., and E. Kuh. 1957. *The Investment Decision*. Cambridge, Mass.: Harvard University Press.

Miller, M., and F. Modigliani. 1961. Dividend Policy, Growth, and the Valuation of Shares. *Journal of Business* 34: 411–433.

Mueller, D.C. 1967. The Firm Decision Process: An Econometric Investigation. *Quarterly Journal of Economics* 81: 58–87.

Peterson, P., and G. Benesh. 1983. A Reexamination of the Empirical Relationship Between Investment and Financing Decisions. *Journal of Financial and Quantitative Analysis* 18: 439–454.

Scherer, F.M. 1965. Firm Size, Market Structure, Opportunity, and the Output of Patented Inventions. *American Economic Review* 55: 1104–1113.

Switzer, L. 1984. The Determinants of Industrial R&D: A Funds Flow Simultaneous Equation Approach. *Review of Economics and Statistics* 66: 163–168.

Chapter 8

Portfolio Theory Models

The purpose of this chapter is to trace the Markowitz development of the mean-variance model of portfolio theory and asset selection. Investors who dislike risk generally price assets such that asset returns are commenserate with their risk of return. Markowitz analysis constructs portfolios with the highest return for a given level of risk or the least amount of risk for a given level of return. The level of risk in Markowitz is measured by the standard deviation of a security's asset.

Individuals' portfolios tend to be characterized as having only two or three stocks and Markowitz analysis is very appropriate for the individual investor. Total risk, or the portfolio variance, is the appropriate measure of portfolio risk when the investor is not adequately diversified in his security holdings.

It is well known in the financial community that generally one must incur higher risks in order to achieve higher returns. It is extremely important that a risk-averse investor or portfolio manager be able to make a proper assessment of the riskiness of a portfolio to ensure that its return is commensurate with the variability or volatility of the return. It is not enough simply to state that common stock returns have been considerably more volatile than bond returns, so that one should expect stock returns to exceed bond returns. Furthermore, the borrowing and lending decision must be made in the context of the risk-return trade-off. The purpose of this chapter is to acquaint the reader with the relationship between the magnitude and the variability of returns on investments.

In this chapter we will focus our attention on the analysis of common stock returns. It has long been known that the returns on common stocks have been greater and more variable than the returns on fixed-income investments, such as corporate and government bonds or U.S. Treasury Bills. Table 8-1, based on the data of Ibbotson and Sinquefield

Table 8-1 Returns on Various Kinds of Investments

Type of Security	Annual Returns, 1926–1981	
	Arithmetic Mean	Standard Deviation
NYSE Common Stocks	11.4%	21.6%
Long-term Government Bonds	3.1	5.7
Long-term Corporate Bonds	3.7	5.6
U.S. Treasury Bills	3.1	3.1
Consumer Price Index	3.1	5.

(1982), compares the returns on different groups of investments during the period 1926–1981.

We develop an example of Markowitz analysis using Air Products and Chemicals, Inc., Exxon, and IBM. The traditional graphical analysis of Markowitz is enhanced by matrix algebra which greatly simplifies model calculation. One can easily invert the covariance matrix of asset returns and determine the optimal weight of a very large number of securities in the portfolio.

Several interesting results emerge from Ibbotson and Sinquefield's data:

1. Common stocks (represented by the S&P 500) earned a risk premium (the nominal return less the inflation rate of 8.3 percent—this risk premium can be useful in establishing hurdle rates (or minimum acceptable rates of return for projects) for capital budgeting);
2. Long-term corporate bonds produced higher returns with less risk than long-term government bonds (one certainly would not have expected this finding);
3. U.S. Treasury Bills produced almost no real return to the investor, though one would have expected them to do so (Fisher 1907, 1911). (It is true that the variability of the return on T-Bills was very slight, but one could not have improved one's real income by investing in them throughout the period 1926–1981.)

Ibbotson and Sinquefield's findings are generally held to establish the historic risk-return relationship. Moreover, the returns on common stocks indicate that, on average, the road to riches may be paved by a more thorough effort at security and portfolio analysis.

Most of the portfolio analysis in this chapter is based on principles developed by Markowitz (1952, 1959). Markowitz was one of the first financial economists to assess the risk and return characteristics of stocks in portfolios and establish their implications for borrowing and lending opportunities. He pointed out the need to be aware of the statistical moments of a security's return. That is, one must be able to estimate the stock's expected return and the mean (or central tendency) and the variability (as measured by the standard deviation) of that return. In this chapter we will examine means and variances of returns, primarily those based on annual data. Besides the variability of the return of each stock in a portfolio, one must be concerned with the covariances among returns of the different securities. Markowitz developed an algorithm for establishing the highest return for a given level of risk or the lowest risk for a given level of return (assuming that investors were risk-averse—that they preferred to hold the least risky assets, holding constant the level of return). Investors must be compensated for holding riskier assets, and the compensation should be proportional to the risk.

Holding-Period Returns and a Brief Statistical Review

Let us briefly review some statistical concepts useful in assessing the risk associated with a portfolio. We first define the holding-period return, R_t, of a single security held for a single period:

$$R_t = \frac{P_{cs_t} - P_{cs_{t-1}} + d_t}{P_{cs_{t-1}}}.$$

d_t = dividend per share at time t,

where

P_{cs_t} = stock price at time t,

and

$P_{cs_{t-1}}$ = stock price at time $t - 1$.

It is assumed that an investor purchased the stock at last period's price, P_{t-1}, and that the stock earned a dividend, d_t, during the current period; the price appreciation has been $P_{cs_t} - P_{cs_{t-1}}$. To calculate the holding period return, an individual can consult many sources. The ten-year history of a security's prices, earnings, and dividends are obtainable from the *Stock Market Encyclopedia*, published by Standard & Poor's. This compilation provides this information as well as current outlooks, yields, bond ratings, and annual balance sheet and income statement data for the largest 750 stocks in the U.S. economy. As an example, a page is reproduced, showing the data for the Exxon Corporation. One notices that the *Encyclopedia* gives the range of stock prices in a given year, rather than the year-end price; in this chapter the midpoint of the trading range is used as the representative price of the stock. Such midrange prices are shown in Table 8-2, which contains data for Air Products & Chemicals, Inc. (APD), Exxon (XON), and International Business Machines (IBM).

From the data in Table 8-2, the holding-period returns in Table 8-3 may be calculated.

The investor or portfolio manager must be aware of the mean and the variance of the return of each security and the covariances among the returns to determine the position of each component of the portfolio, as explained later in this chapter. The mean, or expected, value of a security's return is found by evaluating the formula

$$\bar{R} = E(R_t) = \sum_{t=1}^{T} \left(\frac{R_t}{T} \right). \tag{1}$$

The security's variance is found by measuring its variability about the mean (the second statistical moment):

$$\sigma^2 = E(\text{Variability}) = \frac{\sum_{t=1}^{T} (R_t - \bar{R})^2}{T - 1} \tag{2}$$

One divides by $T - 1$ to adjust the estimation for the degree of freedom "lost" by calculating the security's mean.

The covariance between securities i and j, σ_{ij}, indicates how security i behaves (relative to its mean) as security j is varying about its mean:

$$\sigma_{ij} = \frac{\sum_{t=1}^{T} (R_{it} - \bar{R}_i)(R_{jt} - \bar{R}_j)}{T - 2}. \tag{3}$$

It is extremely difficult to examine a covariance between two securities and say very much about the relationship between them, except that the covariance is positive or negative (or zero). That is, a covariance of 0.350 between two highly variable securities may seem smaller than a covariance of 0.25 between two very stable (low standard deviation) securities. The correlation coefficient, ρ, is very useful in standardizing the covariances between two securities and allowing the portfolio manager to establish the relative riskiness of combinations of securities:

Table 8-2 Stock Prices and Dividends, 1976–1985

Year	APD Price	APD Dividend	XON Price	XON Dividend	IBM Price	IBM Dividend	S&P 500 Price	S&P 500 Dividend
1976	$17.44	$0.063	$24.94	$1.36	$64.00	$2.00	$102.21	$3.85
1977	14.06	0.125	25.19	1.50	66.31	2.50	98.20	4.54
1978	13.63	0.250	24.19	1.65	68.13	2.88	96.02	5.07
1979	15.25	0.325	27.56	1.95	70.81	3.44	103.01	5.64
1980	21.63	0.400	35.25	2.70	61.56	3.44	188.80	6.25
1981	20.75	0.400	35.25	3.00	59.94	3.44	128.05	6.66
1982	16.25	0.400	28.56	3.00	76.81	3.44	119.71	6.96
1983	21.25	0.450	34.13	3.10	113.25	3.71	160.41	7.06
1984	21.31	0.525	40.81	3.35	113.75	4.10	160.46	7.45
1985	28.31	0.635	50.00	3.45	138.10	4.40	186.84	7.94

Table 8-3 Holding-Period Returns, 1976-1985

Holding Period	APD	XON	IBM
1976-77	-0.2154	0.0035	0.0001
1977-78	-0.0031	0.0029	-0.0041
1978-79	0.1123	0.0039	0.1304
1979-80	0.3495	-0.1400	-0.2461
1980-81	-0.0042	-0.0027	0.0000
1981-82	-0.2445	0.2480	-0.2105
1982-83	0.2683	0.3883	0.1781
1983-84	0.0002	0.0004	0.1788
1984-85	0.2840	0.1940	0.2031

$$\rho_{ij} = \frac{\sigma_{ij}}{\sigma_i \sigma_j}.$$

One remembers from a statistics course that the correlation coefficient must lie between -1 and $+1$.

The arithmetic means and variances, the covariance matrix, and the correlation matrix for the returns on three securities, calculated from annual data from 1976 to 1985, are:

Stock	E(R)	σ^2		Covariance Matrix APD	XON	IBM
APD	0.0988	0.0558	APD	0.0558	0.0336	0.0036
XON	0.1756	0.0264	XON	0.0336	0.0264	-0.0029
IBM	0.1487	0.0351	IBM	0.0036	-0.0029	0.0351

	Correlation Matrix APD	XON	IBM
APD	1.0000	0.8764	0.0804
XON	0.8764	1.0000	-0.0952
IBM	0.0804	-0.0952	1.0000

In the covariance matrix, the diagonal elements are the security variances. The average of the three covariances is 0.0114, and the average of the three correlation coefficients is 0.2872. The correlation coefficient between Air Products (APD) and Exxon (XON), 0.8764, is quite high. One would expect that in a risk-minimizing portfolio, if Air Products is held in a long (own) position, that Exxon would be sold short.

The Optimal Combination of Securities in Portfolios

If an investor held only two assets, A and B, in a portfolio, the portfolio return would be the sum of the two returns weighted by the proportions of the respective securities in the portfolio:

$$E(R_p) = W_A E(R_A) + W_B E(R_B). \qquad (4)$$

The portfolio is composed of only the two assets, thus, $W_B = 1 - W_A$. Risk need not be additive in the portfolio because of the variability of the covariance between two securities:

$$\sigma^2(R_p) = W_A^2 \sigma_A^2 + W_B^2 \sigma_B^2 + 2 W_A W_B \sigma_{AB}. \qquad (5)$$

Risk is additive only if the two securities are perfectly positively correlated; an investor would gain no diversification benefits from holding long positions in both securities, given such a correlation coefficient. The diversification benefits from Markowitz analysis lead the investor and portfolio manager to look for assets that have low, or even negative, correlation coefficients.

One can easily solve Equation (5) for the optimal weighting scheme for assets A and B for a given covariance matrix if one remembers that the first-order condition for minimizing a function is that the partial derivative of the function with respect to the decision variable is zero and that σ_{AB} can be written as $\rho_{AB}\sigma_A\sigma_B$.

$$\sigma^2(R_p) = W_A^2 \sigma_A^2 + W_B^2 \sigma_B^2 + 2 W_A W_B \sigma_{AB}$$

Replacing W_B by $1 - W_A$,

$$\sigma^2(R_p) = W_A^2 \sigma_A^2 + (1 - W_A)^2 \sigma_B^2 + 2 W_A (1 - W_A) \rho_{AB}\sigma_A\sigma_B;$$

$$\frac{\partial \sigma^2(R_p)}{\partial W_A} = 2 W_A \sigma_A^2 + 2(1 - W_A)(-1)\sigma_B^2 + 2\rho_{AB}\sigma_A\sigma_B - 4 W_A \rho_{AB}\sigma_A\sigma_B$$

$$= 0.$$

Solving for W_A,

$$2 W_A(\sigma_A^2 + \sigma_B^2 = 2\rho_{AB}\sigma_A\sigma_B) = -2\rho_{AB}\sigma_A\sigma_B + 2\sigma_B^2$$

$$W_A = \frac{\sigma_B^2 - \rho_{AB}\sigma_A\sigma_B}{\sigma_A^2 + \sigma_B^2 - 2\rho_{AB}\sigma_A\sigma_B} = \frac{\sigma_B(\sigma_B - \rho_{AB}\sigma_A)}{\sigma_A^2 + \sigma_B^2 - 2\rho_{AB}\sigma_A\sigma_B}. \qquad (6)$$

Equation (6) produces the optimal weight, W_A, and hence W_B to minimize the risk of a two-asset portfolio. The optimal-weight solution is not intuitively obvious, but if the two assets are independent, ρ_{AB} equalling zero,

$$W_A = \frac{\sigma_B^2}{\sigma_A^2 + \sigma_B^2}.$$

Furthermore, if assets A and B are perfectly negatively correlated, i.e., $\rho_{AB} = -1$, then $W_A = \sigma_B/(\sigma_A + \sigma_B)$ because the denominator is a perfect square, $(\sigma_A + \sigma_B)^2$. It is extremely unusual to find assets that are independent or perfectly negatively correlated, however; thus, Equation (6) should be used by most investors to analyze the weighting scheme of a two-asset portfolio.

The average investor is not well diversified, owning only about 2.7 stocks (Blume and Friend 1975). Such an investor should be acquainted with the three-asset portfolio as well as the two-asset case analyzed in typical textbooks. The three-asset case is much more interesting than the two-asset case because three covariances and correlation coefficients must be analyzed and incorporated into the calculation of the optimal weights. The expected value of the return on the portfolio is

$$E(R_p) = W_A E(R_A) + W_B E(R_B) + W_C E(R_C). \tag{7}$$

Letting $W_C = 1 - W_A - W_B$,

$$E(R_p) = W_A E(R_A) + W_B E(R_B) + (1 - W_A - W_B)E(R_C)$$

$$= W_A[E(R_A) - E(R_C)] + W_B[E(R_B) - E(R_C)] + E(R_C). \tag{8}$$

Equation (8), a rewritten version of Equation (7), will be very useful later in the chapter because it will show various combinations of W_A, W_B, and W_C that produce equal portfolio returns; it is known as the isomean line in Markowitz (1959) analysis. One must again call upon the first-order condition to determine the risk-minimizing security weights in the portfolio:

$$\sigma^2(R_p) = W_A^2\sigma_A^2 + W_B^2\sigma_B^2 + W_C^2\sigma_C^2 + 2W_A W_B \sigma_{AB} + 2W_A W_C \sigma_{AC}$$

$$+ 2W_B W_C \sigma_{BC}. \tag{9}$$

Replacing W_C by $1 - W_A - W_B$,

$$\sigma^2(R_p) = W_A^2\sigma_A^2 + W_B^2\sigma_B^2 + (1 - W_A - W_B)^2\sigma_C^2 + 2W_A W_B \sigma_{AB}$$

$$+ 2W_A(1 - W_A - W_B)\sigma_{AC} + 2W_B(1 - W_A - W_C)\sigma_{BC} \tag{10}$$

$$= W_A^2(\sigma_A^2 + \sigma_C^2 - 2\sigma_{AC}) + W_B^2(\sigma_B^2 + \sigma_C^2 - 2\sigma_{BC})$$

$$+ W_A(-2\sigma_C^2 + 2\sigma_{AC}) + W_B(-2\sigma_C^2 + 2\sigma_{BC})$$

$$+ W_A W_B(2\sigma_C^2 + 2\sigma_{AB} - 2\sigma_{AC} - 2\sigma_{BC}) + \sigma_C^2. \tag{11}$$

To solve for the risk-minimizing security weights, set the partial derivatives with respect to W_A and W_B equal to zero:

$$\frac{\partial \sigma^2(R_p)}{\partial W_A} = 2W_A(\sigma_A^2 + \sigma_C^2 - 2\sigma_{AC}) + (-2\sigma_C^2 + 2\sigma_{AC})$$

$$+ W_B(2\sigma_C^2 + 2\sigma_{AB} - 2\sigma_{AC} - 2\sigma_{BC}) = 0; \tag{12}$$

$$\frac{\partial \sigma^2(R_p)}{\partial W_B} = 2W_B(\sigma_B^2 + \sigma_C^2 - 2\sigma_{BC}) + (-2\sigma_C^2 + 2\sigma_{BC})$$

$$+ W_A(2\sigma_C^2 + 2\sigma_{AB} - 2\sigma_{AC} - 2\sigma_{BC}) = 0. \tag{13}$$

As an example, let us calculate the optimal security weighting scheme for the three-asset case with APD, XON, and IBM stocks. Let APD be security A, XON be security B, and IBM be security C. Substituting the appropriate numbers in Equations (12) and (13),

$$\frac{\partial \sigma^2(R_p)}{\partial W_A} = 2W_A[.0558 + .0351 - 2(.0036)] + [-2(.0351) + 2(.0036)]$$

$$+ W_B[2(.0351) + 2(.0336) - 2(.0036) - 2(-.0029)]$$

$$= 2W_A(.0837) - .0630 + W_B(.1360) = 0 \tag{14}$$

$$.1674 W_A = .0630 - .1360 W_B$$

$$W_A = .3763 - .8124 W_B$$

$$\frac{\partial \sigma^2(R_p)}{\partial W_B} = 2W_B[.0264 + .0351 - 2(.0029)] + [-2(.0351) + 2(-.0029)]$$

$$+ W_A[2(.0351) + 2(.0336) - 2(.0036) - 2(-.0029)]$$

$$= 2W_B(.0673) - .0760 + W_A(.1360) = 0 \tag{15}$$

$$.1346 W_B = .0760 - .1360 W_A$$

$$W_B = .5646 - 1.0104 W_A$$

One can easily solve these simultaneous equations for the optimal weights:

$$W_A = .3763 - .8124W_B$$

$$W_B = .5646 - 1.0104W_A$$

$$W_A = .3763 - .8124(.5646 - 1.0104W_A)$$

$$W_A = .3763 - .4587 + .8208W_A$$

$$.1792W_A = -.0824$$

$$W_A = -.4598$$

The optimal security weight for APD, W_A, in the portfolio is $-.4598$; thus, Air Products is a short sell (you should sell this stock, although you do not own it, through your broker).

The optimal seucrity weight for XON is

$$W_B = .5646 - 1.0104W_A = .5646 - 1.0104(-.4598) = 1.0292.$$

The optimal security weight for IBM is

$$W_C = 1 - (-.4598) - 1.0292 = .4306.$$

The optimal security weights are not equal and not necessarily positive. The negative weight on Air Products results from its very high correlation with Exxon (as we noted earlier). If the investor has a $100,000 portfolio, the optimal allocation of security portions should be:

Stock	Value
Air Products	($45,980)
Exxon	102,920
IBM	43,060

The reader might be surprised to see that the absolute dollar value of the portfolio greatly exceeds $100,000; most brokerage firms do not allow investors the opportunity to maneuver accounts in such a manner. One could use the absolute dollar weights to calculate the security weights (Lintner 1970). Markowitz analysis takes explicit account of the possibility of negative optimal weights, referring to portfolios composed solely of positively weighted securities as legitimate portfolios. One would expect legitimate portfolios to be composed of securities with rather low correlation coefficients.

Another Example: A Legitimate Portfolio

Let us assume an expected return vector and a correlation matrix such that the portfolio that minimizes risk, known as the minimum-variance portfolio (MVP), is legitimate. That is, the portfolio weights of the three asset portfolio are (all) positive.

Stock	E(R)	σ_{ij}			ρ_{ij}		
A	.06	.0900	.0360	.0210	1.000	.3000	.1000
B	.09	.0360	.1600	−.0560	.3000	1.0000	−.2000
C	.12	.0210	−.0560	.4900	.1000	−.2000	1.0000

The isomean line for the assumed three-asset portfolio is

$$E(R_p) = -0.06W_A - 0.03W_B + 0.12, \tag{16}$$

and the portfolio variance is

$$\sigma^2(R_p) = 0.538W_A^2 + 0.762W_B^2 - 0.938W_A - 1.092W_B$$

$$+ 1.122W_AW_B + 0.490. \tag{17}$$

The optimal W_A and W_B are found as follows:

$$\frac{\partial \sigma^2(R_p)}{\partial W_A} = 1.076W_A + 1.122W_B - 0.938 = 0$$

$$1.076W_A = 0.938 - 1.122W_B;$$

$$\frac{\partial \sigma^2(R_p)}{\partial W_B} = 1.524W_B + 1.122W_A - 1.092 = 0$$

$$1.524W_B = 1.092 - 1.122W_A.$$

Solving the two simultaneous equations,

$$W_A = 0.5390, \quad W_B = 0.3230;$$

hence,

$$W_C = 0.1380.$$

The expected return of the MVP is

$$E(R_p) = 0.539(0.06) + 0.323(0.09) + 0.138(0.12) = 0.078,$$

and the variance of the MVP is

$$\sigma^2(R_p) = (0.539)^2(0.0900) + (0.323)^2(0.1600) + (0.138)^2(0.4900)$$

$$+ 2(0.539)(0.323)(0.036) + 2(0.323)(0.138)(-0.056)$$

$$+ 2(0.539)(0.138)(0.04)$$

$$= 0.063.$$

$$\sigma(R_p) = \sqrt{0.063} = 0.251.$$

The expected return and variance of the minimum variance portfolio are 7.8 percent and 6.3 percent, respectively.

One might ask how the optimal portfolio weights, returns, and variances might change if the investor sought to achieve a 10 percent, 15 percent, or 20 percent return on the portfolio. The Markowitz critical line addresses the estimation of optimal portfolio weights along with the risk-return trade-off. In Markowitz treatment (1952, 1959) of the three-asset case, the critical line was estimated by graphing the isomean and isovariance functions and finding points of tangency, corresponding to the maximum return for a specified risk or the minimum risk for a given return. Let us return to the isomean line for the assumed three-asset case, $-0.06W_A - 0.03W_B + 0.12$, and derive values for W_A, holding W_B constant, and for W_B, holding W_A constant, for various expected portfolio returns.

One would graph the isomean lines in W_A, W_B space (See Figure 1). The parallel lines represent combinations of W_A, W_B, and W_C producing equal portfolio returns (along each line). The isovariance ellipses are

Table 8-4 Isomean Line Intercepts

$E(R_p)$	$W_A	W_B = 0$	$W_B	W_A = 0$
0.05	1.167	2.333
0.10	0.333	0.667
0.15	-0.500	-1.000
0.20	-1.333	-2.667

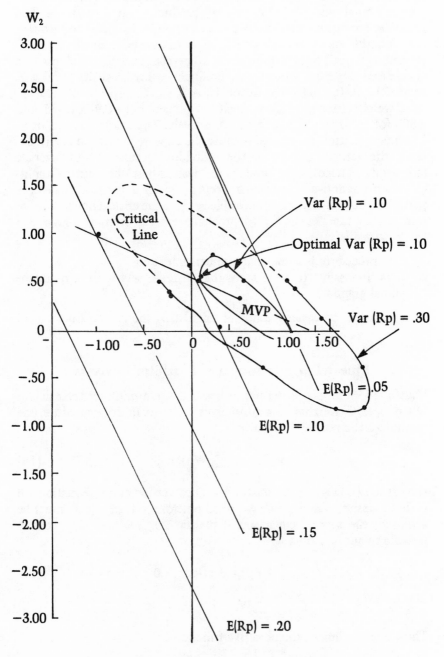

Figure 1 Graphical Markowitz Analysis

calculated by a Fortran program developed by Francis (1985); they represent combinations of W_A, W_B, and W_C producing equal variances. The graphical approach of Markowitz to our example isomean and isovariance functions is shown in Figure 1. Note that the point at which the 10 percent isomean line is tangent to the 10 percent isovariance ellipse (the equal percentages are coincidental) produces optimal security weights of about 0.11, 0.50, and 0.39 for securities A, B, and C, respectively. The optimal weights for a portfolio return of 15 percent are −0.975, 0.975, and 1.000 for securities A, B, and C, respectively. The nonlegitimate, or illegitimate, portfolio is created because the expected portfolio return exceeds the returns of any of the individual securities and leverage (borrowing) is necessary to produce the desired portfolio return. Graphical determination of the optimal security weights for the 20 percent portfolio return is virtually impossible because the critical line has disappeared into the "ozone." Two problems emerge from the graphical Markowitz analysis:

1. The procedure is somewhat cumbersome; and
2. It is impossible to treat more than three assets with two-dimensional graphs.

There must be an easier method of calculating the critical line.

Linear Programming and Portfolio Analysis

Martin (1955) proposed the use of linear programming for the calculation of optimal weights for a multi-asset portfolio. In this procedure, one minimizes the portfolio variance,

$$\sigma^2(R_p) = \sum\sum W_i W_j \sigma_{ij}, \tag{18}$$

subject to two Lagrangian constraints. The first constraint (Equation 19) is that a desired value of the expected portfolio return, $E(R_p)^*$, must be achieved; the second constraint (Equation 20), requires the security weights to sum to unity:

$$\sum W_i E(R_i) - E(R_p)^* = 0 \tag{19}$$

$$\sum W_i - 1 = 0. \tag{20}$$

Thus, one minimizes the objective function Z:

$$Z = \sum\sum W_i W_j \sigma_{ij} + \lambda_i \left[\sum W_i E(R_i) - E(R_p)^* \right] + \lambda_2 \left(\sum W_i - 1 \right). \tag{21}$$

The three-asset example is solved by setting the partial derivatives of Z with respect to W_i and λ_j equal to zero:

$$\frac{\partial Z}{\partial W_1} = 2W_1\sigma_1^2 + 2W_2\sigma_{12} + 2W_3\sigma_{13} + \lambda_1 E(R_1) + \lambda_2 = 0;$$

$$\frac{\partial Z}{\partial W_2} = 2W_1\sigma_{21} + 2W_2\sigma_2^2 + 2W_3\sigma_{23} + \lambda_1 E(R_2) + \lambda_2 = 0;$$

$$\frac{\partial Z}{\partial W_3} = 2W_1\sigma_{31} + 2W_2\sigma_{23} + 2W_3\sigma_3^2 + \lambda_1 E(R_3) + \lambda_2 = 0;$$

$$\frac{\partial Z}{\partial \lambda_1} = W_1 E(R_1) + W_2 E(R_2) + W_3 E(R_3) - E(R_p)^* = 0;$$

$$\frac{\partial Z}{\partial \lambda_2} = W_1 + W_2 + W_3 - 1 = 0.$$

Francis (1979) represents the system more compactly by an equation in vector notation,

$$CW = k,$$

in which C is an extended covariance matrix, W is the weighting vector, and k is the vector of constants. In full, Francis' equation becomes

$$
\begin{array}{ccccc}
2\sigma_1^2 & 2\sigma_{12} & 2\sigma_{13} & E(R_1) & 1 \\
2\sigma_{21} & 2\sigma_2^2 & 2\sigma_{23} & E(R_2) & 1 \\
2\sigma_{31} & 2\sigma_{32} & 2\sigma_3^2 & E(R_3) & 1 \\
E(R_1) & E(R_2) & E(R_3) & 0 & 0 \\
1 & 1 & 1 & 0 & 0
\end{array}
\quad
\begin{array}{c}
W_1 \\
W_2 \\
W_3 \\
\lambda_1 \\
\lambda_2
\end{array}
\quad = \quad
\begin{array}{c}
0 \\
0 \\
0 \\
E(R_p)^* \\
1
\end{array}
$$

$$(22)$$

To solve for the optimal portfolio weights, the inverse of C is multiplied by k to give

$$W_1 = 2.406 - 23.920 E(R_p)^*;$$

$$W_2 = -0.812 + 14.506E(R_p)^*;$$

$$W_3 = -0.594 + 9.414E(R_p)^*; \qquad (23)$$

$$\lambda_1 = 12.328 - 157.700E(R_p)^*;$$

$$\lambda_2 = -1.089 + 12.328E(R_p)^*.$$

Table 8-5 Optimal Weights Determined by Linear Programming

Parameter	Desired Portfolio Return, $E(R_p)^*$		
	0.10	0.15	0.20
W_1	0.014	−1.182	−2.378
W_2	0.639	1.364	2.089
W_3	0.347	0.818	1.289
λ_1	−3.442	−11.327	−19.212
λ_2	0.144	0.760	1.376
$\sigma^2(R_p)$	0.1003	0.4697	1.2332

Once the matrix **C** is inverted, one can easily substitute any desired portfolio return to calculate the optimal weights for the critical line (the SAS program SAS/OR is useful for inverting a matrix).

One notices the extremely variable weighting scheme caused by borrowing to achieve the desired portfolio returns. The Sharpe approach is considerably easier to implement than the graphical technique put forth by Markowitz; it must be noted, however, that Markowitz (1956, 1959) was keenly aware of the linear programming approach to the problem. Note that the matrix **C** can accommodate any number of securities. Elton and Gruber (1987) extended the linear programming approach in a way that specifically addresses the Lintnerian short-selling qualification. In their calculation of the efficient frontier (another term for the critical line), Elton and Gruber seek to maximize θ, the excess return of a portfolio, relative to the portfolio standard deviation. The excess return is defined as follows:

$$\theta = \frac{E(R_p) - R_F}{\sigma_p}, \qquad (24)$$

where R_F is the risk-free rate. Theta is maximized subject to the constraint that the weights must sum to unity. Expanding the numerator in Equation (24), the definition of theta,

$$\theta = \frac{\sum W_i E(R_i) - \sum W_i R_F}{\left(\sum\sum W_i W_j \sigma_{ij}\right)^{1/2}}.$$

Expanding the denominator,

$$\theta = \frac{\sum W_i E(R_p) - \sum W_i R_F}{\left(\sum W_i \sigma_i^2 + \sum\sum_{i \ne j} W_i W_j \sigma_{ij}\right)^{1/2}}.$$

Partial derivatives of θ with respect to the weights take the form

$$\frac{\partial \theta}{\partial W_i} = (\lambda W_1 \sigma_{1i} + \lambda W_2 \sigma_{2i} + \cdots + \lambda W_N \sigma_{Ni}) + E(R_i) - R_F = 0.$$

$$(25)$$

Note that if $Z_k = \lambda X_k$, the partial derivatives may be written

$$E(R_i) - R_F = Z_1 \sigma_{1i} + Z_2 \sigma_{2i} + \cdots + Z_N \sigma_{Ni}. \qquad (26)$$

For the three-asset case,

$$E(R_1) - R_F = Z_1 \sigma_1^2 + Z_2 \sigma_{12} + Z_3 \sigma_{13};$$

$$E(R_2) - R_F = Z_1 \sigma_{21} + Z_2 \sigma_2^2 + Z_3 \sigma_{23};$$

$$E(R_3) - R_F = Z_1 \sigma_{31} + Z_2 \sigma_{32} + Z_3 \sigma_3^2.$$

To solve the Elton and Gruber system, one inverts the covariance matrix and multiples the inverse by the vector of excess returns to determine the vector of security weights. The Zs are scaled into the security weights by:

$$W_R = \frac{Z_R}{\sum Z_i}. \qquad (27)$$

The Lintnerian short solution is

$$W_R = \frac{Z_R}{\sum |Z_i|}. \qquad (28)$$

One disadvantage of the Elton and Gruber algorithm is that the risk-free rate is specified, rather than the desired portfolio return. Many people are accustomed to thinking in terms of desired portfolio returns.

A Further Look at Portfolio Selection Using Monthly Data

Many investors would prefer not to use annual data and would seek instead monthly data. Monthly stock price and dividend data could be found on the CRSP (Center for Research in Security Pricing) tapes developed at the University of Chicago. Monthly data from 1926 on firms composing the NYSE (stocks traded on other exchanges are now available). A reexamination of APD, XON, and IBM, based on monthly data from January 1981 to December 1985, reveals the following risk-return relationships:

If one desires monthly portfolio returns specified by the values of $E(R_p)^*$ shown in Table 8-7, the optimal portfolio weights may be obtained by using the Martin (1955) algorithm.

The erratic behavior of the efficient frontier is due to IBM, which has a much higher return than APD and XON and a much lower variance than APD. The inconsistent risk-return relationship results from the choice of securities examined. We include this example because textbooks generally include only well-behaved numerical examples.

Table 8-6 Monthly Returns and Variances

	Stock		
	APD	XON	IBM
Arithmetic Mean	.0093	.0072	.0165
Variance	.0061	.0027	.0030
Skewness	.3704	.4903	.4885

Table 8-7 Monthly Efficient Frontiers for a Three-Asset Portfolio

Weights	Desired Monthly Returns, $E(R_p)^*$				
	.0073	.008	.009	.010	.015
APD	.039	.221	.200	.180	.078
XON	.961	.745	.653	.561	.102
IBM	.000	.034	.146	.259	.820
$\sigma^2(R_p)$	.0025	.0021	.0019	.0017	.0024

References

Blume, M. and I. Friend. 1975. The Asset Structure of Individual Portfolios and Some Implications for Utility Functions. *Journal of Finance* 30: 585–603.

Elton, E.J., and M.J. Gruber. 1987. *Modern Portfolio Theory and Investment Analysis*. 3rd ed. New York: John Wiley & Sons.

Fisher, I. 1930. *The Theory of Interest*. New York: Macmillan.

_____. 1911. *The Purchasing Power of Money*. New York: Macmillan.

Francis, J.C. 1976. *Investments: Analysis and Measurement*. 2d ed. New York: McGraw-Hill.

_____ and S.H. Archer. 1979. *Portfolio Analysis*. 2d ed. Englewood Cliffs, N.J.: Prentice-Hall.

Ibbotson, R.G., and R.A. Sinquefield. 1982. *Stocks, Bonds, Bills, and Inflation: Historical Returns (1926–1981)*. Charlottesville, Va.: Financial Analysts Research Foundation.

Lintner, J. 1970. The Market Price of Risk, Size of Market, and Investor Risk Aversion. *Review of Economics and Statistics* 52: 87–99.

Martin, A.D. 1955. Mathematical Programming of Portfolio Selection. *Management Science* 1: 152–166.

Markowitz, H.M. 1952. Portfolio Selection. *Journal of Finance* 7: 77–91.

_____. 1956. The Optimization of a Quadratic Function Subject to Linear Constraints. *Naval Research Logistics Quarterly* 3: 111–133.

_____. 1959. *Portfolio Selection: Efficient Diversification of Investments*. New Haven: Yale University Press.

Chapter 9

Market Risk and Shareholder Return Models

In the previous chapter we discussed the development of the Markowitz mean-variance framework for analyzing the optimal weighting of securities in a portfolio. It is a startling fact that if a portfolio manager must maintain at least 20 securities in his portfolio (as required by the Investment Company Act of 1940), he must be prepared to deal with 190 covariances. Moreover, the graphical estimation of the critical line seems quite laborious with only four securities. To facilitate the task, an easier method must be made available to the portfolio manager in the effort to obtain the maximum return for a given level of risk. The single-index model, or market model, was developed by Sharpe (1964), Lintner (1965), and Mossin (1966) to describe a new risk-return relationship.

The market model holds that the return on security *j* can be related by a linear regression line to the return on the market, such as the S&P 500 or NYSE Composite Index:

$$R_{jt} = \alpha_j + \beta_j R_{Mt} + \varepsilon_{jt}, \tag{1}$$

where

R_{jt} = expected return on security *j* at time *t*;

R_{Mt} = expected return on market at time *t*;

α_j, β_j = hypothesized regression coefficients;

ε_{jt} = a randomly distributed error term.

A regression analysis produces estimates, *a* and *b*, for the regression coefficients α and β, respectively. The expected value of the error term is zero because the ordinary least squares regression should be statistically unbiased. Moreover, the regression error term of security j should be independent of the regression error term of security i and of the market:

$$\text{cov}\,(e_i, e_j) = 0;$$

$$\text{cov}\,(e_j, R_M) = 0;$$

$$E(e_j) = 0;$$

$$\sigma^2(e_j) = \sigma e_j^2.$$

The variance of a security return can be broken down into a systematic risk component, a part measuring the association between changes in the security return and the market return, and the residual risk:

$$\sigma_j^2 = \beta_j \sigma_M^2 + \sigma e_j^2, \tag{2}$$

where

σ_j^2 = Variance of the return on security j;
β_j = Security beta;
σe_j^2 = Residual risk or unsystematic risk.

The unsystematic or residual risk of a portfolio is substantially reduced by diversification. The unsystematic risk of a portfolio of 8 to 16 randomly selected stocks generally is only 15 percent of the total portfolio risk. The security beta, β, measures the risk that the inclusion of an additional stock adds to a diversified portfolio because most residual risk has been eliminated in the portfolio. The security beta is the sole determinant of the risk of a security in a well-diversified portfolio. Furthermore, if one remembers that the covariance of securities i and j can be broken down into their respective betas and market risk, one can begin to expand upon the Elton and Gruber theta (1987) developed in the previous chapter.

$$\sigma_{ij} = \beta_i \beta_j \sigma_M^2 \tag{3}$$

The portfolio excess return measure may be expanded as follows:

$$\theta = \frac{E(R_p) - R_F}{\sigma_p}$$

$$= \frac{\sum_{i=1}^{n} W_i E(R_i) - \sum_{i=1}^{n} W_i R_F}{\left[\sum_{i=1}^{n} W_i^2 \sigma_i^2 + \sum_{i \neq j}^{n} \sum_{i \neq j}^{n} W_i W_j \sigma_{ij}\right]^{1/2}}$$

$$= \frac{\sum_{i=1}^{n} W_i E(R_i) - \sum_{i=1}^{n} W_i R_F}{\left[\sum_{i=1}^{n} W_i^2 \beta_i^2 \sigma_M^2 + \sum_{i=1}^{n} \sum_{i \neq j}^{n} W_i W_j \beta_i \beta_j \sigma_M^2 + \sum_{i \neq j}^{n} W_i^2 \sigma e_i^2\right]^{1/2}} \tag{4}$$

The portfolio beta is a weighted average of the security betas, and the portfolio alpha is a weighted average of the security alphas. Diversification tends to drive the third term in the denominator, the portfolio residual risk, to zero. The return and risk characteristics of a portfolio can now be expressed as linear functions of the security or portfolio beta. Whereas the Markowitz critical line examined the risk-return trade-off, using total portfolio variability as the relevant risk criteria, the Sharpe-Lintner-Mossin risk-return relationship can be expressed in terms of systematic risk. Let us briefly trace the relationships between the relevant risk criteria. The Markowitz critical line can be written for the economy as

$$E(R_p) = R_F + \left[\frac{E(R_M) - R_F}{\sigma_M}\right]\sigma_p \tag{5}$$

where

R_F = risk-free (90-day Treasury bill) yield;
$E(R_M)$ = expected return on the market;
σ_M = standard deviation of the market return;
$E(R_p)$ and σ_p = the mean and standard deviation of the portfolio, respectively.

Equation (5) is generally referred to as the Capital Market Line (CML). Let us more closely examine Equation (5) by the use of the estimated market model,

$$R_j = a_j + b_j R_M + e_j. \tag{6}$$

The return on a portfolio can be expressed as a linear function of the portfolio beta. This linear relationship may be referred to as the Security Market Line (SML). Although b is our estimate of the theoretical beta, b is normally written as β in the financial literature. The risk-return relationship is known as the Capital Asset Pricing Model (CAPM):

$$k_p = R_F + [E(R_M) - R_F]\beta_p, \tag{7}$$

where

k_p = required return on the portfolio;

β_p = portfolio beta.

The portfolio beta, the weighted average of the security betas, is defined as

$$\beta_p = \frac{\text{cov}(R_p, R_M)}{\sigma_M^2}.$$

Thus, Equation (7) may be written as

$$k_p = R_F + E(R_M) - R_F\left[\frac{\text{cov}(R_p, R_M)}{\sigma_M^2}\right]$$

$$= R_F + \frac{E(R_M) - R_F}{\sigma_M}\left[\frac{\text{cov}(R_p, R_M)}{\sigma_M}\right]$$

Because cov $(R_p, R_M) = \sigma_p\sigma_M\rho_{pM}$,

$$k_p = R_F + \frac{E(R_M) - R_F}{\sigma_M}\left[\frac{\sigma_p\sigma_M\rho_{pM}}{\sigma_M}\right]$$

$$= R_F + \left[\frac{E(R_M) - R_F}{\sigma_M}\right]\sigma_p\rho_{pM}.$$

Diversification tends to eliminate unsystematic risk and drive the portfolio beta toward unity, so that

$$k_p = R_F + \left[\frac{E(R_M) - R_F}{\sigma_M}\right]\sigma_p. \tag{8}$$

Equation (8), the Capital Market Line (CML) relationship, may be developed from the Security Market Line (SML) and CAPM relationships if the portfolio is diversified [the CML and SML relationships are treated very well in Weston and Copeland (1987)]. Thus, one may measure portfolio performance by estimating only the security alphas and betas and calculating the portfolio alpha and beta. The estimation of efficient betas, however, is not as easy as one might expect.

The Estimation of Betas

There are many ways to estimate betas. Perhaps the most widely accepted method is to employ ordinary least squares (OLS) to determine the alpha and beta coefficients using five years of monthly data (Fama 1976). In the OLS regressions, one assumes that the security returns, R_j, and market returns are normally distributed [the assumption of bivariate normality; see Fama (1976) for a complete discussion of the statistical assumptions of the market model]:

$$E(\tilde{R}_{jt}|R_{Mt}) = \alpha_i + \beta_i R_{Mt},$$

$$\beta_i = \frac{\text{cov}(\tilde{R}_{jt}, \tilde{R}_{Mt})}{\sigma^2(\tilde{R}_{Mt})},$$

and

$$\alpha_j = E(\tilde{R}_{jt}) - \beta_j[E(\tilde{R}_{Mt})].$$

The regression estimators for α_j and β_j are

$$\bar{R}_j = \sum_{t=1}^{T} \frac{\bar{R}_{jt}}{T};$$

$$\bar{R}_M = \sum_{t=1}^{T} \frac{\bar{R}_{Mt}}{T};$$

$$M_{jm} = \frac{\sum_{t=1}^{T}(\tilde{R}_{jt} - \bar{R}_j)(\bar{R}_{Mt} - \bar{R}_M)}{T - 2};$$

$$\tilde{b} = \frac{M_{jM}}{\tilde{M}_{mm}} = \frac{\sum_{t=1}^{T}(\tilde{R}_{jt} - \bar{R}_j)(\bar{R}_{Mt} - \bar{R}_M)}{\sum_{t=1}^{T}(\tilde{R}_{Mt} - \bar{R}_M)^2};$$

$$\tilde{a}_i = \tilde{R}_i - \tilde{b}_i R_M.$$

Let us return to the monthly data for APD, XON, and IBM briefly examined in the previous chapter. The analysis of month-end stock prices and the (value-weighted) NYSE Composite Index produces the means and the covariance matrix shown in Table 9-1. The returns are found by the calculation of logarithm of price changes (relatives). The price relatives method is an alternative form to the return form used in Chapter 8 that incorporated dividends.

$$R_{jt} = \ln\left(\frac{P_{jt}}{P_{jt-1}}\right)$$

The ordinary least squares estimation of betas and alphas produces the results in Table 9-2.

An examination of Table 9-2 reveals that the betas for the three firms are statistically different from zero at the 5 percent level; the estimated t-values exceed 1.96, and therefore the betas are considered "good." One expects the systematic risk measure of a security to be statistically different from zero. The alphas indicate that Air Products and Exxon are priced consistently with the Security Market Line because the alphas are not statistically different from zero at the 20 percent level. IBM appears to be marginally undervalued (at the 13 percent level) because its alpha is statistically significant at the 15 percent level. The goodness-of-fit measure, R^2, indicates that the market models are statistically significant for the three firms (one should review Chapter 2 for the moment matrix approach to R^2).

$$R^2 = \frac{\tilde{b}_i^2 M_{Rm,Rm}}{M_{Rj,Rj}}.$$ (9)

The use of the Standard & Poor's 500 as the relevant market index, as reported in Standard & Poor's *Stock Market Encyclopedia*, produces almost identical betas for the three firms, as shown in Table 9-3. This is not surprising, given the extremely strong correlation between the S&P 500 and the NYSE Composite Index.

A recent Kidder Peabody (1985) research study examined the correlation between various market indices for 1984, using daily price data from January 1979 to December 1984, and reported the results shown in Table 9-4.

One could have calculated betas using the NYSE Composite and S&P500 indices (value-weighted indices), the Dow Jones Industrial

Table 9-1 Summary Statistics of Monthly Data

Stock or Index	$\bar{R}_j$	$\sigma(\bar{R}_j)$		Correlation Matrix			
				R_{APD}	R_{XON}	R_{IBM}	R_{NYSE}
APD	.0093	.0780	R_{APD}	1.0000	.1730	.2494	.6643
XON	.0074	.0513	R_{XON}	.1730	1.0000	.3184	.5257
IBM	.0165	.0551	R_{IBM}	.2494	.3184	1.0000	.5490
NYSE	.0092	.0401	R_{NYSE}	.5490	.5257	.6643	1.0000

Exhibit 9-1
Estimation of Air Products Beta
GENERAL LINEAR MODELS PROCEDURE

DEPENDENT VARIABLE: RETAPD

SOURCE	DF	SUM OF SQUARES	MEAN SQUARE	F VALUE	PR > F	R-SQ
MODEL	1	0.15571430	0.15571430	45.01	0.0001	0.44
ERROR	57	0.19719106	0.00345949		ROOT MSE	
CORRECTED TOTAL	58	0.35290536			0.05881745	

SOURCE	DF	TYPE I SS	F VALUE	PR > F		DF	TYPE III SS
RETNYSE	1	0.15571430	45.01	0.0001		1	0.15571430

PARAMETER	ESTIMATE	T FOR HO: PARAMETER=0	PR > |T|	STD ERROR OF ESTIMATE
INTERCEPT	-0.00249947	-0.32	0.7516	0.00785778
RETNYSE	1.29119052	6.71	0.0001	0.19245636

Source: SAS output

Exhibit 9–2
Estimation of Exxon Beta
GENERAL LINEAR MODELS PROCEDURE

DEPENDENT VARIABLE: RETXON

SOURCE	DF	SUM OF SQUARES	MEAN SQUARE	F VALUE	PR > F	R-SQUARE
MODEL	1	0.04215352	0.04215352	21.77	0.0001	0.276381
ERROR	57	0.11036599	0.00193625		ROOT MSE	
CORRECTED TOTAL	58	0.15251951			0.04400279	

SOURCE	DF	TYPE I SS	F VALUE	PR > F	DF	TYPE III SS	F VALUE
RETNYSE	1	0.04215352	21.77	0.0001	1	0.04215352	21.77

PARAMETER	ESTIMATE	T FOR HO: PARAMETER=0	PR > |T|	STD ERROR OF ESTIMATE
INTERCEPT	0.00126547	0.22	0.8303	0.00587860
RETNYSE	0.67180464	4.67	0.0001	0.14398137

Source: SAS output

Exhibit 9–3
Estimation of IBM Beta
GENERAL LINEAR MODELS PROCEDURE

DEPENDENT VARIABLE: RETIBM

SOURCE	DF	SUM OF SQUARES	MEAN SQUARE	F VALUE	PR > F	R-SQUARE
MODEL	1	0.05299556	0.05299556	24.59	0.0001	0.301358
ERROR	57	0.12286000	0.00215544		ROOT MSE	
CORRECTED TOTAL	58	0.17585556			0.04642670	

SOURCE	DF	TYPE I SS	F VALUE	PR > F	DF	TYPE III SS	F VALUE
RETNYSE	1	0.05299556	24.59	0.0001	1	0.05299556	24.59

PARAMETER	ESTIMATE	T FOR HO: PARAMETER=0	PR > |T|	STD ERROR OF ESTIMATE
INTERCEPT	0.00960063	1.55	0.1272	0.00620243
RETNYSE	0.75326158	4.96	0.0001	0.15191264

Source: SAS output

Table 9-2 Complete Regression Results

Stock	alpha	beta	R^2
APD	−.0025	1.291	.441
(t)	(−.32)	(6.71)	
Probability > |t|	.7516	.0001	
XON	.0013	.672	.276
(t)	(.22)	(4.67)	
Probability > |t|	.8303	.0001	
IBM	.0096	.753	.301
(t)	(1.55)	(4.96)	
Probability > |t|	.1272	.0001	

Table 9-3 Security Betas Using Alternative Indices

Stock	beta, S&P 500 Index	beta, NYSE Composite Index
APD	1.24	1.29
XON	.74	.67
IBM	.69	.75

Average, or the Dow (a price-weighted index of 30 blue-chip stocks begun around 1895) and obtained comparable betas.

Betas estimated using OLS analysis tend to be unstable, or nonstationary, as one might expect, given the random nature of the regression coefficient. Historic betas do not always do a very good job of forecasting future betas. Blume (1971) used an adjustment technique based on the tendency of betas to converge to one. The rise of lower (less than one) betas toward one and the fall of higher (greater than one) betas tends to reduce forecasting errors relative to historic betas (Klemkosky and Martin 1975). A cross-sectional (Bayesian) adjustment technique advocated by Vasichek (1973) relies upon the tendency of betas to converge to a weighted average beta. The betas on securities with larger standard errors (typically larger betas) would be weighted downward while betas on securities with smaller standard errors (smaller betas) would be weighted to produce an increase in the beta. Elton, Gruber, and Urich

Table 9-4 Correlation Matrix

	S&P100	NYSE Composite Index	DJIA	S&P500
S&P100	1.0000	.910	.950	.969
NYSE Composite	.910	1.000	.963	.940
DJIA	.950	.963	1.000	.956
S&P500	.969	.944	.956	1.000

(1978) found no consistent forecasting advantage for either the Blume or Vasichek schemes, although both techniques produced lower forecasting errors than historic betas and a naive rule that set betas equal to one.

The forecasting of betas is particularly important in utility rate cases in which the fair rate of return is determined by the use of beta and the CAPM (Myers 1972, Breen and Lerner 1972, Brigham and Crum 1977, Pettway 1978, and Carleton 1979). Carleton (1979) examined AT&T for the period 1967–76 and found that the intercept of his regressions, the alpha, was very large and quite nonstationary, causing him to question the use of the CAPM in efficient regulation.

One could calculate betas from annual holding-period data (Weston and Copeland 1986, pp. 416–18). The alphas and betas obtained using annual holding-period data from 1977 to 1985 for the three securities examined in the previous chapter.

Table 9-5 Annual Beta Analysis

Stock	$\bar{R}_i$	alpha	beta	t
APD	.0988	−.114	1.351	4.05
XON	.1756	−.015	.732	2.34
IBM	.1487	.009	.532	1.25

The use of annual data, which is not incorrect but not generally accepted in the financial community, might lead one to short Air Products (although the APD alpha is not statistically different from zero, $t = -.93$) and earn positive returns by purchasing IBM (although the IBM alpha only has a t-value of .06). The use of annual, rather than monthly, data to calculate betas gives results that are quite different; the IBM beta is not statistically different from zero (at the 10 percent level). One should generally use five years of monthly data for beta analysis [Fama (1976)].

Empirical Tests of the Single-Index Model

There have been many empirical tests of the single-index model; the reader is referred to Elton and Gruber (1987) for a complete summary of the literature. Sharpe and Cooper (1972) found a very consistently positive relationship between stock returns and betas, once the stocks are classed into deciles on the basis of the previous year's level of systematic risk. The higher beta stocks produced higher stock returns (and higher future realized betas). The majority of the recent statistical tests of the single-index model have formed portfolios (Black, Jensen, and Scholes 1972; and Fama and MacBeth 1973). The creation of portfolios has eliminated the problem of residual risk, heteroscedasticity, that Lintner

(1972) found in his initial Security Market Line estimation. Lintner examined annual data of 301 firms from 1954 to 1963 and, having estimated security betas using the market models, found that security returns were positively associated with beta and residual risk. The regression coefficient on the unsystematic risk variable should have been zero for the CAPM to be "proven"; the t-value on the unsystematic risk variable was 6.8, quite significant and almost equal to the t-value on the beta variable. Lintner found that the intercept, 0.108, exceeded the risk-free rate, and the slope, 0.063, was below the Ibbotson and Sinquefield (1982) market price of risk discussed in the previous chapter. Miller and Scholes (1972) reexamined Lintner's results and, having adjusted alpha for the changing risk-free rate, $\alpha_i = (1 - \beta_i)R_F$, found that measurement error probably created Lintner's finding of residual risk. That is, Miller and Scholes adjusted Lintner's intercept for the negative correlation between the market return and the risk-free rate (which biased the intercept upwards) but found no material change in Lintner's results. Miller and Scholes believed that errors in estimating the "true" betas caused the intercept and slope problems found by Lintner. If the true beta is positively associated with estimated residual risk, one would expect to find the positive relationship between return and unsystematic risk.

Black, Jensen, and Scholes (1972) formed portfolios and examined the excess return on portfolios relative to systematic risk. Black, Jensen, and Scholes (BJS) grouped stock into deciles on the basis of the previous year's systematic risk (to eliminate a possible beta bias). Five years of monthly data were used to estimate a beta, and portfolios were formed as betas were used to divide stocks into deciles in year six. BJS generated betas and returns for the grouped portfolios for 35 years. The BJS regression results of the CAPM tests found excess returns to be positively associated with betas; however, the alphas were ill-behaved as they were negative for high-beta ($\beta > 1$) portfolios and positive for low-beta ($\beta < 1$) portfolios. The two-factor model was supported by the BJS regression results, because in the zero-beta model (the two-factor model) the alpha should be equal to the difference between the zero-beta portfolio return and the risk-free rate.[1]

Fama and MacBeth (1973) formed 20 portfolios using the BJS methodology during the period 1935–68 and found no evidence of

---

[1]
$$R_{jt} = \bar{R}_Z(1 - \beta) + \beta R_{Mt}$$

$$R_{jt} = \alpha_j + R_F(1 - \beta_j) + \beta_j R_{Mt}$$

or

$$\alpha_j = (\bar{R}_Z - R_F)(1 - \beta_j)$$

residual risk, heteroscedasticity, or nonlinearity (the portfolio beta squared). Fama and MacBeth found additional support for the two-factor model because their intercept exceeded the risk-free rate and the slope, statistically significant from 1935 to 1968, was less than expected, given the market price of risk. A closer look at the Fama and MacBeth regression results indicates that the slope term is rather volatile in their Panel A, the simple beta regression. Moreover, the beta variable is not statistically significant in the period 1946–55 and is only marginally significant (at the 10 percent level, $t = 1.73$ and 1.96, respectively) during the periods 1935–45 and 1955–June 1968. In the complete model (their Panel D), the beta variable is statistically significant only during the overall period (at the 10 percent level, $t = 1.85$) and the period 1946–1955 ($t = 2.39$). The overwhelming evidence supporting the risk-return trade-off is not found.[2]

Linear Programming and the Single-Index Model

The excess return of a portfolio, the expected return less the risk-free rate, divided by beta, the Treynor index (which will be discussed in the following chapter) is useful in determining optimal security weighting (Elton, Gruber, and Padberg 1976, 1978, 1987). Securities are included in the portfolio as long as the Treynor index continues to rise. The cut-off point for security inclusion in the portfolio, C^*, is found by grouping stocks on the basis of highest to lowest Treynor indexes and calculating the C_i for a portfolio of the i stocks:

$$C_i = \frac{\sigma_M^2 \sum_{j=1}^{i} \frac{[E(R_j) - R_F]/\beta_j}{\sigma e_j^2}}{1 + \sigma_M^2 \sum_{j=1}^{i} \left(\frac{\beta_j^2}{\sigma e_j^2}\right)} \tag{10}$$

---

[2]The Fama and MacBeth findings on the risk-return tradeoff were examined by Schwert (1983) who found the results surprisingly weak. If one were to ignore the "January effect," in which January monthly returns are significantly higher than the other months, (particularly for smaller-capitalized stocks), one does not find a statistically significant regression coefficient on the beta variable in the Fama and MacBeth analysis [Tinic and West (1984)]. Recent factor analysis modeling of security returns have found up to five factors explain security price movements [Ross and Roll (1980) and McElroy and Burmeister (1988)]. The Arbitrage Pricing Theory (APT) uses factor analysis to model the determinants of returns. The factors, as reported in Berry, Burmeistes and McElroy (1988) are default risk, the term structure, unexpected inflation, unexpected change in growth rate in profits, and residual market risk. However, there is no evidence as to the *ex ante* superiority of the five factor model when compared to the single index model [Chen, Copeland and Mayers (1988) and Dhrymes, Friend, and Gultekin (1984)].

where

σe_j^2 = residual risk.

Securities are added to the portfolio as long as C_i rises. A decrease in C_i indicates that the last stock added to the portfolio should not be included in the optimal set. Optimal security weights are found by the following:

$$Z_i = \frac{\beta_i}{\sigma e_i^2} \left[\frac{E(R_i) - R_F}{\beta_i} \right] - C^*;$$

$$W_i = \frac{Z_i}{\sum_{j=1}^{N} Z_j} \qquad (11)$$

Thus the Elton, Gruber, and Padberg algorithm makes use of both systematic and unsystematic risk measures.

Summary and Conclusions

The single index model has been developed using the original formulations of Sharpe, Lintner, and Mossin. Empirical evidence supports the existence of a risk-return relationship although the estimated regression coefficients do not behave as one might have expected from theory. Optimal security weighting can be developed using the single index model.

Exhibit 9-4 Descriptive Statistics

VARIABLE	N	MEAN	STD DEV
IBM (price)	60	98.27516667	30.25032100
XON (prices)	60	38.08200000	8.56739677
APD (prices)	60	42.97316667	7.92323369
NYSE (index)	60	87.53883333	15.29816153
RETIBM	59	0.01650214	0.05506353
RETXON	59	0.00742066	0.05128008
RETAPD	59	0.00933064	0.07800369
RETNYSE	59	0.00916217	0.04012915

Source: SAS output

Exhibit 9-5

PEARSON CORRELATION COEFFICIENTS/PROB > |R| UNDER H0:RHO=0/NUMBER OF OBSERVATIONS

	IBM	XON	APD	NYSE	RETIBM	RETXON	RETAPD	RETNYSE
IBM (prices)	1.00000	0.77300	0.76291	0.93710	0.14003	0.31282	0.20192	0.19954
	0.0000	0.0001	0.0001	0.0001	0.2901	0.0159	0.1251	0.1297
	60	60	60	60	59	59	59	59
XON (prices)	0.77300	1.00000	0.86066	0.89415	-0.05447	0.21906	0.11177	0.09955
	0.0001	0.0000	0.0001	0.0001	0.6820	0.0955	0.3993	0.4532
	60	60	60	60	59	59	59	59
APD (prices)	0.76291	0.86066	1.00000	0.91144	-0.00957	0.15528	0.29233	0.17405
	0.0001	0.0001	0.0000	0.0001	0.9427	0.2402	0.0247	0.1874
	60	60	60	60	59	59	59	59
NYSE (index)	0.93710	0.89415	0.91144	1.00000	0.06222	0.28157	0.23497	0.21993
	0.0001	0.0001	0.0001	0.0000	0.6397	0.0307	0.0732	0.0942
	60	60	60	60	59	59	59	59

Source: SAS output

						RETIBM	REXTON	RETAPD	RETNYSE
RETIBM	0.14003	-0.05447	-0.00957	0.06222	1.00000	0.31835	0.24944	0.54896
	0.2901	0.6820	0.9427	0.6397	0.0000	0.0140	0.0568	0.0001
	59	59	59	59	59	59	59	59
REXTON	0.31282	0.21906	0.15528	0.28157	0.31835	1.00000	0.17300	0.52572
	0.0159	0.0955	0.2402	0.0307	0.0140	0.0000	0.1901	0.0001
	59	59	59	59	59	59	59	59
RETAPD	0.20192	0.11177	0.29233	0.23497	0.24944	0.17300	1.00000	0.66426
	0.1251	0.3993	0.0247	0.0732	0.0568	0.1901	0.0000	0.0001
	59	59	59	59	59	59	59	59
RETNYSE	0.19954	0.09955	0.17405	0.21993	0.54896	0.52572	0.66426	1.00000
	0.1297	0.4532	0.1874	0.0942	0.0001	0.0001	0.0001	0.0000
	59	59	59	59	59	59	59	59

Exhibit 9-6

Annual APD	Regression Output:
Constant	−0.11406
Std Err of Y Est.	0.124060
R Squared	0.701021
No. of Observations	9
Degrees of Freedom	7
X Coefficient(s)	1.350926
Std Err of Coef.	0.333454

Source: Lotus® Spreadsheet Regression Analysis

Exhibit 9-7

Annual IBM	Regression Output:
Constant	0.008643
Std Err of Y Est.	0.158637
R Squared	0.182205
No. of Observations	9
Degrees of Freedom	7
X Coefficient(s)	0.532497
Std Err of Coef.	0.426392

Source: Lotus® Spreadsheet Regression Analysis

Exhibit 9-8

Annual XON	Regression Output:
Constant	−0.01458
Std Err of Y Est.	0.116281
R Squared	0.439661
No. of Observations	9
Degrees of Freedom	7
X Coefficient(s)	0.732481
Std Err of Coef.	0.312545

Source: Lotus® Spreadsheet Regression Analysis

References

Berry, M.A., E. Burmeister, and M.B. McElroy. 1988. Sorting Our Risks Using Known APT Factors. *Financial Analysts Journal* 29–42.

Black, F., M.C. Jensen, and M. Scholes. 1972. The Capital Asset Pricing Model: Some Empirical Tests. In *Studies in the Theory of Capital Markets*, ed. M.C. Jensen. New York: Praeger Publishers.

Blume, M. 1971. On the Assessment of Risk. *Journal of Finance* 26: 1–10.

———. 1975. Betas and their Regression Tendencies. *Journal of Finance* 30: 785–795.

Breen, W., and E. Lerner. 1972. On the Use of β in Regulatory Proceedings. *The Bell Journal of Economics and Management Science* 3.

Brigham, E., and R. Crum. 1971. On the Use of the CAPM in Public Utility Rate Cases. *Financial Management*.

Carleton, W.T. 1979. A Note on the Use of the CAPM for Utility Rate of Return Determination. In *Portfolio Theory, 25 Years After*, ed. E.J. Elton and M.J. Gruber. Amsterdam: North-Holland.

Chen, N.-F., T.E. Copeland, and D. Mayers. 1988. A Comparison of Single and Multifactor Portfolio Performance Methodologies. In *Stock Market Anomalies*, ed. E. Dimson. Cambridge: Cambridge University Press.

Dhrymes, P.J., I. Friend, and N.B. Gultekin. 1984. A Critical Reexamination of the Empirical Evidence on the Arbitrage Pricing Theory. *Journal of Finance* 39: 323–344.

Elton, E.J., M.J. Gruber, and M.W. Padberg. 1976. Simple Criteria for Optimal Portfolio Selection. *Journal of Finance* 31: 1341–1357.

———. 1978. Simple Criteria for Optimal Portfolio Selection: Tracing Out the Efficient Frontier. *Journal of Finance* 33: 296–302.

Elton, E.J., and M.J. Gruber. 1987. *Modern Portfolio Theory and Investment Analysis*. 3d ed. New York: John Wiley & Sons.

Elton, E.J., M.J. Gruber, and T. Urich. 1978. Are Betas Best? *Journal of Finance* 33: 1375–1384.

Fama, E.F. 1976. *Foundations of Finance*. New York: Basic Books.

Fama, E.F., and J. MacBeth. 1973. Risk Return and Equilibrium: Empirical Tests. *Journal of Political Economy* 71: 607–636.

Klemkosky, R., and J. Martin. 1975. The Adjustment of Beta Forecasts. *Journal of Finance* 30: 1123–1128.

Lintner, J. 1965. The Valuation of Risk Assets in the Selection of Risky Investments in Stock Portfolios and Capital Budgets. *Review of Economics and Statistics* XLVII: 13–37.

McElroy, M.B. and E. Burmeister. 1988. Arbitrage Pricing Theory as Restricted Nonlinear Multiple Regression Model: I T NL SUR Estimates. *Journal of Business and Economic Statistics*, 29–42.

Miller, M.H., and M. Scholes. 1972. Rates of Return in Relation to Risk: A Re-examination of Some Recent Findings. In *Studies in the Theory of Capital Markets*, ed. M.C. Jensen. New York: Praeger Publishers.

Mossin, J. 1966. Equilibrium in a Capital Asset Market. *Econometrica* 34: 768–783.

_____. 1973. *Theory of Financial Markets*. Englewood Cliffs, N.J.: Prentice-Hall.

Myers, S. 1972. The Application of Finance Theory to Public Utility Rate Cases. *Bell Journal of Economics and Management Science* 3: 58–97.

Roll, R. and S. Ross. 1980. An Empirical Investigation of the Arbitrage Pricing Theory. *Journal of Finance* 35: 1073–1104.

Schwert, G.W. 1983. Size and Stock Returns and Other Empirical Regularities. *Journal of Financial Economics* 12: 3–12.

Sharpe, W.F. 1964. Capital Asset Prices: A Theory of Market Equilibrium Under Conditions of Risk. *Journal of Finance* 19: 425–442.

_____. 1963. A Simplified Model for Portfolio Analysis. *Management Science* 20: 277–293.

_____. 1985. Stock Market Indices. 1985. *Quantitative Analysis and Applications*. Kidder, Peabody, & Co.

Sharpe, W.F., and G.M. Cooper. 1972. Risk-Return Class of New York Stock Exchange Common Stocks, 1931–1967. *Financial Analysts Journal* 28: 46–52.

Tinic, S.M. and R.R. West. 1984. Risk and Return: January vs. The Rest of the Year. *Journal of Financial Economics* 13: 561–574.

Vasichek, O. 1973. A Note on Using Cross-Sectional Information in Bayesian Estimation of Security Betas. *Journal of Finance* 28: 1233–1239.

Weston, J.F., and T.E. Copeland. 1987. *Managerial Finance*, 8th ed. Chicago: CBS Publishing.

Appendix to Chapter 9

An Absolute Dollar CAPM

The vast majority of formulations and studies of the CAPM specify the relationship between risk and return in an expected return format. Mossin (1966, 1973) put forth a security market framework that addresses the market value of the firm rather than the required rate of return on the security. We will briefly review the Mossin framework and refer the reader to his seminal text, *Theory of Financial Markets*, for the complete analysis. An investor, i, allocates his wealth, W, among lending activities, m, and investments in corporate equities of security j, Z_j. The market value of equity and debt are given by p_j and d_j. The market value of the firm, v_j, is the sum of the market values of debt and equity,

$$W_i = M_i + \sum_{j=1}^{J} Z_{ij} P_j. \tag{1}$$

Stockholders earn the value of the cash flow X_j after debt principal and interest, rd_j, has been paid. The stockholder income of investor i is

$$Y_i = \gamma_{mi} + \sum_{j=1}^{J} (X_j - rd_j)$$

$$= \gamma W_i + \sum_{j=1}^{J} Z_{ij}(X_j - rd_j - rp_j).$$

The investor allocates investment funds so that the expected utility of an additional dollar of investment in shares is zero. If all firms' shares are owned by individuals, and investors' net lending equals the supply of corporate bonds, then the market is in equilibrium when the sum of investors' wealth equals the total value of firms:

$$\sum_{i=1}^{M} Z_{ij} = 1$$

$$\sum_{i=1}^{M} M_i = \sum_{j=1}^{J} d_j$$

$$\sum_{i=1}^{M} M_i = \sum_{j=1}^{M} \sum_{i=1}^{J} Z_{ij} P_j = \sum_{j=1}^{J} v_j.$$

If investors have quadratic utility functions

$$U_i(Y_i) = Y_i - C_i Y_i^2, \tag{3}$$

then the investors' demand for shares can be written

$$U = E[U(Y)] = \sum_X U[rW + Z(X - p)]f(x) \tag{4}$$

$$E[U'(Y)(X - \gamma_p)] = 0$$

$$E[(1 - 2cY)(X - \gamma_p)] = 0 \tag{5}$$

$$Z = \frac{\mu - r_p}{\sigma^2 + (\mu - r_p)^2} (1 - rW)$$

where

$$\mu = E(X).$$

The market clearing conditions produce an equilibrium in which the investor holds the same percentage of the outstanding stock of all companies, or the balanced portfolio.

$$Z_j^* = \frac{1}{\sum_{i=1}^{M} \frac{1}{Zc_i} - r \sum_{i=1}^{M} W_i} \tag{6}$$

For firm k,

$$\left[\sum_k \sigma_j k + (\mu_j - v_j)(\mu_k - r_{pk})\right] = (\mu_j - rv_j)\left(\sum_i \frac{1}{Zc_i} - r \sum_i W_i\right)$$

$$\sum_k \sigma_i k - (\mu_i - rv_i)\left(\sum_i \left(\frac{1}{Zc_i}\right) - r\sum_i W_i\right) = 0$$

The solution for the value of the firm, v_i, is

$$v_i = \frac{1}{r}\left(\mu_i - \frac{\sum_k \sigma_i k}{\sum_{i=1}^{M} \frac{1}{2c_i} - \sum_k \mu k}\right) \tag{7}$$

or

$$v_i = \frac{1}{r}(\mu_i - Rb_i) \tag{8}$$

where

$$b_i = \sum_k \sigma_i k = \text{Systematic risk,}$$

and

$$R = \frac{1}{\sum_i \left(\frac{1}{2c_i}\right) - \sum_k \mu k} = \text{Market price of risk.}$$

One can use the absolute value CAPM for capital budgeting where one accepts a project, Z, if and only if the change in the market value of equity, $P'_i - P_i$, exceeds the cost of the investment, I:

$$P'_i = P_i + \frac{1}{r}(\mu_z - Rb_z)$$

$$I = (n'_i - n_i)p'_i$$

where $n'_i - n_i$ is the number of new shares.

$$\Delta P_i = \frac{\frac{1}{r}(\mu_z - Rb_z) - I}{n_i}$$

or

$$\frac{1}{r}(\mu_z - Rb_z) > I. \tag{9}$$

Chapter 10

Bond Portfolio Models

The purpose of this chapter is to examine the determinants of bond prices and yields. Particular emphasis is given to default risk, the econometric determination of the debt default premium, and the announcement of changes in bond ratings. Corporate financial officers are greatly concerned with their debt ratings because of the associated costs of borrowing.

In bond pricing, one must be concerned with changing coupon rates and time to maturity. One can manage bond portfolios by analyzing bond price volatilities or elasticities. Bond management is often concerned with the duration of a debt instrument, which is closely related to the bond's elasticity. Corporate financial officers seek to obtain debt financing at the lowest possible cost and attempt to "time" debt issues so that long-term debt issues can "lock in" the lowest rate possible over the relevant time period (up to thirty years). The term structure of interest rates presents several hypotheses concerning the relationships among interest rates over time.

Evidence is presented to support the concept that effective portfolio management should use both debt and equities.

An appendix is included on bond management and duration using Lotus 1-2-3.

The empirical survey of Ibbotson and Sinquefield (1982) might lead an investor to question the appropriateness of ever considering the purchase of bonds or other fixed-income securities. Stocks, as measured by the S&P 500, achieved an arithmetic mean return of 11.4 percent during the period 1926–1981, whereas long-term government bonds, as recorded at the Center for Research in Security Prices (CRSP), appreciated only 3.1 percent. The long-term government bond yields were equal to those of U.S. Treasury Bills, although the standard deviation of long-term bond returns almost doubled that of the Treasury Bills. Moreover, negative returns were quite possible with long-term government bonds, a condition not found by Ibbotson and Sinquefield data for Treasury Bills. The risk premium on long-term corporate bonds (relative

237

to Treasury Bill yields) was 0.6 percent for the period 1926–1981, and the corporate bonds were as risky (in terms of the standard deviations) as long-term government bonds. Ibbotson and Sinquefield noted that the inflation-adjusted long-term bond return was approximately zero during the period 1926–1981, although long-term government bonds achieved a 7.7 percent return between 1932 and 1936, when prices rose very little or even fell (as in 1982). Thus, one might be interested in a bond portfolio or in dividing one's portfolio between stocks and bonds when prices are falling or very slowly increasing. Corporate bond yields were closely comparable to those of long-term government bonds between 1926 and 1981. A reduction in inflation aids fixed-income security managers.

Fogler and Groves (1977) addressed some of the points made by Ibbotson and Sinquefield in a study on managed bond portfolios during the period 1900–1968 and found that although the all-bond portfolio achieved a geometric return of only 3.32 percent and the all-stock (S&P Industrials) portfolio achieved a return of 10.04 percent, nonlinearity in the data led to a condition in which the bond-to-stock ratio of 50:50 produced a portfolio return of 7.26 percent.[1] The nonlinearity resulted from portfolio rebalancing to return to the original percentage strategy, sometimes forcing the sale of stock securities following very bullish years. Thus, Fogler and Groves noted that the incremental returns from increasing the equity percentage of one's portfolio are not as dramatic as one might expect from Ibbotson and Sinquefield's analysis. For example, the overall portfolio return rises from 3.32 percent to 5.42 percent when the portfolio goes from all-debt to a bond-to-stock ratio of 75:25. The corresponding increase is only from 8.81 percent to 10.04 percent when the portfolio manager increases the portfolio mix from 25:75 to an all-equity portfolio. An almost linear risk-return trade-off existed for the debt/equity mix decision in the Fogler and Groves analysis. Risk could be reduced without disabling portfolio performance by including debt in one's portfolio. If one seeks to develop a five-year portfolio (its planning horizon), Fogler and Groves (1977) advocated a 25 to 50 percent debt component in the portfolio.[2]

Bond Default Risk

Default risk can be measured by several methods in bond analysis; we will rely upon the Ibbotson and Sinquefield (1982) definitions, in which

---

[1]Fogler and Groves cite Wilbur (1967) for some of the geometric return bond data. The geometric return is widely used in finance, particularly by Henry Latané and his collaborators (Latane, Tuttle, and Jones 1967).
[2]The debt/equity mix of 50:50 was preferred for a 10-year holding period.

the default premium is found by subtracting the long-term government bond yield from the long-term corporate bond yield, holding time to maturity constant. A bond maturity premium is the difference between the long-term government bond yield and the U.S. Treasury Bill yield. The default premium for the period 1926–1978 was 0.50 percent (the arithmetic mean), whereas the corresponding maturity premium was 0.20 percent. Default premiums and bond maturity premiums tend to follow near random walks (in levels), although the default premiums were relatively high in the early 1930s (with the exception of 1932), the late 1950s, early 1960s, 1967, and 1974–1975. These years of large default premiums should surprise few people (being recessionary and depressionary eras). The maturity premiums on long-term government bonds were extraordinarily high in 1932 and 1934 (15.74 percent and 9.85 percent, respectively), 1940, 1949, 1954, 1959, and 1976. The maturity premiums became strongly negative in the early 1960s, late 1970s, and early 1980s. The negative bond maturity premiums can be extremely troublesome in applying the Capital Asset Pricing Model if one uses only 5- or 10-year market risk premiums, which became negative in the later 1970s.

The classical study of risk premiums on corporate bonds was developed by Fisher (1959), who investigated the yields on corporate debt for the years 1927, 1932, 1937, 1949, and 1953. Fisher examined 366 firms in these years, and the logarithm of the firm's average risk premium (the bond's yield to maturity less the riskless bond's corresponding yield to maturity) was hypothesized to be a function of earnings variability, the equity-to-debt ratio, period of solvency, and amount of debt outstanding. Fisher performed an ordinary least squares regression analysis of the overall (and individual years') data and found the following regression line:

$$x_0 = .987 + .307x_1 - .253x_2 - .537x_3 - .275x_4,$$
$$(t) \qquad (9.59) \quad (-7.03) \quad (-17.32) \quad (-13.10)$$

where

x_0 = debt default premium;

x_1 = earnings variability, the coefficient of variation in net income, for nine years;

x_2 = periods of solvency;

x_3 = market value of equity divided by long-term debt;

x_4 = market value of traded debt outstanding (marketability).

Fisher's overall regression results were very stable, and little variation was found in the individual annual regressions. The variable coefficients were highly significant and had the expected signs: increasing the outstanding debt and the equity-to-debt ratio increased default risk. Increasing earnings variability and decreasing the period of solvency tends to increase default risk and its premium.

When one speaks of default risk in modern finance, one ordinarily refers to a firm's bond rating. Bond ratings are produced by Moody's and Standard & Poor's (S&P). The S&P rating scheme is:

Rating	Quality
AAA	Highest quality
AA	High quality
A	Upper medium grade
BBB	Medium grade
BB	Somewhat speculative
B	Speculative
CCC-CC	Possible default
C	Default
DDD-D	Little possible recovery

Weinstein (1977) examined the effect of bond rating changes on bond prices during the period July 1962 to July 1974 and found small, statistically significant (at the 10 percent level) price changes in the month preceding the announcement of the rating change. Bond prices (relative to a diversified bond portfolio) fell when the rating decreased and vice versa, as one would have expected. The market is relatively efficient with respect to bond rating changes. One cannot significantly profit by buying a bond simply because of the public announcement that its rating has been increased, nor can one profit by shorting debt for a ratings decrease. The majority of the abnormal returns occurred between 19 and 7 months prior to the announcement (the 1.204 cumulative abnormal return has a t-value of only 1.41, hardly statistically significant).

Bond Pricing and Managing a Bond Portfolio

As a manager of fixed-income securities, such as bonds, one can change the riskiness of the fund by altering the quality rating of the debt, the maturity of the debt, or the coupon of the debt instruments. The purpose of this section is to address the well-known bond pricing theorems presented by Malkiel (1962) and discuss their implications for portfolio managers. Let us assume that we are interested in pricing 10-year annual bonds with coupons of 7 percent, 8 percent, and 9 percent.[3] The (initial) current interest rate is 8 percent and is expected to rise or fall by only one point in the coming year. Clearly, if interest rates fall, the present value of the bond interest payments and principal will rise, and the bond manager would earn a higher return than if interest rates were to be constant or rise. On the other hand, a rise in interest rates would reduce the present value of the interest stream and principal and reduce the value of the bond portfolio. If 10-year annual bonds are priced (to the nearest dollar) at market yields of 7 percent, 8 percent, and 9 percent, we have a 3 × 3 bond matrix:

10-Year Annual Bond Prices Market Yields (%)

		7	8	9
Bond coupons	7%	$1,000	$ 933	$ 871
	8%	1,070	1,000	935
	9%	1,140	1,067	1,000

If interest rates fall from 8 to 7 percent, the 7 percent coupon bond rises $67 in price, the 8 percent coupon bond rises $70, and the 9 percent coupon bond rises $63 in price. Note that the percentage (relative to the initial bond price) increases are 7.18, 7.00, and 6.84 percent for the 7, 8, and 9 percent coupon bonds, respectively. If interest rates are expected to fall and bond prices rise, one would prefer to invest in the lowest possible coupon bonds. If the interest rate rose to 9 percent and bond prices fell, the percentage declines would be 6.66, 6.50, and 6.28 for the 7, 8, and 9 percent coupon bonds, respectively. The lowest bond price decline is experienced by the highest coupon bond, while the lowest coupon bond is the most volatile. One notes that when interest rates fall the bond appreciation percentages exceed the bond price depreciation percentages when interest rates rise. Malkiel (1962) derived the mathematics behind the coupon/bond strategies, and the portfolio implications are well known. If interest rates are expected to rise, one shifts the fixed income portfolio to high coupon issues and, if interest rates are expected to fall, to low coupon issues. Furthermore, if the bonds were consol in nature, paying interest indefinitely with the return of principal, the bond price would be more volatile than those of 10-year annual bonds. In terms of the initial 8 percent interest rate, an 8 percent consol would sell at its par value. If the interest rate fell to 7 percent the bond would sell for $1,143, whereas an interest rate increase to 9 percent would cause the price to

---

[3]The vast majority of government and corporate bonds pay interest semiannually but we use annual bonds to simplify the bond theorems.

fall to $889.[4] Thus, if interest rates are expected to fall, a bond portfolio manager seeks to shrink the coupons and lengthen maturities. A bond portfolio manager expecting an interest rate increase will shorten maturities and purchase high coupon bonds.

We may now summarize Malkiel's bond theorems that were used in the previous examples of bond pricing:

1. Bond prices and yields are inversely associated.
2. Bond prices become more volatile as the time to maturity increases.
3. The bond price appreciation when interest rates fall exceeds the bond price depreciation when interest rates rise (holding constant the change in interest rates).
4. Bond price volatilities increase as the bond coupon decreases.

In discussing bond price volatilities, one does not normally use terms such as volatilities based on percentage changes, but one normally speaks of elasticities. The 3 × 3 bond price matrix and the percentage changes can easily be discussed in terms of the elasticity, ELAS:

$$\text{ELAS} = - \frac{(p_1 - p_0)/p_0}{(r_1 - r_0)/r_0} \tag{1}$$

where

p_0 = initial bond price;
p_1 = new bond price;
r_0 = initial market yield;
r_1 = new market yield.

Because the 3 × 3 matrix was created by changing the interest rate by one percentage point in either direction, the bond price volatilities (in terms of percentage price changes and elasticities) are proportional. The bond price elasticities, when the interest rate falls from 8 to 7 percent, are −57.44, −56.00, and −54.72 percent for the 7, 8, and 9 percent coupon bonds, respectively. The bond price elasticities, when interst rates rise to 9 percent from 8 percent, are −53.28, −52.00, and −50.24 percent for the 7, 8, and 9 percent coupon bonds, respectively. The lowest coupon

---

[4]The price of a consol bond is calculated by dividing the annual interest payment by the market yield.

bonds have the highest price volatilities and elasticities.[5] If one wishes to discuss bond management in terms of duration (see the appendix for a more detailed presentation of duration), one may calculate the duration of the bonds in the 3×3 matrix:

$$-\text{ELAS} = \text{duration}\left(\frac{r_0}{1 + r_0}\right) \tag{2}$$

$$-\text{ELAS}/\left(\frac{r_0}{1 + r_0}\right) = \text{duration}$$

The durations of the 7, 8, and 9 percent coupon bonds when interest rates fall from 8 percent to 7 percent are 7.75, 7.56, and 7.39 years, respectively. The corresponding durations when interest rates rise to 9 percent are 7.19, 7.02, and 6.78 years, respectively. One may speak either of price yield volatilities, elasticities, or durations when using equal changes in interest rates. The use of duration has one very large advantage: elimination of the risk due to changing interest rates, known as the immunization of the bond portfolio, may be achieved by selecting a zero-coupon bond with a life equal to the desired bond return (Farrell 1983). That is, to earn a 10 percent return over a three-year period, the bond portfolio manager may purchase a three-year zero-coupon bond with a 10 percent yield or a 10 percent bond with a three-year duration.

In a passive bond portfolio strategy, the manager can use duration to immunize the portfolio. In an active bond strategy, the manager may attempt to forecast interest rates and possible structures of yield curves.

The Term Structure of Interest Rates

When one speaks of the structure of interest rates, one normally talks about the yield curve, which shows the relationship between yield to maturity and time to maturity for a given issue of debt. Because one holds constant the risk of the issuer, one may choose to examine the shape of the yield curve by noting the yields of U.S. government securities, shown daily in *The Wall Street Journal*. On September 24, 1987, *The Wall Street Journal* published the following abbreviated term structure:

---

[5]Bond elasticity concept was formerly referred to as the yield elasticity; see Latané, Tuttle, and Jones (1967) *op. cit.*, for a discussion of the concept. Elasticities are now used and are easily converted into duration, the current term used in bond management. The duration is proportional to the bond price volatility and elasticity because we have held interest rates constant.

Maturity Date	Yield to Maturity
September 1988	7.84%
October 1992	8.97
August 1997	9.37

Such a term structure of interest rates is upward sloping; that is, interest rates are expected to rise. If interest rates are expected to rise, corporations will find it advantageous to issue long-term debt to "lock in" the lower current interest rate, driving down long-term bond prices and increasing long-term debt yields. Investors will prefer short-term bonds so that their funds will be available for reinvestment at the higher future interst rates, driving up short-term bond prices and decreasing short-term bond yields. The term structure thus is dependent upon expectations of future interest rates, sloping upward when interst rates are expected to rise, being flat when interest rates are not expected to change, and sloping downward when interest rates are expected to fall. This theory of interest rates and expectations is known as the expectations theory of the term structure of interest rates.

An interesting case of this theory is the unbiased expectations theory of interest rates, which holds that long-run interest rates are geometrically related to current (spot) interest rates and future (forward) interest rates. Let us return to the term structure of interest rates as of September 24, 1987. In deciding between the purchase of a 10-year versus a five-year bond, an investor must be able to make an educated guess at the five-year loan rate that will prevail five years from now. The investor purchasing the 10-year bond, yielding $_tR_{10}$ (or 9.37% in the example), earns the following during the bond's life:

$$(1 + {_tR_{10}})^{10}.$$

The investor purchasing the five-year bond earns $_tR_5$ annually for five years; however, the choice between the two bonds ultimately comes down to the reinvestment rate five years from now. The interesting aspect of this problem is that the five-year future interest rate will not be known, of course, for five years. The investor purchases the (current) 10-year bond if the implied loan rate of the 10-year bond exceeds the five-year bond and the five-year loan rate five years from now, $_{t+5}r_5$.

$$(1 + {_tR_{10}})^{10} = (1 + {_tR_5})^5(1 + {_{t+5}r_5})^5 \qquad (3)$$

$$(1 + {_tR_{10}})^{10} = (1 + {_{t+5}r_5})^5 \qquad (4)$$

$$\sqrt[5]{\frac{(1 + {_tR_{10}})^{10}}{(1 + {_tR_5})^5}} - 1 = {_{t+5}r_5} \qquad (5)$$

In terms of our numerical example:

$$_{t+5}r_5 = \sqrt[5]{\frac{(1.0937)^{10}}{(1.0897)^5}} - 1 = 0.0977$$

An investor is indifferent between purchasing a 10-year (spot) bond yielding 9.37 percent and a five-year (spot) bond yielding 8.97 percent and a five-year bond five years from now yielding 9.77 percent. If the expected five-year bond (loan) rate five years from now is only 9.50 percent, the implied loan rate in the 10-year bond is greater than that in the current five-year bond and the expected reinvestment opportunity, and the investor should purchase the 10-year bond. If the expected five-year loan rate five years from now is 9.85 percent, then the five-year bond is the better investment. One may calculate any number of investment alternatives in the yield curve relationships. An investor is indifferent between the purchase of the current (spot) 10-year bond yielding 9.37 percent and the one-year bond, yielding 7.84 percent, if one can purchase a nine-year bond one year from now yielding 9.53 percent:

$$\sqrt[9]{\frac{(1.0937)^{10}}{1.0784}} - 1 = 0.0953.$$

The generalized expression for indifference between the purchase of a short-term (p-year) bond versus a long-term l-year bond is

$$_{l-p}\sqrt{\frac{(1 + {}_tR_l)^l}{(1 + {}_tR_p)^p}} - 1 = {}_{t+l-p}r^{l-p}. \tag{6}$$

One may be able to make an educated guess as to whether one should purchase a one- or two-year bond versus a five- or 10-year bond, but an investor would probably be hard-pressed to forecast the 20-year loan rate 10 years from now inherent in the decision to buy a 10- or a 30-year bond.

In the unbiased expectations theory (and the expectations theory), no premium is attached to the purchase of a longer term debt instrument. The interest yields are geometrically determined and one does not earn a higher return from a 30-year bond than from a 10-year bond. This may not make sense to many readers. One generally associates greater risk with returns occurring in the distant future and might expect a risk premium or liquidity premium to be applicable to long-term issues. The liquidity preference theory of the term structure of interest rates, put forth by John Maynard Keynes (1936) and Sir John Hicks (1965), holds that a risk premium, proportional to the time of maturity, should exist in

interest rates.[6] The liquidity preference theory does not seem unreasonable: Who would have expected that the 30-year New York City bond
purchased in 1950 would be so risky in 1976? Certainly returns become
more variable over time, but there is little evidence supporting a consistent liquidity premium in interest rates.

A third theory of the term structure of interest rates is known as
market segmentation, which holds that various financial intermediaries
operate with different time preferences and that interest rates are influenced by the respective supply and demand of funds (Ritter and Silber
1977). Commercial banks, with many short-lived liabilities (deposits), try
to match asset and liability lives and prefer to invest in short-term assets.
The short-term assets tend to earn less than the longer-lived assets, tend-
ing to create an earnings dilemma for many banks (Ritter and Silber
1977). Savings and loan associations, with longer term, less liquid
liabilities, are able to lengthen asset lives, such as mortgages, and be more
profitable. Life insurance companies, with well-behaved, long-term
liabilities are free to invest in very long-lived assets; insurance companies tend to be heavily invested in long-term corporate bonds.

Summary and Conclusions

The bond manager faces a risk-return relationship different from that
confronting the equity manager, the "stock picker." The bond manager
generally encounters less risk than the equity manager, earning a lower
return, but may pursue an active bond strategy of forecasting interest
rates (and the term structure) to enhance return. A passive bond manager
may immunize the portfolio by using duration.

References

Cornell, B. 1977. Spot Rates, Forward Rates, and Exchange Market Efficiency. *Journal of Financial Economics* 5: 55–65.

---

[6]Lord Keynes did not support the risk-premium notion in foreign exchange.
Keynes (1924) developed the interest rate parity theory (IRPT), in which the forward discount on foreign exchange is equal to the difference between the two interest rates. The IRPT holds that there is no risk premium in the foreign exchange market, a hypothesis well supported by the empirical evidence (Granger
1975; Cornell 1977). Keynes (1924) believed that a risk premium should exist in
the commodity markets and this idea became known as the theory of normal
backwardation. The bulk of the empirical evidence supports the absence of a risk
premium in commodity markets (Telser 1958; Dusak 1973). The absence of a
risk premium in commodity markets is the basis of the expectations theory,
which holds that the current (spot) futures price of a commodity is the spot price
that is expected to prevail in the future.

Dusak, K. 1973. Futures Trading and Investor Returns: An Investigation of Commodity Market Risk Premiums. *Journal of Political Economy* 81: 1387–1406.

Farrell, J.L. 1983. *Guide to Portfolio Management*. New York: McGraw-Hill.

Fisher, L. 1959. Determinants of Risk Premiums on Corporate Bonds. *Journal of Political Economy* 67: 217–237.

Fogler, H.R., and W.A. Groves. 1977. How Much Can Active Bond Management Raise Returns? In *Portfolio Management and Efficient Markets: Theoretical Relevance and Practical Applications*, ed. P.L. Bernstein. New York: Institutional Investor Books.

Francis, J.C. 1979. *Investments*. New York: McGraw-Hill.

Granger, C.W.J. 1975. A Survey of Empirical Studies on Capital Markets. In *International Capital Markets*, ed. E.J. Elton and M.J. Gruber. Amsterdam: North-Holland.

Hicks, J.R. 1965. *Value and Capital*. 2d ed. New York: Oxford University Press.

Ibbotson, R.G., and R.A. Sinquefield. 1982. *Stocks, Bonds, Bills, and Inflation: The Past and the Future*. Charlottesville, Va.: Financial Analysts Research Foundation.

Keynes, J.M. 1924. *A Treatise on Money*. London: Macmillan.

Latané, H. 1959. Criteria for Choice Among Risky Ventures. *Journal of Political Economy* 67: 144–155.

Latané, H., D.L. Tuttle, and C.P. Jones. 1975. *Security Analysis and Portfolio Management*. New York: Ronald Press.

Malkiel, B. 1962. Expectations, Bond Prices, and the Term Structure of Interest Rates. *Quarterly Journal of Economics* 76: 197–218.

Pinches, G.E., and K.A. Mingo. 1973. A Multivariate Analysis of Industrial Bond Ratings. *Journal of Finance* 28: 1–18.

Ritter, L.S., and W.L. Silber. 1977. *Principles of Money, Banking, and Financial Markets*. 2d ed. New York: Basic Books.

Telser, L.G. 1958. Futures Trading and the Storage of Cotton and Wheat. *Journal of Political Economy* 66: 233–255.

Weinstein, M.I. 1977. The Effect of a Rating Change Announcement on Bond Prices. *Journal of Financial Economics* 5: 329–350.

Wilbur, L.W. 1967. A Theoretical and Empirical Investigation of Holding Period Yields on High Grade Corporate Bonds. Ph.D. diss., University of North Carolina at Chapel Hill.

Cash Management and Riding the Yield Curve

Cash managers in the last few years have been under increasing pressure to squeeze every possible cent and basis point out of their positions, and to minimize the amount of cash held in their portfolios. These twin considerations have led managers to widen the variety of instruments and techniques used in their jobs. We will examine one particular technique, the yield curve ride, that can satisfy both considerations above. The idea behind riding the yield curve is to let the arithmetic of interest rates, especially those on discount securities, do the work for you.

The typical yield curve is upward-sloping, especially in periods of low or moderately rising interest rates. Thus, as time to maturity increases, so does yield to maturity. In periods of low interest rates, the cash manager has a thankless, indeed almost impossible task: get the best possible yield, but without sacrificing liquidity. No doubt more than one cash manager has asked why the powers that be don't make the same demands when rates are high.

The traditional solution to this problem is to match short-term investments with the time horizon. For instance, buy 90-day Treasury Bills and hold them to maturity. While this strategy eliminates price risk and reinvestment risk over the investment horizon, it neither necessarily minimizes the amount of cash invested nor does it necessarily maximize expected yield.

An alternative solution is to invest for a longer period than the investment horizon, and then sell at the end of the horizon. For instance, the cash manager could buy 180-day Treasury Bills and sell them after 90 days, thus "riding the yield curve" downward. There are, however, some conditions that must be met. First, the yield curve must be upward-sloping. A quick check with numbers for a downward sloping yield curve should be enough to demonstrate that yield curve rides under these circumstances don't work. Second, the yield curve can't rise too much during the course of the investment period. Just how much is "too much" will be discussed below.

Mathematics of Yield Curve Rides

The formulas for discount securities are well known (for instance see Stigum (1981)). Given the discount rate R_d and the face value FV of a discount security maturing after N days, we can find the price P, the dollar discount D, and yield to maturity Y from the following equations:

$$D = FV \times R_d \times N/360 \qquad (1)$$

$$P = FV - D \qquad (2)$$

$$Y = (D/P) \times (365/N) \qquad (3)$$

$$Y = 365 \times R_d/[360 - (R_d \times N)]. \qquad (4)$$

In order to execute a yield curve ride strategy, one must first choose the investment horizon, N. This identifies the instrument that will be used for the buy-and-hold strategy. The second step is to calculate the discount, price, and yield to maturity for the buy-and-hold bill. The third step is to identify possible yield curve ride candidates. At any given time, there are likely to be several choices for riding with time to maturity M_1. The best choice can be found analytically with a personal computer. Graphically the optimal candidate will be at the "shoulder" of the yield curve, the point at which the yield curve flattens out.

Step four is to select the candidate for the ride with maturity M_1 and calculate its purchase price and discount. Step five is to calculate the expected sale price and discount for the ride candidate N days hence. For this one needs the discount rate expected to prevail at that time on the instrument that has $M_1 - N$ days to maturity. For example, if the horizon is 90 days and the 150-day bill is under consideration, the relevant discount rate is the one on a 60-day bill 90 days hence. For the initial analysis, one typically uses the current rate on the bill to calculate the expected price at sale.

Step six is to find the expected dollar profit and yield to maturity of the ride. The dollar profit is simply the difference between the expected sale price (P_S) and purchase price (P_P), while the yield to maturity is given by

$$Y = [(P_S - P_P)/P_P] \times (365/N). \qquad (5)$$

The process can be repeated as often as necessary to find the candidate that maximizes either dollar profit or yield.

This handles the return aspects of a yield curve ride but does not address the risk involved. A simple operational way to look at the risk is to calculate the break-even yield of a ride. The break-even yield is that discount rate at which the ride bill is sold off such that the ride earns exactly the same dollar profit or the same yield to maturity as the buy-and-hold strategy. By calculating the break-even yields, a cash manager can assign a probability that those yields, or higher, will occur. The dollar break-even yield is given by

$$Y_{\$BE} = \$PROF/(.0001 \times M2 \times FV/360) + R_{M2} \qquad (6)$$

where

$\quad Y_{\$BE}$ = break-even yield based on dollars;

$\quad \$PROF$ = expected excess dollar profit from yield curve ride;

$\quad M2$ = number of days left to maturity on the bill at the time of sale;

$\quad R_{M2}$ = current discount rate for the bill of maturity $M2$ days at which the ride is expected to be sold N days hence.

The denominator of the first term on the right-hand side is simply the value of one basis point for $M2$ days. This is added to the original discount rate for the time to maturity at which the bill was originally assumed to be sold to arrive at the break-even yield. This is the rate to which the discount rate—at the time of the sale of the security—can rise so that the buy-and-hold strategy and the yield curve ride strategy will generate the same number of dollars.

The break-even yield in yield to maturity terms is expressed by a longer formula but the idea is just as straightforward. The problem here is to find that discount rate at which the yield curve ride bill would be sold such that the yield to maturity of the yield curve ride equals that of the buy-and-hold strategy. The first step here, therefore, is to use either Equation (3) or (4) above to find the yield to maturity of the buy-and-hold bill. Next, we use the formula for the yield to maturity on a bill sold before maturity (see the instance Stigum [1981], p. 53) and solve for the discount rate at sale:

$$R_{M2} = (360/M2) \times [1 - (1 + \{N \times Y/365\})(1 - \{R_{M1} \times M1/360\})]$$

$$(7)$$

where

R_{M2} = Discount rate on bill of maturity M2 at which yield curve ride bill is sold in order to break even with buy-and-hold bill;

Y = Yield to maturity of the buy-and-hold bill;

R_{M1} = Discount rate at purchase of yield curve ride bill;

N = Investment horizon (days).

An Example

Let us look now at a simplified example. Suppose a company wishes to invest for 90 days, and that the current discount rates on Treasury Bills are as follows:

Time to Maturity (days)	Discount Rate (%)
30	5.00
60	5.25
90	5.50
120	5.75
150	6.00
180	6.25

The 90-day bill is the buy-and-hold bill. Its dollar discount, price, and yield to maturity are (assuming $1 million face amount)

$$D = .055 \times \$1,000,000 \times 90/360 = \$13,750$$

$$P = \$1,000,000 - \$13,750 = \$986,250$$

$$Y = (\$13,750/\$986,250) \times (365/90) = 5.65\%.$$

Suppose the 120-day bill is examined as a potential candidate for the yield curve ride. First we calculate the dollar discount and price at purchase:

$$D = .0575 \times \$1,000,000 \times 120/360 = \$19,167$$

$$P = \$1,000,000 - \$19,167 = \$980,833.$$

Next, we calculate the dollar discount and price at sale 90 days hence, when the bill will have 30 days to maturity, on the assumption that interest rates haven't changed:

$$D = .0525 \times \$1,000,000 \times 30/360 = \$4,375$$

$$P = \$1,000,000 - \$4,375 = \$995,625.$$

The dollar profit of the ride is the difference between the sale and purchase prices:

$$\$PROF = \$995,625 - \$980,833 = \$14,792.$$

The yield curve ride with a 120-day bill therefore yields an additional $1,042 ($14,792 − $13,750) over the buy-and-hold strategy. The yield to maturity of the ride is

$$Y = \$14,792/\$980,833 \times 365/90 = 6.12\%.$$

The dollar break-even yield is

$$Y_{\cdot BE} = \$1,042/(.0001 \times 30 \times \$1,000,000/360) + .0525 = 125\text{bp}$$

$$+ 5.25\% = 6.50\%$$

The yield break-even point is

$$Y_{YTM} = (360/30) \times \{1 - [1 + (.0565 \times 90/360)] \times [1 - .0575$$

$$\times (120/360)]\}$$

$$= 6.60\%.$$

Thus the 30-day T-Bill rate could rise to 6.60 percent and the company would earn the same yield to maturity on the yield curve ride as with the buy-and-hold position. The 30-day T-Bill rate would therefore have to rise 135 basis points from its current level of 5.25% over the next 90 days before the yield curve ride would break even with the buy-and-hold position. The cash manager can now assign some probability to the occurrence of that event or worse, and decide whether that risk is acceptable. In general, the steeper the yield curve, the higher the break-even yields will be, and therefore the more attractive yield curve rides will appear. To the extent that the yield curve contains expectations about future interest rates, however, the steeper the yield curve, the greater the likelihood that rates will rise.

The above discussion seems to suggest that yield curve rides are in general preferable to buy-and-hold strategies. How profitable are yield curve rides, really? Suppose a cash manager had decided on Monday, October 8, 1979, to engage in a policy of buying 26-week Treasury Bills at auction, selling them after 13 weeks, and then buying the new 26-week Bills. By October 1986 he would have earned 66.7 basis points annually in excess of the return from buying and holding the 13-week Bills. Similar results are obtained for any of the 13 possible separate rides starting on the same date. However, there are a couple of points to make concerning these excess yields. First, the cash manager would have to have had a very strong stomach for at least the first year as interest rates gyrated. Indeed, all but one of the yield curve rides would have lost relative to a 13-week buy-and-hold strategy over that first year. Second, the ride strategies had a standard deviation about double that of the buy-and-hold strategies over the time period in question.

These results confirm those of Osteryoung, McCarty, and Roberts (1981), who found that yield curve rides can achieve superior returns, but that rides may not be risk-efficient in the sense of compensating the manager for the duration or maturity mismatch. Thus the manager must evaluate both risk and return in order to determine the advisability of a yield curve ride strategy.

Another potential problem with yield curve rides is accounting procedure, as noted by Stigum. It is perfectly possible for a yield curve ride to generate real dollars but be booked at a loss. Let us use the example above to illustrate this. The 120-day Bill is bought at a price of $980,833. Suppose that when it is sold the rate on the 30-day Bill has risen to the dollar break-even rate of 6.50 percent. The bill is sold at a price of $994,583, so the ride earned $13,750. However, for accounting purposes, the book value of the Bill at the time of sale is purchase price plus accrued interest, or $995,208. This leads to a book loss of $625. The cash manager must determine whether or not he wants to try to justify that loss.

Yield rides need not be limited to discount securities or to short-term securities. Rides can be executed with certificates of deposit (CDs), Eurodollars (E$), and longer term notes and bonds. The formulas given above must be modified, however, for securities quoted on an interest-bearing basis. Again the reader is referred to Stigum.

For interest-bearing securities the use of duration is preferable to maturity. With Treasury Bills, maturity and duration are identical because all cash flows occur at maturity, but notes and bonds will have durations less than maturity. One application here is to calculate the durations of all securities under consideration. Next calculate the additional yield that can be gained by extending duration an additional year. It may very well be that some "yield pick-up" will result from extending the duration. While the maximum increase in yield will likely be out at the long end of the yield curve, the maximum marginal increase per year of additional duration may very well be in the two- to four-year maturity range.

Suppose we have the following term structure for par bonds:

Years to Maturity	Coupon Rate (%)	Duration (yrs.)
1	7.00	0.98
2	7.25	1.90
3	7.50	2.74
4	7.75	3.51
5	7.90	4.23
7	8.00	5.49
10	8.05	7.05
20	8.10	10.22
30	8.10	11.66

The yield pickup based on maturity is given by the following table:

		2	3	4	5	7	10	20	30
						Years to Maturity			
	1	25	50	75	90	100	105	110	110
	2		25	50	65	75	80	85	85
Coupon	3			25	40	50	55	60	60
	4				15	25	30	35	35
	5					10	15	20	20
	7						5	10	10
	10							5	5
	20								0

To calculate the yield pickup per additional duration year, divide the basis point pickup for a particular strategy by the difference in the durations of the two instruments. For instance, the pickup per additional year of duration by going from the two- to the three-year bond is 25/(2.74 − 1.90) = 29.8 basis points. On the other hand, going from the two- to the 20-year bond gives a yield pickup of 85/(10.22 − 1.90) = 10.2 basis points per duration year. The following table summarizes the additional yields for an additional year of duration.

	2	3	4	5	7	10	20	30
1	27.3	36.7	29.6	27.8	22.2	17.3	11.9	10.3
2		29.8	31.1	27.9	20.9	15.5	10.2	8.8
3			32.4	26.8	18.2	12.8	8.0	6.7
4				20.8	12.6	8.5	5.2	4.3
5					7.9	5.3	3.3	2.7
7						3.2	2.1	1.6
10							1.6	1.1
20								0.0

In this case the maximum yield pickup per duration year can be gained by selling the one-year bond and buying the three-year bond.

References

Bierwag, G. 1987. *Duration Analysis.* Cambridge, Mass.: Ballinger Publishing.

Osteryoung, J., D. McCarty, and G. Roberts. 1981. Riding the Yield Curve with Treasury Bills. *The Financial Review* 16, no. 3 (Fall): 57–66.

Stigum, M. 1981. *Money Market Calculations: Yields, Break-evens, and Arbitrage.* Homewood, Ill.: Dow Jones-Irwin.

Chapter 11

Options Pricing Model

The purpose of this chapter is to examine the theoretical determinants of call and put options and trace the development of the Black and Scholes Option Pricing Model (OPM). The Black and Scholes OPM is the accepted procedure on Wall Street (and LaSalle Street) for pricing options and establishing arbitrage positions. Investors and pension fund managers must be aware of the necessary assumptions underlying the model and the implications for estimating the model parameters, the most important parameter being the variance of the security.

The binominal call option model is introduced to make the reader aware of the impact of stock price movements on call options. The assumptions necessary for the convergence of the binominal distribution to the normal distribution (continuous trading) and the lognormal distribution of share prices leads to the development of the Black and Scholes OPM. The empirical tests of the Black and Scholes model are briefly reviewed.

The options portfolio strategies of Merton, Scholes, and Gladstein are reviewed because of their "90/10" strategy for buying out-of-the-money call options that is the basis of many recently-created options mutual funds. Portfolio algorithms for call-buying and -writing and put-purchasing also are examined. Funds managers are deeply involved in these strategies.

An example using a Chrysler call option helps explain the delta, gamma, and theta strategies in playing options. Reference is made to a software (Lotus 1-2-3) package by Bookstaber (1986) that greatly enhances options analysis.

The great growth of options may be attributable to many factors: (1) the lower initial investment and commission for a call option relative to the purchase of the stock makes options popular financial instruments; (2) the computer programs readily available to investors make seemingly difficult calculations very reasonable; and (3) the empirical evidence suggests that the purchase of call options may greatly enhance portfolio performance. The purpose of this chapter is to trace the development of the

Black and Scholes Options Pricing Model (OPM) and briefly examine the risk and return relationships among stocks, bills, bonds, and options.

The reader is referred to excellent and complete treatments of options found in Malkiel and Quandt (1969), Cox and Rubinstein (1985), and Bookstaber (1987). A purchased call option is the opportunity or option, not the obligation, to purchase N shares of stock at a stated price within a specified time period. Call options are traded such that the option commands the opportunity for an investor to buy or sell 100 shares of the stock on which the option is traded at a stated price, known as the exercise or strike price. An investor would purchase a call option if the stock is expected to rise in price within the specified time period. The investor can purchase the call option by paying the call premium or cost of the option, which is generally far less than the cost of purchasing the stock. Furthermore, if the stock price declines, one can lose only the call premium with options (referred to as limited liability) whereas a stock investor may lose considerably more if there is a substantial price decline. Let us elaborate on the previous sentences using an Alcoa call option:

	(Ex) Exercise Price	Maturity dates	
		October	*January*
Call	50	6.75	
Premiums	55	3.00	4.50
	60	1.00	2.75

If the current stock price on September 4, P_{cs}, of Alcoa is $55.75, then one sees that a 50 call option that expires on Saturday following the third Thursday in October, about six weeks until maturity, has a call premium of $6.75. That is, to purchase a call option to control 100 shares of Alcoa, one can pay $675 for the call option whereas the stock investment to own the same 100 shares would cost $5575. Let us suppose that the price of Alcoa rises to $70 by the middle of October. The call buyer would earn a tremendous return on the call option investment:

$$
\begin{aligned}
\text{Call Value} &= 100\,(\$70 - \$50) &= 2000 \\
\text{Call Investment} &= -100\,(\$6.75) &= 675 \\
\hline
\text{Gross Return} &= 100\,(\$20 - \$6.75) &= 1325
\end{aligned}
$$

Note that the option investor earned a 196.3 percent return in six weeks or an annualized return of 1635.8 percent. The stock investor would earn a return of 25.6 percent [($7000 − $5575)/$5575] for the six weeks. One easily sees that an upward movement in the stock price generally produces a much greater percentage return for the option than the stock because of the lower call option investment. However, one must be very careful in this example because if the stock price of Alcoa falls to $50 by the end of October, the call purchaser has lost his entire investment ($675, 100 percent) whereas the stock investor lost only $575 or 10.3 percent. The limited liability of the call purchaser can be shown if the stock price of Alcoa fell to $40. The call purchaser loses only the call premium of $675 if the price falls to $40 whereas the stock investor loses $1575 [($4000 = $55750)/$4454 or 28.3 percent]. When an investor purchases a call option, one purchases the right to walk away from the investment and lose only the premium.

Suppose the investor did not care to risk an investment of $675 but would rather choose to invest only $300 and purchase the 55 call option. If the stock price rises to $70 by October, the call buyer enjoys an even larger percentage return than the 50 call buyer because of the lower investment:

$$100($70 - $55)/300 = 500\%$$

One can carry our example yet further and purchase the 60 call options in which a rise to $70 allows the call purchaser to earn an investment return of 1000 percent in six weeks and enter the "grey poupon" class. Thus, one must decide not only the stock on which one purchases a call option but also the exercise price. The "in the money" (ITM) call options when the stock price exceeds the exercise price, offer more safety and generally lower returns (less probability of loss) than "at the money" (stock price is equal to the exercise price) and "out of the money" (OTM) options, in which the stock price is less than the exercise price [see Cox and Rubinstein (1985) for a treatment of ITM and OTM calls and the security Market Line]. The Merton, Scholes, and Gladstein (1978, 1982) risk-return analyses of call and put option portfolios will greatly extend this brief introduction into option strategies.

One notices in our Alcoa option example that if one selects a 55 call option, one incurs costs of $300 for the October options and $450 for the January option. One would expect the longer-lived option to cost the investor a larger investment than the shorter term option. A call option is worth more as the maturity date of the option increases because there is a greater probability that the stock price will exceed the exercise price.

When one writes (or sells) a call option, one does not believe that the stock price will exceed the exercise price of the option (or at least not exceed it by more than the call premium) within the specified time period. One generally writes a call option when one owns the underlying stock (a covered call writer) and one wishes to enhance one's return. Let us assume that an investor purchased 100 shares of Alcoa when the stock price was $40. Now that the stock price is $55.75, one has earned a nice return. The investor could write an October call option with an exercise price of $55 and receive a premium of $300. If the stock price is at $55 on the maturity date of the option, the call writer earns the $300 and enhances the stock return. Furthermore, call writing may be of interest to investors owning stocks that pay little, if any, dividends. However, if the price rises to $70, the call writer has sold the stock's potential gains above $55 ($1500) for the seemingly low price of $300. Again we see the need for analyzing stock options in a risk-return framework. A naked call-writer, one that does not own the underlying stock, faces very large potential losses if the stock price rises.

A put option is an option to sell stock at a stated price within a specified time period for a specified number of shares. One purchases a call option when one expects a substantial price decline, enabling the investor to sell the stock at the exercise price which would exceed the current market price. The purchase of a put option allows the investor the limited liability luxury as opposed to the unlimited loss potential inherent in a short sale position. One can purchase a put option on a stock if one has a long position in that stock to provide down-side protection, this is, in essence, a term insurance policy. That is, if one owns stock and the current stock price is $60, one can purchase a 55 put option and losses on the stock position as the price declines below $55 are offset buy put option gains. One writes a put option if one does not expect a stock price decline and the premium enhances the portfolio return. Put option premiums increase as the time-to-maturity increases because there is a greater time and probability for the stock price decline below the exercise price.

The Malkiel-Quandt Notation

The authors have long admired the options notation put forth by Malkiel and Quandt (1969) in their very enjoyable and stimulating monograph on options markets. One profits from a stock price rise when one purchases a call option and loses only the premium from a stock price decline. As Malkiel and Quandt write, the option profits lose in terms of stock price advances and declines in a 2×1 matrix.

$$\begin{bmatrix} Pcs \uparrow \\ Pcs \downarrow \end{bmatrix}$$

If one purchases a call option one profits as the stock price advances, and the Malkiel-Quandt notation would be:

$$\begin{bmatrix} +1 \\ 0 \end{bmatrix}$$

Note that the premiums are not included in the analysis and one must be careful in examining option/portfolio strategies. There may be a problem with naked call writing where one loses in the event of a stock price advance in terms of unlimited stock advances and retains only the call premium in the event of a price decline:

$$\begin{bmatrix} -1 \\ 0 \end{bmatrix}$$

However, if one is a covered call writer, the Malkiel-Quandt notation is:

$$\frac{\text{Covered}}{\text{Call}} = \frac{\text{long in}}{\text{stock}} + \frac{\text{call}}{\text{writer}}$$

$$\text{writer} = \begin{bmatrix} +1 \\ -1 \end{bmatrix} + \begin{bmatrix} -1 \\ 0 \end{bmatrix} = \begin{bmatrix} 0 \\ -1 \end{bmatrix}$$

It would appear that the covered call writer never wins; however, if one writes a call option with an exercise price in excess of the stock price, (OTM), one can substantially profit on the stock price advance and receive a call premium to partially offset the stock price decline.

A put buyer return pattern can be written as:

$$\begin{bmatrix} 0 \\ +1 \end{bmatrix}$$

and a put writer return pattern is:

$$\begin{bmatrix} 0 \\ -1 \end{bmatrix}$$

Straddles, straps, and strips, combinations of calls and puts, might pose problems for the Malkiel-Quandt notation. For example, if one purchases one call and one put at the same exercise price on the identical stock, it would appear that the investor will never lose.

$$\frac{\text{straddle}}{\text{buyer}} = \frac{\text{call}}{\text{buyer}} + \frac{\text{put}}{\text{buyer}}$$

$$\begin{bmatrix} +1 \\ 0 \end{bmatrix} + \begin{bmatrix} 0 \\ +1 \end{bmatrix} = \begin{bmatrix} +1 \\ +1 \end{bmatrix}$$

One could purchase a 55 October call on Alcoa for $3 and a 55 October put for $1.375. If the investor buys a straddle, one invests $4.375 (or $437.50 in the 100 share position) in the position. The investor purchases volatility in buying a straddle on profits only if the price rises above $59.38 or falls below $50.63. A straddle buyer does not care which event (advance or decline) occurs as long as the volatility is very large. A strike might lead one to by a straddle on the firm's stock; one could profit on the put if the strike is long and violent and the call if the strike is settled quickly and cheaply. The Malkiel-Quandt positions do not offer the investor an insight into the volatility problems in purchasing a straddle. A straddle writer appears to consistently lose in the Malkiel-Quandt analysis:

$$\begin{bmatrix} -1 \\ 0 \end{bmatrix} + \begin{bmatrix} 0 \\ -1 \end{bmatrix} = \begin{bmatrix} -1 \\ -1 \end{bmatrix}$$

However, in reality, the writer wins as long as the price fluctuates between $50.63 and $59.38. The straddle writer wins as long as the stock volatility is low. Anything that reduces the stock volatility enhances the profitability of the straddle writer; for example a merger, particularly a conglomerate merger reduces systematic risk and total risk. A merger announcement could lend one to write straddles on the acquiring firm's stock.

    A strap is when one has two calls and one put in an option portfolio. A strap buyer is not completely certain about the course of a stock's movement; however, the buyer is leaning toward an upward stock movement. One can easily see this in the Malkiel-Quandt notation:

$$\begin{matrix} \text{strap} \\ \text{buyer} \end{matrix} \quad 2\begin{bmatrix} +1 \\ 0 \end{bmatrix} + \begin{bmatrix} 0 \\ +1 \end{bmatrix} = \begin{bmatrix} +2 \\ +1 \end{bmatrix}$$

One must be aware of the numerous (3) transaction costs and premiums associated with straps. In our Alcoa example, the 55 October strap would cost $737.50 [2($3) + $1.375 = $7.375]. Therefore, the break-even price range is $47.63 and $58.69 [$55 + $7.28/2]. One profits at a 2:1 ratio as the stock price advances above $55. A strip is two puts and one call. A strip purchaser is somewhat confused but more pessimistic than optimistic about the stock price movement. The Malkiel-Quandt notation for a strip purchaser is:

$$\text{strip}\atop\text{purchaser}\quad \begin{bmatrix} +1 \\ 0 \end{bmatrix} + 2\begin{bmatrix} 0 \\ +1 \end{bmatrix} = \begin{bmatrix} +1 \\ +2 \end{bmatrix}$$

Straddles, straps, and strips offer investors and portfolio managers opportunities to alter portfolio return distributions.

The Binominal Option Pricing Model

The binominal option pricing model (OPM) evolved from Sharpe (1978), Rendleman and Bartter (1979), and Cox, Ross, and Rubinstein (1979). Much easier than the Black and Scholes OPM derivation (the limiting case of the binominal OPM is its continuous time partner, the traditional Black and Scholes OPM) the binomial OPM may be developed from a very practical example. Let us assume that the firm's current stock price is P_{cs} and either goes up u in the next period or falls by d. A call option is equal to the maximum of zero or P_{cs} − Ex where Ex is the exercise price. In the King's English, a call option cannot be negative. In a three-period model, the value of the call option, V_c, may be developed:

$t = 0$	$t = 1$	$t = 2$	$t = 3$
P_{cs} − Ex	$P_{cs}(u)$ − Ex	$P_{cs}(u)^2$ − Ex	$P_{cs}(u)^3$ − Ex
			$P_{cs}(u^2d)$ − Ex
			$P_{cs}(udu)$ − Ex
		$P_{cs}(ud)$ − Ex	$P_{cs}(udd)$ − Ex
	$P_{cs}(d)$ − Ex		$P_{cs}(duu)$ − Ex
			$P_{cs}(dud)$ − Ex
		$P_{cs}(du)$ − Ex	$P_{cs}(d^2u)$ − Ex
			$P_{cs}(d)^3$ − Ex
		$P_{cs}(d)^2$ − Ex	

The value of the call option can be found by multiplying the discounted value of the call in each of the eight possible states of nature by the respective probabilities of these states. The probability of an upward price movement, u, is p:

$$p = \frac{r - d}{u - d},$$

where r is one plus the risk-free rate. The probability of a downward movement, d, is q where $q = 1 - p$. Thus the value of the call option:

$$V_c = \frac{p^3[P_{cs}(u^3) - \text{Ex}] + 3p^2q[P_{cs}(u^2d) - \text{Ex}] + 3pq^2[P_{cs}(ud^2) - \text{Ex}] + q^3[P_{cs}(d^3) - \text{Ex}]}{(1 + r)^3}$$

(1)

This equation may seem rather formidable until one remembers that the reader solved this in sophomore statistics class. If k represents the number of upward movements in n periods:

$$V_c = \frac{1}{r^n} \sum_{k=0}^{n} \frac{k!}{(n-k)!} p^k q^{(n-k)}[\max (0, P_{cs}u^k p^{(n-k)} - \text{Ex}]$$

(2)

Let us work a very small numerical example that will illustrate the analysis. Assume the following:

$$P_{cs} = 80$$
$$\text{Ex} = 100$$
$$r = 1.2$$
$$d = .9$$
$$r = 1.08$$

$$p = \frac{1.08 - .9}{1.2 - .9} = .5$$

$$V_c = \frac{1}{(1.05)^3} \{(.6)^3[\max (0,80(1.2)^3 - 100]$$

$$+ 3(.6)^2(.4)[\max (0,80(1.2)^2.(9) - 100]$$

$$+ 3(.6)(.4)^2[\max (0,80(1.2)(.9^2) - 100]$$

$$+ (.4)^3[\max (0,80(.9^3) - 100]\}$$

$$V_c = (.864)[(.216)(38.24) + (.432)(3.68) + (.288)(0.00) + (.064)(0.00)]$$

$$= (.864)[8.26 + 1.59] = \$8.51.$$

The value of the three-period call is \$8.51. The call option, if only two-period, would be:

$$V_c = (1.05)^2\{[(.6)^2 80(1.2)^2 - 100 + 2(.6)(.4)[\max (0,80(1.2)(.9) - 100]$$

$$+ (.4)^2[\max (0,80(.9)^2 - 100]\}$$

$$V_c = (.907)[.36(15.2) + .48(0.00) + (.16)^2(0.00)] = \$4.96.$$

Note, as in the general case of options, as the time to maturity rises, the value of the option increases. The binominal option pricing model convergences to the traditional Black and Scholes Option Pricing Model as the number of periods go to infinity (continuous time), and the binominal approximation of the stock price distribution becomes normally distributed (for price relatives).

$$\log(P_{cs}^*/P_{cs}) = k \log (u/d) + n \log d, \qquad (3)$$

$$E[\log (P_{cs}^*/P_{cs}] = mn,$$

where * denotes the maturity date and mn is the expected mean of the series.

$$\text{Prob} \left[\frac{\log (P_{cs}^*/P_{cs}) - mn}{\sigma\sqrt{n}} < Z \right] = N(Z)$$

The traditional Black and Scholes OPM can be written from the binominal option pricing model as:

$$V_c = P_{cs}N(X) - \text{Exr}^{-t}N(X - \sigma\sqrt{t}) \qquad (4)$$

where

$$X = \frac{\log (P_{cs}/\text{Exr}^{-t})}{\sigma\sqrt{t}} + \frac{1}{2}\sigma\sqrt{t}$$

A More Traditional Black and Scholes Option Pricing Model Derivation

The rudiments of the Black and Scholes OPM were known in the 1960s as shown in the works of Sprenkle (1962), Boness (1964), and Kassouf (1969); however, Black and Scholes (1973), developed their model with a hedge ratio that allowed not only a theoretical value but a risk-free hedging strategy.[1] The Black and Scholes OPM is characterized by rather re-

---

[1] Wall Street quickly adopted the Black and Scholes OPM to the extent that even practitioners into their 50's and 60's who cannot take a derivative, total or partial, have hired "computer jocks" to program the OPM into their computers or use their H-P calculators.

strictive assumptions: (1) the stock price series follows a lognormal distribution; that is, the distribution of price relatives is normally distributed; (2) the risk-free is constant; (3) the variance of the price series is constant and known; (4) the stock pays no dividend; and (5) the call option is a European call option that cannot be exercised prior to expiration (maturity).

The traditional Black and Scholes (1973) Option Pricing Model (OPM) finds a theoretical value of the call option, V_c, by creating a risk-free portfolio composed of a call option and shares of the underlying stock. The value of the portfolio, V_p, is found by the sum of the market values of equity and options.

$$V_p = hnV_c + mP_{cs} \tag{5}$$

where

> h = hedge ratio,
> n = number of call options,
> m = number of shares of stock,
> and P_{cs} = price of common stock.

If there are no transactions in the stock and options, n and m are assumed to be constant, and the value of the portfolio may change as a result of fluctuating stock prices and call option prices. The reader is aware that changes in the stock price affect the price of call, however, the call price is affected by changes in the time to maturity of the option. Although the price of the underlying stock may be unchanged for a trading day, the value of the call will fall as a result of time decay. Without time decay, the change in the portfolio is:

$$dV_p = hndP_{cs} + mdV_c \tag{6}$$

If n and m are selected in this way, the risk-free hedge is created:

$$dV_p = hdP_{cs} - dV_c \tag{7}$$

One notices that if the call option is written ($m < 0$), then the stock is purchased ($n > 0$) to create the hedged portfolios. The stock price and option price changes are:

$$dP_{cs} = P_{cs_{t+dt}} - P_{cs_t},$$

$$dV_c = V_{c_{t+dt}} - V_{c_t}.$$

The change in the stock price series follows a random walk, that is, the stock price series follows a lognormal distribution and the distribution of price relatives. In $(P_{cs_t}/P_{cs_{t-1}})$ is normally distributed. The change in the value of the call option may be written in terms of changes in time and the stock price.

$$dV_c = \frac{\partial V_c}{\partial t} dt + \frac{\partial V_c}{\partial P_{cs}} dP_{cs} + \frac{1}{2} \frac{\partial^2 V_c}{\partial P_{cs^2}} P_{cs}{}^2 \sigma^2 \tag{8}$$

where

σ^2 = variance in stock price relatives.

The change in the value of the hedged portfolio is:

$$dV_p = hdP_{cs} - \left(\frac{\partial V_c}{\partial t} + \frac{1}{2} \frac{\partial^2 V_{c2}}{\partial P_{cs}} \sigma^2 P_{cs}^2 \right) dt \tag{9}$$

The change in the value of the hedged portfolio should equal the risk-free rate, R_F.

$$R_F V_p = R_F P_{cs} \frac{\partial V_c}{\partial P_{cs}} + \frac{\partial V_c}{\partial^t} + \frac{1}{2} \frac{\partial^2 V_c}{\partial P_{cs^2}} \sigma^2 P_{cs}^2$$

$$0 = R_F P_{cs} \frac{\partial V_c}{\partial P_{cs}} + \frac{\partial V_c}{\partial^t} + \frac{1}{2} \frac{\partial^2 V_{c2}}{\partial P_{cs}} \sigma^2 P_{cs}^2 - R_F V_p$$

The value of the V_c is found by solving the above partial differential equation subject to:

$V_c = \max (P_{cs} - Ex, 0), 0 < t < T$ (maturity date), $0 < P_{cs}$.

The Black and Scholes OPM value of the call option is found to be:

$$V_c = P_{cs} N(d_1) - \frac{Ex}{e^{rt}} N(d_2) \tag{10}$$

where

$$d_1 = \frac{\ln (P_{cs}/Ex) + \left(r + \frac{\sigma^2}{2} \right) t}{\sigma \sqrt{t}},$$

$$d_2 = \frac{\ln\left(P_{cs}/Ex\right) + \left(r - \dfrac{\sigma^2}{2}\right)t}{\sigma\sqrt{t}},$$

$N(.)$ = cumulative normal distribution, and $e = 2.71828$.

The optimal hedge ratio, h, to create the risk-free hedge is $N(d_1)$. If the call option is purchased, $N(d_1)$ shares of stock are sold short. If the call is over-valued and written, the stock is purchased in the ratio of $N(d_1)$. The traditional Black and Scholes OPM assumes no dividends are paid. The dividends may be handled in several manners: (1) the present value of the escrowed dividend may be subtracted from the stock price; and (2) the time to ex-dividend is substituted for the same variable and the relevant stock price is the price less the present value of the escrowed dividends (D).

$$0 = \frac{1}{2}\frac{\partial^2 V_{c_2}}{\partial P_{cs}}\sigma^2 P_{cs}^2 + \frac{\partial V_c}{\partial t} + (R_F - D)P_{cs}\frac{\partial V_c}{\partial P_{cs}}R_F V_c \qquad (11)$$

The value of the call option is clearly a function of six variables.

$$V_c = f(\overset{+}{P_{cs}}, \overset{+}{t}, \overset{+}{R_F}, \overset{+}{\sigma^2}, \overset{-}{D}, \overset{-}{Ex})$$

As the stock price rises, the value of the call increases. This is im-mediately clear for an "in the money" call in which the stock price ex-ceeds the exercise price. An increase in the exercise price reduces the value of the call. An increase in the time to maturity creates more time for the stock price to exceed the exercise price and thus raise the value of the option. The risk-free rate is used to discount the exercise price in determining the value of the call; an increase in the risk-free rate reduces the present value of the exercise price and increases the value of the call option. The dividend reduces the ex-dividend price and reduces the call. The variance of the price relative series positively affects the value of the call because an increase in the variability serves the probability that stock price will exceed the exercise price and raise the value of the call option.

Let us use the Black and Scholes Option Pricing Model to determine the value of a Chrysler call option and the hedge ratio. On January 4, 1988, Chrysler's stock price was \$22.25 and an April call option with an exercise price of 20 was selling for \$3.88. Given a risk-free rate of 5.98 percent (the April 20, 1988, Treasury Bill yield) and approximately 60 trading days prior to maturity, the Black and Scholes value of the 20

April call option should be $2.41. Thus, the call option should be written and the written call option should be hedged by purchasing 86.6 shares of Chrysler stock (the hedge ratio is $N(d_1)$ which equals $-.866$). An alternative method of valuing options is to compare the variance that the market is using to price the call option (its implied volatility) with the historic volatility. The annualized 90-day standard deviation of Chrysler's price relatives as of January 4, 1988, was 30.24, up substantially from the 90-day annualized standard deviation of 17.12 for the first 90 trading days of 1987, (the 180-day annualized standard deviation of Chrysler's price relatives was 24.83) whereas the implied volatility was 74.83. The implied volatility is so great (reflecting the lingering effects of October 19th) relative to the historic volatility that one must question the implied volatility and write the call, just as one did when the call price was calculated. One can hedge the short call by purchasing a Chrysler call with an implied volatility that is less than the historic standard deviation. If one is not available, one might purchase an index call option in proportion to Chrysler's beta. The implied volatility in this example was estimated using the Lotus 1-2-3 worksheet program described in Bookstaber (1987).

In call options analysis, one traditionally examines the delta of a call option which represents the change in the value of the call option relative to the change in the stock price. The delta of a call option is zero for an OTM option and one for a deep ITM option. Of course, the delta of a call option is the hedge ratio or $N(d_1)$. The gamma of a call option represents the change in the delta relative to the change in the stock price. The gamma of the April 20 Chrysler is .09 (using the 24.83 volatility for 180 days) and the positive gamma implies that additional volatility is needed for option profitability. The theta of a call option represents the change in the value of the call option with respect to the change in time to the maturity of the call. A positive theta, 1.87 for the April 20 Chrysler call, implies that as time to maturity increases, the value of the call increases and one will write a "short" term call and purchase a "longer" term call (buying a horizontal spread). The kappa of a call option represents the change in the call price relative to a one percent change in volatility. The kappa of the Chrysler call option is $-.74$ and implies that volatility of the Chrysler option is expected to decrease. The reader is referred to Bookstaber (1987) for a complete and excellent discussion of options.

The put option price is developed from the put-call parity relationship in which the purchase of a put is equal to the price of the call plus the present value of the strike price less the stock price. That is, the purchase of a put is analogous to the purchase of a call, shorting the stock, and borrowing the discounted exercise price.

$$V_c - P_{cs} - V_p + \frac{Ex}{1 + R_F} = 0$$

$$V_p = V_c + \frac{Ex}{1 + R_F} - P_{cs}$$

The empirical results of Klemkosky and Resnick (1979) and Gould and Galai (1974) substantiate the put-call parity theory and options market efficiency [Galai (1977) and Phillips and Smith (1980)]. One may wonder why options trading firms have emerged in options analysis. One can easily find and agree upon the stock price, exercise price, risk-free rate, time to maturity, and dividends. The relevant variance to be used in pricing the option is of great concern and interest as is the role that options and stocks play in diversified portfolio. Latané and Rendleman (1976) found that if one assumes that the call option is correctly priced and solves the Black and Scholes OPM for the implied variance, the implied variances were superior to historic variances if forecasting future variances. Schmalensee and Trippi (1978) found that variances are not constant but are first-order negatively serially correlated, i.e., mean reverting. In one of the best studies of options market efficiency, Whaley (1982) found: (1) the American call and European call options less the es-crowed present values of dividends produced values within 3–5 cents of observed values (far within transactions costs, bid-ask spread) with good-ness of fit measures exceeding 0.98. Furthermore, the option pricing errors are due to variance errors and not to dividends, time to maturity (particularly the American call option), or the "in the moneyness" of the call option. Whaley noted the conclusion about the in the money nature of option problems. Whaley's option regression results indicated a ten-dency for "out of the money" ($P_{cs} <$ Ex) to be underpriced by the traditional Black and Scholes models at the 10 percent level (although the regression coefficient = .04 − .10). Black (1976) noted that out of the money options tended to be underpriced. Most options theorists agree that implied variances are relevant variance for options investing and these variances are not constant but rather mean-reverting.

The two major topics of option analysis concerns the area of option portfolios and portfolio insurance. Merton, Scholes, and Gladstein (1978, 1982) developed portfolio models to analyze option portfolios. In their earlier price, Merton, Scholes, and Gladstein found using an option simulation period from June 1963 to December 1975, that "in the money" covered calls ($P_{cs} >$ Ex) earned less return than merely owning the stock. This is hardly surprising because further stock price apprecia-tion above the exercise price (above the current option premium) is called away by the option buyer. The "out of the money" covered calls earned higher returns than the "in the money" covered calls, but were still less than stock returns. The right tail of the stock price distribution is eliminated by writing calls on the held stock. Although covered call writing reduced returns relative to holding stock, the portfolio standard deviations also were lower involving call writers. The principal contribution of the Merton, Scholes, and Gladstein (1978) call option study was that portfolios composed of 90 percent commercial paper and 10 percent purchased out of the money calls outperformed stock returns, also producing much higher portfolio variances. The out of the money calls produced tremendous returns, despite the fact that 70 percent of the options expired unused, earning approximately 400 percent. One notes that out of the money option premiums, when the exercise price is 1.2 times the stock price (i.e., Ex = 96, P_{cs} = 80), should be very small. Therefore, if the stock price raises slightly over the exercise price, the corresponding percentage option returns would be very large.

The Merton, Scholes, and Gladstein (1982) put study found that in the money puts (Ex > P_{cs}) provided portfolio insurance that was too costly for investors (reducing portfolio returns) whereas out of the money puts (Ex < P_{cs}) offered downside protection (protective puts) at a very reasonable (.4 percent) cost to the portfolio manager. Writing uncovered puts was far less variable than fully covered call writing, although both strategies had identical Malkiel-Quandt notation; the stock variance led to the higher variability in covered call writing. If one combines protective put purchases with out of the money call writing one could effectively shape the desired portfolio distribution. Bookstaber and Clarke (1983) developed a portfolio algorithm to set exercise price levels for puts and calls to manage an options portfolio (with as few as five options).

References

Black, F. 1975. Fact and Fantasy in the Use of Options. *Financial Analysts Journal* 36–72.

Black, F., and M. Scholes. 1973. The Pricing of Options and Corporate Liabilities. *Journal of Political Economy* 8: 637–654.

Boness, A.J. 1964. Elements of a Theory of Stock Option Value. *Journal of Political Economy* 72: 163–175.

Bookstaber, R. 1987. *Options Pricing and Investing Strategies.* Chicago: Probus Publishing.

Bookstaber, R. 1981. *Option Pricing and Strategies in Investing.* Reading, Mass.: Addison-Wesley Publishing.

Bookstaber, R., and R. Clarke. 1983. An Algorithm to Calculate the

Return Distribution of Portfolios with Option Positions. *Management Science* 29: 419-429.

Cootner, Paul, ed. 1964. *The Random Character of Stock Market Prices.* Cambridge, Mass.: MIT Press.

Cox, J.C., and M. Rubinstein. 1985. *Options Markets.* Englewood Cliffs, N.J.: Prentice-Hall.

Cox, J.C., S. Ross, and M. Rubinstein. 1979. Option Pricing: A Simplified Approach. *Journal of Financial Economics* 6: 229-263.

Galai, D. 1977. Tests of Market Efficiency of the Chicago Board of Options Exchange. *Journal of Business:* 167-197.

Gould, J.P., and D. Galai. 1974. Transactions Costs and the Relationship Between Put and Call Prices. *Journal of Financial Economics* 1: 105-130.

Jarrow, R.A., and A. Rudd. 1983. *Option Pricing.* Homewood, Ill.: Dow Jones-Irwin.

Kassouf, S.T. 1969. An Econometric Model for Option Price with Implications for Investors' Expectations and Audacity. *Econometrica* 37: 685-694.

Klemkosky, R.C., and B.G. Resnick. 1979. Put-Call Parity and Market Efficiency. *Journal of Finance* 34: 1141-1157.

Latané, H., and R. Rendleman. 1976. Standard Deviations of Stock Price Ratios Implied in Option Prices. *Journal of Finance* 31: 369-381.

Malkiel B.G., and E. Quandt. 1969. *Strategies and Rational Decisions in the Securities Options Market.* Cambridge, Mass.: MIT Press.

Merton, R., M. Scholes, and M. Gladstein. 1978. The Returns and Risks of Alternative Call Option Portfolio Investment Strategies. *Journal of Business* 51: 183-242.

Merton, R., M. Scholes, and M. Gladstein. 1982. The Returns and Risks of Alternative Put-Option Portfolio Investment Strategies. *Journal of Business* 55: 1-55.

Merton, R.C. 1973. Theory of Rational Option Pricing. *Bell Journal of Economics and Management Science* 4: 141-183.

Phillips, S., and C. Smith. 1980. Trading Costs for Listed Options: Implications for Market Efficiency. *Journal of Financial Economics* 8: 179-201.

Schmalensee, R. and R. Trippi. 1978. Common Stock Volatility Expectations Implied by Option Premia. *Journal of Finance* 33: 129-148.

Sharpe, W.F. 1978. *Investments*. Englewood Cliffs, N.J.: Prentice-Hall.

Smith, Clifford W. 1976. Option Pricing. *Journal of Financial Economics* 3: 3-51.

Sprenkle, C.M. 1961. Warrant Prices and Indicators of Expectations and Preferences. *Yale Economic Essays* 1: 179-231.

Stroll, H.R. 1969. The Relationship between Put and Call Option Prices. *Journal of Finance* 24: 801-824.

Whaley, R. 1982. Valuation of American Call Options on Dividend-Paying Stocks. *Journal of Financial Economics* 10: 29-58.

Chapter 12

Security Analysts and Composite Earnings Forecasting Models

Recent studies have shown that composite forecasts are superior to individual forecasts. Portfolio managers may not be able to produce profitable investment strategies by using only analysts' forecasts; however, composite earnings models—combining analysts' forecasts with mechanical earnings forecasts—may produce superior earnings forecasts. Security analysts' forecasts are improved when combined with time series forecasts for a diversified sample of 261 firms with a 1980–82 postsample estimation period. The mean square error of analyst forecasts may be reduced by combining analyst and univariate time series model forecasts in an ordinary least squares regression model. This reduction is very interesting when one finds that the univariate time series model forecasts do not substantially deviate from random-walk-with-drift models. Multicollinearity exists between analyst and time series model forecasts, and ridge regression techniques are used to estimate composite earnings models; ridge regression, however, does not improve upon the ordinary least squares composite models.

Introduction

The majority of the financial literature supports the conclusion that earnings forecasts prepared by security analysts are more accurate than time series model forecasts (Armstrong 1983). Fried and Givoly (1982) and Givoly and Lakonishok (1984) stated that: (1) analyst forecasts are superior to mechanical earnings prediction models; (2) analyst forecasts are used by investors to forecast future returns; and (3) analyst forecasts can be used by investors to formulate investment strategies. Not all of the economic studies have supported the forecasting efficiency of analysts, however, Cragg and Malkiel (1968), Elton and Gruber (1972), and Guerard (1987,a,b,c) have questioned the superiority of analysts. The purpose of this study is to develop models combining analyst and time series forecasts to forecast corporate earnings more effectively. The majority of researchers analyzing the annual-earnings-generating process have found that a random walk with drift model best describes the earnings series (Watts and Leftwich 1977). Analysts' forecasts may be combined with univariate time series model forecasts in order to produce superior models for estimating earnings. Guerard demonstrated for a 261-firm sample that time series earnings forecasts may be combined with analyst forecasts to produce more efficient earnings forecasts.

The recent statistical literature is rich with examples of composite modeling. Granger and Ramanathan (1984) proposed a method of combining forecasts with no restrictions on the weights; a constant term is estimated. The weighting scheme of combining forecasts with a constant term produces an unbiased forecast and will produce the lowest estimated mean square error. Multicollinearity exists between analyst forecasts and time series forecasts and leads one to examine the application of ridge regression techniques. Guerard (1987a) did not find that the use of biased regression improved upon ordinary least squares composite modeling in forecasting earnings.

Security Analyst Forecasts

The one-year-ahead security analyst forecasts used in this chapter are those published in the *Earnings Forecaster*, published by Standard & Poor's. Many studies use a computerized database, the I/B/E/S system, which presents means, modes, and variability statistics for concensus analysts' earnings forecasts. The I/B/E/S database is available from Lynch, Jones, & Ryan, a New York City-based brokerage service. Analyst forecasts are collected and published in the weekly periodical. Elton, Gruber, and Gultekin (1981) have shown that (I/B/E/S) analysts forecasts are immediately incorporated into the share prices, so that one cannot earn an excess return by purchasing securities forecasted to have the highest growth prospect; one can profit only by purchasing securities achieving a higher-than-expected earnings growth. The purpose of this study is to develop composite earnings models. Better forecasting models may identify potentially high-growth securities overlooked by analysts, or may produce forecasts of growth rates more accurate than those produced by analysts. The identification of such securities could produce high portfolio yields to the investor. The mid-April *Earnings Forecaster* issues are used in this chapter because the annual earnings of the previous year are generally known in the March–April period.

Univariate Time Series Model Building and Forecasting

Univariate time series models are estimated for 261 randomly selected firms, during the period from 1959 to 1979. The span of 21 years may seem quite short for time series modeling (Newbold and Granger 1974), but the Ljung-Box statistics and residual plots indicate that the models are adequately fitted and the first difference models are stationary. Moreover, the accounting literature supports series modeling using only 25 annual observations (Albrecht et al. 1977).

Annual data on earnings per share are taken from the COMPU-STAT tapes and from Moody's *Industrial Manual* for the 261 firms. The general form of the models is that of an ARIMA (0,1,1) process, a random-walk-with-drift series. Although many of the models possess moving-average parameters of higher orders than the first, the estimated model forecasts are so highly correlated with random-walk-with-drift forecasts that one cannot reject the Little (1962) hypothesis of random earnings changes. Logarithmic transformations were applied to all earnings series because of the linear relationship between the series ranges and means in 10-year intervals (Jenkins 1979).

Composite Earnings Estimations

The use of ordinary least squares (OLS) in estimating composite earnings models, as developed by Granger and Ramanathan (1984), reduces the average estimated mean square regression error relative to the analyst forecasts of the 261 firms for the 1980–1982 postsample period. The estimated composite earnings models are summarized in Table 12-1, and the 1980–82 average mean square estimation errors are shown in Table 12-2. The use of a large sample of firms produced an interesting result for relative estimating efficiency; the average three-year analyst (SEC) mean square forecasting error of 1.270 is approximately equal to the univariate time series (BJU) mean square forecasting error of 1.277 shown in Table 12-2. This result supports the early work of Cragg and Malkiel (1968), Elton and Gruber (1972), and Guerard (1987) previously described in analyzing analyst forecasting efficiency.

The work of Granger and Ramanathan (1984) and Bopp (1985) leads to using OLS analysis to estimate composite earnings models. The cross-sectional composite earnings model is of the form

$$EPS_t = a + b_1 BJU_t + b_2 SEC_t + e_t, \qquad (1)$$

where

> EPS = logarithm of actual earnings per share,
> BJU = logarithm of univariate time series model forecast,
> SEC = logarithm of consensus analyst forecast,
> e_t = randomly distributed error term.

Table 12-2 shows that the OLS composite earnings model produces an estimated mean square error, MSE (using the analyst and univariate time series forecast), of 1.040, some 18.1 percent less than the analyst forecasts. The relatively poor (nondominant) analyst forecasting performance was due to the 1982 analyst forecasts. The regression coefficients on the univariate time series forecast variable in 1980 through 1982 are such that the variable could not be omitted from the regression equation, Equation (1). That is, omission of the time series variable significantly decreases the adjusted (for degrees of freedom) R^2. Fried and Givoly (1982) did not find support for the construction of composite earnings models using time series and analyst forecasts. The principal difference between the Fried and Givoly study and this chapter is that Fried and Givoly used a linear correction technique to examine the incremental value of the time series forecast, whereas this chapter examines the estimation of OLS and biased regression models using both raw variables and avoids the inappropriate application of the incremental value technique (Christie et al. 1984).

The linear correction technique allows one to subtract the linear dependence from both sides of the regression equation

$$y = \beta_1 X_1 + \beta_2 X_2 + \ldots \beta_k X_k.$$

That is, if one independent variable, X_1, can be expressed as a linear combination of the other independent variables,

$$X_1 = C_2 X_2 + C_3 X_3 + \ldots + C_k X_k,$$

then the linear dependence may be subtracted from both sides of the regression equation to determine the new dependent variable

$$y - \beta_1 X_1 = \beta_2 X_2 + \ldots + \beta_k X_k + \varepsilon.$$

The new X vector has full-column rank.

The near-multicollinearity existing between analyst forecasts and univariate time series forecasts in the sample period (1959–79) and

Table 12-1 Regression Analysis Summary

Year	Regression Equation	Dependent Variable	Constant	BJU	SEC	MSE	k	R2
1980	OLS	EPS (t)	-.255 (-2.85)	.610 (6.53)	.523 (6.98)	.236		.595
	Ridge	EPS	.181	.452 (12.91)	.371 (13.25)	.262	.67	
	Robust	EPS	-.147 (-1.92)	.583 (7.30)	.484 (7.56)	.170		
	Ridge (Robust)	EPS	.138	.485 (15.20)	.379 (14.60)	.138	.42	
1981	OLS	EPS	-.256 (-2.88)	.427 (4.56)	.648 (7.82)	.276		.576
	Ridge	EPS	.219	.363 (12.10)	.378 (13.64)	.316	.83	
	Robust	EPS	-.225 (-3.00)	.423 (5.35)	.641 (9.09)	.193		
	Ridge (Robust)	EPS	.200	.365 (12.20)	.391 (14.50)	.300	.78	
1982	OLS	EPS	-.271 (-2.26)	.435 (3.49)	.564 (5.05)	.540		.370
	Ridge	EPS	.166	.337 (8.43)	.341 (9.47)	.574	.85	
	Robust	EPS	-.258 (-3.02)	.403 (4.51)	.619 (7.64)	.272		
	Ridge (Robust)	EPS	-.048	.413 (13.80)	.456 (16.90)	.185	.46	

Table 12-2 Mean Square Forecasting Errors, 1980-1982

BJU	1.277
SEC	1.270
Combined Model; OLS	1.040
Ridge	1.139
Equal Weighted	1.147
Robust	0.729[a]
Ridge (Robust)	0.619[a]

[a] = statistically different from security analyst (SEC) forecasts at the 5 percent level.

postsample periods (1980–82) leads one to question the appropriateness of OLS; near-multicollinearity inflates the estimated standard error of the regression coefficients, and t-values are biased downward. One would expect that analysts use some variation of a first-order exponential smoothing model [which, of course, approximately equals the ARIMA (0,1,1)]. Thus, one would expect multicollinearity, given that the forecasts are not truly derived from independent sources of information. Fried and Givoly (1982), as noted earlier, found little support for composite model building with time series and analysts' forecasts; however, they used a linear correction technique rather than biased regression to reduce multicollinearity. The use of ridge regression techniques on the unstandardized (raw) variables using the iterative procedure of Hoerl, Kennard, and Baldwin (1975) to estimate the biasing parameter, k, produces more stable regression coefficients, particularly in 1982 (see Table 12-1). The regression coefficients on analyst and time series forecasts tend to equality in the ridge regression, as one would have expected, given the approximately equal standard deviations of the variables (Bates and Granger 1969). However, the more stable regression coefficients of the raw (unstandardized) ridge regression do not estimate earnings as well as the OLS regressions (the 1980–1982 average mean square estimation error is 1.139 using ridge regression); see Guerard (1987) for a more complete discussion of biased regression analyses.

Robust Regression and Composite Model Building

The ordinary least squares regression and ridge regression analyses produce 5 to 10 outliers (observations not within two standard deviations of the regression lines) in each annual regression; given a normal distribution of 261 observations, one would have expected at least 12 or 13 observations to lie outside of the confidence intervals. One could use the Beaton-Tukey (1974) biweight (robust) procedure for iteratively reweighting the regressions. Large residuals lead to very small observation weights. The biweight function is:

$$w_i = (1 - (r/B)^2)^2 \text{ if } |r| \leqslant B, \tag{2}$$

$$0, \text{ otherwise}$$

where

r = absolute value (residual/standard deviation of error),

B = a tuning constant, 4.685.

The use of the iteratively reweighted least squares regression and ridge regression techniques substantially reduces the 1980–1982 mean square forecast errors (0.729 and 0.619, respectively, as shown in Table 12-2). Security analyst forecast errors can be substantially (and statistically significantly) reduced by 42.6 percent and 51.3 percent, respectively, by the use of weighted least squares and weighted ridge regression techniques.

The regression coefficients on the time series and analyst forecast variables for the ridge regression on the robust-weighted data in 1981 and 1982 are approximately equal; one would have expected this, given the respective (approximately equal) standard deviations of the variables (Bates and Granger 1969). The ridge-estimates coefficients are slightly (not statistically different) better forecasting coefficients than those based on equal variable weights; with equal weighting, the average mean square error is 1.149. The superiority of the estimated weighting scheme has been advanced by Winkler and Makridakis (1983).

Forecasting, Not Estimating, Composite Earnings Models

The composite models developed in the previous section were constructed by regressing time series forecasts and time series model forecasts upon earnings per share. The regression models discussed in the previous section involved contemporaneous variables, and "nonforecasting" models were estimated. However, the use of composite earnings models at time t, based on estimated weights at time $t - 1$, improve upon security analyst forecasts (see Table 12-3).

The composite earnings models are quite useful for forecasting, particularly in 1982. The application of robust regression techniques is statistically significant in reducing analyst forecasting errors. Moreover, the calculation of firm (observation) weights proves useful in forecasting corporate earnings.

Composite Models and Information Coefficients

The application of ordinary least squares and ridge regression analyses on the robust-weighted data produced the lowest mean square forecast-

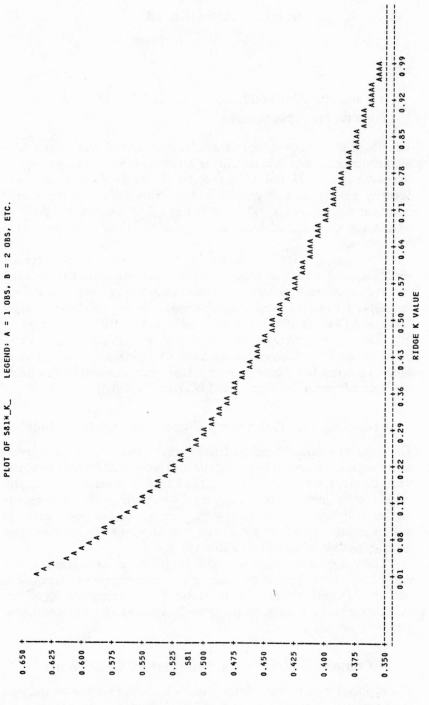

TYPE OF OBSERVATION=RIDGE

PLOT OF B81*K_ LEGEND: A = 1 OBS, B = 2 OBS, ETC.

Table 12-3 Mean Square Forecasting Errors Forecasting Years

Source (Year of Weights)	1981	1982
SEC (t)	.328	.656
Combined Model, OLS (t)	.273	.534
Ridge (t)	.312	.568
Robust (t)	.437	.167
Ridge (Robust) (t)	.391	.183
OLS (t − 1)	.283	.550
Robust (t − 1)	.273	.173[a]
Ridge (Robust) (t − 1)	.289	.213[a]

[a] = statistically significant different from analyst forecasts at 5 percent level.

ing errors among the composite forecasting models. The reweighted regression techniques also aided in the identification of the relative-ranking of the firms' earning growth rates. The information coefficient, IC, measures the efficiency of identifying the relationship between actual and forecasted rankings among the sources of information. One would want to maximize the information coefficient, b, where

$$\text{Actual ranking} = a + b \text{ (Forecasted ranking)}.$$

The information coefficients shown in Table 12-4 show the efficiency of the composite ordinary least squares, minimum absolute deviations, ordinary least squares regression on the robust-weighted data (Robust), and ridge regression on the robust-weighted data [Ridge (Robust)] relative to the analyst ICs. The reweighted regression techniques would substantially aid analysts in forecasting 1981-1982 earnings.

In a more recent *Composite Modeling and Portfolio Performance* study of 648 year-end firms, Guerard and Stone (1988) found that security analyst forecasts produced excess returns of 1.3-3.9 percent annually during the 1981-1985 period. Moreover, composite modeling using ARIMA(0,1,1) forecasts and analyst forecasts produced additional excess returns of 1.5-3.5 percent annually during the 1981-1985 period.

Table 12-4 Information Coefficients

	1980	1981	1982
BJU	.347	.386	.391
SEC	.468	.384	.364
Combined Model, OLS	.353	.280	.312
Ridge	.482	.455	.507
Robust	.448	.299	.355
Ridge (Robust)	.493	.464	.532

The excess returns from analysts' forecasts and composite modeling were statistically significant. Further evidence was produced to cast doubt on the incorporation of all information by analysts as one would expect in an efficient market.

Summary and Conclusions

Composite earnings per share models may be developed using analysts' forecasts and univariate time series forecasts. The OLS composite earnings models substantially reduce the mean square forecasting error present in the analyst forecasts despite the fact that the univariate time series models are not significantly different from random-walk-with-drift formulations. The use of biased regression techniques aids in forecasting earnings, once the analyst and time series forecast variables are weighted in a robust regression-formulated scheme. The estimation of composite earnings models may be an avenue of potential profit; univariate time series models complemented the analyst forecasts in this study. Furthermore, the results of this study indicate that analysts may not necessarily use all information available at the time of their forecasts. Moreover, executive compensation may be associated with earnings growth, although the timing of the association may be difficult to statistically validate.

References

Albrecht, W.S., L.L. Lookabill, and J.C. McKeown. 1977. The Time-Series Properties of Annual Earnings. *Journal of Accounting Research* 15: 226–244.

Armstrong, J.S. 1983. Relative Accuracy of Judgmental and Extrapolative Methods in Forecasting Annual Earnings. *Journal of Forecasting* 2: 437–447.

Ball, R., and R. Watts. 1979. Some Additional Evidence on Survival Biases. *Journal of Finance* 34: 197–206.

Bates, J.M., and C.W.J. Granger. 1969. The Combination of Forecasts. *Operational Research Quarterly* 20: 451–468.

Beaton, A.E., and J.W. Tukey. 1974. The Fitting of Power Series, Meaning Polynomials, Illustrated on Band-Spectroscopic Data. *Technometrics* 16: 147–185.

Belsley, D.A. 1984. Demeaning Conditions Diagnostics Through Centering. *American Statistician* 38: 73–77.

Bopp, A.E. 1985. On Combining Forecasts: Some Extensions and Results. *Management Science* 31: 1492–1498.

Box, G.E.P., and G.M. Jenkins. 1970. *Time Series Analysis: Forecasting and Control.* San Francisco: Holden-Day.

Brown, L.D., and M.S. Rozeff. 1978. The Superiority of Analyst Forecasts as Measures of Expectations: Evidence from Earnings. *Journal of Finance* 33: 1–16.

Bunn, D.W. 1975. A Bayesian Approach to the Linear Combination of Forecasts. *Operating Research Quarterly* 26: 325–329.

Christie, A.A., et al. 1984. Testing for Incremental Information Content in the Presence of Multi-collinearity. *Journal of Accounting and Economics* 6: 205–217.

Clemen, R.T. Linear Constraints and the Efficiency of Combined Forecasts. *Journal of Forecasting,* forthcoming.

Clemen, R.T., and R.L. Winkler. 1986. Combining Economic Forecasts. *Journal of Economic and Business Statistics* 4: 39–46.

Cragg, J.G., and B. Malkiel. 1968. The Consensus and Accuracy of Some Predictions of the Growth of Corporate Earnings. *Journal of Finance* 23: 67–84.

Elton, E.J., and M.J. Gruber. 1972. Earnings Estimation and the Accuracy of Expectational Data. *Management Science* 18: 409–424.

Elton, E.J., M.J. Gruber, and M. Gultekin. 1981. Expectations and Share Prices. *Management Science* 27: 875–887.

Fried, D., and D. Givoly. 1982. Financial Analysts' Forecasts of Earnings: A Better Surrogate for Market Expectations. *Journal of Accounting and Economics* 4: 85–107.

Givoly, D., and J. Lakonishok. 1984. The Quality of Analysts' Forecasts of Earnings. *Financial Analysts Journal* 40–47.

Givoly, D. and J. Lakonishok. 1988. Divergence of Earnings Expectations: The Effect on Stock Market Response to Earnings Signals. In *Stock Market Anomalies,* ed. E. Dimson. Cambridge: Cambridge University Press.

Granger, C.W.J., and P. Newbold. 1977. *Forecasting Economic Time Series.* New York: Academic Press.

Granger, C.W.J., and R. Ramanathan. 1984. Improved Methods of Combining Forecasts. *Journal of Forecasting* 3: 197–204.

Guerard, J.B. Composite Forecasting Using Ridge Regression. *Communications in Statistics*, forthcoming.

Guerard, J.B. 1987. Linear Constraints, Robust-Weighting and Efficient Composite Modeling. *Journal of Forecasting* 6: 193-199.

Guerard, J.B. Composite Forecasting and Analysts' Forecasts of Annual Earnings. *Financial Analysts Journal*, forthcoming.

Guerard, J.B., and B.K. Stone. 1988. Compound Forecasting of Annual Corporate Earnings. Drexel Burnham Lambert, Inc. Working paper.

Guerard, J.B., and R. Ochsner. 1987. Composite Earnings Forecasting Efficiency and Executive Compensation. In *Robust Regression Techniques*, Ed., K.D. Lawrence and J. Arthur. New York: Marcel Dekker.

Hoerl, A.E., and R.W. Kennard. 1970. Ridge Regression: Biased Estimation for Nonorthogonal Problems. *Technometrics* 12: 55-67, 69-82.

Hoerl, A.E., R.W. Kennard, and K.F. Baldwin. 1975. Ridge Regression: Some Simulations. *Communications in Statistics* 4: 105-123.

Jenkins, G.M. 1979. Practical Experiences with Modelling and Forecasting Time Series. In *Forecasting*, ed. O. Anderson. Amsterdam: North-Holland.

Kang, H. 1986. Unstable Weights in the Combination of Forecasts. *Management Science* 32: 683-695.

Little, I.M.D. 1962. Higgledy Piggledy Growth. *Oxford University Institute of Statistics* 24: 387-412.

Montgomery, D.C., and E.A. Peck. 1982. *Introduction to Linear Regression Analysis*. New York: John Wiley & Sons.

Newbold, P., and C.W.J. Granger. 1974. Experience with Forecasting Univariate Time Series and the Combination of Forecasts. *Journal of the Royal Statistical Society* 137: 131-146.

Vinod, H.D., and A. Ullah. 1981. *Recent Advances in Regression Methods*. New York: Marcel Dekker.

Watts, R.L., and R.W. Leftwich. 1977. The Time Series of Annual Accounting Earnings. *Journal of Accounting Research* 15: 254-271.

Winkler, R.L., and S. Makridakis. 1983. The Combination of Forecasts. *Journal of the Royal Statistical Society* 146: 150-157.

Chapter 13

Managing Portfolios: An Efficient Market Model

The purpose of this chapter is to examine the managing of portfolios in an efficient market. In an efficient market, security prices fluctuate randomly around their fair market value, providing few opportunities for investors to outperform a buy-and-hold strategy. A very large empirical literature reveals very few stock market anomalies. In a weak form of the efficient markets hypothesis (EMH), stock prices reflect the past stock history and volume information. The weak form of the EMH cast doubt on the efficiency of technical analysis. The semi-strong form of the EMH holds that all publicly-available information is incorporated into share prices, public announcements, such as dividend, earnings, merger and accounting changes, are incorporated in prices such that fundamental analysis is of little value.

In a strong efficient market, all information is incorporated in share prices such that no participants can earn excess returns. The strong form of the EMH holds that insiders and professional money managers do not produce superior profits.

The empirical evidence is supportive of the weak and semi-strong forms of the EMH; however, insiders earn excessive profits and the strong form evidence is not conclusive.

Few academic hypotheses are as unwelcome in the practitioner-oriented financial community as the concept of the efficient markets hypothesis (EMH). Members of the investment community generally perceive finance academicians as frustrated statisticians who can't make money in the market (with the exception of the late Henry Latané), while many academicians regard practitioners as beneficiaries of the transactions costs creating some of the random deviations of prices from the equilibrium levels.[1] The purpose of this chapter is to provide a brief review of the theory and evidence of the EMH and discuss the implications for portfolio managers.

The EMH is based on the hypothesis that stock prices fully reflect the information available at some time t (Fama 1970, 1976). Businessmen base dividend, investment, and other financial decisions on stock prices, and it is very important that the stock prices reflect equilibrium prices if proper financial decisions are to be made. Investors purchase and sell shares in the belief that the price at which the transaction occurs is, on average, a "fair" price. Generally the EMH is discussed in terms of its weak, semistrong, and strong forms. Each form addresses the information that is incorporated into the stock price. The weak form holds that historic information of prices and volume is incorporated into the stock price. The semistrong form holds that all publicly available information is reflected in stock prices. In the strong form, all information is incorporated into share prices.

The EMH is generally discussed in terms of "fair-game" or "expected-returns" theories. In a fair-game setting, there is no way to process available information to earn an above-average return. The fair-game model may be expressed in terms of market prices, information sets, and excess returns:

$$X_{j,t+1} = P_{csj,t+1} - E(P_{csj,t+1}|\phi_t),   (1)$$

where

$X_{j,t+1}$ = excess return on security j at time $t + 1$,
$P_{csj,t+1}$ = price of security j at time $t + 1$,
$\tilde{P}_{csj,t+1}$ = expected price of security j at time $t + 1$,
ϕ_t = information set at time t.

In an efficient market, the excess return on security j should be zero:

$$E(\tilde{X}_{j,t+1}|\phi_t) = 0   (2)$$

The market is efficient in processing the information set, ϕ_t, such that the expected price of security j in the coming period should be equal to the actual price. That is, the best guess of the actual price next period is

---

[1]For a stronger version of this point, see Malkiel (1981).

the expected price next period given the currently available information. The tilde $(\sim)$ denotes that security prices and excess returns are random variables with zero means.

The reader recognizes that the information set concept refers to the information inherent in the weak, semistrong, and strong forms of the EMH. If one can express the one-period return on security j at time t as

$$\tilde{R}_{j,t} = \frac{P_{csjt} - P_{csj,t-1}}{P_{csj,t-1}}, \tag{3}$$

then one can express the fair-game model in terms of expected returns on securities:

$$Z_{j,t+1} = R_{j,t+1} - E(\tilde{R}_{j,t+1}|\phi_t)$$

$$E(\tilde{Z}_{j,t+1}|\phi_t) = 0. \tag{4}$$

The fair-game model is very similar to the expected-return theory in which the expected price in the next period, given the currently available information set, is equal to the current price of the security multiplied by 1 plus the random rate of return for the security in the next period:

$$E(\tilde{P}_{csj,t+1}|\phi_t) = [1 + E(R_{j,t+1}|\phi_t)]P_{cs_t}. \tag{5}$$

The stochastic process found in Equation (5) is said to be a martingale process. If Equation (5) is written as an inequality, then the process is said to be a submartingale process (Granger 1975):

$$E(\tilde{P}_{csj,t+1}|\phi_t) > P_{cs_t}.$$

Empirical Tests of the Weak Form of the EMH

Some of the earliest tests of the weak form of the EMH, that stock prices fully reflect all historic price information, were performed on the premise that expected returns are constant, i.e., the martingale form of Equation (5). The martingale form has generally been tested by an examination of the autocorrelation function (as we discussed in Chapter 2) of the security's return time series. In essence one regresses the current security return against previous values of the security's returns (with k lags). One would expect, in an efficient market, that the regression coefficients, the autocorrelation function estimates would not be statistically different from zero. The random-walk theory of returns and stock prices, a restricted form of the weak form of the EMH, may be tested using raw (RRW) or logged (LRW) data (Granger 1975). The early empirical pricing tests of Kendall (1953), Alexander (1964), Cootner (1964), and Fama (1965), among others, found few statistically significant deviations from randomness for stock price series and stock index series (see Table 12–1). The average correlation coefficients reported in Granger (1975) and implied R_s^2 (the correlation coefficient squared) of less than 2 percent. Thus, one is hard pressed to reject the random nature of stock prices and indexes. Granger (1975) and Granger and Morganstern (1963) found slight deviations from randomness with the use of spectral analysis. In spectral analysis, one attempts to identify persistent patterns in the data by fitting sine and cosine functions. The spectrum of the error term series was not completely flat, as one would expect to find in a pure random-walk environment, but showed evidence of slight monthly cycles and seasonal harmonics at very low frequencies. This is not terribly different from arguing that stock prices (or corporate earnings) do not follow a random walk but rather a random walk with drift, an ARIMA (0,1,1) process. The Granger and Morganstern (1963) found few deviations from randomness in stock prices.

The random-walk theory of prices holds that successive price changes should be identically and independently distributed (a condition not required in the fair-game model). Each period's security return should be a random variable, as Markowitz illustrated with his roulette wheel (as discussed in Chapter 8). To accept the random-walk hypothesis leads one to accept the weak form of the EMH; however, the acceptance of the weak form of the EMH does not necessarily imply that one accepts the randomness of stock prices (hence the restricted form). Fama (1965) used nonparametric statistics tests, runs tests, to find few statistically significant deviations from randomness in stock price changes.

A final test of the weak form of the EMH involves the testing of the submartingale form of Equation (5), implying that expected returns are positive (Fama 1976). The primary test of the expected returns of the positive form are the filter rule tests examined by Alexander (1964) and Fama and Blume (1966). In the filter rule test, one buys a security if it rises at least x percent (hopefully on large volume) and holds it until it falls x percent from a subsequent high when the investor should sell the stock and assume a short position. Alexander found a filter of one percent outperformed a buy-and-hold strategy, whereas the Fama and Blume (1966) study supported the weak form of the EMH [although their 0.5 percent filter earned a slightly larger than normal rate of return (for 0.5 percent, .115 > .104)]. There is a possibility of earning slight profits on daily price swings. The introduction of transactions costs, such as the floor trader's paying a 0.1% per turnaround clearinghouse fee eliminates the very small advantage of the small filter rule relative to the buy-and-hold strategy (Fama 1976). The overwhelming evidence of the martingale and submartingale forms of Equation (5) supports the existence of a weakly efficient market and tends to discourage technical analysis.

Empirical Tests of the Semistrong Form of the EMH

The semistrong form of the EMH holds that security prices reflect all publicly available information, such as stock splits, earnings and dividend announcements, accounting changes, and mergers. The premiere test of the semistrong form of the EMH is known as the FFJR test of stock splits (Fama et al. 1969). Fama and his colleagues examined all stock splits in which at least five shares were distributed for every four formerly outstanding, for (almost all) NYSE firms from January 1927 through December 1959. The sample included 622 firms and 940 splits. The primary conclusion of the study was that security returns were adjusted for general market conditions. That is, the extraordinary effects of the split were analyzed by subtracting the market return from the security return.

$$E(\tilde{R}_{j,t}|\phi_{t-1}, R_{Mt}) = \alpha_j + \beta_j \tilde{R}_{MT} \tag{6}$$

Equation (6) is known as the market model, and the market is composed of all stocks on the NYSE.

$$\beta_j = \frac{\text{covariance}(\tilde{R}_{j,t} \tilde{R}_{M,t})}{\text{Variance}(\tilde{R}_{Mt})} \tag{7}$$

$$\alpha_j = E(\tilde{R}_{j,t}|\phi_{t-1}) - \beta_j E(\tilde{R}_{M,t}|\phi_{t-1}) \tag{8}$$

The reader immediately recognizes Equation (7) as the beta produced using the market model developed in the previous chapter and Equation (8) as producing the alpha, or excess return. Fama and his collaborators cumulated the excess returns for each month, starting 29 months before the split and ending 30 months after the split. The betas and alphas were estimated, omitting 15 months prior to and following the split because the regression coefficients might be biased because of the rising stock condition preceding most stock splits. They tested the "old wives' tale" that stock splits increase shareholder wealth by adjusting the security's price to a more attractive trading range.

Stock splits usually occur when stock prices are rising; thus, one would not be surprised to find cumulative average residuals (CARs) that are statistically different from zero (positive) prior to the split. The FFJR study presented evidence that positive excess returns were produced in the 29 months prior to the split, although the majority of the excess returns were produced during the 12 months immediately preceding the split. The rising prices one year prior to the split might be associated with a sharp improvement in firms' earnings prospects, according to FFJR. Furthermore, FFJR hypothesized that the market anticipated that splits are generally associated with rising dividends. One notices that the large (34.07%) excess return does not increase following the split. Support is found for the semistrong form of the EMH because following the split announcement, one cannot earn an excess return by purchasing the shares of the firm engaging in the split. There is no significant change in the CARs of the splitting firm unless a change occurs in the firm's dividend behavior. FFJR defined a (relative) dividend change as total dividends paid by the firm in the 12 months after the split divided by total dividend paid in the 12 months before the split, relative to the same ratio for all NYSE firms. Firms generating relative dividend increases maintain the presplit appreciation, even experiencing a slight addition (1.5%). However, firms producing relative dividend decreases experienced substantial excess return decreases (from 26.40% to 19.46%). The FFJR study produced evidence that if firms do not generate the anticipated dividend increase, the stock price plummets, and much of the presplit gain is eliminated.

Earnings announcements are a very interesting test of the semistrong form of the EMH. Ball and Brown (1968) studied 261 firms during the period 1946–66 and, using an Abnormal Performance Index (API), found that almost all (85–90%) of the excess returns were produced prior to the earnings announcement. The importance of Ball and Brown's study is that firms producing "increased" earnings generated positive excess returns throughout the year, with few adjustments following the annual announcement. The firms producing "decreased" earnings produced negative excess returns throughout the year. The actual earnings announcement added little to the relative excess return behavior.

An earnings study concerned with earnings forecasts was developed by Elton, Gruber, and Gultekin (1981) to analyze the effectiveness of security analysts in forecasting earnings and enhancing shareholder wealth. Elton, Gruber, and Gultekin (EGG) analyzed the Lynch, Jones, and Ryan database of consensus earnings estimates, the I/B/E/S service, for 1973, 1974, and 1975, and 710 two-year forecasts for 1974–76. EGG found that excess returns could not be earned by purchasing stock forecasted by analysts to produce the highest expected growth rates; the consensus forecasts were incorporated into share prices as one would expect in a semistrong efficient market. One could make excess returns by correctly forecasting the firms producing the highest earnings growth.

The EGG results supported the Niederhoffer and Regan (1972) results that the 50 best performing stocks produced "good" earnings increases, far higher than anticipated by analysts, whereas the 50 worst performing stocks suffered rather large decreases in earnings although analysts actually had forecast rather large earnings growth. Thus, one must select firms achieving earnings growths, but to secure large excess returns, one must select firms that produce earnings growth in excess of analysts' forecasts. EGG found that the upper 30 percent of firms having the highest earnings growth earned an excess return of 7.75 percent for 12 months following the March data, whereas the bottom 30 percent of firms in earnings growth lost a corresponding 7.31 percent. The middle 40 percent lost slightly more than 1.0 percent. Thus, earnings are a very important determinant of share prices. Malkiel (1981) has referred to earnings forecasting as the *raison d'être* of analysts. Fundamental research appears to be an avenue worth pursuing if one can effectively forecast earnings or, as EGG noted, the consensus forecasts. The EGG study of earnings forecasts is supportive of the semistrong form of the EMH.

One might expect accounting changes that affect earnings to be of concern to investors and portfolio managers, given the influence of earnings on prices. Kaplan and Roll (1972) found that firms that switched to the flow-through method of reporting investment credit and switched from accelerated depreciation to straight-line depreciation did not produce any statistically significant permanent change in stockholder wealth. These firms generally produced negative abnormal returns, as one would have expected, given that these accounting changes generally were designed to produce higher reported earnings. The negative abnormal returns were diminished for several weeks about the time of the announcement, but no long-term inefficiencies in the market were discovered.

Mergers represent an additional area where the semistrong efficient markets hypothesis may be tested. Mandelker (1974), studying major mergers during the period 1947–1966, found that acquiring firms' shareholders did not earn a statistically significant excess return. The lack of profitability reflects the fact that the acquiring firms paid a price in which all potential merger profits had been bid away. The lack of merger profits for the acquiring firms is known as the Perfectly Competitive Acquisitions Market (PCAM). The acquired firms' shareholders earn statistically significant excess returns (24 percent) because of the merger premiums (Dodd and Ruback 1977). The selection of takeover targets represents an area of potential profitability.

Empirical Evidence Concerning the Strong Form of the EMH

The strong form of the EMH addresses the question of whether all information is incorporated in share prices. The strong form tests the immediate adjustment of the market to public and nonpublic (potentially monopolistic) information. The empirical evidence is mixed on the strong form tests: corporate insiders and stock exchange specialists consistently earned above-normal returns, whereas money managers (primarily mutual funds) have not generally outperformed the market.

Corporate insiders must report purchases and sales of securities to the SEC, as required by the securities and Exchange Act of 1934, every month (Jaffe 1974a, 1974b). Corporate insiders, generally corporate officers and major stockholders, earned excess returns of about 4% per trade during the period 1961–1967. Furthermore, Jaffe (1974b) found that government regulation of insiders during the 1960s [the Cady, Roberts decision, 1961; the Texas Gulf Sulphur indictment, 1965; and the Texas Gulf Sulphur decision, 1966] did not affect the volume or profitability of insider trading. In fact, given his evidence on profitability and the value of regulation to society, Jaffe questioned whether insider trading regulation was cost-effective. The strong form does not hold with respect to corporate insiders who clearly have access to quite lucrative information that is not available to the public at the same time (there is about a six-week delay).

Stock specialists are required to maintain an orderly market in their stocks; thus, specialists should buy on the "down-tick" and sell on the "up-tick." Specialists have access to information concerning unfilled orders that is very productive in generating above-average returns (Niederhoffer and Osborne 1966). An SEC report (1963) found that a specialist sells above his last purchase on 83 percent of his sales and buys below his last sell on 81 percent of his purchases. Stock specialists represent another violation of the strong form of the EMH.

Money managers may be able to take advantage of monopolistic access to security information. Three indexes are generally used to measure portfolio performance of money managers. Sharpe (1966) developed a variability index, known as the Sharpe Index, to measure relative performances of 34 mutual funds during the period 1954–1963. The Sharpe Index, S_I, is constructed by dividing the excess return on the portfolio by the standard deviations of the annual returns:

$$S_I = \frac{E(R_p) - R_F}{\sigma_p}. \tag{9}$$

The Sharpe Index is a Capital Market Line (CML) measure, as it depends on total risk or variability. Sharpe found that the average S_I for the 34 funds was 0.633 during the period 1954–1963, whereas the Dow enjoyed a Sharpe Index of 0.667.

Treynor (1965) used beta, or systematic risk, to rank mutual funds and created the Treynor Index, T_I, by finding the excess return of the portfolio by the portfolio beta:

$$T_I = \frac{E(R_p) - R_F}{\beta_p}.$$ (10)

Treynor also found that only one of 57 mutual funds significantly beat the market. The Jensen Index, J_I, (1968) is a variation of the Security Market Line (SML) that measures portfolio performance in terms of the security's excess return, relative to the market's excess return:

$$E(R_p) - R_F = \alpha + \beta_p[E(R_M) - R_F].$$ (11)

The Jensen Index uses alpha, α, to measure the ability of a mutual fund manager to outperform the market. A manager must produce a positive alpha to beat the market. Jensen (1969) analyzed a sample of 115 mutual funds during the period 1955–1964, finding an alpha of -1.1 and an average beta of 0.84. It is interesting to note the relatively low beta of the money managers. Jensen found that 45 of the 115 money managers produced alphas (net returns) between -1.0 percent and 1.0 percent. Thus, the majority of the money managers earned alphas that did not beat the market but were not destructive of investor wealth. The original results of Sharpe, Treynor, and Jensen showed support for the strong form of the EMH, as money managers could not outperform the market despite the possible availability of nonpublic information. Recent evidence by McDonald (1974) suggests that funds in the 1960s, seeking to maximize capital gains, outperformed the market (as measured by the Treynor Index), while income-growth, growth-income, income, and balanced funds underperformed the market.

The Rationality of Market Forecasts

An interesting recent analysis of efficient markets modeling can be found in Mishkin (1983). One can test the rationality of financial market forecasts by examining the forecast error and analyzing the error's correlation with combinations of information available at the time the forecast was developed. Mishkin (1983) is primarily concerned with examining the efficiency of the bond market; testing the hypothesis that interest rates are rational during the 1954.1–1976.4 period. The methodology used by Mishkin is the Macro Rational Expectations (MRE) model which examines the effects of unanticipated movements in economic variables. Mishkin found an efficient bond market in which unanticipated (increases) movements in 90-day Treasury Bill rates were associated with higher long-term U.S. government bonds. Additional analysis of prior bill movements would not have led to more efficiency in the bond market. The constant liquidity premium was not statistically different from zero in the Mishkin study. However, Mishkin found irrationality in inflation forecasts in the bond market. In an efficient market environment, unanticipated inflationary increases should produce higher long-term rates. Mishkin's results of inflationary expectations imply that increases in inflation would continue which he attributed to the very low inflation at the beginning of the period and unusually high inflationary rates prevailing in the mid-1970s. Mishkin found no statistically significant deviations from rationality in the joint tests of inflation and interest rate forecasts during the 1954–1976 period.

Conclusions and Implications of the EMH for Portfolio Managers

It is extremely difficult to outperform the market. It appears that technical analysis is of little value because the market is weak-form efficient. The efficiency of the market might appear to cast doubt on fundamental analysis; the results of Elton, Gruber, and Gultekin, however, support the search for improved methods of forecasting corporate earnings and consensus analysts' forecasts. The market for mergers appears to be efficient, although merger premiums provide excess returns to stockholders of the acquired firms. The strong-form efficiency tests support the profitability of insiders and stock specialists.

Portfolio managers are unlikely to produce consistently positive alphas unless they are superior at forecasting earnings or takeover targets. Most money managers should set their portfolio betas and earn a risk-adjusted return commensurate with the SML. Moreover, market-timing using portfolio betas will probably produce little profitability. Analysts in an efficient market can produce positive alphas by correctly identifying stocks producing the highest earnings growth.

References

Alexander, S. 1964. Price Movements in Speculative Markets: Trends or Random Walks. In Cootner, ed., *Random Character of Stock Market Prices*. Cambridge, Mass.: MIT Press, 338–372.

Ball, R. 1972. Changes in Accounting Techniques and Stock Prices. *Empirical Research in Accounting*, (supplement to *Journal of Accounting Research* 10 (1972).

Black, F. 1972. Implications of the Random Walk Hypothesis for Portfolio Management. *Financial Analysts Journal* 27 (March–April): 16–22.

Ball, R.P., and P. Brown. 1968. An Empirical Evaluation of Accounting Income Numbers. *Journal of Accounting Research* 6 (Autumn): 159–178.

Cootner, P. 1964. *The Random Nature of Stock Prices.* Cambridge, Mass.: MIT Press.

Dodd, P., and R. Ruback. 1977. Tender Offers and Stockholders Returns. *Journal of Financial Economics* 5: 351–374.

Elton, E.J., and M.J. Gruber. 1981. *Modern Portfolio Theory and Investment Analysis.* 3d ed. New York: John Wiley & Sons.

Elton, E.J., M.J. Gruber, and M. Gultekin. 1981. Expectations and Share Prices. *Management Science* 9: 975–87.

Fama, E.F. 1965. The Behavior of Stock Prices. *Journal of Business* 38: 34–105.

———. 1970. Efficient Capital Markets: A Review of Theory and Empirical Work. *Journal of Finance* 25: 383–417.

———. 1970. Random Walks in Stock Prices. *Financial Analysts Journal* 21, no. 5: 55–58.

———. 1976. *Foundations of Finance.* New York: Basic Books.

Fama, E.F., and M. Blume. 1966. Filter Rules and Stock Market Trading Profits. *Journal of Business* 39: 226–244.

Fama, E.F., et al. 1969. The Adjustment of Stock Prices to New Information. *International Economic Review* 10: 1–21.

Granger, C.W.J. 1975. A Survey of Efficient Capital Markets. In *International Capital Markets*, ed. E.J. Elton and M.J. Gruber. Amsterdam: North-Holland.

Granger, C.W.J., and O. Morganstern. 1963. Spectral Analysis of New York Stock Market Prices. *Kyklos*, 1–27.

Jaffe, J.F. 1974. Special Information and Insider Trading. *Journal of Business* 47: 410–428.

———. 1974. The Effect of Regulation Changes on Insider Trading. *Bell Journal of Economics and Management Science* 45: 93–121.

Jensen, M.C. 1968. The Performance of Mutual Funds in the Period 1945–1964. *Journal of Finance* 23: 389–416.

Jensen, M.C. 1969. Risk, The Pricing of Capital Assets, and the Evaluation of Investment Portfolios. *Journal of Business* 42: 167–247.

Kaplan, R.S., and R. Roll. 1972. Investor Evaluation of Accounting Information: Some Empirical Evidence. *Journal of Business* 45: 225–257.

Kendall, Maurice G. 1953. The Analysis of Economic Time Series. *Journal of the Royal Statistical Society* 96: 11–25.

Latané, H.A., O.M. Joy, and C.P. Jones. 1970. Quarterly Data Sort—Rand Routines and Security Evaluation. *Journal of Business* 43: 427–438.

Lorie, James H., and V. Niederhoffer. 1968. Predictive and Statistical Properties of Insider Trading. *Journal of Law and Economics* 11: 35–53.

Malkiel, B. 1981. *A Random Walk Down Wall Street.* New York: W.W. Norton.

Mandelker, G. 1974. The Case of Merging Firms. *Journal of Financial Economics* 1: 303–335.

Mishkin, F.S. 1983. *A Rational Expectations Approach to Macroeconomics.* Chicago: The University of Chicago Press.

Niederhoffer, V., and M.F.M. Osborne. 1966. Market Making and Reversal on the Stock Exchange. *Journal of the American Statistical Association* 61: 897–916.

Niederhoffer, V., and Regan, P. 1972. Earnings Changes, Analysts' Forecasts and Stock Prices. *Financial Analysts Journal.* 65–71.

Report of the Special Study of the Security Markets. 1963. Washington, D.C.: Securities and Exchange Commission.

Sharpe, W.F. 1966. Mutual Fund Performance. *Journal of Business* 39, no. 1: 119–139.

Treynor, J.L. 1965. How to Rate Management of Investment Funds. *Harvard Business Review* 43: 63–75.

Chapter 14

Models for Corporate Acquisitions

The purpose of this chapter is to briefly review the merger history of the United States and the merger-stock price correlations. The corporate acquisitions market is characterized as the Perfectly Competitive Acquisitions Market (PCAM) in which the price paid is such that no merger profits result for the acquiring firm's stockholders. The lack of consistent merger profits is not obvious given the recent merger activity. The merger history of the United States is reviewed and the relationship between mergers and stock prices is examined. The associations among mergers, price-earnings multiples, and stock prices are examined because of the possible measurement of synergistic effects. The Larson-Gonedes price-earnings multiple model is very useful in identifying necessary stock price movements for producing synergy.

Merger theories, including reduction in bankruptcy risks, are reviewed and an appendix is included to analyze risk reduction impacts on equity valuation in mergers.

History of Mergers in the United States

The first major merger movement began in 1879, with the creation of the Standard Oil Trust, and ended with the depression of 1904. During the merger movement, giant corporations were formed by the combination of numerous smaller firms. The smaller companies represented nearly all the manufacturing or refining capacity of their industries. The 40 largest firms in the oil-refining industry, comprising more than 90 percent of the country's refining capacity and oil pipelines for its transportation, combined to form Standard Oil. In the two decades following the rise of Standard Oil, similar horizontal mergers created single dominant firms in several industries. These dominant firms included the Cottonseed Oil Trust (1884), the Linseed Oil Trust (1885), the National Lead Trust (1887), The Distillers and Cattle Feeders (1887), and the Sugar Refineries Company (1887). The trust form of organization was outlawed by court decisions, but merger activities continued to create near-monopolies as the single-corporation or holding-company organization became dominant. The Diamond Match Company (1889), the American Tobacco Company (1890), the United States Rubber Company (1892), the General Electric Company (1892), and the United States Leather Company (1893) were created by the development of the modern corporation or holding company.

The height of the merger movement was reached in 1901, when 785 plants combined to form America's first billion-dollar firm, the United States Steel Corporation. The series of mergers creating U.S. Steel allowed it to control 65 percent of the domestic blast furnace and finished steel output. This growth in concentration was typical of the first merger movement. The early mergers saw 78 of 92 large consolidations gain control of 50 percent of their total industry output, and 26 secure 80 percent or more.

The first major merger movement occurred during a period of rapid economic growth. The economic rationale for the large merger movement was the development of the modern corporation, with its limited liability, and the modern capital markets, which facilitated the consolidations through the absorption of the large security issues necessary to purchase firms. Nelson (1959) found the mergers were highly correlated with the period's stock prices (.613) and industrial production (.259) during the 1895–1904 period. The expansion of security issues allowed financiers the financial power necessary to induce independent firms to enter large consolidations. The rationale for the first merger movement was not that of trying to preserve profits despite slackening demand and greater competitive pressures. Nor was the merger movement the result of the development of the national railroad system, which reduced geographic isolation and transportation costs. The first merger movement ended in 1904 with the depression, with whose onset coincided the Northern Securities case. Here it was held, for the first time, that antitrust laws could be used to attack mergers leading to market dominance.

A second major merger movement stirred the country from 1916 until the Depression of 1929. This merger movement was only briefly interrupted by the First World War and the recession of 1921 and 1922. The approximately 12,000 mergers of the period coincided with the stock market boom of the 1920s. Although mergers greatly affected the electric and gas utility industry, market structure was not as severely concentrated by the second movement as it had been by the first. Stigler (1950) concluded that mergers during this period created oligopolies, such as Bethlehem Steel and Continental Can. Mergers, primarily vertical and conglomerate in nature as opposed to the essentially horizontal mergers of the first movement, did affect competition adversely. The conglomerate product-line extensions of the 1920s were enhanced by the high cross-elasticities of demand for the merging companies' products (Lintner 1971). Antitrust laws, though not seriously enforced, prevented mergers from creating a single dominant firm. Merger activity diminished with the Depression of 1929 and continued to decline until the 1940s.

The third merger movement began in 1940; mergers reached a significant proportion of firms in 1946 and 1947. The merger action from 1940 to 1947, although involving 7.5 percent of all manufacturing and mining corporations and controlling 5 percent of the total assets of the firms in those industries, was quite small compared to the merger activities of the 1920s. The mergers of the 1940s included only one between companies with assets exceeding $50 million and none between firms with assets surpassing $100 million. The corresponding figures for the mergers of the 1920s were 14 and 8, respectively. Eleven firms acquired larger firms during the mergers of the 1920s than the largest firm acquired during the 1940s.

The mergers of the 1940s affected competition far less than did the two previous merger movements, with the exception of the food and textile industries. The acquisitions by the large firms during the 1940s rarely amounted to more than 7 percent of the acquiring firms' 1939 assets or to as much as a quarter of the acquiring firm's growth from 1940 to 1947. Approximately $5 billion of assets were held by acquired or merged firms over the period 1940–1947. Smaller firms were generally acquired by larger firms. Companies with assets exceeding $100 million acquired, on average, firms with assets of less than $2 million. The larger firms tended to engage in a greater number of acquisitions than smaller firms. The acquisitions of the larger acquiring firms tended to involve more firms than did those of smaller acquiring firms. Mergers added relatively less to the existing size of the larger acquiring firms. The relatively smaller asset growth of the larger acquiring firms is in accordance with the third merger movement's generally small effects on competition and concentration. One factor contributing to the maintenance of competition was that many mergers were initiated by the owners of the smaller firms. Financiers and investment bankers did not play a prominent part early in the third merger movement.

The current merger movement, an extension of the 1940s conglomerate movement beginning in 1951 and continuing to the present, the forecast period of this study, was becoming a movement of conglomerate mergers. One of the nine mergers occurring in 1951 involved acquired firms with assets exceeding $10 million, four were con-

glomerate mergers, of which three were product-line-extension combinations. The growth of the large conglomerate mergers continued
throughout the forecast period. In 1954, 21 of the 37 mergers involving
acquired firms with assets exceeding $10 million were conglomerate in
nature; 14 of the 21 conglomerate mergers were product-line extensions,
while only two of the mergers were market-extension combinations. The
mergers of the 1960s, 1970s, and 1980s were almost purely conglomerate
in nature.

The Accounting Basis

If one company purchases another company and only the acquiring company survives, the combination is a merger. A consolidation involves the
combination of at lesat two firms in which a new firm is created.

A company can acquire another firm by the *purchase* accounting
method, in which the acquired firm is valued as the amount of assets
given in exchange (Davidson et al. 1976). The parent firm records the acquired assets at their current market value. If the current value of the acquired firm exceeds its book value, the excess is goodwill that will be
amortized over a period of no more than 40 years.

A second accounting practice, the *pooling-of-interests* method, is
allowed for acquisitions in which interests of both firms' stockholders
are merged. No assets are revalued and no goodwill is recognized as
assets, and liabilities of the new firms are recorded as such on the unmerged firms' books. The pooling-of-interests method may be used only
when one firm issues voting stock for the acquisition; no cash transactions are allowed. The stock issuance for the acquisition must be a single
transaction, and the acquiring firm must acquire at least 90% of the acquired firm's stock.

The Economic Basis for Acquisitions

Firms seek to acquire other firms for three reasons: to pursue profits
through monopoly power, to generate economies of scale in operations,
and to contribute managerial abilities lacking in the acquired firm's
management. This chapter will present some of the leading theories of
corporate mergers. The empirical tests of the effects of mergers on stockholder welfare will be discussed.

Expectations of the three economic benefits of mergers can explain
horizontal mergers, in which a firm acquires a firm in its own industry.
But the economic reasons cannot explain the post-war trend of conglomerate mergers, in which a firm acquires a firm in an unrelated industry. Economists have held that mergers do not exhibit synergism, the

"2 + 2 = 5" effect. The absence of synergism leads to the acceptance of the additive property of value: the value of the merged film is the sum of the market values of the unmerged firms (Mossin 1973):

$$MV_{ab} = MV_a + MV_b \qquad (1)$$

where

MV_{ab} = market value of the merged firm, a and b;

MV_a = market value of firm a;

MV_b = market value of firm b.

If no synergism exists, there would not seem to be any economic rationale for conglomerate mergers.

Conglomerate mergers were explained by Mueller (1969) as resulting from firms' attempts to maximize growth. If a larger, more mature firm wants to consider the more profitable investment opportunities and the higher rates of return on projects of a smaller, younger firm, the larger firm must purchase the smaller firm. By purchasing the smaller firm, the larger firm has internalized the investment opportunities, and the more profitable marginal investment contributes to the larger firm's growth. Synergism, in which the merged firm's market value exceeds the sum of the unmerged firms' market values, would rarely be found in a conglomerate merger. Mueller hypothesized that the conglomerate merger could be justified only if the managers of the acquiring firm could find investment opportunities currently overlooked by the acquired firm's management. Mueller's theory of mergers has been questioned since its premise is that firms maximize growth. Corporate benefits tend to be distributed on the basis of profits, not growth of sales. Management should try to maximize profits if profits serve as the basis for benefits.

Gort (1969) put forth a theory of mergers based on valuation discrepancies. Acquisitions of other firms occur when a higher value is placed on the firm's assets by the potential purchaser than by the current owners. The valuation discrepancies tended to occur in times of high stock prices, as purchasers tend to believe the rapid changes in stock prices represent an increased economic disturbance. The higher disturbance increases the distribution of the firm's assets' valuations, raising the probability that an investor will place a higher value on the firm than the current owners. The empirical evidence has revealed that mergers occur during periods of high stock prices; thus there could be a basis for Gort's disturbance theory.

One of the principal theories of conglomerate mergers is that mergers reduce the probability of bankruptcy for the merged firm. Lewellen (1971) advanced the theory that mergers reduce the variance of the merged firm's cash flow, lessen the possibility of default on its debt, and increase the debt capacity of the firm. Debt capacity is increased as lenders are willing to establish a higher corporate lending limit to the merged entity. However, the merger must involve firms with less than perfectly correlated income streams. The merging firms must not have cash flows such that defaults on their borrowings occur simultaneously.

Assume that firms A and B are considering a merger. Given the following probability estimates of the possible states of the world, would the risk of default be lessened by the merger?

Probability	State	Cash Flow Firm A	Firm B
0.2	Depression	$ 100	$920
0.3	Recession	300	700
0.4	Normal	700	240
0.1	Boom	1,000	0

It is obvious that the cash flows of firms A and B are negatively correlated. Firm A could be a venture capital firm that profits from a rising economy while firm B could be a gold mining company that profits when gold prices are high, the economy falling.

Firms A and B have the same expected values $E(CF)$ and essentially the same standard deviations of cash flows, σ_{CF}. The expected cash flow is of the form

$$\sum_{i=1}^{4} p_i CF_i,$$

where p_i = probability of the occurence of state of nature, i.

and the variance is of the form

$$\sum_{i=1}^{4} [CF_i - E(CF)]^2 p_i. \tag{2}$$

We may calculate the expected values of the two cash flows, CF_A and CF_B:

$$.2(\$80) \quad = \$\ 16 \qquad .2(920) = \$184$$
$$.3(\$280) \quad = \quad 84 \qquad .3(700) = \quad 210$$
$$.4(\$700) \quad = \quad 280 \qquad .4(240) = \quad 96$$
$$.1(\$1,000) = \quad 100 \qquad .1(0) \quad = \quad 0$$
$$E(\mathrm{CF}_A) = \$490 \qquad E(\mathrm{CF}_B) = \$490$$

and the variances:

$$.2(\$80 - \$490) \quad = \$\ 33,620$$
$$.3(\$280 - \$490) = \quad 13,230$$
$$.4(\$700 - \$490) = \quad 17,640$$
$$.1(\$1,100 - \$490) = \quad 37,210$$
$$\mathrm{Var}(\mathrm{CF}_A) = \$101,700$$
$$\sigma(\mathrm{CF}_A) = \quad \$319$$

$$.2(\$920 - \$490) = \$36,980$$
$$.3(\$700 - \$490) = \quad 13,230$$
$$.4(\$240 - \$490) = \quad 25,000$$
$$.1(\$\ 0 - \$490) = \quad 24,010$$
$$\mathrm{VAR}(\mathrm{CF}_B) = \$99,200$$
$$\sigma(\mathrm{CF}_B) = \quad \$315$$

The covariance of A's and B's cash flows, the covariance being

$$\sum_{i=1}^{4} p_i[\mathrm{CF}_{A_i} - E(\mathrm{CF}_A)][E(\mathrm{CF}_{B_i} - E(\mathrm{CF}_B)], \qquad (3)$$

is calculated:

$$.2(\$80 - \$490)\ (\$920 - \$490) = \$-35,260$$
$$.3(\$280 - \$490)\ (\$700 - \$490) = \quad -13,230$$
$$.4(\$700 - \$490)\ (\$240 - \$490) = \quad -21,800$$
$$.1(\$1,100 - \$490)\ (\$0 - \$490) = \quad -29,890$$
$$\mathrm{Cov}(\mathrm{CF}_A,\ \mathrm{CF}_B) = \$-99,380$$

The correlation coefficient, r, of the cash flows of firms A and B will establish that these are imperfectly correlated firms.

$$r = \frac{\mathrm{Cov}(\mathrm{CF}_A,\ \mathrm{CF}_B)}{\sqrt{\mathrm{Var}(\mathrm{CF}_A) \times \mathrm{Var}(\mathrm{CF}_B)}}$$

$$= \frac{\$-99,380}{\sqrt{\$101,700 \times \$99,200}} = \frac{\$-99,380}{\$100,452} = -.989$$

The correlation coefficient of $-.99$ shows that the cash flows of firms A and B are almost perfectly negatively correlated.

If firms A and B are assumed to have assets of \$10,000 each, a debt of \$6,000 each, with each firm's debt having a 4 percent cost, the unmerged firms should have essentially the same default probability. The interest costs for each firm are \$240, that is, \$6,000(.04), and the probabilities of default, given by the area under the normal curve, are essentially equal. The general form is

$$Z = \frac{x - \mu}{\sigma} \tag{4}$$

where

Z = Standardized normal variable;

x = Interest cost, \$240;

μ = Expected value, \$490 of cash flow;

σ = Standard deviation of cash flow, \$319 and \$315 for firms A and B, respectively.

P_r (Firm A's cash flow > \$240)

$$z_A = \frac{\$240 - \$490}{\$319} = -.784$$

$$z_B = \frac{\$240 - \$490}{\$315} = -.794$$

The Z-values of $-.784$ and $-.794$ correspond to bankruptcy probabilities of .2187 and .2175 for firms A and B, respectively. The Z-value of $-.78$ indicates an area under the normal curve such that there is a .2823 probability that the outcome cash flow will fall between \$240 and \$490. There is a probability of .5000 that the cash flow will exceed \$490. Summing up these probabilities gives .7823, the probability that firm A's cash flow will exceed \$240. Thus $(1 - .7823) = .2187$, the probability of firm A's cash flow falling below its interest obligations and bankruptcy ensuing.

The merger of firms A and B yields a cash flow of:

Probability	State	(M) Merged Firm's Cash Flow
.2	Depression	$1,020
.3	Recession	1,000
.4	Normal	940
.1	Boom	1,000

The expected value and the variance of the cash flow may be calculated:

$$.2($1,020) = $204$$
$$.3($1,000) = 300$$
$$.4($940) = 376$$
$$.1($1,000) = 100$$
$$E(CF_M) = $980$$

$$.2($1,020 - $980) = $320$$
$$.3($1,000 - $980) = 120$$
$$.4($940 - $980) = 640$$
$$.1($1,000 - $980) = 40$$
$$Var(CF_M) = $1,120$$

The variance of the merged firm's cash flow is only $1,120. Its standard deviation is $33.47, and the probability of bankruptcy goes to zero:

$$z = \frac{$480 - $980}{$33.47} = -14.94 > -3.0$$

Even though the merged firm's interest cost is $480, the sum of the un-merged firms' interest expenses, the standard deviation is so reduced that the probability of bankruptcy is zero. The Z-value far exceeds -3.0, the minimum value of the normal curve. With less than perfectly cor-related cash flows, mergers reduce the merged firm's variance and risk of default.

Another way of examining the reduction in variance is to look at the merger in a portfolio approach. Assume that firms A and B have cash flow variances of 30 percent and a correlation coefficient of .40. If the merged firm is made up of 50 percent of firm A and 50 percent of firm B, the merged firm's variance and standard deviation will be

$$\sigma(CF_M) = \sqrt{Var(CF_M)}$$

$$= \sqrt{W_A^2\sigma_A^2 + W_B^2\sigma_B^2 + 2W_AW_B\sigma_{AB}\sigma_A\sigma_B}$$

$$= \sqrt{(.50)^2(.30) + (.50)^2(.30) + 2(.50)(.50)(.40)(\sqrt{.30})(\sqrt{.30})}$$

$$= \sqrt{.075 + .075 + .06}$$

$$= \sqrt{.21}$$

$$= .4583.$$

The unmerged firms A and B had variances of 30 percent, whereas the merged firm has a variance of 21 percent. Firms A and B had standard deviations of .5477, that is, $\sqrt{.30}$, and the merged firm's standard deviation is only .4583. The portfolio approach reveals that mergers reduce the risk of the merged firm relative to the risks of the unmerged firms.

Since the variance of the merged firm falls, the merged firm could sustain a higher debt level than the sum of the unmerged firms. The existence of additional debt capacity creates more highly leveraged firms. The leverage increases the total market value of the firm, leading to a higher stock price. The higher stock price increases the wealth of the firm's stockholders.

The Larson-Gonedes Exchange Ratio Model

Larson and Gonedes (1969) developed an exchange ratio model that is both theoretical and highly testable. The model can be developed from an assumption that the acquiring firm wants to project a growth image so that the market will capitalize its earnings at a high price-earnings multiple. As the firm acquires smaller firms (in terms of the firms' price-earnings multiples), the earnings of the acquired firms are capitalized at the acquiring firm's higher price-earnings multiple. The merger results in a higher market price for the acquiring firm.

Assume two firms, A and B, can be represented by the following data:

	Firm A	Firm B
Earnings (E)	$20 million	$ 5 million
Shares Outstanding (S)	2 million	1 million
Earnings Per Share (EPS)	$10	$ 5
Stock Price Per Share (P)	$160	$50
Price-Earnings Multiple (P/E)	16	10

Firm A is interested in acquiring firm B and is willing to pay firm B's stockholders $60 per share for their stock. Firm B's stockholders are delighted, because they have immediately profited $10 per share. If firm A is willing to pay $60 per share for firm B, the exchange ratio, ER, is

$$ER = \frac{P_B}{P_A} = \frac{\$60}{\$160} = .375.$$

To pay firm B's stockholders, firm A can issue firm B's stockholders (.375) 1,000,000 shares or 375,000 shares of firm A's stock. If a stockholder in firm B before the merger owned 100 shares of stock, worth $5,000, he now owns 37.5 shares of firm A's stock. Following the merger, the former stockholder of firm A has holdings worth $6,000, that is, 37.5 × ($160). His gain is $1,000 because of the merger.

We must now examine whether firm A's stockholders will profit. If firm A pays firm B's stockholders $60 per share and issues 375,000 shares, the merger is very profitable for firm A's stockholders as long as the market allows firm A's price-earnings multiple to remain at 16. Following the merger, firm AB is represented as follows:

Firm AB

Earnings = $20 million + $5 million = $25 million
Shares Outstanding = 2,000,000 + 375,000 = 2,375,000
EPS = $10.53
Price = P/E (EPS) = 16 ($10.53) = $168.48

Firm A's stockholders have profited $8.48 per share because of the merger. Notice, however, that firm A's stockholders profited only because the market did not adjust the firm's price-earnings multiple after the merger. A decrease in the price-earnings multiple of the merged firm could well wipe out the acquiring firm's gains.

In the absence of synergy, Larson and Gonedes held that firm A's price-earnings multiple should fall as a result of the merger. The price-earnings multiple of the merged firm, θ, should be the weighted average of the merging firms' price-earnings multiples in the absence of synergy:

$$\theta = \frac{P_A(S_A) + P_B(S_B)}{E_A + E_B} \tag{5}$$

$$= \frac{\$160(2,000,000) + \$60(1,000,000)}{\$20,000,000 + \$5,000,000}$$

$$= 15.2.$$

If the price-earnings multiple of the merged firm is equal to θ, there are no profits for the acquiring firm's stockholders; the price of firm A's stock remains at $160:

$$P_A = \$10.53(15.2) = \$160.06$$

The presence of synergy would be shown in a price-earnings multiple of the merged firm exceeding θ. If the price-earnings multiple of the merged firm is less than θ, the acquiring firm's stockholders suffer a loss and would oppose the merger.

Firm A's shareholders should be willing to pay firm B's stockholders a price dictated by a maximum acceptable exchange ratio, ER_A. Larson and Gonedes derived this to be

$$ER_A = \frac{\theta(E_A + E_B) - (P/E)_A(E_A)}{(P/E)_A E_A \left(\dfrac{1}{S_A}\right)(S_B)} \tag{6}$$

For example, if the market were to allow the merged firm's price-earnings multiple to remain at 16, firm A's stockholders could afford to pay firm B's stockholders a price far exceeding $60 per share and still reap merger profits:

$$ER_A = \frac{16(\$25,000,000) - 16(20,000,000)}{16(\$20,000,000)\left(\dfrac{1}{2,000,000}\right)(1,000,000)}$$

$$= .500.$$

An exchange ratio of .500 implies a maximum acceptable price of $80 per share for firm B's stock:

$$P_B = ER_A(P_A) = .500(\$160) = \$80.$$

If firm A pays firm B stockholders a price of exactly $80 per share, firm A's stockholders are indifferent to the merger because the price of firm A's stock remains at $160 per share. Firm A must issue 500,000 shares, that is, .5(1,000,000), to acquire firm B. Following the merger, firm A is represented as:

	Firm A
Earnings	$25,000,000
Shares Outstanding	2,500,000
EPS	$10
P/E	16
Price = $160	= $10(16).

Firm A's stockholders profit as long as the exchange ratio is below .500. If the market allows a price-earnings multiple of the merged firm to remain at 16, firm A cannot pay a higher price than $80 per share for firm B and still profit from the merger. Of course, firm A would prefer to offer firm B's stockholders as small a price as possible for their stock to consummate the merger. If firm A paid firm B's stockholders a price of $60 per share, the merger premium, MP, would be given in terms of the actual exchange ratio, AER:

$$MP = \left(\frac{AER(P_A) - P_B}{P_B} \right)(100) \qquad (7)$$

where

$$AER = \frac{\$60}{\$160} = .375$$

$$MP = \left(\frac{.375(\$160) - \$50}{\$50} \right)(100) = 20$$

A 20 percent merger premium would have been paid.[1]

---

[1]The minimum θ consistent with the profitability constraint, that the merged firm's price must be at least as great as the acquiring firm's price, is given by

$$\theta = \frac{P_A[AER(S_B) + S_A]}{E_A + E_B}$$

$$= \frac{\$160[.375(1,000,000) + 2,000,000]}{\$20,000,000 + 5,000,000}$$

$$= 15.2.$$

Notice the minimum θ consistent with the acquiring firm's profitability constraint equals the weighted average price-earnings multiple for the merging firms.

If firm A paid firm B's stockholders $70 per share for their stock, the actual exchange ratio would be .4375 and the merger premium would be 40 percent. The minimum θ consistent with merger profitability would be

Synergism will result only if θ exceeds the weighted average of the merging firm's price-earnings multiples. If

$$\theta > \frac{P_A(S_A) + P_B(S_B)}{E_A + E_B},$$

the market value of the merged firm exceeds the market values of the unmerged firms. If $ER > P_B/P_A$, the acquired firm profits more proportionally than the acquiring firm. The reverse occurs if $ER < P_B/P_A$. A firm should engage in a merger only if it benefits its stockholders. The relative bargaining strengths of the acquiring and acquired firms determine the distribution of the merger gains. Note that high price-earnings multiples, generally resulting from high stock price, allow more mergers to be profitable. The history of mergers in the United States substantiates the positive association between stock prices and number of mergers.

Testing for Synergism

Research has established that the market anticipates mergers at least seven months before the mergers occur. Mergers generally occur during rises in stock prices, and thus tests for synergy must consider market movements. Adjusting for systematic risk, Halpern (1973) found that the merger gains before the announcement are divided equally between the acquiring and acquired firms.

Conn and Nielsen (1977) tested evidence of merger synergism, as defined by the Larson and Gonedes model, at the month of the merger announcement, the month of the merger consummation, and the month following merger consummation; they found support for the Larson and Gonedes model. Harris, Stewart, and Carleton (1982) provide evidence in 1970s mergers that the price-earnings multiples of the acquired firms were significantly less than the price-earnings multiples of non-acquired firms.

$$\theta = \frac{\$160[(.4375)1,000,000 + 2,000,000]}{\$25,000,000}$$

$$= 15.6.$$

If firm A is willing to pay firm B's stockholders a 40 percent merger premium, the market must allow the merged firm to maintain at least a 15.6 price-earnings multiple for the merger to profit the acquiring firm's stockholders.

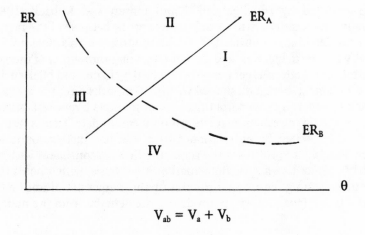

$$V_{ab} = V_a + V_b$$

In terms of the Larson and Gonedes exchange ratio model and the ER–0 diagram, mergers in quadrant 1 profit both firms' stockholders. Above the ER_B rectangular hyperbola, the acquired firm's stockholders win since the merger premium is relatively large. To the right of ER_A, the acquiring firm's stockholders win as the market maintains

$$\theta > \frac{P_A(S_A) + (S_B)}{E_A + E_B}. \qquad (8)$$

Conn and Nielsen found that 78 of 131 mergers between 1960 and 1969 occurred in quadrant 1 in the month of announcement, supporting Larson and Gonedes' model.

However, by the months of the merger consummation and the month following the merger consummation, only 72 and 67 of the 131 mergers were profitable to both firms. In the month following consummations, only 51 percent of the mergers were profitable to both firms' stockholders. The acquired firms' stockholders lost in 24 of the 131 mergers in the month following consummation whereas the acquiring firms' stockholders lost in 58 cases. There was no difference in the merger behavior of conglomerates and nonconglomerates.

Tests have revealed that mergers do not produce synergism when within 10 months following the merger (Haugen and Langetieg 1975). The Haugen and Langetieg evidence is consistent with the Perfectly Competitive Acquisitions Market hypothesis (PCAM), which holds that the expected NPV of the merger should be zero. The PCAM is generally associated with Mandelker (1974) and is supported by the merger survey results reported by Mueller (1977) and Jensen and Ruback (1983). Generally, the acquired firm's stockholders profit because of the merger premiums (Dodd and Ruback 1977). The acquiring firm's stockholders generally lose from mergers, and the net effect on profitability of mergers is neutral. The slight merger benefits reported by Conn and Nielsen and other scholars have been dissipated within 10 months after the mergers. The lack of synergism supports the efficient markets hypothesis since a merger is public information at the announcement date. Excess returns cannot be generated by purchasing a firm that has just announced a merger. The lack of profits for the acquiring firms is consistent with the perfectly competitive acquisitions market hypothesis, which holds that competition among acquiring firms bids up the merger premiums for the acquired firm's stockholders, neutralizing the benefits from the merger.

Conclusion

Mergers do not produce synergism, although the acquired firms profit from the merger premiums. Before the announcement date, profits from mergers are split evenly by the acquired and acquiring firms. The Larson and Gonedes model's synergism is questionable in significance in the month following the consummation of the merger. Researchers have not found sufficient synergism to violate the efficient markets hypothesis.

References

Beckenstein, A.R. 1979. Merger Activity and Merger Theories: An Empirical Investigation. *The Antitrust Bulletin* 105–128.

Butters, J.K., J. Lintner, and W.L. Cary. 1951. *Corporate Mergers*. Cambridge, Mass.: Graduate School of Business, Harvard University.

Conn, R., and J. Nielsen. 1977. An Empirical Test of the Larson-Gonedes Exchange Ratio Determination Model. *Journal of Finance* 32: 749–760.

Davidson, S., et al. 1976. *Financial Accounting: An Introduction to Concepts, Methods, and Uses*. Hinsdale, Ill.: Dryden Press.

Dodd, P. and R. Ruback. 1977. Tender Offers and Stockholders Returns: An Empirical Test. *Journal of Financial Economics* 4: 351–374.

Gort, Michael. 1969. An Economic Disturbance Theory of Mergers. *Quarterly Journal of Economics* 83: 724–742.

Guerard, J.B. 1985. Mergers, Stock Prices, and Industrial Production: An Empirical Test of the Nelson Hypothesis. In *Time Series Analysis:*

Theory and Practice 7, Ed. O.D. Anderson. Amsterdam: North-Holland Publishing Company.

Halpern, P. 1973. Empirical Estimates of the Amount and Distribution of Gains to Companies in Mergers. *Journal of Business* 46: 554–575.

Harris, R.S., J.F. Stewart, and W.T. Carleton. 1982. Financial Characteristics of Acquired Firms. In *Mergers and Acquisitions*, Ed. Keenan and White. Lexington, Mass.: Lexington Books.

Haugen, R., and T. Langetieg. 1975. An Empirical Test for Synergism in Mergers. *Journal of Finance* 30: 1003–1013.

Hayes, S.L., and R. Taussig. 1967. Tactics in Cash Takeover Bids. *Harvard Business Review* 67: 135–148.

Jensen, M.C., and R.S. Ruback. 1983. The Market for Corporate Control: The Scientific Evidence. *Journal of Financial Economics* 11: 5–50.

Larson, K., and N. Gonedes. 1969. Business Combinations: An Exchange Ratio Determination Model. *Accounting Review* 44: 720–728.

Lewellen, W.G. 1971. A Pure Financial Rationale for the Conglomerate Mergers. *Journal of Finance* 26: 521–537.

Lintner, J. 1971. Expectations, Mergers, and Equilibrium in Purely Competitive Markets. *American Economic Review* 61: 101–112.

Mandelker, G. 1974. Risk and Return: The Case of Merging Firms. *Journal of Financial Economics* 1: 303–335.

Melicher, R., J. Ledolter, and L.J. D'Antonio. 1983. A Time Series Analysis of Aggregate Merger Activity. *Review of Economics and Statistics* 65: 423–430.

Mossin, J. 1973. *The Theory of Financial Markets*. Englewood Cliffs, N.J.: Prentice-Hall.

Mueller, D.C. 1969. A Theory of Conglomerate Mergers. *Quarterly Journal of Economics* 83: 743–759.

Nelson, R.L. 1959. *Merger Movements in American Industry 1895–1954*. Princeton: Princeton University Press.

Opinions of the Accounting Review Board, No. 16. New York: American Institute of Certified Public Accountants, August 1970.

Shugert, W.F., and R.D. Tollison. 1984. The Random Character of Merger Activity. *Rand Journal of Economics* 12: 500–509.

Stigler, G.J. 1950. Monopoly and Oligopoly by Merger. *American Economic Review* 40: 23–34.

Appendix to Chapter 14

The Options-Pricing Model and Mergers

A European call is an option to buy a stated number of shares of stock for a stated amount (the exercise price) at the maturity date of the contract. Intuitively, the call option will be of greater value the higher the market price of common stock and the lower the exercise price. As the market value of the stock rises above the exercise price at the maturity date of the option, the option is exercised and the shares are purchased at the exercise price, sold at the market price, and a profit is realized.

Black and Scholes (1973) derived an economic value of the European call option, assuming no taxes or transactions costs, log-normally distributed stock prices, and a known and constant risk-free rate:

$$W = XN(d_1) - Ce^{-r_f t}N(d_2), \tag{1}$$

where

W = Price of the call;

X = Current value of the underlying asset, the stock price;

C = Exercise price of the call option;

t = Time to maturity;

r_f = Instantaneous risk-free rate;

$N(\dots)$ = Standardized normal cumulative probability density function;

$$d_1 = \frac{\ln\left(\dfrac{x}{c}\right) + \left(r_f + \dfrac{\sigma^2}{2}\right)t}{\sigma\sqrt{t}};$$

$d_2 = d_1 - \sigma\sqrt{t}$;

σ^2 = Instantaneous variance of V's returns.

The firm's equity can be viewed as a European call option in which stockholders sell the firm to the bondholders with an option to buy back the firm at time period t. The exercise price is the face value of the debt. The equity will have a positive value only if the teminal value of the firm exceeds the face value of the debt. The face value of the debt can be thought of as the "limited liability" of the equity; it is the protection against the depreciation of the firm's value below the face value of the debt.

Merton (1974) used the Black and Scholes options model to price corporate liabilities where the value of equity, f, may be expressed

$$f = h(\overset{+}{V}, \overset{-}{B}, \overset{+}{r_f}, \overset{+}{\sigma^2}, \overset{+}{t}).$$

The value of equity increases with the value of the firm, the risk-free rate, the variance, and the time to maturity of the debt. The equation for the value of equity can be written

$$\text{dist. } 1 = \frac{\ln\left(\dfrac{V}{B}\right) + \left(r_f + \dfrac{\sigma^2}{2}\right)t}{\sigma\sqrt{t}};$$

$$\text{dist. } 2 = d_1 - \sigma\sqrt{t};$$

$$f = V[N(d_1)] - Be^{-r_f t}[N(d_2)].$$

Assume that a firm has a current market value of $5 million and that the face value of its debt is $2 million. The firm's variance of return is 10 percent and the risk-free rate is 5 percent. The firm's debt will mature in 20 years. The market values of its debt and equity can be found:

$$\text{dist. } 1 = \frac{\ln\left(\dfrac{5,000,000}{2,000,000}\right) + \left(.05 + \dfrac{.10}{2}\right)20}{\sqrt{.10}(\sqrt{20})}$$

$$= \frac{.9163 + 2.000}{.3162(4.4721)}$$

$$= 2.0623.$$

From the table of areas under the normal curve,

$$N(d_2) = .2422 + .5000 = .7422.$$

The .5000 representing the area under the left-hand side of the normal curve is added as the cumulative normal function is employed. To find the value of equity,

$$S = \$5,000,000(.9803) - \$2,000,000(.7422)e^{-(.05)20}$$

$$= \$4,901,500 - \$546,080.24$$

$$= \$4,355,419.76$$

The market value of the firm's equity, from the options pricing model, is $4,355,419.76. Since its current market value is $5,000,000, the current market value of its debt must be $644,580.24. The market value of debt is the minimum of the value of the firm or the face value of debt.

If the firm engages in a merger that reduces its variance to 8 percent, the value of its debt will rise and the market value of its equity will decrease:

$$\text{dist. 1} = \frac{\ln\left(\dfrac{5,000,000}{2,000,000}\right) + \left(.05 + \dfrac{.08}{2}\right)20}{\sqrt{.08}(\sqrt{20})}$$

$$= \frac{2.7163}{1.2647}$$

$$= 2.1478$$

$$N(\text{dist. 1}) = .9842$$

$$\text{dist. 2} = 2.1478 - \sqrt{.08}(\sqrt{.20}) = .8831$$

$$N(\text{dist. 2}) = .8106$$

The value of equity is found:

$$S = \$5,000,000(.9842) - \$2,000,000(.8106)e^{-rft}$$

$$= \$4,324,560.52$$

The value of equity has fallen from $4,355,419.76 to $4,324,560.52 entirely because of the reduction in the variance resulting from the merger. The value of the debt has risen:

$$\$5,000,000 - \$4,324,560.52 = \$675,439.48$$

Debt's value rises from \$644,580.24 to \$675,439.48 because of the reduction in the firm's variance.

If investors hold the market portfolio (equal amounts of the firm's debt and equity) a change in the market values of corporate liabilities will not affect the market value of their total holdings. The loss on equity holdings will be offset by the gain on debt holdings. If investors do not hold the market portfolio, wealth transfers from bondholders to stockholders must be made to leave stockholders indifferent to mergers. The merged firm will have a higher debt-to-equity ratio. Because interest on debt is deductible and the value of the firm rises with debt, the higher debt-to-equity ratio increases the value of the firm.

References

Black, F. and M. Scholes. 1973. The Pricing of Options and Corporate Liabilities. *Journal of Political Economy* 81: 637–654.

Merton, R. 1974. On the Pricing of Corporate Debt: The Risk Structure of Interest Rates. *Journal of Finance* 29: 449–470.

Chapter 15

Mergers and Equity Valuation Models

The purpose of this chapter is to apply valuation techniques to determine fair-market prices for possible take-over targets. Discounted cash flow techniques such as the Rappaport valuation model, are useful in projecting cash flow from potentially-acquired firms that are determined from sales forecasts and operating margins.

Least squares forecasting is used to project future sales levels and historic profit margins allow the forecasting of cash flow. The cost of capital analysis discussed in Chapters 5 and 6 are used to discount the projected earnings and cash flow. The market model discussed in Chapter 9 is employed to examine post-merger profitability. The acquisition of Superior Oil by Mobil serves as an interesting application of the integration of many techniques of financial modeling.

Merger Analysis

One cannot help noticing the interest excitement produced in our economy by mergers and acquisitions. Nowadays it is not unusual for a billion-dollar firm to acquire another billion-dollar firm. The purpose of this chapter is to analyze techniques of determining reasonable prices for merger candidates. In Chapter 14 we briefly discussed the generation of merger profits, synergy, in the merger process, i.e., the Perfectly Competitive Acquisitions Market (PCAM). Given the very large number of corporate mergers and acquisitions, it is difficult to believe that the expected net present value of the mergers is zero (Mandelker 1974; Franks, Broyles, and Hecht 1977; Mueller 1977; and Jensen and Ruback 1983). Financial managers are well aware of the Rappaport (1979) cash flow framework for merger analysis, and yet it may seem rather strange that merger premiums are generally around 100 percent. Moreover, financial economists still speak of an efficient market and yet the acquired firms' prices may have been substantially undervalued for a considerable period of time. The authors are well aware that the efficient markets hypothesis (EMH) applies to the market for corporate control in that one cannot abnormally profit from buying stock in an acquiring firm; however, does it not seem unlikely that the acquired firm could have been so substantially undervalued in an efficient market? We will take a closer look at merger valuation in this chapter.

Let us examine Mobil Corporation's acquisition of Superior Oil in 1984. Mobil acquired Superior Oil for $5.7 billion in 1984 by (1) purchasing 22.6 percent of Superior's outstanding stock from the heirs of the founder at $45 per share; (2) offering to purchase up to 36 million shares of Superior Oil in exchange for $20 in cash and $25 principal amount of a 14.4 percent Mobil debenture for each Superior Oil share; (3) merging the two companies by the terms explicit in (2) except that the coupon rate on a second debenture was tied to the U.S. Treasury bond market. One notes the use of large amounts of debt in this merger, which is not unusual in the 1980s.

Sales Forecasting and Cash Flow

In attempting to determine the appropriate price to offer for a potential merger candidate, the management of the acquiring firm must forecast sales, discounted future profits and cash flow, and estimate a reasonable residual value. Let us apply merger evaluation techniques to the Superior Oil Company. The sales and net income history of Superior Oil, reflecting previous mergers and accounting changes, was:

Year	Sales Revenues ($millions)	Net Income ($millions)
1974	$333	$61
1975	382	52
1976	441	50
1977	545	63
1978	731	31
1979	1,085	200
1980	1,498	334
1981	2,057	361
1982	2,041	233
1983	1,793	235

The application of ordinary least squares (OLS) to the forecasting of sales revenues for Superior Oil produces the following equation:

$$(t) \qquad (-.66) \qquad (8.06)$$
$$\text{Sales} = -110.933 + 218.461 \,(\text{Time}), \quad R^2 = .891. \qquad (1)$$

The Durbin-Watson statistic of 1.06 reveals statistically significant autocorrelation ($\rho\varepsilon_t$, $\varepsilon_{t-1} > 0$); however, application of the Cochrane-Orcutt procedure produces only a slight improvement in the Durbin-Watson statistic that is still autocorrelated.[1] One also could use non-linear least squares (NLLS), but the R^2, or goodness of fit, from this technique is only marginally higher than the OLS regression:

$$\begin{matrix} (t) & \wedge & (44.24) & (11.47) \\ \end{matrix}$$
$$\log \text{Sales} = 5.511 + .231 \ (\text{Time}), R^2 = .943. \qquad (2)$$

The Durbin-Watson statistic of the nonlinear least squares, 0.94, shows statistically significant evidence of autocorrelation.[2] The Cochrane-Orcutt procedure, applied to the nonlinear least squares regression line, produces the following results:

$$\begin{matrix} \wedge & (7.90) & (2.18) \\ \end{matrix}$$
$$\log \text{Sales} = 5.847 + .177 \ (\text{Time}), R^2 = .945, \hat{\rho} = .736. \qquad (3)$$

The Cochrane-Orcutt procedure for use in the case of Superior Oil, sales and nonlinear least squares regression produces a t-value of the time variable in Equation (3) is not statistically different from zero at the 10 percent level.

Thus, in sales forecasting, one might use the OLS or the nonlinear least squares, although both model error terms are autocorrelated. The respective Superior Oil forecasts are ($millions):

Year	OLS	CORC(OLS)	NLLS	CORC(NLLS)
1984	2292.1	2298.6	3140.1	2426.0
1985	2510.6	2532.8	3956.0	2895.8
1986	2729.0	2767.0	4984.1	3456.5
1987	2947.5	3001.3	6279.2	4125.7
1988	3165.9	3235.5	7910.9	4924.6

One immediately notices that seemingly unreasonable sales forecasts are produced by the NLLS regressions.

---

[1]The Cochrane-Orcutt (CORC) procedure least squares regression line is:

$$\begin{matrix} \wedge & (-.81) & (4.90) \\ \end{matrix}$$
$$\text{Sales} = -277.906 + 234.227 \ (\text{Time}), R^2 = .908, \hat{\rho} = .393.$$

[2]The nonlinear least squares estimators are derived from $Y = ab^X$ and the minimization of the sum of squared errors: $\Sigma(\log Y - \log a - X \log b)^2$. If $\Sigma X = 0$, $\log a = (\Sigma \log Y/N)$ and $\log b = (\Sigma X \log Y/\Sigma X^2)$.

During the period 1979–1983, Superior Oil averaged a 16.5 percent return on sales, ranging from 10.9 percent in 1979 to 22.3 percent in 1982. Superior Oil had depreciation charges of $457 million in 1983. If one held the depreciation charge constant during the period 1984–1988 and used the 16.5 percent return on sales to forecast net income, one could derive the following results ($MM):

Year	OLS	CORC(NLLS)
1984	835	857
1985	871	935
1986	907	1027
1987	943	1138
1988	979	1270

The residual value of cash flow is found by discounting the profits of 1988, using the Mobil Corporation's cost of capital, and finding its present value. In the Rappaport (1979) model for valuing merger candidates, one normally derives cash flow forecasts by subtracting changes in capital expenditures and net working capital from earnings plus depreciation (and other noncash charges). Superior Oil engaged in very unusual net working capital management (Rappaport's net working capital adjustment, W, ranged from 1.462 to -35.313 and will be assumed to be zero during the 1984–1988 period).

Mergers and the Cost of Capital

One should use Mobil Corporation's cost of capital to discount the expected future profits of Superior Oil. One could use the reciprocal of Mobil's price-earnings multiple, 8, to find an approximation of the firm's cost of capital, or use Mobil's beta.[3] Mobil's cost of capital at the end of 1983 was approximately 10.2 percent (the price-earnings ratio is 8 and the tax rate is 64.3 percent), using the constant-growth assumption and

---

[3]In the absence of leverage, the market value of the firm is its market value of equity, its price per share, P_{cs}, times shares outstanding, N, and is equal to the discounted, at k_e, earnings of the firm.

$$P_{cs}(N) = \frac{\text{Eat}}{k_e}\,; P_{cs}(N)k_e = \text{EAT};$$

$$(P_{cs})k_e = \text{EAT}/N; k_e = \frac{\text{EPS}}{P_{cs}}.$$

with leverage and constant growth, $k_e = (\text{EPS}/P_{cs})(1 - tL)$ where L is long-term debt divided by assets. (Lewellen 1969).

the price-earnings (*P/E*) multiple approach. The *P/E* approach and the 10.2 percent cost of capital do not seem reasonable, given the December 1983 U.S. Treasury Bill yield of 9.1 percent. A more reasonable cost of capital is found by using an asset beta in which the Mobil equity beta, .93 at the end of 1983, is weighted by the debt-to-equity ratio (13,952:19,442). The Ibbotson and Sinquefield market risk premium of .088 may be used:

$$k_c = .091 + (.088)(.93)\left(\frac{13,952}{19,442}\right) = .150.$$

The discounted future earnings and residual values of the Superior Oil company, discounted at 15 percent, using OLS and CORC(NLLS), produced $4.738 billion and $6.103 billion, respectively. The use of OLS, CORC(NLLS) analysis, and the CAPM-based cost of capital produce very reasonable market values for Superior Oil. If the stockholders of Superior Oil used the firm's *P/E* of 18.5 to value its future earnings and residual value, the market value of Superior would be so large, given the approximate 5.0 percent cost of capital, that its stockholders would never engage in merger. (The Modigliani and Miller market value of the firm would be $6.5 billion to Superior Oil stockholders.) In the early 1980s, Superior Oil had a beta of 1.25, an expected growth rate of 13 percent, and a $2 dividend in 1983.[4] The equilibrium stock price to Superior Oil's shareholder was

$$P_{cs} = \frac{\$2(1.13)}{.201 - .130} = \$31.83,$$

where

$$k_e = .091 + .088(1.25) = .201.$$

Thus, the merger greatly enhanced shareholder wealth for Superior Oil's equity holders because the Superior stock traded around 30 in 1982.

It appears that Mobil Corporation paid a reasonable price for Superior Oil given that Mobil paid $5.7 billion for a firm worth between $4.738 billion (using OLS-sales forecasting) and $6.103 billion (using CORC(NLLS)-sales forecasting), and one would not expect Mobil to earn a (positive or negative) abnormal excess return as a result of the merger. Let us examine the CAPM and performance measures and return to the Mobil-Superior merger.

---

[4]Merrill Lynch, *Monthly Research Review*, January 1983.

The CAPM and Excess Performance Measures[5]

The CAPM gives a formula for the expected one-period return of a security in terms of two factors: (1) a riskless return for time and (2) a return for systematic risk that is a scale factor of the expected return of the market:

$$E(R_j) = R_F + \beta_j[E(R_M) - R_F], \tag{4}$$

where

$E(R_j)$ = expected return on security j;

R_F = return for a riskless asset;

$E(R_M)$ = expected return on the market portfolio;

β_j = cov $[E(R_j), E(R_M)]/\text{Var } E(R_M)$.

The CAPM gives only a formula for expected return. Closely related are several stochastic models of security returns.

The Market Model

A common description of returns can be written as

$$E(R_j) = a_j + \beta_j^T E(R_M) + E_j \tag{5}$$

where

$E(R_j)$ = return on security j;

$E(R_M)$ = return on the market portfolio;

E_j = nonmarket component of return on security j;

a_j = a constant;

β_j^T = the market responsiveness of stock j.

The superscript T on the beta symbol indicates a total return beta. It is assumed that

$$E(E_j) = 0, \tag{6}$$

$$\text{Cov } (E(R_M), E_j) = 0. \tag{7}$$

---

[5]This section draws heavily from Stone (1988).

The important assumption in Equation (5) is that a stock's return can be represented as a linear scaling of the market return (or possibly just a broad-based market index such as the NYSE composite or the S&P 500). That is, a single risk measure is sufficient to describe the riskiness of an asset.

A special and more restrictive model of the return generating process has played a prominent role in the development of modern portfolio theory. If one adds to Equation (5) and assumptions the previously discusses two (Equations 6 and 7) the following restriction:

$$\text{Cov } (E_j, E_t) = 0 \text{ for all securities } j \text{ and } t \text{ whenever } j \neq t.$$

one finds that a single index model should adequately describe the systematic risk of the security. This assumption says that the only correlation between any two securities arises from their joint dependence on the market return, as we discussed in Chapter 9. This assumption ignores industry or sector effects not included in the market index. Farrell (1983) makes the violation of this assumption the basis of this multi-index model, but the assumption is not unreasonable aside from non-market industry effects and other common factors such as interest rates and inflation.

Relation of Market Model to the CAPM

Taking expected values of both sides of Equation (5) gives

$$E(R_j) = a_j + \beta_j^T E(R_M) \tag{8}$$

if one assumes $E(E_j) = 0$. If it is assumed that the CAPM beta value equals the market model beta value, then comparison of Equations (4) and (7) for $E(R_j)$ requires that

$$\alpha_j = R_F(1 - \beta_j^T) = 0. \tag{9}$$

This expression can be viewed as the intercept value predicted by the CAPM. This is the intercept consistent with a fair return for time and risk (Black, Jensen, and Scholes 1972). Hence, an intercept greater than this would imply superior risk-adjusted returns from the CAPM viewpoint of fair return.

It is common to discuss performance by comparing the actual intercept in a market-index model of returns with the CAPM prediction, i.e.,

$$\text{PERFORMANCE}_j = \hat{\alpha}_j - [R_F(1 - \hat{\beta}_j)], \tag{10}$$

where $\hat{\alpha}_j$ and $\hat{\beta}_j$ are measured values of the intercept and slope coefficients for security j over some time period, e.g., 60 months.

What is called "performance" in Equation (10) is often called the stock's "adjusted alpha" and sometimes simply its "alpha." Thus, there is considerable ambiguity in the term "alpha" in assessing abnormal returns. It may be (1) the intercept in a regression of stock return on market return, (2) the measured regression intercept corrected for the theoretical fair-return intercept from the viewpoint of the CAPM, or (3) the intercept in a regression of excess stock return on excess market return, as discussed subsequently.

The Two-Factor Return-Generating Process

Equation (4) expresses security return as a function of a single factor—the market-index return. A stochastic return-generating process that is more closely congruent with the CAPM and that allows for cross-time variation in the value of the riskless rate is

$$E(R_{jt}) = R_{Ft} + \beta_j^E E(R_{MT}) + U_{jt}. \tag{11}$$

This is often called a two-factor return-generating process since it expresses return in terms of both the market return and the riskless rate. Equation (11) can be rewritten in excess-return form as

$$E(R_{jt}) - R_{Ft} = \beta_j^E[E(R_{Mt}) - R_{Ft})] + U_{jt}. \tag{12}$$

It is assumed that $E[U_jt] = 0$ and $\text{Cov}[E(R_{MT}) - R_{Ft}, U_{jt}] = 0$. Thus, U_{jt} can be viewed as the nonmarket component of "excess return," where excess return here means a return in excess of a fair return for time. The beta value in Equations (11) and (12) is denoted β_j^E to emphasize that it is the beta value for the excess return version of the return-generating process. It is not necessarily the same as the total return beta, which has been denoted β_j^T for security.

The essence of the estimation for β_j^E is to regress excess return on stock j, $E(R_{jt}) - R_{Ft}$, on the excess market return, $[E(R_{Mt}) - R_{Ft}]$. The associated regression equation is

$$E(R_{jt}) - R_{Ft} = E\gamma_j + \beta_j[E(R_{Mt}) - R_{Ft})] + U_{jt}. \tag{13}$$

Expression (13) differs from (12) by the intercept term α_j^E. This intercept is the "excess return alpha. From the viewpoint of the CAPM, the theoretical value of α_j^E is zero. Hence, it measures abnormal return in the sense of return in excess of a fair return for time and risk from the viewpoint of the CAPM value of expected return. In contrast to the intercept in the total return regression, the excess return intercept should not depend on either R_F or a stock's beta value. The absence of any need to adjust the excess return alpha in using it as a performance measure is one reason for preferring the excess return measure, namely simplicity.

There are two closely related stochastic models of the return-generating process that express security return in terms of a market-index return. These are (1) a total-return one-factor model that does not reflect variation in the riskless rate over an estimation period and (2) an excess-return two-factor model that expresses security return in terms of a fair return for time, plus a fair return from nondiversifiable risk, plus a nonmarket component of excess return.

The formulas for the two beta measures are:

$$\beta_j^T = \text{Cov} \ [E(R_M), \ E(R_j)]/\text{Var} \ E(R_M) \qquad (14)$$

$$\beta_j^E = \text{Cov} \ [E(R_M) - R_F, \ E(R_j) - R_F]/\text{Var} \ (E(R_M) - R_F). \qquad (15)$$

In general these two betas are not equal, although they are often close. A sufficient condition for equality is that R_F be constant over the estimation period.

Since R_F is not constant, is generally not uncorrelated with R_M, and is clearly never uncorrelated with all stock returns, these two alternative estimates of market sensitivity are functionally not equivalent either numerically or in terms of rank ordering. Differences in the two alternatives can generally be expected to increase (1) as the cross-time variation in R_F increases and (2) as the magnitude of correlation between R_F and either R_M or R_s increases. In the pre-1965 world of fairly stable short-term interest rates, these sufficient conditions were not violated significantly. In the post-1975 period, these conditions may not have been met, and the excess-return beta and performance measure are the more appropriate measures.

The two alternative measures of abnormal return from the regression intercepts for security j are

$$\text{Total-return estimate} = \alpha_j^T - R_F(1 - \beta_j^T);$$

and

$$\text{Excess-return estimate} = \alpha_j^E.$$

Excess Returns and the Mobil Corporation

One would expect the larger issuance of debt associated with Mobil's acquisition of Superior Oil to drive up its beta (as discussed in Chapter 7) and not affect its abnormal return a la the CAPM. A 60-month beta (estimated using the NYSE Composite Index) and alpha, γ^E, were estimated for the Mobil Corporation for 1983–1985 using data from the Center for Research in Security Pricing (CRSP) tapes at the University of Chicago. The effects of the merger will not be completely reflected in the risk-adjusted alpha because Mobil restructured Montgomery Ward in 1985 to provide for the sale of its Jefferson Ward division, and thus it is not possible to completely identify only the merger-induced abnormal wealth effects. However, annual risk-adjusted alphas and betas indicate that Mobil stockholders earned the abnormal returns during the period 1983–1985 that one would have expected in an efficient market: zero. The beta of Mobil rose to 1.16 in 1985, and the abnormal stockholder return (the performance measure previously discussed) became slightly negative.

The Mobil Corporation

Year	Beta	Excess-Return Alpha
1983	.93	.004
1984	1.00	.003
1985	1.16	−.004

The arithmetic mean performance measure, .001 for the three years, is not statistically different from zero. The Mobil Corporation's financial strategies have yet to increase stockholder wealth.

Summary and Conclusions

The purpose of this chapter is to analyze merger valuation techniques as applied to Mobil Corporation's acquisition of Superior Oil. It is necessary to apply sales forecasting and pro forma statement analyses in the valuation of merger candidates. The CAPM and the market model are used to measure the creation of abnormal wealth for the stockholders. The evidence in the Mobil case supports an efficient acquisitions market.

References

Black, F., M.C. Jensen, and M. Scholes. 1972. The Capital Asset Pricing Model: Some Empirical Tests. *Studies in the Theory of Capital Markets*, Ed. M.C. Jensen. New York: Praeger Publishers.

Blume, M. 1971. On the Assessment of Risk. *Journal of Finance* 26: 1–10.

Dodd, P., and R. Ruback. 1977. Tender Offers and Stockholder Returns: An Empirical Test. *Journal of Financial Economics* 4: 351–374.

Fama, F., and J. MacBeth. 1973. Risk, Return and Equilibrium: Empirical Tests. *Journal of Political Economy* 607–636.

Farrell, J. 1983. *Guide to Portfolio Management.* New York: McGraw-Hill.

Jensen, M.C. and R. Ruback. 1983. The Market for Corporate Control: The Scientific Evidence. *Journal of Financial Economics* 11: 5–50.

King, F. 1966. Market and Industry Factors in Stock Price Behavior. *Journal of Business,* 39: 139–189.

Lewellen, W.G. 1969. *The Cost of Capital.* Belmont, Calif.: Wadsworth.

Mandelker, G. 1974. Risk and Return: The Case of Merging Firms. *Journal of Financial Economics* 1: 303–335.

Rappaport, A. 1979. A Strategic Framework for More Profitable Acquisitions. *Harvard Business Review* 57: 99–106.

Roll, R. 1969. Bias in Fitting the Sharpe Model to Time Series Data. *Journal of Financial and Quantitative Analysis,* 4: 271–289.

Sharpe, W.F. 1963. A Simplified Model for Portfolio Analysis. *Management Science,* 9: 277–293.

———. 1964. Capital Asset Prices: A Theory of Market Equilibrium Under Conditions of Risk. *Journal of Finance,* 19: 425–442.

———. 1970. *Portfolio Theory and Capital Markets.* New York: McGraw-Hill.

Stone, B.K. 1988. Lecture Notes on Efficient Beta Estimations. Brigham Young University.

Chapter 16

Leasing Models

The purpose of this chapter is to introduce the reader to how leasing may affect the firm's cash flow and capital investment decision. Management (often the chief financial officer) prefers to lease assets rather than purchasing these assets if the net present value resulting from the leasing decision exceeds that of the capital investment or purchase decision. The leasing models involve cost of capital and cash flow considerations that are governed by accounting standards. The Miller and Upton and Weingartner models are reviewed in this chapter.

Definitions and Types of Leases

Lease terms usually obligate organizations to make a series of payments over a future period of time. The big question for a least is: Do the features of the lease agreement in effect make it a purchase or do they in fact retain the nature of a true rental contract? In either case the cash flow consequences of leasing and borrowing are similar.

Until 1976 leases were off balance sheet financing. This means a firm could lease an asset and neither show an asset nor a liability on its balance sheet. At this time the only information disclosed on the financial statements was a brief footnote to its accounts describing its lease obligation. Now, accounting standards require that all financial or capital leases be capitalized (see 'Accounting for Leases', Statement of Financial Accounting Standards No. 13, Financial Accounting Standards Board, 1976). The FASB issued Statement 13 to provide guidelines as to how lease should be characterized.

In the case of the lessee, the Statement requires that leases be classified as a **capital lease** if at the beginning of the lease it meets one of four criteria:

1. The lease transfers ownership of the property to the lessee by the end of the lease term.
2. The lease contains an option to purchase the property at a bargain price.

3. The lease term is equal to 75 percent or more of the estimated economic life of the property, or
4. The present value of the rentals and other minimum lease payments, at the beginning of the lease term equal 90% of the fair value of the lease property less any related investment tax credit retained by the lessor.

If the lease does not meet any of those criteria, it is classified as an **operating lease.**

In the case of a capital lease the lessee records an asset and a liability at an amount equal to the present value of the minimum lease payments during the lease term excluding executory costs such as insurance, maintenance, and taxes to be paid by the lessor together with any profit. The amount capitalized is subject to the limitation that it does not exceed the fair value of the lease property at the inception of the lease.

Operating leases are generally short term and cancellable during the period of the contract if the lessee desires. Leases that extend over the estimated economic life of the asset and that can generally not be canceled unless the lessor is reimbursed for losses are **capital leases** (also known as financial leases).

Evaluation of the Leasing Alternative

Why should a firm lease an asset? Generally, from a common sense standpoint, one might think that owning is always better than leasing. Well, this is not the case. Since leases are a source of financing they must be evaluated in terms of the alternatives available. In some cases leasing is the best financing alternative available. Consider that when a firm obtains equipment or an asset under other than a capital lease the conventional measures of financial leverage (illustrated in Chapter 1), such as the debt-equity ratio, understate the actual extent of leverage. Even though it is reasonable to think that analysts would notice and adjust for this difference this is not always the case. Furthermore, because of the additional fixed charge (for the lease payment) this increases the degree of variability of earnings given a change in sales.

Leasing may offer the least cost alternative in many situations. It is important to note that evaluation of leasing as a financing alternative does not imply that the asset itself is a good choice. The only choice that is confirmed by conducting the leasing analysis is whether the financing choice is a good one.

Leasing an asset may imply different service alternatives than owning the same asset. For example, under a full service or rental lease the lessor pays for maintenance and insurance. However, under a net lease, the lessee agrees to pay for maintenance and insurance.

Other reasons to lease an asset include the following:

- Convenience. For example, if a firm is only interested in having an asset for a short period of time it may be simply more convenient to lease the asset rather than purchase it.
- Ability to cancel a lease. Nowhere is this more evident than in the computer equipment leasing industry. If a particular model should become outdated then the lessee may simply invoke his ability to cancel the lease and, hopefully, get an updated newer model computer.
- Maintenance provisions. Under certain types of leases, for example, a full-service lease, the user receives maintenance and other services. Typically, the lessors are well-equipped to provide the maintenance.

There are many factors to consider in evaluating a lease. In summary, however, the single most important formula in evaluating a lease is the following:

$$\begin{array}{lll} \text{Net Value} = & \text{Initial Financing} & - \text{ Present Value of Liability} \\ \text{of Lease} & \text{Provided} & \text{Created by the Lease} \\ & \text{by the Lease} & \end{array}$$

OR

$$\begin{array}{ll} \text{Net Value} = & \text{Initial Financing} \\ \text{of Lease} & \text{Provided} \\ & \text{by the Lease} \end{array} - \sum_{i=1}^{N} \frac{\text{LCF}}{(1 + r(1 - T_C))^t}$$

where

    LCF = cash outflow attributable to the lease in period t
    N = duration of the lease
    r = discount rate
    t = tax rate

The underlying principle is that a financial lease offers a better financial advantage than buying and borrowing if the financing provided by the lease exceeds the present value of the liability created by the lease.

    The Initial Financing Provided equals the cost of the leased asset minus any immediate lease payment or other cash outflow attributable to the lease. This formula applies only to net financial leases. Any other benefits provided through a lease (such as salvage value, maintenance costs, etc.) should be factored into the lease evaluation by considering the present value impact of these benefits. Note that the value of leasing is its **incremental value** relative to buying and borrowing.

Now, lets consider an example problem. Assume that a company is considering buying equipment costing $100,000 with a life of three years. The manufacturer of the equipment has offered to lease the equipment for three years for an annual payment of $36,000. The company is responsible for all maintenance, insurance, and operating expenses. The direct cash flow consequences of obtaining the asset through a lease are as follows:

1. A cash inflow of $100,000 because the company does not pay for the equipment.
2. Loss of the investment tax credit since the company does not own the equipment. The investment tax credit is 10 percent of the cost of the equipment or $10,000. Since the investment tax credit is taken it reduces the depreciable investment in the business by one-half of the investment tax credit taken. Thus, the depreciable investment equals $100,000 − ½($10,000) or $95,000.
3. Obligation of the lease payment of $36,000 a year for three years. The first payment is due when the equipment is received. The lease payments are fully deductible as a business expense and the marginal tax rate is 46 percent. The tax savings is $16,560 ($36,000 • .46). Thus, the after tax cost is $19,440 or $36,000 − $16,560.
4. The company does not have the ability to depreciate the truck. Assume the depreciable base of the truck is $95,000 (see 2 above) and the depreciation is evenly incurred throughout the three year life of the equipment. Thus, depreciation is $31,667 per year.

In summary the direct cash flow consequences of the lease are as follows.

	Year 0	Year 1	Year 2	Year 3
1. Cost of new equipment	+100,000			
2. Investment tax credit Loss	−10,000			
3. Lease payment	−19,440	−19,440	−19,440	
Payment = 36,000				
Tax savings = 16,560				
Net cost = 19,440				
4. Lost Depreciation	−14,567	−14,567	−14,567	
Tax Shield				
Depreciable cost = 95,000				
Annual Depreciation = 31,667				
Tax Savings = 14,567				
TOTALS	+53,460	−36,540	−36,540	

Now that we have identified the cash flows the next step is to apply a discount rate to each flow. Typically, the cash flows associated with the lease payment may be discounted at about the same after-tax rate of interest as the interest payments on a secured bond issued by the lessee. The cash flows associated with the tax shields might be subject to greater risk (because we do not know whether the firm makes a profit in the year the tax savings are estimated to be realized) and thus be subject to a higher discount rate. For our purposes, we will assume the discount rate will be the same for all cash flows.

$$NPV = +53,460 - \frac{36,540}{(1 + (.1)(1 - .46))} - \frac{36,540}{(1 + (.1)(1 - .46))^2}$$

$$NPV = +53,460 - \frac{36,540}{(1 + .054)} - \frac{36,540}{(1 + .054)^2}$$

$$NPV = +53,460 - 34,667 - 32,892$$

$$NPV = -14,099$$

Substituting in our equation we have

$$\begin{array}{c} \text{Net Value} = \text{Initial Financing} - \sum_{i=1}^{N} \frac{\text{LCF}}{(1 + r_c(1 - T))^T} \\ \text{of lease} \qquad \text{Provided} \\ \text{by the lease} \end{array}$$

Based on this information, leasing is the preferred financing alternative. However, this analysis does not fully consider all the information that should be evaluated in this decision.

   Additional information that must be incorporated into this analysis is the effect of leasing on the firm's borrowing ability. Basically, firms that lease more will end up borrowing less, other things being equal. This is true because leasing displaces borrowing. Finally, we have assumed the company has taxable income and thus there is a deduction for the lease payment and there would be a deduction for depreciation. If the firm did lose money and therefore paid no taxes, then we would not calculate any savings due to taxes.

Weingartner Approach to Leasing

Weingartner's (1987) *Financial Management* presents a slightly different approach to leasing that analyzes the differences between leasing and owning. Basically, he identifies the decision as focusing on trade-offs between an asset's disposition rights versus the reduced costs of obtaining its use rights. He suggests that this analysis permits easier treatment of uncertainty over the asset's economic life in the hands of the user. The calculations required to support the analysis include the following:

(1) Expected discounted lease costs
(2) Asset's acquisition cost
(3) Expected disposition rights (including the residual value, tax shields due to depreciation, adjustments for recapture of excess depreciation expense, and capital gains taxes, if any)

If (1) exceeds the sum of (2) and (3) then the cost of leasing is higher than the cost of owning and the decision should be to purchase; it is the correct decision to not lease. The appropriate discount rate is the cost of capital.

In the following paragraphs we will review in detail Weingartner's approach.

History of Leasing—Differences in the Marketplace Between Lessors and Lessees

According to Weingartner the practice of leasing is primarily related to the asymmetries between lessors and lessees. These asymmetries include the following:

• Lessors typically specialize in a limited number of assets. This specialization results in the lessor's knowing more about the market for the asset than the lessee.
• Lessors typically have larger economies of scale than lessees (both in terms of buying and selling power for the leased assets and often in terms of collecting information about the asset itself);
• Lessors are typically better connected to the marketplace for the assets, hence, they are in a better position to re-market and offlease assets. This lowers the cost of bearing this type of risk.

Basically, the lease gives the lessee the right to use the asset for a period of time in exchange for an agreed upon single payment or series of payments. Ownership implies bearing the risk of obsolescence and retention of **disposition** rights. According to Weingartner, the separate valuation of use rights versus disposition rights is helpful in simplifying a leasing problem. In most finance texts the importance of making such a split in ownership rights is not even noticed because of many of the assumptions made (these assumptions include that the lease term is identical with the projected economic life of the asset). Lessors and lessees have different beliefs about the life of the asset as well as differences in the degree of confidence with which those beliefs are held.

Use Rights and Disposition Rights

Consider a project with a single asset for which the firm foresees a given life. The net present value of the project assuming purchase of the asset is:

$$V_p = -I + \sum_{j=1}^{L} \frac{n_j}{(1+k)^j} + \sum_{j=1}^{L_d} \frac{t_{dj}}{(1+k)^j} + \frac{R}{(1+k)^L} - \frac{A}{(1+k)^L}$$

where

L = asset life,

n_j = after tax revenues or $(r_j - c_j)(1-t)$,

j = period,

r = revenues,

c = costs,

t = marginal corporate income tax,

I = asssets cost,

R = residual value at the end of period L,

d_j = depreciation tax shield in period j for depreciable life L_d,

k = the firm's (or project's) cost of capital,

V = net present value assuming purchase of the asset.

Another way of expressing this equation is:

$$V_p = -I + U + D$$

where

D = Disposition rights, that is, the third, fourth, and fifth terms above relating to the residual value, depreciation tax shield, and the adjustments from possible depreciation recapture and capital gains taxes

$$D = \frac{R}{(1+k)^L} + \sum_{j=1}^{L_d} \frac{t_d}{(1+k)^j} - \frac{A}{(1+k)^L}$$

U = use rights

I = initial outlay

Oftentimes the assumption is made that if $U > I$, then we should purchase. However, this is not true. Because D (the disposition rights) are often a positive contribution to present worth. **For the simplest case, in which the project's life and the asset's economic life are equal, the lease versus purchase decision reduces to an evaluation of $I - D$ or $U - I$.**

The Discount Rate for the Leasing Evaluation

Weingartner argues that the discount rate for the lease payments should be the same as that for depreciation tax shields and all other cash flows. In contrast, some financial managers argue that the tax shield should be discounted at a lower rate since there is less uncertainty associated with this cash flow. One of the reasons advanced for using the same discount rate is that the tax shield is merely a component of the project's net after-tax cash flow which is to be discounted at the cost of capital. Other flows are subject to the same analysis.

Uncertainty Associated with the Evaluation

Weingartner (1987) further notes that the equations presented so far ignore the fact that the amounts used are implied to be certain. However, these amounts are estimates. In fact, we could attach a probability, P, distribution to each of the individual estimates to more correctly state the equation in terms of expected values. Thus:

$$E[V_p(L)] = -I + E[U(L)] + E[D(L)]$$

where, for example:

$$E[D(L)] = \sum_i p_i D(L_i)$$

In fact, drawing this argument further can involve cases in which the estimated life of the asset differs from the lease term. In this case, the additional cash flows must be considered and incorporated into the evaluation.

References

Johnson, R.W. and W.G. Lewellen. 1972. Analysis of the Lease-or-Buy Decision. *Journal of Finance* 27: 815–823.

Levy, H. and M. Sarnat. 1979. Leasing, Borrowing, and Financial Risk. *Financial Management* 8: 47–54.

Lewellen, W.G., M.S. Long, and J.J. McConnell. 1976. Asset Leasing in Competitive Capital Markets. *Journal of Finance* 31: 787–798.

Miller, M.H. and C.W. Upton. 1976. Leasing, Buying and the Cost of Capital Services. *Journal of Finance* 31: 761–786.

Myers, S.C., D.A. Dill and A.J. Bautista. 1976. Valuation of Financial Lease Contracts. *Journal of Finance* 31: 799–819.

Schall, L.D. 1974. The Lease-or-Buy and Asset Acquisition Decisions. *Journal of Finance* 29: 1203–1214.

Weingartner, H.M. 1987. Leasing, Asset Lives and Uncertainty: Guides to Decision Making. *Financial Management* 16: 5–12.

Chapter 17

Composite Forecasting: A New Look at GNP Forecasting Models

The purpose of this chapter is to examine the efficiency of composite modeling of GNP forecasting. Regression analysis is used to develop composite models of GNP forecasts made by Chase, Wharton, DRI, and the BEA. Multicollinearity among the GNP forecasts leads to the application of latent root regression techniques. Composite modeling techniques should be measured against an "equal-weighting" scheme to establish forecasting efficiency.

The financial and statistical literature is rich with studies showing that decision making may be enhanced by combining several forecasts. Granger and Newbold (1986), Winkler and Makridakis (1983), Figlewski and Urich (1983), and Clemen and Winkler (1986) have examined the effectiveness of combined economic forecasts relative to individual forecasts. The majority of these studies examining composite modeling have questioned the incremental value of analyzing the correlation matrix and estimating forecast variable weights. Composite modeling using simple arithmetic weighting schemes have tended to outperform estimated weighted schemes (Clemen and Winkler 1986). The best estimated weighting schemes employed the assumption of independent forecast variables, rather than estimating variable weights using the correlation matrix (Bates and Granger 1969). An excellent literature review is found in Clemen (1988).

The questions examined in this chapter are: (1) How many of the economic forecasts are employed in estimating the most effective post-sample forecasting models? (2) Is the Granger and Ramanathan (1984) methodology enhanced by the use of latent root regression? and (3) Are simplistic schemes preferred to more complex and variable weighting schemes?

Financial economists suggest modeling the forecast errors with a multinormal process, but the normal model performed poorly. One possible problem is that the covariance matrix must typically be estimated with small quantities of data. The sparse data observations produce a very unstable correlation matrix and even more unstable estimates of the combining weights (Kang 1986). Furthermore, for economic forecasting, the problem is exacerbated by the multicollinearity that typically plagues economic forecast errors; correlations in the neighborhood of 0.90 are not at all unusual. The Bayesian approach developed by Clemen and Winkler worked well in terms of mean squared error (MSE) or mean absolute error (MAE), and the approach tended to "break up" the multicollinearity of the forecast errors.

In the next section a discussion of the regression approach to combining forecasts is followed by a brief discussion of latent root regression. Latent root regression is used in the combination of the highly collinear GNP forecasts studied by Clemen and Winkler and by Kang.

The Theory of Combining Forecasts

The optimal combination of forecast variables has been examined since an initial investigation by Bates and Granger (1969), who found that two unbiased one-step forecasts, $f_{n,1}$ and $g_{n,1}$, of X_{n+1}, made at time n, could be combined as follows to outperform the individual forecasts:

$$C_{n,1} = wf_{n,1} + (1 - w)g_{n,1}. \tag{1}$$

The composite forecast, $C_{n,1}$, was formed by first calculating the optimal weight, w, for the forecast variable $f_{n,1}$:

$$w = \frac{\sigma^2(g_{n,1}) - \rho_{f_{n,1}g_{n,1}}\sigma(f_{n,1})\sigma(g_{n,1})}{\sigma^2(f_{n,1}) + \sigma^2(g_{n,1}) - 2\rho_{f_{n,1}g_{n,1}}\sigma(f_{n,1})\sigma(g_{n,1})} \tag{2}$$

Bates and Granger found that the optimally calculated weights did not improve upon the weights constructed from the assumption of independent forecast variables. Thus, the composite weights, using the independence assumption, should be proportional to the standard deviations of the respective forecast error variables.

A slightly more complex weighting scheme is the Granger and Ramanathan (1984) methodology, in which a single series X_{t+1} is forecast using k forecasts for the $0, 1, 2, \ldots, n-1$ time periods. The Granger and Ramanathan notation was:

$$\boldsymbol{X}^T = (X_1, X_2, X_3, \ldots, X_n)$$

is a $1 \times n$ vector of the X to be forecast;

$$\boldsymbol{f}_j^T = (f_{j0}, f_{j1}, \ldots, f_{j,n-1})$$

is a $1 \times n$ vector of forecasts from the jth model;

$$\boldsymbol{F} = (f_1, f_2, \ldots, f_k)$$

is an $n \times k$ vector of forecasts, and l is a vector of 1s. Granger and Ramanathan's method C had no restriction on the forecast variable weights, and a regression constant, δ_0, was estimated. The optimal variable forecast weights, δ, were found by:

$$\min(X - \delta_0 1 - F\delta)^T(X - \delta_0 1 - F\delta) \tag{3}$$

The normal equations were solved to determine the optimal weights

$$\hat{\delta} = \hat{\alpha} - \hat{\delta}_0 (F^T F)^{-1} F^T 1, \tag{4}$$

where

$$\hat{\alpha} = (F^T F)^{-1} F^T X$$

$$\hat{\delta}_0 = (1^T X - 1^T F \hat{\delta})/n$$

Thus, the combined forecast was

$$X_C = \hat{\delta}_0 1 + \hat{\delta} F. \tag{5}$$

Granger and Ramanathan's method C produces the smallest mean squared error and an unbiased composite forecast. A constant term should be estimated rather than obtaining a weighted average of the forecasts.

An Introduction to Latent Root Regression Analysis

It is well known that multicollinearity produces unstable regression coefficients with inflated standard errors (Gunst, Webster, and Mason 1976). The standard ordinary least squares (OLS) regression model is

$$Y = B_0 1 + XB + E, \tag{6}$$

where

Y is an $n \times 1$ vector of observable variables;

B_0 and B^T are unknown parameters; 1 is an $n \times 1$ vector of ones;

X is an $n \times k$ matrix of standardized known independent variables;

E is an $n \times 1$ vector of random variables.

The least squares estimator B is well known:

$$\hat{B} = (X^1 X)^{-1} X^1 Y \tag{7}$$

The expected value of the OLS estimator is B, the true-value, minimum-variance unbiased estimator. Multicollinearity, the condition of highly correlated independent variables, produces an almost exact linear dependence among the independent variables. The near singularity of the independent variables produces inflated estimated standard errors of regression coefficients because the ill-conditioning distorts the $(X^1 X)^{-1}$ calculation. Biased regression techniques, such as ridge regression and latent root regression (Gunst, Webster, and Mason 1976; Webster, Gunst, and Mason 1974) were developed in an attempt to obtain stable regression coefficients.

Whereas ridge regression is concerned with the determination of the biasing parameters, k, whether by coefficient ridge plotting or estimation by an iterative procedure (Hocking 1976), latent root regression seeks to identify near singularities in the independent variables, determining the predictive value of the near singularities, and estimate modified regression coefficients adjusted for nonpredictive near singularities.

The correlation matrix $(A^1 A)$ of dependent and independent variables has latent roots, λ_i, and latent vectors, α_{0i}, defined by the equations

$$|A^1 A - \lambda_i I| = 0;$$

$$(A^1 A - \lambda_i I)\alpha_i = 0.$$

The OLS estimator of B can be written (Gunst, Webster, and Mason 1976) as

$$\hat{B} = -n \sum_{i=0}^{k} a_i \alpha_{i}, \tag{8}$$

in which

$$a_i = \alpha_{0i}\lambda_i^{-1} / \left(\sum_{r=0}^{k} \alpha_{or}^2 / \lambda_r \right).$$

Multicollinearity is present when the latent roots and vectors are near zero. Exact linear dependence exists among the independent variables when some $\lambda_i = 0$; in practice, it is very rare for some $\lambda_i = 0$, but some λ_i may be very small, indicating near singularities. Webster, Gunst, and Mason (1974) found that near singularities are present when the latent roots are less than the 0.30 and the latent root vectors are less than 0.10.

In a geometric interpretation, the latent root of a particular latent vector measures the spread of data points in the direction defined by the latent vector. The latent root represents the sum of squares, and a small latent root indicates little variability in the orthogonal axis direction (Webster, Gunst, and Mason 1974). A small latent vector means that the orthogonal axis is nearly orthogonal to the independent variable axis. Small latent roots and variables reveal nonpredictive near singularities.

The latent root regression estimator should dominate the OLS estimator when the collinear variables produce coefficients in which a linear combination of vectors is orthogonal to the elements of the latent vector corresponding to the smallest latent root of the correlation matrix, V_1. That is, the subvector of regression coefficients, B, whose elements correspond to collinear variables is a small multiple of the elements of the latent vectors of the smallest latent root. Latent root regression adds a biased term while removing the ill-conditioning. As $B^{*1} = cV^1$ and $|c|$ is small, the bias term is small and the mean square error of the latent root regression estimator is less than the mean square error of the ordinary least squares estimator. Thus, LRR analysis is preferred to OLS analysis as long as the parameter vector is not parallel to the latent vector corresponding to the smallest latent root of the correlation matrix.

Combining GNP Forecasts

Wharton Econometrics (Wharton), Chase Econometrics (Chase), Data Resources, Inc. (DRI), and the Bureau of Economic Analysis (BEA) make quarterly forecasts of many economic variables. We used their level forecasts of nominal, N, GNP (1970–83) (obtained directly from Wharton and BEA and from the *Statistical Bulletin* published by the Conference Board for Chase and DRI) to construct growth rate forecasts (in percentage terms), and we calculated the deviations from actual growth as determined from GNP reported in *Business Conditions Digest*. Forecasts with four different horizons (1, 2, 3, and 4 quarters) were analyzed. For example, the one-quarter GNP forecast predicts the percentage change for the three-month period four quarters in the future. We label the data by year and quarter; for example, 75.3 refers to the third quarter of 1975. Details regarding the analysis of the individual forecasters are presented in Clemen and Winkler (1986). The correlations are uniformly high, ranging from 0.82 to 0.96. Thus, the data are automatically suspected of multicollinearity.

The data were divided into two periods, one for estimation and one for forecast evaluation. For the estimation period (up to 79.4 for each horizon), the combining weights (*B*) are estimated using both OLS and latent root regression (LRR) techniques. The results of the estimation are shown in Table 17–1. Stepwise OLS regression is performed for each forecast horizon. One notices that as two economic forecast variables enter into the OLS regression equations for each forecast horizon, the *t*-values are not statistically significant for both variables. Multicollinearity tends to produce this effect (Gunst, Webster, and Mason 1976). The latent root regression results for the two forecast (the LRR analysis is performed on the variables used in the OLS stepwise regression) variables analyses indicate that both regression variables are statistically significant for $N1$ and $N2$, whereas only BEA and DRI forecasts are statistically significant in the $N3$ and $N4$ regressions. In the three-variable OLS regression analyses, the only statistically significant (at the 10 percent level) forecast variables are the Chase and BEA variables in the $N1$ analysis, BEA in the $N3$ analysis, and DRI in the $N4$ analysis. The three-variable LRR analysis produces more efficient estimates of parameters; BEA in $N1$, DRI and BEA in $N2$, and DRI and BEA in $N4$ are statistically significant at the 5 percent level. Moreover, the Wharton forecast is statistically significant at the 10 percent level in the $N3$ LRR regression.

In the four-variable OLS analyses, the only statistically significant variable is the DRI forecast variable in the $N4$ regression at the 10 percent level. The regression coefficients are extremely unstable in the OLS regressions; the unstable weights have been noted by Kang (1986). The statistically significant forecast variables in the LRR analyses are Chase and DRI in $N1$, DRI and BEA in $N2$, DRI and BEA in $N3$, and DRI in $N4$. The LRR analysis produces many more statistically significant variables than does the OLS regression analysis. Moreover, the variables that are statistically significant in the four-variable LRR analysis are not always significant in the two- or three-variable OLS forecast variable analyses (the significant OLS variables are Chase in $N1$, at the 5 percent level, DRI in $N2$, BEA in $N3$, and DRI in $N4$). Thus, the use of stepwise OLS analysis

Table 17-1 Stepwise Regressions

Method	Series	EQ	Constant	Wharton	Chase	DRI	BEA	R^2	Vector Deletion
OLS	N1_{[t]}	1.1	.80		.56 (1.66)		.44 (1.42)	.43	
LRR	N1	1.2	.82		.49 (4.56)		.51 (5.05)	.43	1,1,0
OLS	N1	1.3	1.37		.75 (1.94)	-.36 (-1.00)	.55 (1.67)	.45	
LRR	N1	1.4	1.42		-.14 (-.94)	.29 (1.13)	.78 (2.23)	.34	1,1,1,0
OLS	N1	1.5	2.18	-.53 (-1.28)	.65 (1.66)	.33 (.92)	.48 (1.43)	.46	
LRR	N1	1.6	1.30	-.23 (-.58)	.96 (2.83)	.37 (4.93)	-.11 (-1.78)	.40	1,1,0,0,0
OLS	N2	2.1	1.23			.38 (2.68)	.52 (1.09)	.23	
LRR	N2	2.2	1.35			.54 (3.23)	.39 (2.81)	.23	1,1,0
OLS	N2	2.3	-.25		-.07 (-.72)	.62 (.93)	.52 (1.09)	.24	
LRR	N2	2.4	1.70		-.20 (-.65)	.42 (2.81)	.65 (2.49)	.24	1,1,1,0
OLS	N2	2.5	1.48	.06 (.20)	-.28 (-.76)	.59 (.87)	.52 (1.10)	.24	
LRR	N2	2.6	1.71	.08 (.24)	-.25 (-.69)	.41 (2.52)	.63 (2.31)	.24	1,1,1,1,0

(continued)

Table 17-1 Continued

Method	Series	EQ	Constant	Wharton	Chase	DRI	BEA	R^2	Vector Deletion
OLS	N3	3.1	4.85		-.51 (-1.43)		1.07 (2.96)	.18	
LRR	N3	3.2	7.34		-.15 (-.82)		.47 (2.90)	-.07	1,1,0
OLS	N3	3.3	4.12	.29 (.65)	-.55 (-1.51)		.90 (1.75)	.18	
LRR	N3	3.4	4.68	.77 (1.85)	-.02 (.06)		-.19 (-1.36)	.05	1,1,1,0
OLS	N3	3.5	4.17	.21 (.46)	-.59 (-1.53)	.20 (.34)	.82 (1.47)	.18	
LRR	N3	3.6	4.17	.16 (.39)	-.62 (-1.60)	.32 (2.56)	.76 (5.56)	.18	1,1,1,0
OLS	N4	4.1	7.75		-.54 (-1.35)	.82 (2.01)		.12	
LRR	N4	4.2	8.34		.38 (2.30)	-.14 (-.86)		-.07	1,1,0
OLS	N4	4.3	10.72		-.40 (-.94)	.99 (2.22)	-.60 (-.96)	.14	
LRR	N4	4.4	7.36		.20 (1.69)	-.30 (-2.49)	.43 (2.33)	-.12	1,1,0,1
OLS	N4	4.5	10.92	-.06 (-.28)	-.47 (1.10)	1.10 (2.39)	-.63 (-.96)	.17	
LRR	N4	4.6	8.69	-.09 (-.40)	-.60 (-1.69)	.96 (2.03)	-.08 (-.36)	.12	1,1,1,0,1

may not be appropriate for identifying effective forecasting services. Furthermore, if the F-statistic for variable entrance is set at the 10 percent level, only one forecast variable enters into each of the four OLS regressions. An examination of regression diagnostics (as discussed in Chapter 2) shows evidence of multicollinearity because the condition numbers are nearly equal to 30 (Belsley 1984).

The LRR technique generally resulted in more efficient estimates of the parameters (judging by the t-statistics), but the difference between the two techniques in this regard is somewhat less dramatic for the more distant horizons. The LRR weights turned out to be less stable than the OLS weights; for each forecaster, the range of the weights for the three estimation periods is greater under LRR than OLS. We attribute this to the nature of the estimation procedure. The LRR technique requires sensitive estimation of a correlation matrix as well as latent roots and vectors, all of which will change rapidly for small changes in a highly collinear data matrix. Small changes in the estimated latent roots and vectors can lead to changes in the decision of which latent roots and vectors (components) to eliminate. Table 17-1 also demonstrates the interesting empirical result that, for the longer horizons, LRR eliminated only one of the components. With the uniformly high correlation coefficients, one might have expected to see more components eliminated.

The true test of a forecasting procedure is how well it performs outside of the fitting data. Table 17-2 presents the results obtained by using the estimated models to predict actual nominal GNP for the evaluation periods shown. We also include "equal weights" as one of the combining procedures, as a benchmark for the other two. For three out of four horizons for the four-variable case, the equal weights procedure performed better than both OLS and LRR, a result foreshadowed by Clemen and Winkler (1986). Comparing OLS and LRR, they are roughly equivalent. LRR outperformed OLS two out of four times, and the performance measures for the two techniques are very close. Moreover, the equal variable weighting scheme is generally preferred in the analyses that involve two and three forecast variables. The forecasting errors provide additional implications for stepwise analysis: (1) Only two variables in an equal weighted fashion are optimal for forecasting $N1$; (2) Three equally weighted variables should be used to forecast $N2$; (3) The four variables should be equally weighted in the $N3$ forecasting; and (4) Four variables should be weighted with the OLS regression coefficients in forecasting $N4$.

Summary and Conclusions

Latent root regression is an appropriate technique to combine forecasts that are highly collinear. The main argument in favor of this technique is

**Table 17-2 Composite Post-Estimation Mean Errors where
Error = |(Actual-Forecast)|Actual|Horizon**

Equation	N1	N2	N3	N4
1.1	2.65	4.07	4.54	3.85
	(5.21)	(7.12)	(8.18)	(7.45)
1.2	2.66	4.01	4.52	4.26
	(5.08)	(7.66)	(8.22)	(8.80)
Equal	2.36	3.80	4.29	4.33
	(4.34)	(6.52)	(6.51)	(8.86)
1.3	2.73	3.93	4.75	3.85
	(5.04)	(6.81)	(8.65)	(7.69)
1.4	2.98	4.39	5.07	4.19
	(5.89)	(8.07)	(9.09)	(8.53)
Equal	2.38	3.54	4.51	4.26
	(4.49)	(5.55)	(7.14)	(8.68)
1.5	2.90	4.20	4.62	3.65
	(5.81)	(7.79)	(8.31)	(7.20)
1.6	2.75	4.42	4.44	3.73
	(4.87)	(8.19)	(7.96)	(7.14)
Equal	2.47	3.60	4.35	4.45
	(4.63)	(5.69)	(6.76)	(9.30)

The numbers in parenthesis are the standard derivations of the errors.

that it provides a structured way to deal with the multicollinearity. In the empirical combination of GNP forecasts, latent root regression performed well (compared to OLS) in its ability to produce significant parameter estimates. In forecasting out-of sample, on the other hand, LRR and OLS performed at equivalent levels, and both generally were outperformed by the equal-weights procedure. The strong performance of equal weights was anticipated, given that the econometric forecasts were developed from more or less equivalent econometric models. Performance of the LRR technique is determined to some extent by the selection of criteria for the deletion of components. Gunst, Webster, and Mason (1976) delete component i if $|\lambda_i|$ is not greater than 0.3 and $|\alpha_{0i}|$ is not greater than 0.1, but there is no guarantee that these criteria are appropriate for the particular forecast-combining situation. A possible avenue for future research is the exploration of alternative bounds on λ_i and α_{0i} in determining the components to include in the parameter estimate. We suspect that it may be possible to improve forecast performance by relaxing these bounds somewhat.

References

Armstrong, J.S. 1985. *Long Range Forecasting: From Crystal Ball to Computer.* 2d ed. New York: John Wiley & Sons.

Ashton, A.H., and R.H. Ashton. 1985. Aggregating Subjective Forecasts: Some Empirical Results. *Management Science* 31: 1499–1508.

Bates, J.M., and C.W.J. Granger. 1969. The Combination of Forecasts. *Operations Research Quarterly* 20: 451–468.

Belsley, D.A. 1984. Collinearity and Forecasting. *Journal of Forecasting* 3: 183–196.

Clemen, R.T., and R.L. Winkler. 1986. Combining Economic Forecasts. *Journal of Business and Economic Statistics* 4: 39–46.

Clemen, R.T. 1988. Combining Forecasts: A Review and Annotated Bibliography. Unpublished working paper. University of Oregon.

Figlewski, S., and T. Urich. 1983. Optimal Aggregation of Money Supply Forecasts: Accuracy, Profitability and Market Efficiency. *Journal of Finance* 28: 695–710.

Granger, C.W.J., and P. Newbold. 1986. *Forecasting Economic Time Series*, 2nd ed. New York: Academic Press.

Granger, C.W.J., and R. Ramanathan. 1984. Improved Methods of Combining Forecasts. *Journal of Forecasting* 3: 197–204.

Guerard, J.B., and R.T. Clemen. Collinearity and Latent Root Regression in Combining Forecasts. *Journal of Forecasting*. Forthcoming.

Gunst, R.F., J.T. Webster, and R.L. Mason. 1976. A Comparison of Least Squares and Latent Root Regression Estimators. *Technometrics* 18: 75–83.

Gupta, S., and P.C. Wilton. 1986. Combination of Forecasts: An Extension. *Management Science* 33: 356–372.

Hocking, R.R. 1976. The Analysis and Selection of Variables in Linear Regression. *Biometrics* 32: 1–49.

Kang, H. 1986. Unstable Weights in the Combination of Forecasts. *Management Science* 32: 683–695.

Makridakis, S., and R.L. Winkler. 1983. Averages of Forecasts: Some Empirical Results. *Management Science* 29: 987–996.

Newbold, P., and C.W.J. Granger. 1974. Experience With Forecasting Univariate Time Series and the Combination of Forecasts. *Journal of the Royal Statistical Society* Ser. A, 137: 131–164.

Webster, J.T., R.F. Gunst, and R.L. Mason. 1974. Latent Root Regression Analysis. *Technometrics* 16: 513–522.

Winkler, R.L. 1981. Combining Probability Distributions From Dependent Information Sources. *Management Science* 27: 479–488.

Winkler, R.L., and S. Makridakis. 1983. The Combination of Forecasts. *Journal of the Royal Statistical Society* Ser. A, 146: 150–157.

Index

357

11; Return on Sale, 120; Sales of
Assets, 11; Sales to Net Working
Capital, 11–12; summary of
common ratios, 47–49; Taxes
Paid/Net Income, 11; Times Fixed
Charged Coverage Ratio, 28; Times
Interest Earned, 14
Regan, P., 295
Regression analysis, 51–79;
Cochrane-Orcutt (CORC)
procedure, 325–326; composite
earnings estimations, 277, 279;
corporate acquisitions/mergers and,
304–324; Durbin-Watson statistic,
325–326; forecasting models,
51–79, 92–94, 103–117, 277–285,
345–354; line of best fit, 52; linear
least squares regression, 53;
nonlinear least squares analysis,
57–58; ordinary least squares
regression, 52–67; regression line,
55; robust regression and
composite model building,
280–281; *See also* ARMA
modeling; Formulas
Reilly, D. P., 88
Relaxing, in Modigliani and Miller
assumptions, 160–161
Rendleman, R., 263, 270
Required rate of return, 137
Resnick, B. G., 270
Retained earnings, 132; investment
capital and, 132
Retained earnings from the
stockholders viewpoint of internal
operation, 135–136
Retained earnings in terms of the
potential for investment in a
similar firm, 136–137
Return on Assets, 11, 120; data of
Chrysler Corporation, 22–23
Return on a bond, 133–134; measure
of: current yield, 134; yield to
maturity, 134
Return on a debt, 134
Return on Equity, 11, 120; data of
Chrysler Corporation, 22
Return on investments: holding-
period returns, 193–196;
Markowitz analysis, 191–206
Revenue growth, data of Chrysler
Corporation, 18
Ritter, L. S., 246
Roberts, G., 254
Robust regression: and composite
model building, 280–281; *See also*
Regression analysis

Roll, R., 295
Ross, S., 263
Rozeff, M. S., 95, 102
Ruback, R., 295, 323
Rubinstein, M., 258–259, 263

Sales to Assets, 11
Sales to Net Working Capital, data
of Chrysler Corporation, 24–25
Sales to Networking Capital, 11–12
SCFP, *See* Statement of changes in
financial position
Schmalensee, R., 270
Scholes, M., 222–223, 257–259,
263–268, 270–271, 319–320, 329
Scientific Computing Associates, 84
Seasonality, of time series, 116–117
Securities: efficient markets
hypothesis (EMH), 289–298;
holding-period returns, 193–196;
Markowitz analysis, 191–206; as
sources of capital, 132; *See also*
Portfolio theory
Security analyst forecasting models,
275–277
Security Market Line (SLM), formula,
214–215
Security Market Line (SML), 297
Shareholder return models, 211–235
Sharpe, W. F., 206, 211, 213, 222,
225, 263, 296–297
Sharpe index, 296
Sharpe-Lintner-Mossin risk-return
relationship, 213
Silber, W. L., 246
Simple linear regression, 69–74
Simultaneous equation estimation
results, 174–187
Single-index model, 222–231
Sinquefield, R. A., 191–192, 237–239,
327
Smith, C., 270
Sources of capital, 132
Sources of funds, 36–37
Sprenkle, C. M., 265
Standard Oil, 301
Standard and Poors, 123, 138, 148,
193, 240, 276; market index
formulas, 211–234
Statement, sources on, 33
Statement of changes in financial
position, 8; analysis, 33–45;
Chevron data, 41–42; example
analysis, 39–45; explanation of,
34–39; reporting requirements,
33–34
Statements: balance sheet, 7–8;